Ancient Romans

EXPANDING THE CLASSICAL TRADITION

Ancient Romans

EXPANDING THE CLASSICAL TRADITION

ROSALIE F. AND CHARLES F. BAKER III

OXFORD UNIVERSITY PRESS
NEW YORK · OXFORD

For our good friend,
the Reverend Scott H. Helferty

Oxford University Press
Oxford New York
Athens Auckland Bangkok Bogotá Bombay
Buenos Aires Calcutta Cape Town Dar es Salaam Delhi
Florence Hong Kong Istanbul Karachi
Kuala Lumpur Madras Madrid Melbourne
Mexico City Nairobi Paris Singapore
Taipei Tokyo Toronto Warsaw
and associated companies in
Berlin Ibadan

Published by Oxford University Press, Inc.
198 Madison Avenue, New York, New York 10016

Oxford is a registered trademark of Oxford University Press

Library of Congress Cataloging-in-Publication Data

Baker, Rosalie F.
Ancient Romans : expanding the classical tradition /
Rosalie F. Baker and Charles F. Baker III.
p. cm.—(Oxford profiles)
Includes bibliographic references and index.
ISBN 0-19-510884-1
1. Rome—Biography—Juvenile literature.
[1. Rome—Biography.]
I. Baker, Charles F., III. II. Title. III. Series.
DG203.B35 1998
937' .0099—dc21
[b]   97-21531
                                                                          CIP
                                                                           AC

1 3 5 7 9 8 6 4 2
Printed in the United States of America
on acid-free paper

On the cover: (clockwise from top left) Cato, Livia, Augustus, and Constantine the Great.

Frontispiece: In 1812, the French artist Jean-Auguste-Dominique Ingres painted his interpretation of Romulus, the legendary first king of Rome, celebrating his victory over Acron, the king of neighboring Caenina, a Sabine town in Latium.

Design: Sandy Kaufman
Layout: Loraine Machlin
Picture research: Marty Baldessari,
Patricia Burns

Contents

List of Maps

Preface

The influence of the ancient Romans on the western world has been immeasurable and continues to affect our architecture, government, military, engineering, language, law, and literature. Although the Romans themselves adopted or adapted many Greek ideas, they were quite innovative on their own as they sought to manage an empire that spanned the Mediterranean world and beyond.

Ancient Romans will introduce you to the key men and women responsible for nurturing Rome's political and cultural life. Had the ancient Romans themselves written a book like this, they would have started with the story of Aeneas, the legendary founder of the Roman nation, and then continued with biographies of the revered heroes and heroines of early Rome. Because these tales are so steeped in legend and tradition, however, and because it is impossible to know with certainty which details are facts and which are patriotic embellishments, we decided to tell the story of these characters in Appendix 1 and allow the main text to focus on Rome's historical figures.

Many of the Romans profiled here are more commonly known by their Anglicized names or by just one of their Roman names, so we have chosen to use that more familiar name throughout the essays. Each person's full Roman name appears in parentheses in the title of each essay. In addition, Appendix 2 presents a table of the Roman emperors profiled in this book, with the dates of each emperor's reign, his original name, and his official name.

The subject of the first essay is Camillus, the Roman general who defied the Gallic tribes that attacked Rome in the early 4th century B.C. and threatened its very existence. Not until the 5th century B.C., about 800 years later, did another enemy—also from the north—assault and sack the city. Therefore, as the final entry in Part 5's "More Ancient Romans to Remember," we tell the story of Stilicho, the last Roman general to keep the hostile Visigoths from taking Rome.

To be sure, there were many others who either laid the foundation for the accomplishments of the people reviewed in this book or who played roles that were less important, but our pages are limited. To locate more information about Roman civilization and the people who shaped it, consult the Further Reading that appears at the end of the volume. In addition, specific Further Reading entries appear at the end of each biography to direct you to more sources about these particular people.

Throughout the book you will also encounter several maps of the ancient Roman world designed to help you locate the places and structures mentioned in the essays and understand the action taking place. Many of the place names used by the ancient Romans have changed over the centuries. To avoid confusion, we have used the current English name for sites that continue to exist as cities and countries. For example, we use *Rome* (not *Roma*), *Britain* (not *Britannia*), and *Spain* (not *Hispania*). For sites whose ancient names are unfamiliar today or whose names do not at all resemble their ancient names, we have used the ancient name followed by the present-day name in parentheses—as in *Helvetia* (*Switzerland*). For sites that are no longer strategically important or are considered ancient sites—Pergamum in northwest Turkey, for example—we have used the Latin name. Only on the map entitled "Roman Provinces at the Height of the Empire" (on page 160) have we kept the official Latin name of each province. Note that the word *et* in provincial names such as *Creta et Cyrenaica* means "and" and indicates that the province consisted of two distinct areas.

Rosalie F. and Charles F. Baker
New Bedford, Massachusetts

THE MEDITERRANEAN WORLD
218 B.C. – 201 B.C.

SPAIN

Baecula

BAETICA

Carthago
Nova

AFRICA

| 0 | 100 | 200 | 300 | 400 | 500 kilometers |

| 0 | 100 | 200 | 300 | 400 | 500 miles |

A l p s

Ticinus River

Po River

Metaurus River

Tiber River

Adriatic Sea

CORSICA

Rome

CAMPANIA

Cannae

Capua

Tyrrhenian Sea

Tarentum

SARDINIA

Mediterranean Sea

Lilybaeum

SICILY

Utica

Syracuse

Carthage

NUMIDIA

Zama

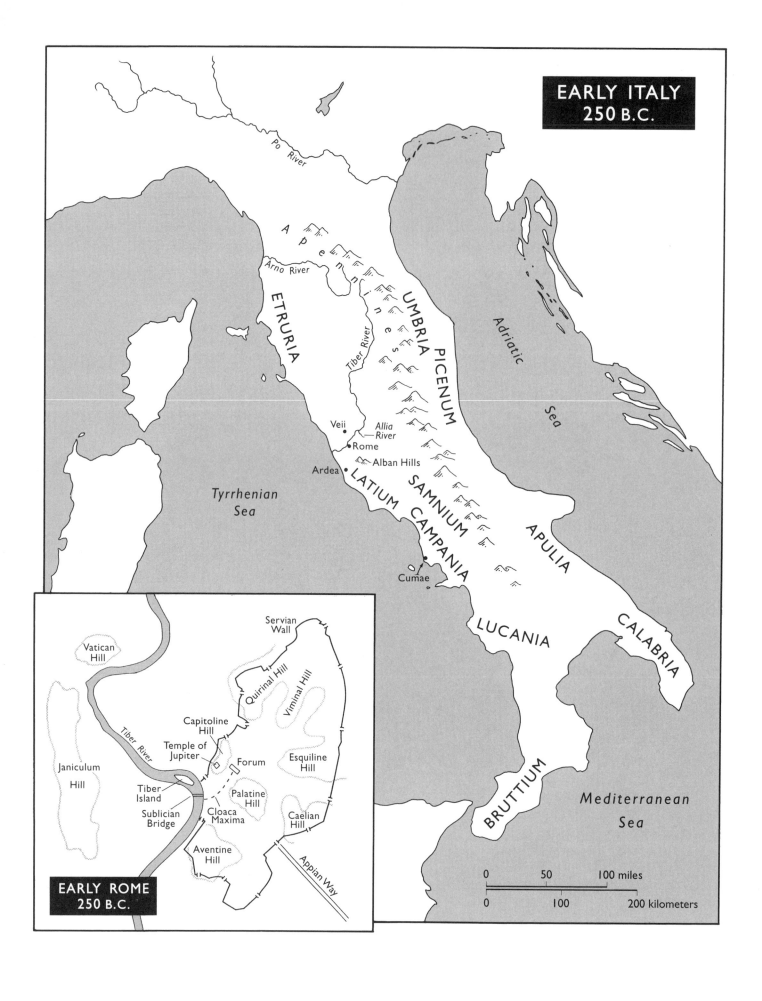

EARLY ITALY
250 B.C.

Po River

Apennines

Arno River

ETRURIA

Tiber River

UMBRIA

PICENUM

Adriatic

Sea

Veii

Allia
River

Rome

Alban Hills

Ardea

Tyrrhenian
Sea

LATIUM

SAMNIUM

CAMPANIA

APULIA

Cumae

LUCANIA

CALABRIA

BRUTTIUM

Mediterranean
Sea

0   50   100 miles

0   100   200 kilometers

EARLY ROME
250 B.C.

Vatican
Hill

Servian
Wall

Quirinal Hill

Viminal Hill

Tiber River

Capitoline
Hill

Temple of
Jupiter

Forum

Esquiline
Hill

Janiculum
Hill

Tiber
Island

Palatine
Hill

Sublician
Bridge

Cloaca
Maxima

Caelian
Hill

Aventine
Hill

Appian Way

1 The Relentless Rise to Power (396–78 B.C.)

 The early Romans were never content to remain within the boundaries of the Palatine and Capitoline hills on the Tiber River. They quickly expanded their control over the neighboring five hills: first the Esquiline and Caelian, then the Quirinal and Viminal, and finally the Aventine. The Capitoline, however, with its great temple to Jupiter (king of the gods), Juno (queen of the gods), and Minerva (goddess of wisdom), continued to be the heart of the community, while the Palatine became home to the city's aristocrats and rulers. In the valley between the two hills the Romans conducted most of their commercial, religious, and political business. Because this land lay in the open area beyond their homes, they called it the *Forum*, from *foras*, meaning "out of doors."

Before long, the Romans outgrew their "seven hills" and sought to overpower their neighbors. To the west they met little resistance, because few people had settled on the narrow, 17-mile strip of land between Rome and the Tyrrhenian Sea. But in the south they had to contend with the Latins, and in the east they confronted the Sabines—both of whom refused to yield their independence willingly. Determination and refusal to admit defeat finally brought victory and, by 300 B.C., the Romans controlled most of central Italy. They now looked north and farther south. But again, both areas proved difficult to subdue.

First the Romans moved north into Etruria. Though the Etruscans possessed a powerful and advanced civilization, they lost their independence when the leaders of their city-states refused to unite against the common enemy, Rome. The defeated Etruscans had a lasting influence on their conquerors, however: The Romans incorporated the Etruscan arch and dome into their buildings, adapted the Etruscan system of irrigation, and used a traditional Etruscan garment as the model for their national toga. While conquest remained Rome's primary goal, adopting and adapting a conquered people's traditions and ideas became a Roman trait in the centuries that followed.

With Etruria subdued, the Romans looked south to the land called *Magna Graecia*, or "Great Greece," where thousands of Greek settlers had established colonies. By 272 B.C.—little more than a century after the fall of Etruria—southern Italy belonged to Rome. But Roman rejoicing was short-lived, because Carthage, a rising power on the coast of North Africa, stood ready to challenge the power of Rome. Over the next 100 years, the two nations engaged in a series of conflicts called the Punic Wars, from the Latin word for "Carthaginians," *Poeni*.

The Romans found Carthage a most dangerous foe. Many Romans feared that the Carthaginian general Hannibal would outmaneuver their troops and take Rome itself. But there were courageous and determined Romans—Scipio Africanus, for example—who refused to consider anything but victory. As a result, the struggle against Carthage changed Rome politically. In the preceding centuries, the glory of victory had belonged to Rome as a whole. Beginning with the Punic Wars, Rome's history began to focus more on those credited with achieving a military triumph.

Rome also changed in other ways after defeating Carthage. Slave labor increased, as did the money in the public treasury, with taxes and tribute (payment of money) pouring into Rome. The growth in Rome's prosperity and power had both a negative and a positive effect.

There had always been animosity between plebeians (the common people) and patricians (the aristocrats), but now these differences intensified. Tensions also increased between those who possessed the coveted rights of Roman citizenship and those who were Rome's subjects but still possessed few rights. Consequently, as Rome evolved into the dominant power of the ancient world, a struggle for equality affected its growth and development.

Part 1 of *Ancient Romans* tells this story as it focuses on the people who molded Rome's first centuries.

Camillus
(Marcus Furius Camillus)

SECOND FOUNDER
OF THE CITY

As General Camillus listened to the Roman envoy's desperate plea for help, he thought of his own past services to Rome. Just six years earlier, in 396 B.C., the Romans had hailed him a national hero after his victory at Veii, the stronghold of the Etruscans. For years the Romans had laid siege to Veii, but only after they appointed Camillus dictator and granted him full decision-making power did they succeed in forcing the inhabitants to surrender.

Decades earlier, the Romans had outlawed the monarchy. They had, however, made a provision that in times of national emergencies a dictator could be appointed for the duration of the crisis.

Camillus' success had vindicated this decision, and his victories had won him the praise and admiration of all Romans. Ever since its founding in 753 B.C., Rome had been expanding and acquiring new lands to the east and south. Those who willingly accepted Roman control or chose to ally themselves with the Romans were treated with respect. Their cities and towns were not plundered, nor were their people enslaved.

But Veii had been different. There the Etruscan people had refused to submit. Because Roman philosophy dictated that anyone who resisted Rome's might should be punished, Camillus had ordered Veii's inhabitants killed or sold into slavery and allowed his troops to loot and destroy the city. This policy became standard procedure when dealing with those who opposed Rome.

Forgetting past insults, Camillus (on horseback) answered Rome's desperate plea for help and led the attack against the brazen Gauls who were intent on capturing and sacking the city.

At first, the Romans had supported Camillus' actions, especially when other Etruscan cities fell to Roman might. But in 391 B.C., Camillus felt Rome's power turn against him. He was charged with appropriating some of the booty from Veii for himself. According to Roman law, this was a serious offense. Proclaiming his innocence and hurt that the Romans would even consider condemning him, Camillus chose to leave Rome and go into voluntary exile in Ardea. His staunchest supporters went with him.

Soon after, Gallic invaders from beyond the Alps (present-day France) crossed into Italy. Without much difficulty, these fierce warriors overran northern Italy and headed for Rome.

On July 18, 390 B.C., a day marked forever after on all Roman calendars as unlucky, the Gauls defeated the Roman army on the banks of the Allia River, just 11 miles north of Rome. With no other forces to hinder their march, they entered the city's gates a few days later, looting and burning at will. The inhabitants escaped to the neighboring hills, except for a few old senators who sat silently in their senatorial (*curule*) chairs in the Forum, the city's public meeting area.

Thinking these white-haired men to be statues or gods, one Gallic soldier reached to stroke Senator Papirius' beard. Instantly, the senator reacted to the insult and slapped the enemy invader. Minutes later, all the senators lay dead.

But the Gauls were not yet masters of the city. A small band of patriotic Romans under the leadership of Marcus Manlius still controlled a fortress on the Capitoline Hill. Here the early Romans had built a great temple to their three chief deities, Jupiter, the king of the gods, Juno, the queen of the gods, and Minerva, the goddess of wisdom and war. This was the heart of Rome; as long as it remained under Roman control, Rome was undefeated.

Camillus, no doubt, had heard of Rome's fate and the slaughter of the senators, but he had not anticipated being asked to help the very people who had turned against him. Yet how could he refuse and still consider himself a Roman?

Camillus looked at the envoy who was nervously awaiting his answer and said yes—but there was a condition. Camillus would aid Rome only after Manlius' troops formally approved him as their leader. After much hesitation, Pontius Cominius, one of Camillus' soldiers, agreed to cross enemy lines and seek the required approval.

Slowly Cominius climbed a secret pathway leading to the Capitoline, inadvertently breaking a few branches of the underbrush as he went. Gallic scouts later followed the trail of broken branches and found the hidden pathway. But the cackling of geese that were sacred to Juno and lived at the temple alerted the Romans. Within minutes, the attack was foiled.

The Gauls, however, were determined to capture the fortress and continued their siege. Tradition says that Camillus and his hastily recruited army of 40,000 arrived at the gates of Rome just as Manlius was offering the Gauls gold in return for peace. Later Roman authors wrote that Camillus calmly approached the bargaining table and said, "Rome buys its peace with iron, not gold."

After a fierce battle, Camillus and his troops prevailed, and the Gauls retreated north. Not for another 800 years would the city of Rome be attacked and looted by invading troops. The rejoicing Romans honored Camil-

Camillus

At the far west end of the Roman Forum, the remains of the great Temple of Concord still stand as a memorial to Camillus' determination to bring peace to the people of Rome.

BORN

Around 450 B.C.
Rome, Italy

DIED

Around 365 B.C.
Rome, Italy

PROFESSION

Statesman and general

ACCOMPLISHMENTS

Held the dictatorship and the military tribuneship; awarded four outstanding military triumphs; according to tradition, routed the Gauls from Rome; ordered construction of the temple to Concord at the foot of the Capitoline Hill

lus with the titles of Romulus, after the founder and first king of Rome, and Second Founder of the City.

Following the defeat of the Gauls, Camillus chose to remain in Rome and promote legislation that would help the city recover. Although his policies tended to favor the patricians (nobility) over the plebeians (common people), Camillus was highly respected by all Romans. The plebeians especially appreciated his belief that an individual's worth depended to a great extent on accomplishments rather than on rank in society. They also approved of his plan to pay individuals for public service and to open the highest-ranking offices to all Roman citizens.

In 367 B.C., while playing a major role in settling internal struggles between warring factions, Camillus—now at least 80 years old—vowed to build a temple to Concord (peace) if the Romans settled their differences. After they did, Camillus kept his promise and ordered the temple constructed at the foot of the Capitoline Hill. Soon after, sometime around 365 B.C., Camillus died in an epidemic that swept Rome.

FURTHER READING

Livy. *Ab Urbe Condita*. Book 6. Edited by Christina Shuttleworth Kraus. New York: Cambridge University Press, 1994.

Plutarch. *Plutarch's Lives*. Vol. 2. Translated by Bernadotte Perrin. Loeb Classical Library. Cambridge: Harvard University Press, 1968.

Scipio Africanus (Publius Cornelius Scipio Africanus)

DARING MILITARY STRATEGIST

Few Roman families produced as many outstanding citizens as the Scipios. Their loyalty and courage became proverbial, and every Roman historian included their achievements in his works. The most famous, Publius Cornelius Scipio, first proved his valor on the battlefield when he was only 18.

In 218 B.C., Rome was embroiled in a major struggle against the Carthaginians for control of Spain and the western Mediterranean. In the decades since Camillus had defeated the Etruscans in northern Italy, the Romans had extended their power across all of Italy and even into Sicily. This had brought them into conflict with Carthage, whose rulers claimed land in Sicily. The Romans won the battle for Sicily and were now contending with Carthage for control of

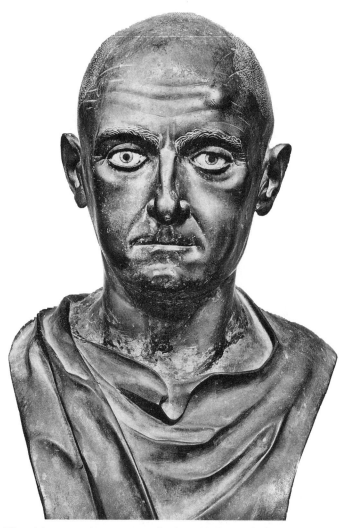

The debate continues as to whether this bust of a Roman represents Scipio Africanus. Most historians agree that the narrow face, prominent ears, and piercing eyes (here inlaid with enamel and semiprecious stones) are commonly associated with Scipio.

Spain. But the famed Carthaginian general Hannibal—who according to tradition vowed at age nine to devote his life to defeating the Romans—suddenly changed tactics, crossed the Alps, and began marching into Italy. Scipio's father, Publius Cornelius Scipio, led the Romans' defense against this attack.

The elder Scipio sent his army to Spain under the leadership of his brother, while he himself recruited more troops and prepared to meet Hannibal. In 218 B.C., the Romans and Carthaginians clashed near the Ticinus River, in northern Italy. The fighting was fierce. Gradually, Hannibal's forces encircled the Romans and the tide of the battle turned in favor of the Carthaginians.

Since this was the younger Scipio's first campaign, his father had given him charge of a cavalry unit positioned away from the thick of the action. When young Scipio saw that enemy troops had surrounded his father's contingent and that his father was gravely wounded, he immediately pulled on his horse's reins to redirect his course, yelled to his comrades to follow, and raced to his father's side. The others hesitated to charge into the teeth of the enemy, but when they saw the daring courage of their young commander they rushed forward and rescued the elder Scipio. By this one deed, Scipio won the admiration of Rome's army and was hailed as a hero.

Such heroics, however, had no effect on Hannibal, who continued his march through Italy, ravaging and plundering as he went. In 216 B.C., the Romans sent the largest army they had ever assembled to meet the Carthaginians at Cannae, south of Rome. Instead of following the tradition whereby one consul took command of the army sent to fight an enemy, both consuls now led Rome's forces against Hannibal. (The two consuls, elected annually, were the chief magistrates of the Roman republic.) The outcome was disastrous: only one consul, some officers, and a few thousand soldiers escaped slaughter or captivity. The defeat was so overwhelming that many Romans began to feel Hannibal was invincible.

Scipio, now 20, was among those determined to avenge the disaster at Cannae. When he heard that a few officers were considering abandoning Italy to the Carthaginians, Scipio immediately marched north to confront them. Before their eyes, he brandished his sword and vowed never to desert Rome. With this show of courage, he rallied the survivors of Cannae and began to make plans for the next encounter with the enemy.

Meanwhile, the elder Scipio had joined his brother in Spain, where the two had sought in vain to defeat the Carthaginians and Hannibal's brother Hasdrubal. When news reached Rome that both Scipios had been killed in battle, in 211 B.C., the Senate feared that Hasdrubal might now cross the Alps to join Hannibal in Italy. This had to be prevented. But whom could the Senate appoint to head the Roman army in Spain? None of the seasoned senior officers volunteered their services.

Only young Scipio was ready and willing, but at 25 he was legally too young to assume command. In addition, he had not been elected to any of the public offices that were prerequisites for taking such a post. Disregarding the rules, Scipio volunteered, claiming he had a right to the post as the close relative of two prominent generals killed in action in Spain. The Senate accepted his offer.

Once in Spain, Scipio moved cautiously as he reviewed his options. In Rome, he had begun collecting information about troop movements, the Carthaginian position in Spain, and the loyalties of the peoples under Carthaginian control. His strategy was

"Give your enemy not only a road to use in retreat, but also the means to defend it."

—Scipio Africanus, quoted by Frontinus in *De Aquae-ductibus Urbis Romae* (About the Aqueducts of the City of Rome, sometime between A.D. 81 and 96)

to understand his enemies, not fear them. After much thought, Scipio chose the port city of Carthago Nova (New Carthage), Spain, as his probable target.

Hasdrubal had established Carthago Nova as the base for all Carthaginian operations and had housed a large treasury within the city's fortifications. He also recognized the value of the city's protected harbor, which provided perfect shelter for supply ships from Carthage. However, Scipio noted that a force of only 1,000 soldiers guarded the garrison and that all three Carthaginian armies stationed in Spain were at least 10 days' march from Carthago Nova.

Scipio's strategy focused on the lagoon that bordered the city—it was very shallow at low tide and could be crossed in many places. If Scipio timed his attack correctly, his men could wade into the lagoon and scale the unprotected side of the fort. Because Scipio knew surprise was often synonymous with success in military campaigns, he told no one of his plan except Laelius, a trusted friend and the commander of the Roman fleet.

In the spring of 209 B.C., Scipio rallied his forces and prepared for battle. His positive attitude and careful assessment of every situation had already won the respect of the troops, and many felt his series of successes proved he had divine protection. Scipio himself always credited the gods with

approving his plans, and before any undertaking he spent time alone in prayer.

After a seven-day march, Scipio made camp just north of Carthago Nova. In his rallying speech before the battle, he promised crowns of glory to those who first scaled the city's walls and similar rewards to those who proved themselves especially courageous. He then added that the plan of attack had come to him in a dream during which the god Neptune had promised a spectacular omen foretelling victory.

At about nine the next morning, Scipio signaled the buglers to sound the attack. Mago, Hannibal's younger brother and the general in charge of Carthago Nova, rushed his troops to the ramparts, leaving the side facing the lagoon unprotected. After arming the town's civilians, Mago opened the main gates and ordered them to charge the Romans. Scipio had anticipated such a move and kept his troops about a quarter of a mile distant from the fort. This move allowed the Romans to replace their killed and wounded soldiers, but prevented the enemy from doing the same.

Once the civilians realized they were in trouble, many panicked and retreated, trampling others in their rush to find safety within the fortress. When the Romans saw that the troops manning the ramparts were deserting their posts, they rushed forward and tried scaling the walls. But the walls were so high that many of their ladders broke under the weight of the numbers of soldiers climbing at the same time. The few Romans who did manage to scale the walls were overcome with dizziness as they neared the top and were easily knocked down by the defenders. Finally, Scipio called a retreat.

Retreat, however, did not mean defeat. Scipio knew that the Romans had the advantage, because he had been in the middle of the battle, cheering on his men while three soldiers holding large shields protected him. Scipio now proceeded to the second part of his plan and ordered one contingent of soldiers to take their scaling ladders and head for the lagoon. He also ordered other Roman soldiers to launch a second assault on the walls. Just as this second attack was at its height, the tide began to ebb and Scipio gave his specially picked soldiers the signal to cross the shallow water and scale the unprotected ramparts. The troops, remembering what Scipio had said about Neptune, believed the receding water was the omen from Scipio's dream and immediately redoubled their efforts. Under such an assault, the Carthaginians were forced to surrender.

Scipio now concentrated his efforts on securing the friendship of the Spaniards. He returned those who had been taken prisoner to their families and promised them fair treatment in return for their loyalty. As a result, many Spaniards who had pledged their support to Hasdrubal switched their allegiance to Scipio.

Now it was Hasdrubal's turn to take the offensive. Deserted by the Spaniards and threatened with attack by the Romans, he decided to fight Scipio. If he won, he would consider his options; if he lost, he would head for Italy to join Hannibal.

When the two forces met at Baecula, just south of Carthago Nova, Scipio was ready. He had studied the Carthaginians' tactics and prepared counter-offensives. Instead of advancing with heavily armed soldiers as support for the front-line troops, Scipio sent lightly armed infantry ahead as a screen and divided his main troops into two groups, deploying one to each side of the enemy. Surprised by such a move, Hasdrubal was unable to react quickly enough to prevent confusion and panic among his men. Realizing that defeat was imminent, Hasdrubal

gathered as many survivors as he could and retreated north.

Scipio seems to have decided against pursuing the Carthaginians. If the other Carthaginian generals in Spain were to join Hasdrubal, Scipio would be outnumbered and might lose all he had just won. Furthermore, by order of the Roman Senate, Scipio had been sent to Spain to win control of the area—his job was now to defeat the Carthaginian forces still in the country. This he did, using Hannibal's own strategy of outflanking the enemy's main forces. As was his custom, Scipio freed the Spanish prisoners without demanding ransom and allowed them to return home. The Carthaginians he sold into slavery. By 206 B.C., Scipio controlled all of Spain.

Throughout his career in Spain, Scipio tried to act responsibly and fairly. Yet once, when he fell seriously ill, a group of disgruntled Romans mutinied. As soon as he had recovered, Scipio assembled both his loyal followers and those who had sided with the leaders of the mutiny. After addressing the latter and condemning their treasonous behavior, Scipio read the names of the head conspirators. As he did so, the loyal soldiers began striking their shields with their swords. Then, without warning, the 38 leaders were dragged in and executed. Their followers were asked to step forward individually and swear an oath of loyalty. Each man who did so was given his back pay and promised forgiveness for his involvement in the conspiracy. Scipio's handling of such potentially dangerous situations brought him even more respect and devotion from the troops.

Scipio had hoped the Senate would grant him a formal triumph in Rome for his conquest of Spain. This honor of leading a grand procession through Rome to the temple of Jupiter on the Capitoline Hill was awarded to generals who achieved a major victory over a foreign enemy and had been

Scipio Africanus

BORN
Around 236 B.C.
Rome, Italy

DIED
184 or 183 B.C.
Liternum, Italy

PROFESSION
General and statesman

ACCOMPLISHMENTS
Drove the Carthaginians out of Spain and won control of Spain for Rome; defeated Hannibal at the Battle of Zama in 202 B.C., ending the Second Punic War; transformed Rome's military into a semiprofessional army

The long, and at times desperate, struggle between Rome and Carthage for supremacy has captured the imagination of artists through the centuries. In this design for a tapestry prepared by the Flemish painter Geraert van der Strecken, Scipio and Hannibal are pictured speaking with one another as their troops listen and prepare for battle.

elected previously to one of Rome's top-level public offices. Scipio satisfied the first requirement, but because of his youth he had not proceeded through the ranks of public office. Therefore, when the Senate made no effort to declare a triumph he did not insist. Instead, he deposited more than 14,000 pounds of silver in Rome's treasury as the state's share of Spain's spoils.

The Roman people, however, were well aware of Scipio's accomplishments and made known their approval. When he returned home in 206 B.C., they elected him to Rome's highest office, the consulship. This was a great honor, as Scipio had not held the lower political offices that were prerequisites for the consulship.

For Scipio, the position of consul was key to his master plan, which involved crushing Carthage's military might and preventing further attacks on Roman territory. He now urged the Roman leaders to ignore Hannibal, who was still encamped on Italian soil, and attack Carthage directly. Because such action required the Senate's per-

mission, Scipio saw his consulship as the first step to winning this approval.

According to Roman law, the two consuls had both administrative and military duties. Each had legions under his command and was empowered to lead them against Rome's enemies. However, as Rome's territory increased and the two consuls found it impossible to perform all the tasks originally required of them, changes were made in the laws. By 205 B.C., when Scipio was consul, it had become the practice for the Senate to assign each outgoing consul a province where he continued his duties under the title of proconsul. With the number of provinces constantly increasing, new laws were passed to create more officers who could serve beyond Rome's borders. It also became the practice to send each outgoing consul to a province where there was turmoil or outright revolt.

Scipio hoped to be posted to Africa because he had a strategy he believed would lead to Hannibal's defeat. There were some senators, however, who disagreed with his reasoning. The most vocal was Quintus Fabius Maximus, who argued instead for a defensive strategy against Carthage. After much debate, the Senate awarded Scipio the province of Sicily with the stipulation that he could sail to Africa if Rome's safety required it.

This was enough for Scipio. In 204 B.C., when his term as consul ended, he proceeded to Sicily with the few troops granted him, recruited several thousand volunteers there, and then enlisted the help of Rome's Italian allies to build a fleet of 30 warships. All he needed now was cavalry. Contemporary accounts tell how Scipio conscripted 300 Sicilian nobles for a cavalry corps, then allowed them to excuse themselves from active duty, provided they left their horses and equipment for those who would take their place.

Still, Scipio was not ready to attack. He recognized the need to have a friendly Sicily behind him and attempted to correct some of the injustices suffered by the Sicilians under previous Roman magistrates. He also ordered several contingents to explore the African coast. Wisely, Scipio gave the scouts the older vessels and saved the new ones for the upcoming battles.

In the spring of 204 B.C., Scipio's expeditionary force of 35,000 set sail for Africa, landing a few miles north of Carthage, near Utica. When he found that he was unable to break Utica's defenses, he decided to retreat before winter storms threatened his troops. On a point of land that jutted out into the water, the Romans set up camp and Scipio used the time to plan his next move. After learning that the Carthaginian camps were built with branches and reeds, Scipio ordered hand-picked teams of his soldiers to set them on fire. The Carthaginians thought the blazes were accidental and rushed to put them out without taking up their weapons, allowing Scipio's

troops to swoop down and annihilate them. Scipio's bold strategy won him control of the surrounding countryside, and he was able to harass the Carthaginians on land and on sea. When Scipio learned that the Carthaginians were massing their forces on the Great Plains, a five-day march from Utica, he attacked them unexpectedly. Thus, Scipio benefited both from the element of surprise and from an innovative strategy that enabled him to outflank and finally encircle the enemy.

For the first time, the leaders in Carthage began to fear for their own city. Finally, after much discussion, they decided to send envoys to Scipio, asking for peace. Scipio welcomed the messengers, but he made Hannibal's withdrawal from Italy a condition of any treaty.

The Carthaginians agreed to Scipio's terms, and Hannibal returned to Africa. Unfortunately, at the same time the treaty was being ratified in Rome, a convoy bearing supplies for Scipio's troops was struck by a storm off the coast of Africa and forced into a bay near Carthage. The Carthaginians, who were also in dire need of supplies, considered keeping everything for themselves. They knew that doing so meant certain war, however, for they realized that the Romans would not tolerate the theft of their goods. But the times were desperate, and with Hannibal now in Carthage the Carthaginians felt a victory might be possible. By the time the envoys returned to Carthage in 202 B.C. to announce that Rome had ratified the peace treaty, the battle lines had been drawn between Scipio and Hannibal.

Historians generally agree that the battle took place at the town of Zama. Scipio again maneuvered his troops to outflank his enemy, the very tactic Hannibal had used in so many victories against the Romans. As the Roman cavalry closed the circle around Hannibal's troops and attacked his rear, the Carthaginians were forced to yield. Scipio had won, but he did not gloat over his victory. His goal was to disarm the enemy, not to destroy the city or harm the inhabitants. Scipio saw Carthage and the Carthaginians as allies of Rome in future ventures.

The Senate applauded Scipio's great military achievement. Because he now had held all the required offices, the Senate awarded him an official triumph. As a further honor, the Senate granted him the honorary title *Africanus*, meaning "African," for his conquest had been in that land. After adopting the title as a personal name, Scipio was known thereafter as Scipio Africanus.

For years, Scipio had experienced absolute power: first in Spain, then in Rome, and now in Africa. The Roman people clamored for him to accept the title of consul for life or dictator for life. But the astute Scipio knew well how fickle the public could be. He therefore continued to be involved in Roman politics and was elected to several political offices, including that of the consulship, but he refused all offers of "lifetime" posts.

Scipio's distrust of public acclaim was proved correct when rivals accused him and his brother Lucius of taking bribes from Antiochus III, a king of Asia Minor defeated by the Romans in 193 B.C. They were also accused of not reprimanding Antiochus for trespassing on Roman lands, and of misappropriating money earmarked for the struggle against Antiochus. The brothers immediately denied the charges. After making an accounting of all the funds received and spent, Lucius appeared before the authorities and was about to give them his findings when Scipio snatched the papers from his hands and tore them to pieces, a gesture expressing his fury that the authorities could

believe such an accusation against him. Lucius was then brought to trial, found guilty, and sentenced. Shortly thereafter, however, he was released. According to some accounts, Scipio's detractors also brought him to trial. However, when he was summoned to appear in court, he turned to the people, reminded them that the day was the anniversary of his victory at Zama, and asked all to follow him to the temple to thank the gods for their help. All did so, and Scipio was later acquitted.

But there was still much resentment against Scipio and his family, many of whom were also active in politics. A Roman statesman named Cato especially sought to discredit the Scipios, principally because he condemned Scipio's lifestyle and values, particularly his devotion to Greek culture. Cato believed that Greek culture was greatly responsible for a decline in Roman morals.

Tired of the quarreling and jealousy he encountered in Rome, Scipio left for his country home at Liternum. Never again did the hero return to Rome. He died within a year after his departure. As he requested, his body was buried at Liternum and not in what he called the "ungrateful city of Rome."

FURTHER READING

Caven, Brian. *The Punic Wars.* New York: St. Martin's, 1980.

Cottrell, Leonard. *Hannibal, Enemy of Rome.* New York: Holt, Rinehart & Winston, 1961.

Lamb, Harold. *Hannibal: One Man Against Rome.* Garden City, N.Y.: Doubleday, 1958.

Nardo, Don. *The Battle of Zama.* San Diego, Calif.: Lucent, 1996.

Scullard, Howard H. *Scipio Africanus: Soldier and Politician.* Ithaca, N.Y.: Cornell University Press, 1970.

Cato the Elder (Marcus Porcius Cato)

"I PREFER TO STRIVE IN COURAGE"

To his contemporaries, Cato the Elder was a *novus homo*, a "new man." That meant he had not inherited money and did not trace his ancestry to Rome's oldest and noblest families. Rather, he owed his success and reputation to his own hard work and study.

Cato spent his youth just north of Rome on a farm that was either his father's or his grandfather's. As a young boy, Cato listened to tales of Rome's great military heroes and heard friends and neighbors tell how his father and grandfather had distinguished themselves fighting for their homeland. Cato's father had schooled him at home, determined to teach his son Rome's history as well as the values he believed were essential to living a good and moral life. In addition to reading, writing, and accounting (all necessary for a successful farm owner), Cato senior also taught his son how to swim, ride a horse, throw a javelin, and fight fully armed.

While Cato was still a youth, his father died, and he inherited the Sabine estate. Because his family owned property and fought in the cavalry divisions, which meant they had enough money to buy the required equipment (including a horse), they were not poor. But they lived quite frugally. Cato himself seems to have adopted this trait at a very early age. Following the example of his father, he worked alongside his slaves in the fields, ate simple meals, and spent his

Stern and sometimes unbending, Cato sought to preserve Rome's traditional values of integrity, diligence, and loyalty to the state.

money carefully. In later years, when speaking of his youth, Cato said that he had only two ways of increasing his wealth: one was work, the other thrift.

In 216 B.C., the Carthaginian general Hannibal changed Cato's life. A sense of despair and hopelessness hung over Rome, because Hannibal had just defeated the largest Roman army ever gathered, killing tens of thousands on the battlefield at Cannae. That this disaster followed several other defeats—all to Hannibal—was making Rome's allies question their allegiance to a power that seemed incapable of defeating the wily Carthaginian. Yet the Roman spirit prevailed and a new call for soldiers echoed across Italy. In this time of crisis, rules were relaxed and recruits as young as 17 were accepted. Naturally, the patriotic Cato, just 17, enlisted.

Cato fought bravely against the Carthaginians, sustaining a number of chest wounds. He took advantage of free moments to walk about the countryside where he was stationed and study the local farming practices. His dutiful manner, trustworthy character, and courageous spirit soon won him a promotion to military tribune. This position carried much power, because the six tribunes who led a Roman legion (the major military unit, approximately 3,000 soldiers at this time) were second only to the consul who served as the legion's commander-in-chief.

Cato's first assignment as tribune was in Sicily, fighting under Marcus Claudius Marcellus against the Carthaginians. The campaign was difficult, especially when the Romans laid siege to the city of Syracuse and had to face the ingeniously designed war machines of the famed mathematician Archimedes. When victory finally came, in 211 B.C., Cato was asked to remain another year to help maintain order.

In 210 B.C., Cato returned to his farm. It must have been a lonely return, for he had no family to welcome him, only his slaves and the overseer who had taken charge during his absence. Nevertheless, Cato applied himself as diligently as before to his fields and crops. He now began to study the art of oratory, for he saw eloquence as the key to achieving success. Often he would set out early in the morning and travel from one village to another, pleading cases in court for defendants who sought his advice, before returning to work on his farm. He maintained this rigorous routine for the practice rather than for money, since it was illegal to charge for such services.

Naturally Cato's friends and acquaintances spoke about him, and his name soon came to the attention of a senator named Publius Valerius Flaccus, who owned land abutting Cato's. Valerius asked to meet Cato, and the two quickly became close friends. In fact, Valerius probably taught Cato his social manners and the rules of protocol; no ancient writer ever mentioned Cato making mistakes socially or politically, as was often the case with other citizens raised to the rank of *novus homo*.

But Rome and a political career were still a few years away for Cato. The threat of the undefeated Hannibal preoccupied Rome as he continued his encampment on Italian land. In 209 B.C., Cato fought against the Carthaginians at Tarentum in southern Italy and then, in 207 B.C., marched north to meet the enemy at the Metaurus River. Hannibal's brother Hasdrubal had crossed the Alps into northern Italy and was planning to crush Rome in a pincer movement. But Rome had quickly raised another army and sent it north under the consul Gaius Claudius Nero. Nero reasoned that if his troops could join the Roman army already in the north without Hasdrubal finding out, the outnumbered Carthaginians would find it difficult to win. His theory proved correct; Hasdrubal was killed and his army crushed. As a sign of Roman strength, Roman officers ordered Hasdrubal's head thrown into Hannibal's camp.

All these incidents naturally had their effect on Cato, who became firmly convinced that the Romans needed to practice the conservative values of the early Roman heroes if Rome was to continue being a great nation. This became Cato's political platform, which he carried everywhere. He detested luxury and condemned anyone who lived in a luxurious manner. He also argued against the Greek influence and the Greek way of life (relaxed, not very frugal, and with a preference for luxury), which he had experienced as a soldier in southern Italy and Sicily, because he felt they were contributing to Rome's moral decline.

One of Cato's staunchest supporters was his neighbor Lucius Valerius Flaccus, who eventually convinced Cato to move to Rome. Once there, Cato met many of Rome's leading figures, who knew of his stern and honest character and his courage on the battlefield. These new acquaintances helped Cato launch his political career and advance up the ladder known as the *cursus honorum* ("course of honor"), which included the offices of quaestor, aedile, praetor, and consul.

It was probably when Cato was serving as quaestor that he met one of Rome's most celebrated citizens, Scipio Africanus. At the time, Scipio was preparing to take an army from Sicily directly to Carthage and fight the Carthaginians in their homeland. Since quaestors were in charge of the public money, Cato was responsible for the funds granted to Scipio for the campaign as well as for settling accounts after the battle. When Cato saw that Scipio Africanus represented everything he detested—a fondness for Greek culture, a preference for luxury, and a desire to enjoy leisure time—he developed an intense dislike for the man.

The custom in Rome's political system was for a Roman working his way up the *cursus honorum* to spend the year following his term as magistrate in Rome as a public official in a Roman province. In this way, the Romans hoped to broaden their political leaders' outlook and give them experience in governing both at home and abroad. Cato spent time in Africa, Spain, and Sardinia. Everywhere, his ability to handle responsibility won him the respect of his superiors.

While serving as propraetor (provincial praetor) in Sardinia in 198 B.C., Cato attacked the practice of usury (charging exorbitant rates to borrow money) and punished those found guilty of this practice. He also took the opportunity to learn Greek, which was spoken throughout the Mediterranean world. His teacher was the poet Ennius, who had fought with Cato against the Carthaginians and then later accompanied Cato on his return to Rome.

Cato the Elder

BORN

234 B.C.
Tusculum, in the area known as Latium

DIED

149 B.C.
Probably in Rome or in the Sabine country

PROFESSION

Statesman and writer

ACCOMPLISHMENTS

First major Latin prose writer and founder of Roman prose literature; put down a revolt in Spain and reorganized the province; pushed through legislation that taxed luxury; revised the list of those eligible for the Senate; inspired the Third Punic War; wrote *De Agri Cultura* (About Agriculture)

In 195 B.C., Cato was elected to Rome's highest office, the consulship. Serving as co-consul was his long-time friend Lucius Valerius Flaccus. Cato used his power to argue vehemently but unsuccessfully against the repeal of the Oppian Law, which forbade women from owning more than a half ounce of gold, wearing multicolored clothes, or riding in two-horse vehicles in the streets of Rome. Throughout his political career, Cato always sought to forbid or, at the least, lessen the opportunities fo Romans to display their wealth publicly. Such extravagance, he felt, weakened the spirit.

Cato's attention soon turned from legislating morality in Rome to putting down an insurrection in Spain. Always a man of action, Cato quickly trained a hastily assembled army into an effective fighting force, suppressed the revolt, and reorganized the province under Roman rule. For this masterful achievement the Senate awarded Cato a triumph through the streets of Rome and up to the temple of Jupiter, on the Capitoline Hill.

Not long after his triumph, Cato found himself headed back to the battlefield—this time to the East, where Antiochus III, king of Syria, was trying to win control of Greece. Aware that all previous attempts to break the enemy's defenses at the pass at Thermopylae had proven unsuccessful, Cato planned his own strategy.

The night before the battle, Cato and a small contingent scouted the area near Antiochus' camp. After advancing to a hill just above the campsite, Cato asked his troops to capture one enemy soldier for interrogation. Several soldiers immediately dashed down the hill and soon returned with a prisoner. After questioning the enemy soldier about the location of Antiochus' sentinels and scouts, Cato prepared his attack.

The enemy troops were so surprised that they were easily defeated. Hit in the mouth by a large stone, Antiochus was overwhelmed by pain and forced to abandon the fight. Thermopylae now belonged to the Romans. Cato's commander hugged him in front of the entire army and declared that no one could grant him anything that would be equal to the service Cato had just rendered his country.

Although the Greek writer Plutarch later wrote that Cato enjoyed the praise he received for his part in the victory and even looked for it, he again became an archconservative once he returned to Rome. In his determination to revive the moral standards of the past, Cato sought to discredit the Scipios, publicly accusing Lucius and Africanus of misusing public funds.

Angered by the seeming unjustness of the accusation, Scipio Africanus tore up the charges and left Rome, never to return. Lucius escaped a jail sentence only through the intervention of other Roman officials. Cato, having eliminated the Scipios as a powerful public force, could now pursue his goal of returning Rome to the moral standards of the past.

In 184 B.C., Cato was elected to the powerful office of censor and, because of his activities while holding this position, he became known to history as Cato the Censor. As censor, Cato had the right to judge whether citizens acted correctly in both public and private matters. Although the term of office was only 18 months, Cato ac-

complished many of his goals. He ruled that luxury items of clothing, carriages, women's jewelry, and household furniture be revalued at 10 times their worth and then taxed accordingly. He also imposed a double tax on property assigned a high value by public officials.

Cato then turned to other reforms: He revised the list of those eligible for the Senate, checked abuses by the tax collectors, and initiated an ambitious public building program, including the upgrading of Rome's sewage system. At times he seemed too zealous, once expelling someone named Manlius from the Senate because he was seen kissing his wife in front of his daughter. But most Romans praised him for his efforts and admired his sincerity.

Even after his term as censor had ended, Cato continued to bring charges against those whose standards of living he deemed harmful to Rome. Some of these people filed countercharges and records show that Cato was brought to trial at least 50 times. He was acquitted each time. The last charge brought

against him was in 149 B.C., just before he died at age 85.

Throughout his eventful political career, Cato continually thought of his farm. Sometime around 160 B.C., he wrote a treatise titled *De Agri Cultura* (About Agriculture), the oldest surviving complete prose work in Latin. This 162-chapter treatise covers the cultivation of vineyards, olive groves, and fruit orchards and also includes several recipes. In Chapter 1, Cato gives his advice on how to buy a farm: "The vineyard is the first consideration, if the quality or quantity of the wine is good; in second place is a well-watered garden; third, a willow plantation; fourth, an olive grove; fifth, a meadow; sixth, grain fields; seventh, a timber forest; eighth, an orchard; ninth, an acorn forest [for hogs]."

Abrupt and unadorned in style, Cato's prose vividly reflects the shrewd, hard, conservative traits of his personality. Pliny the Elder, a later Roman writer and a naturalist, quoted Cato as saying: "The agricultural population produces the bravest individuals, the

Cato loved his farm and even worked alongside his servants in the fields. From observing animals such as the ones represented by these small ancient Roman figures, Cato gathered much information for his book on agriculture.

most courageous soldiers, and a body of citizens who are the least prone to conceive evil thoughts."

A few fragments of Cato's orations and his *Origines* have survived, but nothing remains of his book of maxims or the encyclopedia he wrote as a guide for his son, whom he educated at home. Unfortunately, Cato's son died before he did, but the traits of the elder's personality seemed to have been passed on to his descendants. His great-grandson, also named Cato, was likewise known for his honesty and conservatism.

As the years passed, Cato appears to have become less frugal with his own money, inviting friends young and old to dine with him on a daily basis. Yet his reputation was always above reproach and his conduct as a father and husband was also exemplary. There were those, however, who criticized his practice of selling old slaves so that he would not be burdened with their care.

Sometime around 153 B.C., the Carthaginians accused Rome's ally Masinissa of Numidia of taking their land illegally. Because the peace agreement that ended the Second Punic War prohibited Carthage from entering into any conflict without Rome's approval, the Carthaginians asked Rome to settle the problem. When asked to be a peace negotiator, Cato eagerly accepted. However, when he arrived in Africa and noted the prosperity and wealth everywhere, he saw that the Carthaginians could be a potential threat to Rome.

After discussing the situation, the Romans decided in favor of Masinissa, even though he had been the illegal aggressor, and returned home. Once in Rome, Cato approached the Senate and, turning his steel-gray eyes on his fellow countrymen, declared, *"Carthago delenda est!"* ("Carthage must be destroyed!") To make his point even clearer, he opened the folds of his toga, the traditional garment worn by Roman men, and let two beautiful ripe figs fall on the ground. The Romans immediately understood his meaning— a country that had been crippled just 10 years earlier was once again a power with which to be reckoned. From that day onward, Cato never failed to end his speeches to the Roman Senate with *"Carthago delenda est!"*

In 149 B.C., the Romans followed Cato's command and declared war on their old enemy. Cato died shortly after the beginning of the Third Punic War, not knowing that it would take Rome three years to defeat the Carthaginians and plow the very land on which the proud city had once stood. Cato surely would have approved.

FURTHER READING

Astin, Alan E. *Cato the Censor.* New York: Oxford University Press, 1978.

Cato. *De Re Rustica.* Translated by H. B. Ash and W. D. Hooper. Loeb Classical Library. Cambridge: Harvard University Press, 1934.

Forde, Nels W. *Cato the Censor.* New York: Twayne, 1975.

Plutarch. *Plutarch's Lives.* Vol. 2. Translated by Bernadotte Perrin. Loeb Classical Library. Cambridge: Harvard University Press, 1968.

Plautus (Titus Maccius Plautus)

THE PEOPLE'S PLAYWRIGHT

The early Romans loved Plautus and eagerly awaited the yearly public festivals when his newest comedy would be performed. Yet little is known about this man who could make the Romans laugh. The authenticity of his name has even been questioned, with some sources suggesting that all three were stage names. Most likely he came from a poor family and traveled to Rome to find a job. Once there, he found work first as an actor, then as a playwright. Using profits from his comedies, Plautus apparently went into business for himself. When this failed, he worked in a baker's shop, turning the hand-mill that ground the grain. During this period he again began writing comedies. After selling three plays to the manager of the public games, Plautus was able to quit the mill job and begin a full-time literary career. This took place about 224 B.C., when he was around 30 years old.

Of some 130 plays credited to Plautus, only 21 have survived, 19 of these complete or nearly so. As was the practice of the time, his plays were translations, imitations, or adaptations of original Greek plays, only fragments of which have survived.

In this very free interpretation of ancient Roman life, Plautus takes time from his work as a miller to sit on the grindstone and read a passage from his plays to his fellow workers. The scene painted on the rear wall is probably meant to represent the patron deities of the mill.

> *"Alas, we recognize our good fortune only after we lose what we had."*
>
> —from *Captivi* (The Prisoners, date unknown)

Unlike other writers of his day, Plautus did not slavishly imitate the Greek playwrights. Rather, he handled the Greek texts freely, changing words, reshaping the order of events, and even combining plots from different plays. This latter technique was called *contaminatio*, or contamination. As a result, Plautus was able to infuse a vigor into his characters that was often lacking in the original works. Nevertheless, Roman purists argued that *contaminatio* served only to discredit and ruin the original plays.

Despite this criticism, Plautus followed his idea of how comedy should be written and performed. Unlike the Greek playwrights, who believed that each play should be a coherent whole, with the action proceeding logically from one scene to the next, Plautus concentrated more on individual scenes, working them as he saw fit, regardless of how well each blended with the next. His style was lively and energetic, with sharp contrasts and inconsistencies in the action. Plautus' language was colloquial, fanciful, spirited, and even racy at times.

Although Plautus' references to Roman street names, Italian cities, Roman law courts, and Roman public officials made his plays seem Roman, the actors wore the large cloak worn by all Greeks as their outer garment. In fact, using the Latin name for this cloak, *pallium*, as a base, the Romans called their plays *fabulae palliatae*, or *pallium stories*. The names of the characters were also Greek, and the stage setting mirrored that of the Greek plays. The long, narrow stage represented a street, and three house fronts formed the background. All the action took place outdoors; whatever did happen inside was reported by actors standing on the street or in the doorways. Plautus also enjoyed having his actors comment from the small alleys between the houses. These asides were meant only for the audience and not the other actors to hear, a technique that added suspense to the action.

Critical to every Greek play was the prologue, in which an actor presented the background of the plot. Plautus seems to have found prologues unnecessary, as several of his plays do not include one. To help the audience understand the action, Plautus occasionally had an actor step out of character and address the audience directly.

In modern editions, Plautus' plays are divided into five acts, as are most Roman plays. These divisions are not Plautus' but were made by editors in the 1500s. Roman play action was continuous, and there was no dropped curtain when a play ended. An actor would announce the end of a production with a phrase such as *"Spectatores, plaudite."* ("Spectators, clap!")

Plautine plays were all in verse. The *senarii*, or conversational lines, were spoken, but the rest were sung or chanted to the accompaniment of reed pipes. It is impossible to imagine what the sound was like, because no written accounts or instruments have survived.

Scholars continue to debate whether Plautus' actors wore masks as Greek actors did. The Romans did not follow the Greek custom of using only a few actors, with each taking more than one part, but preferred to use as many actors as there were characters. Both Greek and Roman comedies used stock characters, each representing a type of individual found in society: the braggart soldier, the angry father, the permissive mother, the sly servant, and so on.

In the centuries following Plautus' death, his plays were performed regularly. With the fall of Rome in the fifth century A.D. and the onset of the so-called Dark Ages, interest in Plautine comedy waned. However, when the Renaissance spread across Europe in the 1400s, Plautus' comedies were again read, performed, and adapted. Today audiences can still laugh at Plautus' jokes, for acting companies continue to perform his plays in theaters and universities in the United States and abroad.

Perhaps the most frequently performed of all of Plautus' plays today is the *Menaechmi*, used by Shakespeare as the basis of *A Comedy of Errors*. In the *Menaechmi*, the plot focuses on twin boys. One twin was kidnapped at age seven; the other was renamed after his kidnapped brother. Thus, the main characters are Menaechmus I and Menaechmus II.

When Menaechmus I begins searching for his lost brother and enters the town where Menaechmus II lives, the brother's girlfriend mistakes Menaechmus I for her lover. Menaechmus II happens to be married and has secretly taken a dress from his wife to give to this girlfriend. To complicate matters further, each brother has a servant. There is so much confusion of identity and so many upheavals when each brother denies knowledge of what the other has done that Roman audiences must have laughed from beginning to end. Finally, the two Menaechmi manage to be in the same spot at the same time and the situation is resolved, with Menaechmus II returning home with Menaechmus I.

Another popular play by Plautus is the *Miles Gloriosus* (The Braggart Soldier), in which a blustering soldier kidnaps an Athenian courtesan and takes her to Asia Minor. At the same time, the courtesan's boyfriend is captured at sea and given as a present to this soldier. With the help of a clever slave and the old man in the house next door, the two lovers are able to meet in a secret passageway without the soldier knowing. But one of the soldier's guards catches the pair together and reports the affair to his master. However, the clever slave manages to convince the guard that the pair he saw were not the ones being held by the soldier but their twins, recently arrived from Athens. Then, to win freedom for the girl and her boyfriend (who also happens to be the slave's master), the slave devises a plan. He tells the soldier that the wife of the old man next door loves him, but that he, the soldier, must get rid of the kidnapped maiden if he wishes to meet with her. Meanwhile, the kidnapped boyfriend disguises himself as a ship captain and takes the captured maiden away with him on his ship. The soldier attempts to win the neighbor's wife and is discovered, caught, and beaten. Finally, the soldier realizes how he was tricked by the clever slave.

A passage from the *Mostellaria* (The Haunted House) combines comedy with philosophy when the maiden Philematium and her old servant Scapha discuss beauty:

> PHILEMATIUM: Look at me, Scapha, and see whether you think this outfit looks well on me. Do you think my dear Philolaches will find me attractive?

> SCAPHA: Why do you spend so much time dressing yourself when your manners alone make you pretty? Lovers love not the dress, but what's in the dress.

If Plautus knew his lines would still be making audiences smile more than 2,000 years after his death, he might not have written the epitaph he did: "Plautus has died, comedy is in mourning, the theater is deserted. Laughter, fun, and jest have all broken into tears."

FURTHER READING

Gillingham, Allan G. *Plautus for Reading and Production.* Glenview, Ill.: Scott, Foresman, 1968.

Nixon, Paul, trans. *Plautus.* 7 vols. Loeb Classical Library. Cambridge: Harvard University Press, 1977.

Sandbach, F. H. *The Comic Theatre of Greece and Rome.* London: Chatto & Windus, 1977.

Sutton, Dana Ferrin. *Ancient Comedy: The War of the Generations.* New York: Twayne, 1993.

Plautus

BORN

Around 254 B.C.
Probably Sarsina, Umbria, Italy

DIED

184 B.C.
Probably Rome

PROFESSION

Comic playwright

ACCOMPLISHMENTS

One of Rome's most successful and popular comic playwrights; according to tradition, wrote 130 comedies, 21 of which have survived: *Amphitryon* (Amphityron, the Trickster), *Asinaria* (Comedy of Asses), *Aulularia* (The Pot of Gold), *Bacchides* (Twin Sisters), *Captivi* (The Prisoners), *Casina* (The Male-Bride Drawn by Lot), *Cistellaria* (The Casket Comedy), *Curculio* (The Stolen Seal), *Epidicus*, *Menaechmi* (The Brothers Menaechmus), *Mercator* (The Merchant), *Miles Gloriosus* (The Braggart Soldier), *Mostellaria* (The Haunted House), *Persa* (The Girl from Persia), *Poenulus* (The Little Carthaginian), *Pseudolus* (The Cheat), *Rudens* (The Rope), *Stichus* (The Rebuffed Parasite), *Trinummus* (The Three Penny Day), *Truculentus* (The Taming of the Churl), and *Vidularia* (The Traveling Trunk)

Terence
(Publius
Terentius Afer)

GENIUS OF
THOUGHTFUL
LAUGHTER

An African by birth, Terence came to Rome as a slave and was bought by a senator named Terentius Lucanus. The latter soon realized that the young man he had purchased was not only physically fit and handsome but also very intelligent. After providing him some schooling, Lucanus freed his slave, who followed the custom of adopting the name of his former owner. As a surname, the newly freed slave used Afer, most likely a reference to his birthplace, Africa. Officially, Lucanus' former slave was now known as Terentius Afer, or Terence the African.

According to the Roman biographer and historian Suetonius, Terence was of medium height, dark skinned, and well mannered. While in his early 20s, he presented a comedy entitled *Andria* (Lady of Andros) to the Roman officials responsible for the public festivals at which plays were presented. These officials, known as aediles, then asked Terence to show his work to Caecilius Statius, a well-known writer of comedies.

It so happened that Terence arrived at Caecilius' house just as the latter was having dinner. Terence was admitted to

A keen observer of life around him, Terence used his experiences, both as a slave and then as a freedman, to create characters that reflected his understanding of human nature.

the house, but because he was poorly dressed he was given a seat set aside for those whose social class was beneath that of the assembled guests. As was the custom at such gatherings, all present were invited to recite passages from works they had written. When Terence began to quote from his *Andria*, Caecilius immediately recognized his literary genius and invited Terence to recline on the dining couch near him—one of the most honored positions in the dining room. From there Terence continued his recitation, much to the delight of the respected playwright.

Though it is uncertain when this meeting might have taken place, the *Andria* was first performed in 166 B.C. and was well received. Five more comedies followed, the last being the *Adelphoi* (Brothers) in 160 B.C. That same year Terence's *Hecyra* (Mother-in-Law) was produced for a third time. The first two performances had been complete failures, with the audience leaving the theater while the actors were still on stage. Rumors that a tightrope walker and boxers were performing nearby emptied the theater during the first production, and a gladiatorial performance had the same effect during the second one.

Competition from crowd-pleasing spectacles was not Terence's only concern. An older playwright named Luscius Lanuvinus was always ready to criticize Terence's style of writing and dramatic technique. Roman playwrights were accustomed to using original Greek plays as the model for their own works. Plautus, Naevius, and Ennius had followed this practice, as had Caecilius. All, however, had taken liberties and made changes in their translations. Lanuvinus, on the other hand, believed that Roman writers should use the earlier Latin playwrights, not the Greeks, as their models. When Terence combined plots from two Greek plays, Lanuvinus was furious and accused Ter-

ence of committing *contaminatio*, the process of taking sections of two or more Greek plays and using them in one Roman play. For Lanuvinus, this practice was not to be condoned. Terence, on the other hand, felt that the practice added suspense and drama to the plot. He seems to have ignored Lanuvinus' accusations, even though he once referred to him in a play as a "mean old poet."

Lanuvinus, however, continued to find fault with Terence and even charged that Terence's high-ranking friends collaborated with him on the writing. It was true that Terence enjoyed the patronage of Scipio Aemilianus and his friends, who belonged to what history has termed the Scipionic Circle. The members of this group all promoted the arts and met regularly to discuss literature and philosophy, with a special emphasis on Greek culture and customs. They also helped young writers whose work showed great promise. Because Caecilius was associated with this group and Terence was one of the first writers to come under their patronage, it was only natural that Terence would try to please his patrons and write in a manner of which they approved.

As a result, Terence's style differed considerably from that of his renowned predecessor Plautus. The latter had used slapstick and colloquial language, both of which appealed to the common people of Rome. Terence, however, used a refined Latin that appealed more to the educated Romans such as Scipio and his friends.

Conversations in Terence's plays mirrored everyday situations, but without the exclamations and boisterousness found in Plautus. Terence also incorporated into his Latin verse the short philosophical comments found in the original Greek plays. (Plautus had usually omitted these phrases.)

Terence's idol was the Greek comic playwright Menander; much of his

Terence

BORN

Before 185 B.C.
North Africa, perhaps in Carthage

DIED

159 B.C. or later
Place unknown

PROFESSION

Comic playwright

ACCOMPLISHMENTS

Wrote six comedies: *Andria* (Woman of Andros), *Adelphoi* (The Brothers), *Heautontimoroumenos* (The Self-Tormentor), *Eunuchus* (The Eunuch), *Phormio*, and *Hecyra* (The Mother-in-Law)

In this scene from the *Adelphoi* found in a 9th-century manuscript in the Vatican Library, Aeschinus, with the aid of the cunning slave Syrus, has taken the girl Bacchis from her owner Sannio and plans to give her to his brother Ctesipho.

work was an adaptation of Menander's plays. Yet Terence was far more than just a translator. He was very successful at interweaving into one coherent unit plots and scenes from two or more plays. He also made some adjustments of his own to the action.

To heighten the suspense and drama and keep his audience as unaware of future events as the actors were, Terence broke with the Greek tradition of beginning a play with a prologue that gave an overview of past as well as future events. When there were details he felt the audience needed to know he placed them within the play itself. Terence did use prologues, but only to defend his style against the critics of the day and to ask the audience to give his play a fair and unbiased hearing.

To heighten the drama and suspense, Terence added more dialogue and eliminated monologues. He omitted Greek place names and details that would be unfamiliar to Romans but, unlike Plautus, he never introduced Roman customs or objects.

Terence's characters too are always Greek in name and manner. Quiet and subdued, they rarely show spontaneity or express strong emotion. All speak in very refined Latin. In fact, Terence chose as his models the most refined of the Greek writers of comedy. Coherence and attention to detail were essential ingredients in all of Terence's plays. Unlike Plautus and other Roman playwrights, he did not allow breaks in the action so that an actor could turn and address the audience directly.

Although Terence's *Andria* is not as polished and technically complete as his later works, it is still a charming play and clearly illustrates Terence's ability to portray the characters of romantic young men. The simple plot involves a young Greek named Pamphilus and his girlfriend, Glycerium, who lives next door with Chrysis, a woman said to be her sister. (Chrysis is a newcomer to Athens, having recently moved there from the Aegean island of Andros.) Pamphilus' father, Simo, learns of his son's feelings for Glycerium, but follows through with his own plans for Pamphilus and betroths him to Philumena, the daughter of his friend Chremes. Pamphilus, however, has no intention of marrying anyone but Glycerium. The plot becomes more involved when it is announced that Glycerium is expecting Pamphilus' child and that Pamphilus' friend Charinus wants to marry Philumena. A marriage date is set for Philumena and Pamphilus, but the latter's slave uses trickery in an attempt to stall the wedding. At first he meets with success, but then events begin to unfold too rapidly and the birth of Glycerium's baby adds further complications. Just in time, Crito of Andros arrives in Athens and reveals Glycerium's true identity. She is not Chrysis' sister but the daughter of Chremes and an Athenian citizen. The plays ends as Simo gives his blessing to the marriage of Pamphilus and Glycerium.

In the following scene from the *Andria*, Charinus, his servant Byrria, and Pamphilus discuss the latter's upcoming wedding to Philumena.

> PAMPHILUS: Hello, Charinus.
> CHARINUS: Hi! I need hope, help, advice from you.
> PAM: I'm really rushed, but, what is it?
> CHAR: Are you getting married today?
> PAM: So I'm told!
> CHAR: If you do, you'll never see me again. Byrria, you tell him.
> BYR: He loves your future wife.
> PAM: Well, I don't.
> CHAR: Then, please, as my friend, don't marry her.
> PAM: I'll try not to.
> CHAR: At least postpone the wedding.
> PAM: Believe me, I want out of this marriage more than you want in.
> CHAR: Oh, you have given me hope, life . . .

Following the custom, Terence ended the play with an actor asking the audience, "Applaud us, please!"

Sometime around 159 B.C., Terence visited Greece, most likely to gather more original Greek plays. He was about 30 years old at the time, with many years of playwriting ahead. No one knows what happened to him in Greece, but he never returned to Rome and was never heard of again. Some ancient writers claimed that he died of an illness, others that he was shipwrecked on the return voyage. A few maintained that Terence died of grief after hearing that the translations of the Greek playwright Menander he had completed and sent ahead were lost at sea.

What is certain, however, is that Rome lost a master playwright, one with a sense of tolerance and empathy for human nature that had been lacking in strictly Roman works. Both these traits became part of his legacy as his successors incorporated them into their writing. Terence's influence on Roman education and scholarship was also strong, because his vocabulary and grammatical constructions were considered models of pure Latin.

In the decades that followed Terence's death, many of his lines became Roman proverbs, including "Nothing is being said today that has not been said before" and "A word to the wise is sufficient."

Numerous playwrights have imitated Terence throughout the centuries. They include the French dramatist Molière, who in 1671 wrote an adaptation of *Phormio* entitled *Les Fourberies de Scapin* (The Cheats of Scapin); the 18th-century English writer Henry Fielding, who based his novel *The Fathers* on Terence's *Adelphoi*; and the 20th-century American novelist and playwright Thornton Wilder, who modeled his novel *Woman of Andros* directly on Terence's *Andria*.

FURTHER READING

Sandbach, F. H. *The Comic Theatre of Greece and Rome.* London: Chatto and Windus, 1977.

Sutton, Dana Ferrin. *Ancient Comedy: The War of the Generations.* New York: Twayne, 1993.

Terence. 2 vols. Translated by John Sargeaunt. Loeb Classical Library. Cambridge: Harvard University Press, 1925.

"And so it is that life may be compared to playing with dice. If whatever you especially hope to have does not fall with the throw, then you must use skill to correct that which does fall."

—from *Adelphoi* (160 B.C.)

The Gracchi Brothers (Tiberius Sempronius Gracchus and Gaius Sempronius Gracchus)

CHAMPIONS OF THE PEOPLE

Few people can claim such upright, loyal, and widely respected parents and grandparents as the Gracchi brothers could. Their father, Sempronius Gracchus, had been elected twice to the consulship and once to the office of censor, and he had enjoyed the honor of celebrating two triumphs in Rome for outstanding victories over a foreign enemy. Yet he was respected more for his honesty and moral character than for his political credentials. The mother of the brothers was Cornelia, the daughter of Scipio Africanus, the Roman general who defeated Rome's archenemy Hannibal.

According to the Greek historian Plutarch, Sempronius once found two snakes coiled in his bed. After asking soothsayers their opinions of this omen, he was advised not to kill the snakes—nor to let them escape. If the male snake was killed, they claimed, Sempronius would die. If the female was killed, Cornelia would die. Refusing to think about the possibility of his wife dying and reasoning that he was much older and therefore closer to death, Sempronius killed the male snake. Shortly thereafter, the story goes, Sempronius died.

The widowed Cornelia decided to devote her life to raising her 12 children. Even when Ptolemy, ruler of Egypt, sought her hand in marriage, Cornelia refused. Unfortunately, only three children survived to adulthood: a daughter, Sempronia, who married Scipio Aemilianus (grandson by adoption of Scipio Africanus), and two sons, Tiberius and Gaius.

The older brother by nine years, Tiberius was calmer and more controlled than Gaius. When speaking in public, Tiberius was gentle but persuasive, and he always took pains to speak in clear and grammatically correct Latin. Gaius, on the other hand, was much more fiery and emotional; once, he even pulled his toga off his shoulder when emphasizing a point. Yet he realized that if his speech became too abusive and angry, he would offend his audience. Therefore, according to Plutarch, Gaius kept with him a servant named Licinius, who stood quietly behind him with a sort of pitch pipe. If Gaius became too loud or abusive, Licinius was to blow a soft note on the pipe, the signal to calm down. On the battlefield and in public office, however, the brothers' temperaments were the same—both were fiercely loyal to Rome.

In comparison with their contemporaries, the brothers' lifestyles were quite frugal and simple (especially Tiberius'), habits they had learned at home. There, too, they were introduced to Greek culture, for Cornelia often entertained visiting scholars as well as Greek philosophers and writers.

As a young man, Tiberius was committed to winning rights for the common people and to establishing a policy of humanitarian aid. While these concerns definitely reflected the many philosophical discussions he had heard at home, his battlefield experience had also strengthened his belief in these ideas.

Tiberius' first tour of active duty was in Africa from 147 to 146 B.C., when he served as a junior officer under his cousin and brother-in-law Scipio Aemilianus in the Third Punic War. All the historical accounts told of Tiberius' great courage and of his being the first to climb the enemy's walls.

Tiberius' second major command came in 137 B.C., when he was sent to Numantia in Spain to serve under the Roman consul and general Gaius Hostilius Mancinus. In one key battle, Mancinus was forced to retreat. He then inadvertently maneuvered his army into such a position that they were easily surrounded by the enemy and in danger of annihilation. All appeals for peace were refused, until finally the Numantians agreed to negotiate—not with Mancinus but with Tiberius. The Spaniards felt they could trust Tiberius, for they remembered that his father had ruled wisely while in Spain and had brought an honorable peace to the Numantians.

In the agreement that followed, the Numantians were allowed to keep everything they had confiscated in the area and the Roman army was set free. Tiberius, however, had one matter he still wished to negotiate.

The records of all the transactions Tiberius had made as a public official were part of the property to be kept by the Numantians, and he wanted them back. Determined, Tiberius entered the enemy camp and asked that his materials be returned. He explained that if

his enemies should find fault with any of his activities, he would need his accounts to prove their charges false. The Numantians not only granted his request; they also invited him to eat with them. They then offered him additional gifts, but he accepted only some incense, which he planned to burn at the temple to offer thanks to the gods for their help.

Upon returning to Rome, Tiberius found that the Senate had followed the advice of his cousin, Scipio Aemilianus, and nullified his agreement with the Numantians. Tiberius withdrew his support for Scipio and his friends. He then aligned himself with the second most powerful political group in Rome, headed by Appius Claudius, and married Claudius' daughter.

In 133 B.C., Tiberius began his active political career as a tribune, an office created centuries earlier to protect the rights of the people. Tribunes, elected by the people, had the authority to veto any law they felt violated the people's rights. Always on duty, a tribune could not travel more than one mile beyond the city's walls.

As tribune, Tiberius was ready to push for legislation he felt would address many of the ills afflicting Rome and its territories. In Spain, he had noticed widespread discontent among the

Disturbed by the injustices and burdens suffered by the common people who fought the battles to preserve and expand Rome's power, both Gracchi brothers gave their lives to change the laws and extend political and social rights.

Tiberius Gracchus

BORN

Between 169 and 164 B.C.
Rome

DIED

133 B.C.
Rome

PROFESSION

Statesman

ACCOMPLISHMENTS

Promoted and backed a land reform law that redistributed public lands among poor Romans; established a commission to carry through a land reform bill

soldiers. On his return to Rome through northern Italy he had crossed large tracts of land owned by wealthy Romans and worked by slaves. In Rome, he saw great numbers of people who owned no land and had come to the city to earn a living. Something in the system was wrong, he reasoned.

Rome had been following a practice of allowing a conquered people to retain some of its land. The remainder of the land, which became the property of Rome, was sold, leased, allotted to discharged soldiers, or left unused. In practice, however, only the rich could afford to buy or work these lands, so naturally their holdings continued to increase. As a result, Rome was becoming a land of rich and poor. The old terms *patrician* and *plebeian* fell into disuse and new ones were coined: *optimates* (the best) and *populares* (the people).

Aggravating the situation was an increasing number of slaves. After each conquest, more slaves flooded the market, making slave labor so cheap that many slaveholders simply worked their slaves until they died, then bought new ones, because to care for a sick or aged slave was more expensive than buying replacements. This practice reflected the attitude of many landholders, who considered slaves property, not fellow human beings.

Owners of small farms and poor people who were not slaves both found life difficult. Because it was cheaper to buy slaves than to hire free laborers, workers were unable to find jobs in the countryside and came to Rome seeking employment. Tiberius saw in this the seeds of mutiny, revolt, and revolution and resolved to right the wrongs committed against these people.

Working with his father-in-law and several others who believed reform necessary, Tiberius developed a plan to redistribute public lands. He based his proposal on an existing, but rarely invoked, law stating that ownership of more than 500 *iugera* (approximately 300 acres) by any one person was illegal. Over the years, many landowners had gradually increased their holdings far beyond this quota by taking possession of neighboring empty lands. Because these landowners had spent money improving the lands, they now considered them their own.

To make his law more palatable, Tiberius included in it a provision allowing a landowner with one son to retain possession of 750 *iugera* and one with two sons to keep 1,000 *iugera*. Any land that exceeded these quotas reverted to the public, to be assigned in small parcels to poor citizens. (A similar redistribution policy that involved giving public lands to landless soldiers after a war had been in effect for decades. But this practice had been abandoned after the Carthaginians under Hannibal swept through Italy and killed tens of thousands of Roman soldiers.)

Most landowners bitterly opposed Tiberius' plan, but the poor were elated and flocked to Rome to register their vote. Because Tiberius feared a negative vote in the Senate, he chose to bypass the senators and win approval of the law directly from the people. Not to be outmaneuvered, the senators convinced Tiberius' partner in office, the tribune Octavius, to veto the measure. Tiberius then appealed directly to the Senate for approval. When the senators refused, he tried a different approach.

Roman law stated that only male citizens who owned property could be in the army. The early Romans had set this requirement because they believed landowners would fight harder than those who had no land to lose.

Furthermore, Roman law required that all soldiers provide their own equipment. This meant that the richest citizens made up the cavalry, because only they could afford a horse and the other necessary equipment. The citizens meeting the minimum land requirement became the light-armed foot soldiers. In times of national emergency, however, slaves and men who owned no land could be drafted.

Tiberius saw clearly that as the number of landless individuals increased, the number of recruits would decrease. Then, if the slaves should mass together, as they had recently in Sicily, the Roman army might not be strong enough to defend Rome against attack. Tiberius argued that by granting thousands of poor men enough property to qualify them for military service, Rome would be protecting itself.

Tiberius' next tactic was to urge the impeachment of the tribune Octavius who, he argued, had acted contrary to the wishes of those whom he was elected to represent. When Tiberius brought this argument to the People's Assembly, the delegates agreed and voted Octavius out of office. This was a new strategy in Roman politics, and one which alienated some of Tiberius' supporters.

Meanwhile, Tiberius' land bill became law. Tiberius named himself, his brother Gaius, and his father-in-law to oversee the law's implementation. The Senate, however, continued to oppose Tiberius and refused to grant him the necessary funds. Fortunately for him, the last king of Pergamum in Asia Minor died just at this time, leaving his entire kingdom to the Roman people. Tiberius seized the opportunity and asked that the People's Assembly be given the right to use some of the money to fund the new law and buy the necessary equipment for the new

landholders. Again, Tiberius bypassed the Senate and took his proposal directly to the people.

In response, a number of senators threatened to prosecute Tiberius for misconduct after his year as tribune was over. (Roman law prohibited trying a tribune on any charges while in office.) To avoid this possibility, Tiberius defiantly opposed custom and ran for a second term. Soon rumors began circulating that Tiberius was aiming at the dictatorship. This time, even some of his own supporters urged him to rethink his decision. Soothsayers also warned him that the omens were unfavorable. But Tiberius, determined to complete what he had started, walked to the Assembly meeting.

When the consul Publius Mucius Scaevola refused to stop the Assembly from voting on Tiberius' candidacy, tempers began to fray. Scipio Nascia led the opposition. Tiberius' followers were just as determined, and a violent quarrel broke out in the Assembly over the legality of the proceedings. Words gave way to blows and soon the opposing sides were fighting with sticks and clubs. In the course of the brawl, Tiberius and approximately 300 of his supporters were killed. Their bodies were thrown into the Tiber River.

In the days that followed, the Senate prosecuted and executed many of Tiberius' supporters. However, the tremendous opposition of the people toward the Senate forced the *optimates* to continue implementing Tiberius' land reform law.

At the time of his brother's murder, Gaius Gracchus was in his early 20s. Other than asking that Tiberius' body be returned to the family (a request that was refused), Gaius did not immediately involve himself in political affairs. He did, however, retain his

Gaius Gracchus

BORN

Between 160 and 153 B.C.
Rome

DIED

121 B.C.
Rome

PROFESSION

Statesman

ACCOMPLISHMENTS

Sought to curb injustices in the provinces and gave the *equites* (cavalrymen) power to try provincial governors; provided for a steady distribution of wheat in Rome at a subsidized price; promoted the establishment of self-governing colonies in Italy and overseas, at Carthage; transferred the right to collect Rome's taxes in the provinces from the provincials to the *equites*; argued unsuccessfully for the revision of laws concerning the rights of Latins and Italians

position on the commission to oversee the implementation of his brother's land reform bill.

According to the Roman statesman and orator Marcus Tullius Cicero, Gaius turned to politics only after Tiberius appeared to him one night in a dream asking, "Gaius, why do you delay? There is no escape. One life and one death is appointed for us both: the one to spend, the other to meet, in the service of the people."

In 126 B.C., Gaius was sent as a quaestor (the public official in charge of finance) to Sardinia. The *optimates* were relieved, for they feared Gaius' ability to sway the people with references to his murdered brother. In Sardinia, Gaius proved himself an honest and capable official. When Rome refused to have the cities of Sardinia provide much-needed clothing for the Roman soldiers stationed there, Gaius personally went from city to city asking for help. Everywhere, the people rallied to his cause.

Normally, a quaestorship was a one-year term, but the Senate purposely delayed recalling Gaius to Rome and even considered charging him with mismanagement of funds. Aware that the *optimates* were stalling, Gaius returned unannounced and presented the records of all his transactions in Sardinia. Unable to refute the facts or counteract his eloquently presented defense, the *optimates* dropped their charges. Gaius then presented himself as a candidate for the office of tribune.

Plutarch later wrote that so many of the *populares* journeyed to Rome to vote for Gaius that there were no vacant lodgings anywhere. On election day, so many thronged into the voting place that some had to climb to the roofs of houses to make sure their oral vote was heard and recorded.

In 123 B.C., Gaius assumed the tribuneship and introduced a program that was broader and far more radical than his brother's. Gaius well understood the political system and used the class divisions within each group to his advantage. Much more farsighted than Tiberius, Gaius knew the power of the spoken word to sway people's thinking. Yet he always was forthright in his intentions and honest in his actions.

Gaius was not always successful, however. His proposal to prohibit anyone driven from office by popular vote from running for another office was so unpopular that he withdrew the measure. Nevertheless, he did manage to win passage of a law allowing a tribune to run for re-election. Shortly after, he himself took advantage of this new law, ran, and won.

Gaius then introduced the novel policy of establishing colonies where poor Romans might achieve success—first in the southern Italian towns of Capua and Tarentum and later in North Africa, on the site where Carthage had once stood. This was Rome's first overseas colony. Gaius also took steps to provide a steady wheat supply for all citizens at a reasonable, subsidized price and supported a law requiring Rome to outfit its soldiers, thus opening the military to men who lacked the funds to purchase equipment.

Realizing that his strongest opposition always came from the Senate, Gaius often brought his measures before the Assembly. He also sought to strengthen the growing numbers of wealthy Roman citizens who were not senators but businessmen and landowners. Members of this group were known as *equites* (cavalrymen), because in ancient times they had formed the Roman cavalry units, and Gaius believed they would be more politically responsible than others might be.

Gaius also attempted to curb the widespread corruption among the public officials in the provinces. Too often, Rome's provincial magistrates were charged with bribery and other crimes, brought to Rome to stand trial, and then acquitted. The fault lay with a court system in which the jurors were senators and friends or acquaintances of the accused. Gaius combated this abuse by making only *equites* eligible to be jurors in such cases. He also placed tax collecting under the jurisdiction of the *equites* rather than local officials.

Gaius next addressed the problems of the Latins who inhabited central Italy and the Italians who occupied the rest of Italy. Both were allies of Rome and had sent tens of thousands to fight in the great wars against the Carthaginians, but politically and socially the two groups had few rights. Gaius proposed that the Latins be given full rights of Roman citizenship and that the Italians be given Latin rights, meaning that all their local public officials would become Roman citizens. This historic step was the first in a series of measures that would lead to making all Italy Roman. In Gaius' time, many Roman citizens strongly opposed such a law, fearing for their own rights and privileges.

At this critical moment in his career, Gaius left for Carthage to help establish the new colony there. During his two-month absence, his opponents successfully attacked his laws and proposals. Once back in Rome, Gaius tried to regain the approval of the people. He even moved from his large residence to a small house near the Forum in order to be closer to the people, but it was not enough. His insistence on allowing the Italians to remain in Rome during a vote on a bill affecting their citizenship rights further distanced the people from him. When Gaius ran for a third term as tribune, he was defeated.

In 121 B.C., the consul Lucius Opimius proposed dissolving the newly founded colony in Carthage. To show his opposition, Gaius led an illegal demonstration to the Capitol, where the Senate was meeting. When one of Opimius' attendants rudely addressed the demonstrators, he was attacked and killed. Fortunately, a sudden rainstorm ended the threat of a full-scale battle.

The following day, Opimius asked the Senate to enact a *senatus consultum ultimum* (the highest decree of the senate). This decree, which could be enacted only during a state of public emergency, gave the Senate the power to use any means necessary against public enemies. After little deliberation, the Senate did as Opimius asked. This was the first time in Rome's history that the decree had been invoked.

Gaius then asked for a truce to discuss the situation peacefully, but his request was denied. Instead, Opimius personally led his troops against "Rome's enemies," killing all they met. Except for a short dagger at his side, Gaius was unarmed, because he had not expected such a confrontation. Determined not to be taken alive, Gaius ordered his faithful servant Philocrates to kill him. The loyal Philocrates did so, then took the dagger to his own heart.

Plutarch later wrote that Opimius' friend Septimuleius was so determined to win the reward offered for Gaius' head that he decapitated Gaius' corpse and brought the trophy to Opimius. True to his word, the consul weighed the head and rewarded Septimuleius with 17 pounds of gold.

Still Opimius was not satisfied. In the weeks that followed, he authorized his troops to kill as many of Gaius' followers as possible, approximately 3,000 in all, and throw their bodies into the Tiber, depriving them of a proper burial.

Many of the policies that had so angered the Senate, such as making the Latins citizens with the right to vote, became laws during the decades that followed. The distribution of land under Tiberius' land bill also continued, as did the subsidizing of the grain supply.

Unfortunately, the fate of the Gracchi indicated that a dangerous precedent had been set. Force had become an acceptable means of solving problems, especially of changing unwanted results from the ballot box. As a result, Rome was to become far different from the nation envisaged by the founders of the Republic.

FURTHER READING

Boren, Henry C. *The Gracchi*. New York: Twayne, 1968.

Plutarch. *Plutarch's Lives*. Vol. 10. Translated by Bernadotte Perrin. Loeb Classical Library. Cambridge: Harvard University Press, 1968.

Scullard, H. H. *From the Gracchi to Nero: A History of Rome from 133 B.C. to A.D. 68*. New York: Methuen, 1982.

Stockton, David L. *The Gracchi*. New York: Oxford University Press, 1978.

Marius
(Gaius Marius)

"A SWORD THAT RUSTS IN PEACETIME"

Toward the end of the 2nd century B.C., Rome witnessed major changes in its political system. The sword became more powerful than the word, and political assassination became the means to a desired goal. Although many Romans disagreed with this new approach, their numbers were too few to prevent the abuses of power that followed. One of the most avid proponents of the new system was Gaius Marius.

All that is known of Marius' family is that his parents owned property in Arpinum, a prosperous town near Rome. Although Marius did not trace his lineage to Rome's aristocratic families, he did join the Roman cavalry, indicating that he had enough money to buy the expensive equipment required of the cavalrymen. Marius and his supporters probably spread the story that he came from the poorest classes in an attempt to win the affection of this large and politically important group.

Like all young men of his social class, Marius studied Latin, Greek, and other traditional disciplines such as literature, astronomy, geometry, and logic. Public speaking, however, was never one of his strong points, and he was later to show a preference for the battlefield over intellectual pursuits.

For reasons unknown to us, Marius' public career began later than most. The historian Plutarch indicates that Marius held his first military post at Numantia in Spain in 134 B.C. There his military prowess gained him the recognition of his commander, Scipio Aemilianus. When asked where another Roman might be found to replace as distinguished a commander as himself, Scipio gently tapped Marius on the shoulder and said, "In this man, perhaps." Inspired by this vote of confidence and by his own ambition, Marius spent the next few years working his way up the military and political ladder.

Marius seemed to have an uncanny sense about when to absent himself from Rome so that he would not become involved in political battles, especially those surrounding the murders of the Gracchi brothers. At the same time, he was managing his economic affairs so successfully that he had become one of the richest members of the class known as the *equites*. Originally these were members of the Roman cavalry, but in time the group came to include businessmen and tax collectors. Many attribute Marius' wealth to wise investments, especially in Spain's copper and gold mines.

Sometime around the age of 35, Marius first ran for political office. In 122 B.C., he won the quaestorship with the help of his friends and patrons the influential and aristocratic Metelli family. In 119 B.C., the Metelli backed Marius for the office of tribune. Only plebeians (who at this time were becoming known as *populares*) could hold this office, the purpose of which was to counteract the power of the aristocrats and ensure proper treatment of the people.

Unfortunately, Marius proved himself an ineffectual politician, alienating the *optimates*, the *equites*, and the *populares* alike. The *optimates* strongly opposed Marius' plan to pass legislation that would have made it more difficult for them to control elections. Marius angered the other two groups when he threatened to curtail the distribution of subsidized grain. The *equites* feared losing money if his proposal passed, and the *populares* feared increases in the price of food.

At the next election, Marius was defeated twice on the same day: first when he ran for the aedileship (aediles were the elected officials in charge of public buildings, the grain supply, and the games) of the *optimates* and then, after seeing that as an impossibility, when he ran for the aedileship of the *populares*.

Marius refused to admit that his political career was over. He spent the next two years managing his financial affairs and planning a run for the praetorship. Even though it was a tradition to pass from one office to another, Marius had no intention of standing for the aedileship again. Instead, he made his own rules, in such a way that he changed Roman politics forever.

When Marius won the praetorship (of the six praetors elected, he got the fewest votes) his enemies brought him to trial on a charge of bribing voters. By invoking ancient laws and twisting the rules to his advantage, Marius managed to get himself acquitted. He was now in the grip of fierce ambition and was determined to reach the pinnacle of Roman politics. He set his sights on the office of consul, even though the

position was open only to *optimates*. To surmount this obstacle, Marius married Julia, a member of one of Rome's oldest and most aristocratic families. The political and financial fortunes of her family had lately suffered reverses, and an alliance with one of Rome's richest men—even one from a lower social class—was very much in their interest.

In 110 B.C., Rome confronted Jugurtha, a North African ruler to whom it had granted a portion of Numidia. Jugurtha now wished to control all of Numidia. When he ordered the murder of Italian merchants living in Numidia because they opposed his ambitions, Rome declared war. The renowned military leader Quintus Metellus won two solid victories over Jugurtha's forces but he was unable to stop Jugurtha's bid for power. In Rome, the *populares* demanded a general with the courage and cunning to finish the war. Marius believed he was that man.

Twelve days before the consular election in Rome, Marius obtained military leave from his post in Africa so that he could return to the city and

Convinced of his skills as an effective military leader, Marius (seated) saw his defeat of the Numidian king Jugurtha (far right) as a means of advancing his political career. Therefore, Marius showed no mercy as he prepared to lead the king in chains through the streets of Rome in a grand procession.

present himself as a candidate for the office of consul. The office was now open to him, because his wife was one of the *optimates*. Favorable winds and luck brought him to the city just in time for the elections. Supported by the *populares* and the *equites*, who applauded his promise to kill Jugurtha or bring him back alive, Marius was elected to Rome's highest office.

Stunned though they were at Marius' election, the *optimates* used their power to vote the continued command of the war in Africa to Metellus, not as consul but as proconsul. (By custom, an outgoing consul was given a proconsulship over one of Rome's provinces.) But once again, the *populares* made their feelings known and, with the help of the *equites*, vetoed the Senate's bill and passed their own, naming Marius, not Metellus, the commander.

Disregarding the rule that soldiers had to be property owners, Marius began recruiting anyone who wished to volunteer, including landless men and even slaves. He believed that professional soldiers dependent on the army for their livelihood would fight more efficiently than amateurs. This new policy completely changed Rome's military system. Now there was no longer any need for a draft, because volunteers eagerly signed up to serve. However, their allegiance was not primarily to Rome but to the generals who granted them the most favors, such as booty after a victory or a grant of land upon completing a tour of duty.

Marius also revamped the rules concerning equipment. Usually, horses or mules pulled all the necessary supplies for a campaign in a long baggage train that often slowed troop movement. Marius ordered each soldier to fasten his personal equipment to a forked stick, known as a *furca*, and carry the load over his shoulder. This simple measure considerably shortened the supply line, because the animals now had to carry only large items such as tents and siege equipment. According to tradition, the new marching order earned Roman soldiers the nickname of "Marius' mules."

Marius next tackled the construction of the Roman *pilum*, or thrusting spear. Because the spears were held together by metal rivets, the enemy could often reuse captured Roman spears. By ordering wooden pegs to replace the metal rivets, Marius created a spear whose head would either separate from the shaft or become so twisted upon impact that it was unusable.

With these changes in place, Marius returned to Africa as consul and commander. However, like his predecessor Metellus, he was unable to capture Jugurtha. Then, in 105 B.C., an ally of Jugurtha treacherously betrayed the Numidian king to one of Marius' lieutenants named Sulla. Jugurtha's capture ended the war, but the glory went mostly to Sulla, who even had a representation of the incident engraved on his personal seal. The Senate did grant Marius a grand triumph through the streets of Rome, but it voted the honor of using the surname *Numidicus* to Metellus, not Marius.

Politically, however, Marius was the winner. His success in Africa led to a second consulship. It was against the law for a consul to serve successive terms, but the Romans believed Marius' leadership was necessary because they were confronting another national emergency. Even before Jugurtha had been caught, Germanic tribes had been invading Italy from the north. Every army sent to meet them had met with defeat. Discouraged, the Romans feared that their city would be invaded and looked to Marius, their most trusted general, for help.

Marius immediately accepted the command and left for northern Italy with Sulla as his lieutenant. His assignment was a daunting one, especially because his troops were new recruits. (Most of those who had fought under him in Africa had remained there, waiting for the land allotments he had promised.)

Marius quickly proved himself a capable leader and shaped his new army into a well-disciplined, efficient force. He abolished the distinction between light-armed and heavy-armed troops, permitting each soldier to carry only the traditional short sword and a javelin. As a result, the fighting units were much more flexible and compact and could maneuver more efficiently on the battlefield. According to Pliny the Elder, Marius sought to instill a sense of belonging and pride in his troops by making the eagle the official symbol of the Roman military. (The eagle was also the symbol of Jupiter, the king of the Roman gods.) Each legion, the strength of which had increased to 6,000 soldiers, marched behind its eagle, which was held by a specially assigned standard bearer. In the decades to come, the eagle would lead Rome's troops across Europe, into Asia, and across northern Africa.

Marius had time to prepare his troops well, because the invaders suddenly halted their advance into Italy. The tribes known as the Cimbri turned toward Spain, while the others, the Teutones, remained in central Gaul (present-day France). Marius marched his army into Gaul and, for six days, followed as the Teutones marched south toward the Alps and Italy. From a distance, the Teutones taunted their pursuers, shouting that they would soon be masters of Rome and asking if the Romans had any messages for their wives.

Using the self-control Marius had taught them, the Romans did not rush headlong into battle. They took heart from omens that seemed to foretell victory, especially the arrival of two vultures with bronze collars about their necks. Plutarch wrote that these same birds had appeared before Marius when he led his troops to victory in Africa.

Now all believed they would have the same effect in Italy.

Finally, Marius saw his opportunity and engaged the Teutones at Aquae Sextiae (now Aix-en-Provence). Using a clever bit of strategy, he positioned 3,000 troops high above the battlefield where the enemy could not see them. At a given signal, these troops swooped down and joined the fighting, slaughtering thousands of Teutones. After allowing his soldiers to take what booty they wanted, Marius collected the rest and placed much of it in a huge pile to be burned in the customary victory celebration.

But Marius' work was not done. The Cimbri were advancing into Italy and had already defeated one Roman army sent against them. Marius hastened back to the capital, where he learned of revolts against Roman forces in Sicily and Macedonia. He had to act quickly. After dispatching reinforcements to Sicily and Macedonia, Marius led his army against the Cimbri.

Carefully choosing his terrain, he positioned his men with the wind and sun to their backs. When the two armies clashed, the dust kicked up by the Roman troops blew into the faces of the Cimbri and the sun blinded their vision. Adding to the enemy's distress were the iron chains looped through the belts of their front-line soldiers. This strategy was meant to prevent the Romans from crashing through the lines, but it severely hampered the Cimbri's ability to maneuver.

Once again, Marius' tactics worked. The Romans overwhelmed the Cimbri—the death toll reached into the thousands, with many Cimbri women killing their children and themselves rather than face the prospect of slavery. Plutarch wrote that even the Romans recoiled at the horror of the scene as they entered the enemy camp.

At Rome, Marius was hailed as the third founder of the country. (Romulus

Marius

BORN
Around 157 B.C.
Arpinum, in central Italy

DIED
86 B.C.
Rome

PROFESSION
General and statesman

ACCOMPLISHMENTS
Created a professional army by enabling citizens who owned no land to become soldiers; allowed freedmen and slaves to enlist in the army in national emergencies; defeated Jugurtha and kept North Africa a province of Rome; successfully prevented the Cimbri and Teutones from conquering northern Italy and entering Rome

Marius made the eagle the official symbol of the Roman army. Each legion, a Roman military division, had its own eagle, usually of bronze or silver, on a wooden staff. Each cohort, a subdivision of the legion, also had its own standard, generally referred to as a *signum* (center). The cavalry and light-armed troops had their own banner, called a *vexillum* (right), which was white or red and attached to a short horizontal piece of wood or metal on a staff.

was the first, Camillus the second.) The honors heaped on him soon made him proud and boastful. He abandoned his simple way of life and became an arrogant spendthrift. He no longer considered himself bound by Rome's laws but made his own. For example, he illegally conferred Roman citizenship on 1,000 soldiers for their valiant efforts on the battlefield. He also used his money to gain a sixth consulship. Only one other Roman, Valerius Corvinus, had served six terms as consul, but these periods were spaced out over a span of 45 years. Marius' almost continuous service was unprecedented.

Marius was not as astute a politician as he was a general. Because he wanted to please everyone, he found it difficult to make decisions. In addition, he chose as political partners men who lacked moral values and whose disregard for rules antagonized many Romans.

On one occasion, when Metellus refused to act on a bill before the Senate because the correct proceedings had not been followed, Marius' agents had Metellus exiled. For a while, the Senate ignored Marius' actions, but its members finally reacted when it was revealed that two of Marius' political allies, Saturninus and Glaucia, were planning to assassinate a man who had defeated them in an election.

A group of senators went to Marius' house, demanding that he take action against the conspirators. Again Marius hesitated, even feigning illness to break off the conversation. When the people joined the senators asking for justice, Marius finally ordered that Saturninus and Glaucia be held in the Senate building. But the angry crowd was not to be deterred. Plutarch relates that rioters climbed to the roof, tore off the tiles, and pelted the two men to death.

Although Marius had not ordered this act, many *populares* turned against him, believing that he was a man who betrayed even his close associates. Taking advantage of this change in attitude, members of the Senate arranged to recall Marius' archrival, Metellus. Humiliated by this proposal, Marius refused to remain in Rome for the arrival of Metellus and left for the East, where he believed that Mithridates, king of Pontus, was preparing to declare war on Rome. Marius believed that he could reclaim his prestige on the battlefield. Plutarch later quoted Marius as saying, "The Romans treat me as a sword that rusts in peacetime." Unfortunately for Marius, Mithridates chose to remain at peace with Rome.

Rome's Italian allies, on the other hand, chose war. For decades, they had fought in Rome's legions, yet they were refused citizenship and its privileges. In 90 B.C., believing they had no other recourse, the Italians withdrew all support from Rome, established their own state and government, and named their capital Italia. Following tradition, Rome's consuls assumed command of the legions. Marius received a minor post, but this was not the war he wished to fight. He had commanded many of the Italian troops, knew their families, and had tasted victory because of their strength and devotion to duty. Though he now defeated them in a major battle, he relied on his lieutenant Sulla to complete the rout. The *optimates*, who had always favored Sulla, granted him the honor of the victory. Soon after, Marius resigned his command and Sulla took charge of his troops.

At this moment Mithridates took advantage of the turmoil in Italy to seize Roman territory in Asia Minor, killing tens of thousands of Romans in the area. Wishing to end the so-called Social War with the Italians, the Senate first offered the rights of citizenship to those Italian allies who had remained faithful to Rome, then to all Italians who pledged their allegiance within 60 days. The Italians accepted the terms. However, when a tribune named Sulpicius Rufus proposed legislation giving the Italians the same rights as the citizens of Rome and extending the right to vote to freedmen (ex-slaves), he met bitter opposition. Sulpicius appealed to Marius for political support, promising to see that Marius was given command of the forces against Mithridates.

The Senate, however, followed the law and awarded the post to Sulla, who was now consul. With the help of his armed bodyguard, Sulpicius then forced Sulla to leave Rome. Sulla went immediately to the legions he was to command against Mithridates, rallied their support, and led them to the gates of Rome. For the first time in Rome's history, Roman troops marched on their own city.

Marius had no troops at his command and chose to flee the city rather than face certain death. Plutarch later wrote that Marius kept his spirits high by telling his loyal companions of an omen he had received as a young man: An eagle's nest had fallen into his cloak, and in the nest were seven fledglings. This, Marius asserted, was the gods' way of telling him that he would be consul seven times. Since he had held the office only six times, he assured his followers that he would survive this crisis.

The opposition, meanwhile, offered a reward for the capture and return of Marius and Sulpicius. Marius outsmarted the troops sent to capture him by hiding in the woods and then swimming to a ship offshore. When the sailors on this ship understood the consequences of harboring a wanted man, they ordered Marius ashore. A short time later, Sulla's men discovered Marius hiding in a swamp, took him prisoner, and prepared to carry out the death sentence imposed on him. Plutarch claims that when the man sent to kill Marius entered the room where he was being held, the darkness was so great that all he saw was two eyes staring at him, like the embers in a smoldering fire. From the depths of the darkness, the man heard Marius say, "Will you dare to kill Gaius Marius?"

Overcome with fear, the man ran from the room, shouting that he could not kill Marius. The officials of Minturnae then rethought their judgment against a man who had saved Rome in the past. They decided to spare his life and gave him a ship and provisions. Marius immediately set sail for North Africa. Even there, he was forced to escape assassins and took refuge on an island.

Meanwhile, Rome was in turmoil. Sulla had killed many of Marius' followers and had taken control of the city. But the newly elected consuls were divided in their allegiance. Octavius favored the *optimates* and Sulla, while Cinna favored the *populares* and Marius. Once again, blood flowed in Rome as the two factions clashed in the Forum. Cinna proved the loser, and the Senate deposed him from the consulship. He then marshaled the Italians and laid siege to Rome.

When the news of this development reached Marius in Africa, he immediately set sail for home—and the seventh consulship he believed awaited him. Once in Italy, Marius joined forces with Cinna. More troops rallied to their side when the Italians learned that the two generals promised to reinstate Sulpicius' law expanding the rights of all Italians.

In the weeks that followed, the combined forces of Marius and Cinna retook Rome. What happened next has been a subject of controversy for centuries. Most accounts, tracing their sources to enemies of Marius and Cinna, indicate that the two men unleashed a massacre unprecedented in Roman history, executing all their personal and political enemies. With little or no opposition remaining, Marius and Cinna were elected consuls. Marius' omen had proved correct.

There was little time for rejoicing however. News reached Rome that Sulla had defeated Mithridates and was planning to return home. This meant war, and for once Marius was unequal to the challenge, either because of advancing age or because he was tired of constant turmoil. Perhaps he simply feared death. Whatever the reason, his actions became increasingly irrational, and on the 17th day of his consulship he died. According to Plutarch, all Rome rejoiced.

FURTHER READING

Kildahl, Philip A. *Caius Marius*. New York: Twayne, 1968.

McCullough, Colleen. *Fortune's Favorites*. New York: Morrow, 1993.

Plutarch. *Plutarch's Lives*. Translated by Bernadotte Perrin. Loeb Classical Library. Cambridge: Harvard University Press, 1968.

Smith, Richard P. *Caius Marius: A Tragedy*. Philadelphia: University of Pennsylvania Press, 1968.

Sulla
(Lucius
Cornelius Sulla)

THE LAST REPUBLICAN

As a young man, Sulla must have found life quite frustrating. He traced his ancestry to one of Rome's oldest aristocratic families, yet no relative had ever accomplished anything particularly significant. He received a good education and led a rather carefree life until his father died, when everything changed abruptly.

Inheriting nothing (there may in fact have been nothing left to inherit), Sulla was forced to move into a rundown neighborhood, where he rented an apartment next door to a former slave. While enjoying a steady income from

The expression on what is believed to be the bust of Sulla shows a determined and forceful individual; Sulla himself carefully reviewed his plans before acting.

financial investments, Sulla still did not have enough money to qualify him for the rank of military service open to members of his social class. This rank was a prerequisite for election to Rome's top political offices.

Perhaps because of these circumstances, Sulla sought companionship in the theater, where money and family background did not govern friendships or social position. Even after he succeeded in becoming one of Rome's leading citizens, he never forgot these early friends. Their company even inspired him to write a few short comedies during this early period.

Sulla was a determined man, with a personality that was both pleasant and commanding. Although no definitive likeness of him survives, his appearance must have been striking. Accounts tell of his red hair, piercing blue eyes, and pale complexion mottled with red blotches (the result of a disease that became worse as he grew older).

Shortly before his 30th birthday, Sulla's fortunes changed. First, his stepmother died and left her considerable fortune to him. Then his mistress died, and he also inherited her property. With the financial resources he needed, Sulla now began his political career, running successfully for the office of quaestor in 108 B.C.

Soon after his election, Sulla served under the consul Gaius Marius in a war against Jugurtha, the king of Numidia in North Africa. Jugurtha had been Rome's ally during wars in Spain, but in later years he had extended his control over Roman possessions in Africa. All Rome's efforts to conquer Jugurtha had failed, but Sulla provided them with an advantage when he won the admiration of Bocchus, the king of neighboring Mauritania and also Jugurtha's father-in-law.

Because Bocchus felt threatened by Jugurtha's continuing conquests, he considered betraying his son-in-law to the Romans. He sent a request to Marius asking that Sulla be designated the intermediary in negotiations. This was a dangerous mission for Sulla, who not only had to cross enemy territory but also had to trust a foreign king planning to betray a relative. There was no way of knowing whether Bocchus would surrender Jugurtha once he had Sulla in his kingdom or use Sulla as a bargaining chip with Rome. After long deliberation, Bocchus finally sided with Sulla. When Jugurtha was summoned to Bocchus' court, Bocchus' soldiers seized the unsuspecting king and handed him over to the Roman.

Naturally, Sulla saw himself as the real victor in the campaign against Jugurtha and proudly commissioned a signet ring for himself. Carved into the seal was an image of Bocchus surrendering Jugurtha to Sulla. This irked Marius, and relations between the two became strained. Ultimately, however, Rome's safety proved more important than personal feelings. When Germanic tribes headed south to invade Italy and capture Rome, Marius once again chose Sulla as his lieutenant, and once again Sulla proved a capable military leader and administrator. But the enmity between the rivals continued, and Sulla soon requested a transfer to the army led by Marius' co-consul.

After the defeat of the Germans, Marius and Sulla returned to Rome and politics. Instead of running for the next office open to him, the aedileship, Sulla opted to stand for the praetorship, the second-highest position in Rome. Undaunted when he lost, Sulla tried again the next year and won.

After completing his year in office, Sulla spent a year in the provinces, as was the custom. Awarded the province of Cilicia in Asia Minor by the Senate, Sulla left Rome to assume his new duties. But the scheming of Mithridates, king of neighboring Pontus, forced the Senate to send Sulla back to the battlefield. Because his original assignment

Sulla

BORN
138 B.C.
Perhaps in or near Rome

DIED
78 B.C.
Puteoli, Campania

PROFESSION
Statesman and general

ACCOMPLISHMENTS
Captured Jugurtha, king of Numidia, ending the war in Africa; retook Greece from Mithridates; won the battle for Rome against the *populares*; ruled as dictator of Rome and its possessions; instituted a score of reforms, political and administrative; extended full Roman rights to the Italians

had been political, Sulla did not have a full army with him and had to recruit soldiers hastily from Rome's allies in the area. His ability to accomplish this and then drive Mithridates back into his own kingdom testify to Sulla's skill as a military leader.

Sulla's campaign against Mithridates proved important in other ways. It brought him to the banks of the Euphrates River and the boundaries of the powerful Parthian Empire, a nation with which Rome had had no contact. After several meetings, Sulla was able to conclude a treaty of friendship between Rome and Parthia. This momentous political occasion also proved to be a personal milestone for Sulla.

A number of Chaldean (from southern Babylonia, between the Tigris and Euphrates rivers) astrologers, well known for their ability to foretell the future, attended Sulla's meeting with the Parthians. Sources relate that one astrologer began studying Sulla's face, finally proclaiming that he was destined to become the greatest man who had ever lived and that he would die at the height of his glory. Sulla would never forget this prediction, which he mentioned just before his death.

Sulla's immediate concern, however, was the consulship, Rome's highest office. Yet, Rome proved to be much less receptive than Sulla had anticipated. His archrival Marius had convinced another Roman to accuse Sulla of extortion while he was in Asia Minor. Although the charge was dropped because Sulla's accuser failed to appear in court, Sulla was discredited. As a result, he chose not to run for the consulship and stayed out of politics for four years.

Then, in 91 B.C., Sulla's old friend Bocchus appeared in Rome, asking the Senate's permission to place some statues on the Capitol as a way of showing his friendship and support. The senators agreed—but were surprised when the statuary showed Bocchus handing over Jugurtha to Sulla, not Marius. Understandably, Marius was furious and prepared to order the removal of the statues. Before he could do so, though, news reached Rome that allied Italian forces had declared war on the city. Determined to have full Roman political and civil rights, the Italians had lost faith in Rome's leaders and seceded. After setting up their own capital at Corfinium, east of Rome, they had elected consuls and were preparing to become an independent nation.

Once again, a national crisis made Marius and Sulla forget their differences. In 90 B.C., the two joined forces to protect their city. Marius' contributions were insignificant, because he was angry at not being appointed commander-in-chief. Sulla, on the other hand, won recognition for his efforts. The invasion of Rome's province in Asia Minor by Mithridates brought the Social War (the name given to the conflict between Rome and the Italian allies, from the Latin word for allies, *socii*) to a quick close. In 89 B.C., the two sides signed a treaty, but the stipulations attached to it actually withheld equal rights from the Italians, a point that would cause much dissent in the future.

For the time being, the focus was on the East and Mithridates. Judging Sulla to be their most competent leader, the Romans elected him consul for the year 88 B.C. The Senate also named him commander of the forces against Mithridates. Marius, who had wanted the command for himself, was determined to revoke the Senate's decree. Convincing the tribune Sulpicius to work with him, Marius persuaded the People's Assembly to give the Italian allies full rights with no restrictions and award him command of the expedition against Mithridates.

Sulla was training his troops in Campania, south of Rome, when he learned of these maneuvers. Knowing that Marius had enough votes to swing any election, Sulla led his army against Rome. This was the first time Roman soldiers had placed duty to their commander above allegiance to Rome—and the first time that Romans had ever marched against their own city.

Sulla quickly took control of the city. Summoning all the inhabitants to a meeting, he explained that as consul he had acted rightly to protect Rome from its enemies. However, because Sulla saw the enemy as belonging mostly to the class of the *populares*, he took steps to establish the *optimates* as the party in power. One measure included revoking legislation recently pushed through by Marius. An astute politician, Sulla knew he could not win the support of everyone in Rome, so he did not push for passage of all the legislation he felt necessary. Instead, he focused on his army and a plan to defeat Rome's enemies in the East.

Soon after Sulla's departure for Asia Minor in 88 B.C., the *populares* wrested control of Rome from the *optimates*. Marius returned triumphantly to the city and ordered the execution of scores of Sulla's followers. Then, after declaring himself consul, Marius took steps to have himself named commander of the forces in the East in place of Sulla, but he died before his appointment could be confirmed.

News of Marius' death and the return of the *populares* to power must have been relayed to Sulla. He also must have heard that he had been declared an outlaw in Rome, which meant that anyone had the right to kill him. His house was destroyed, his family and friends forced to flee Italy. Nevertheless, Sulla continued to follow the orders he had been given when he left Rome: defeat Mithridates and reconquer the Roman lands that he had captured.

Sulla began his campaign in Greece, which Mithridates had boldly occupied. In 86 B.C., after a long and difficult siege, Sulla captured Athens and expelled Mithridates' forces from Greece. Refusing to join with other Roman troops in the area for fear that their officers might be political enemies, Sulla turned his army toward Asia Minor.

Instead of carrying the war into Mithridates' territory, Sulla opted to negotiate a treaty with the wily king. Sulla must have recognized that Mithridates' extensive empire was rich in resources, allowing Mithridates the money and soldiers to continue fighting for an extended period of time. Sulla, on the other hand, was far from home, had few resources, and his troops were weary from the long battle in Greece. In addition, Rome was in turmoil, and Sulla had been declared a public outcast. A long war would work to his disadvantage.

In 85 B.C., Sulla met with Mithridates at Dardanus on the Hellespont. Mithridates agreed to withdraw his troops from the lands he had conquered and pay Rome a fine. In return, Rome agreed to consider Mithridates a friend and ally and allowed him to remain king of Pontus. The leniency of the terms infuriated many Romans, especially Sulla's troops, who knew how much booty Mithridates had taken home from his conquests.

Sulla, meanwhile, attributed all events to his good fortune and the favor of the gods. Short of money during the siege of Athens, he had ordered the treasuries at the sacred temples in Greece to send contributions. When his envoy sent word that he feared taking anything from Apollo's temple at Delphi because he had heard the sound of a lyre being played within, Sulla replied that such a sound was a sign of joy, not anger. In fact, Sulla was so sure of divine favor that he saw the gods as contributors to his cause. After the *populares* appointed Lucius Valerius Flaccus to replace Sulla as general in 86 B.C., the gods appeared to confirm their preference for Sulla—Flaccus'

T H E
CATILINE
A N D
JUGURTHINE WARS.
TRANSLATED FROM
SALLUST.
BY HUGH MAFFETT, Esq.
LATE OF THE MIDDLE TEMPLE.

Nec tamen exprimi verbum e verbo neceffe erit, ut interpretes
indiferti folent.   CICERO DE FINIBUS.

D U B L I N :
PRINTED BY STEWART AND SPOTSWOOD, COLLEGE-GREEN.
M,DCC,LXXII.

Sometime after 40 B.C., the Roman historian Sallust wrote his account of how the plotting of two individuals, Catiline and Jugurtha, caused much turmoil and dissent throughout Rome. Rome's efforts to conquer Jugurtha, the king of Numidia, had failed until Sulla captured him, thereby ending the war in Africa.

own lieutenant murdered him before he could arrive at Sulla's camp.

Even with his good fortune, Sulla was still short of money. To remedy the situation, he decided to exact fines from the Asian cities that had allied themselves with Mithridates. In addition, each city was required to treat Roman tax collectors and envoys graciously, offering them every convenience available and even supplying them with pocket money. Naturally, these concessions made Sulla's troops happier, but discontent was brewing among Rome's subjects in Asia.

Sulla now turned his thoughts to home. With a force of approximately 40,000 men and much plunder from the Asian cities, he entered southern Italy and advanced toward Rome. In 82 B.C., Sulla stood outside the Colline Gate. The battle lines had been drawn, and neither he nor the leaders of the *populares* were about to yield. For the second time, Sulla led an army of Romans against the city, and for the second time he won.

In the months that followed, Sulla's agents murdered thousands of his opponents and confiscated their property. There were cases in which someone added a name to the list of condemned people just to get the person's land. Sulla contributed to the chaos and terror by freeing 10,000 slaves, most of whom had belonged to his enemies. These ex-slaves adopted Sulla's family name, Cornelius, and promised to protect their new benefactor with their lives.

That same year, Sulla had himself appointed dictator, with the right to rewrite the laws and re-establish the Republic. However, in his determination to carry out his plan Sulla set no time limit on his dictatorship. This set another precedent in Roman history, because such limits had been required by law.

In keeping with his belief that the Senate should be the principal political body in Rome, Sulla curtailed the rights of the tribunes and granted them only the power to protect individual citizens from unjust imprisonment or execution. (Originally, this had been the tribunes' only right, but over the years their powers had increased tremendously.) Now, under Sulla's rules, the tribunes could no longer exercise a veto against the Senate or bring matters to a vote before the people without gaining the Senate's approval. Sulla also decreed that tribunes could not run for any other high-ranking public office, a provision that naturally stopped many ambitious young Romans from considering a tribuneship.

To prevent anyone from rising too quickly, Sulla established minimum age requirements for each of the high-ranking offices. A Roman had to be at least 30 for the quaestorship, 36 for the aedileship, 39 for the praetorship, and 42 for the consulship. Furthermore, everyone had to proceed from office to office, the aedileship being the only one that could be omitted. Finally, Sulla decreed that an elected official could not run again for the same office until a 10-year period had elapsed.

Fully aware of how he had used his soldiers' allegiance to gain power, Sulla acted to prevent any other Roman official from doing the same. He forbade provincial governors from extending their stay beyond the normal one-year term of office, from waging unauthorized wars beyond their borders, and even from leaving their province without the approval of the Senate or Assembly. To ensure adherence to this new constitution, Sulla invoked the law of *maiestas* (treason) against anyone who disobeyed.

Sulla also was convinced that new policies were needed to reverse what he considered a decay in morals throughout Rome. By establishing criminal courts to pursue and punish wrongdoers, he hoped to dissuade Romans from committing crimes such as murder, forgery, embezzlement of public funds, and electoral bribery. Sulla even tried to ban extravagant weddings and funerals. A veteran of the Social War, Sulla understood why the Italians felt that Rome discriminated against them. He therefore extended full rights to these people, a measure that ensured their future participation in Roman politics.

With his constitution in place and the Republic reorganized, Sulla felt the time appropriate to celebrate his triumph over Mithridates. As the ceremony came to a close, Sulla gave an account of his achievements, then requested that he be granted the honor of using the surname *Felix*, which meant "fortunate."

In 81 B.C., Sulla gave up the dictatorship and ran for consul, confident that his laws would be obeyed and that the gods would continue to bless him. When his term as consul ended, he did not seek an extension, nor did he run again. Even so, he remained Rome's most powerful citizen.

Toward the end of 80 B.C., Sulla's fourth wife, Metella, died of an illness. (His first wife had died years earlier. He had divorced his third wife and possibly his second.) Soon afterward, Sulla happened to be attending a theatrical performance when a woman walked past him and plucked some wool threads from his garment. According to Plutarch, when Sulla turned to her with an inquiring glance, the woman said, "Sir, what harm can there be if I should want to partake, albeit in a small way, of your good luck?" With that, she walked away and took her seat. After finding out that she was of high birth and recently divorced, Sulla sought her hand in marriage.

Their time together proved quite brief. The following year, 79 B.C., Sulla retired from public office and moved to his estate in Puteoli, Campania. Perhaps he felt his death imminent, for he had never forgotten the prediction of the Chaldean astrologer that he would die at the height of his fame. Certainly he was considered the master of Rome. Or, perhaps he was just being true to his word, because he had promised to relinquish his titles as soon as his reforms were in place.

As a private citizen, Sulla began writing his memoirs, completing them just two days before he died in the spring of 78 B.C. of a fever and hemorrhaging. Good fortune seemed to accompany him even in death. The Senate decreed a public funeral for Sulla, but the appointed day was overcast and gloomy. After delaying the ceremony for several hours because of the threat of rain, the officials finally decided to begin. Suddenly, a strong wind blew up around the funeral pyre and set it all ablaze. Then, as the last embers were smoldering, a violent rain poured down on the city.

Sulla the Fortunate was dead, but his reforms continued to affect the course of Roman history for decades. The Senate erected a monument to his memory and inscribed it with the words Sulla had written for his own epitaph: "Here lies Sulla Felix, a man who never forgave an enemy or forgot a friend."

FURTHER READING

Baker, George P. *Sulla the Fortunate: The Great Dictator*. New York: Dodd, Mead, 1927.

Keaveney, Arthur. *Sulla: The Last Republican*. London: Croom Helm, 1982.

Plutarch. *Plutarch's Lives*. Vol. 4. Translated by Bernadotte Perrin. Loeb Classical Library. Cambridge: Harvard University Press, 1968.

More Ancient Romans to Remember

Cincinnatus (active around 458 B.C.) was revered as one of Rome's noblest national heroes. In 458 B.C., when Rome's archrivals the Aedui had surrounded the Roman army encamped on the Alban Hills just south of Rome, a general was needed to raise an army and lead the troops to victory. Immediately, all thoughts turned to Cincinnatus, who had proved himself an outstanding leader when he had held the office of consul years earlier. The envoys sent to fetch him found him plowing the fields of his small farm. Hurriedly, they explained the reason for their visit and offered him the position of dictator for as long as it might take to defeat the Aedui. Without hesitating, Cincinnatus laid down his plow, traded his work clothes for military equipment, and rode out to raise an army.

According to tradition, Cincinnatus and his army defeated the Aedui in a single day of fighting and freed the besieged Romans. After celebrating the customary triumph given a Roman general who had defeated an enemy, Cincinnatus felt his mission was complete. Following the law stating that a dictator should hold office only as long as the national emergency required, he relinquished his title and returned to his plowing.

Marcus Manlius (active 387–86 B.C.) was another of Rome's early heroes whose achievements were documented and not completely bound up in legend. When the Gauls sacked Rome in 387 B.C. and were preparing to capture the fortress on the Capitoline Hill, the Roman commander Manlius barricaded his troops within its walls, knowing that to lose the Capitoline was to lose Rome.

Unfortunately, a messenger making his way up the hill had broken a few branches. Using these tracks as clues to guide them, the Gauls stealthily crept up the hill. They were about to attack when a flock of sacred geese, quartered in the goddess Juno's temple on the Capitoline, heard the men's footsteps and began to cackle.

Manlius immediately roused his soldiers to action and foiled the attack, holding out through the ensuing siege until reinforcements arrived. Following the Roman victory, Manlius was honored as the preserver of the Capitoline and granted the privilege of using *Capitolinus* as his surname.

Fabricius (active 280s–270s B.C.) served Rome as consul in 282 B.C. and as a victorious general on several occasions. In 280 B.C., the Romans were at war with the Greeks in southern Italy. So many thousands had been killed on both sides that when Pyrrhus, the leader of the Greeks, finally claimed victory, he wondered if he had won at all. This is the origin of the term "Pyrrhic victory," meaning a victory gained at too great a price.

Fabricius was one of the Roman envoys sent to Pyrrhus to ransom prisoners or negotiate a prisoner exchange. Judging Fabricius to be a poor man from his appearance, Pyrrhus offered him gold and other gifts in the hope of persuading him to switch his allegiance. Fabricius rejected every offer Pyrrhus made, until finally the Greek king dismissed the loyal Roman.

The following day, Pyrrhus again invited Fabricius into his tent. This time Pyrrhus intended to use scare tactics to win the Roman's support. Unaware that a huge war elephant dressed in armor stood behind the curtain near the chair assigned to him, Fabricius sat down. At the signal, Pyrrhus' slave raised the tent flap and the elephant trumpeted right above Fabricius' head.

According to Plutarch's account of the incident, Fabricius replied, "Pyrrhus, neither your bribes yesterday, nor your war elephant today will turn me from Rome. Poverty combined with honesty is worth far more than wealth. Let us proceed with the business at hand!"

Impressed with Fabricius' courage, Pyrrhus then invited the Roman to become one of his own advisors. "I think not," replied Fabricius, "for, if your loyal citizens experience my manner of ruling, they will prefer me to you."

Several ancient writers relate another incident proving the upright character of Fabricius. One night, Pyrrhus' doctor secretly approached Fabricius and offered to kill the Greek king. Believing that no traitor could be trusted, Fabricius ordered the doctor arrested and sent back to Pyrrhus with an explanation of his treacherous act. So overwhelmed was Pyrrhus by this noble act that he freed the Romans he held prisoner. Considering it improper to accept prisoners without a negotiated agreement, Fabricius ordered an equal number of Greek prisoners released.

Fabricius became the model of virtue for all Romans and came to represent the honest and upright character of their forefathers, the founders of their nation.

Regulus (active around 256–249 B.C.) was another of Rome's early heroes. As consul in 256 B.C., Regulus and his co-consul, Lucius Manlius Vulso, led the Roman forces against the Carthaginians in North Africa. Their first endeavors met with such great success that Manlius was able to return with his army to Rome while Regulus remained to continue the war.

Shortly thereafter, Regulus advanced his troops to within a day's march of Carthage. He then offered peace terms that were so demanding that the Carthaginians opted to continue the war, even if it meant certain death. Fortunately for the Carthaginians, a mercenary Spartan general named Xanthippus offered his help and reorganized the Carthaginian army. At the next battle, his troops completely routed the Romans, capturing Regulus and 500 of his soldiers. For five years, Regulus remained a prisoner in Carthage. Only after a Roman army invaded North Africa and defeated the

For the Romans, Cincinnatus embodied all the traits of a true patriot. Other nations have also used the story of Cincinnatus' unwavering devotion to his country to instill loyalty in their citizens. Here, an Italian artist shows Cincinnatus leaving his plow midfield to accept the task of leading his fellow Romans in a time of crisis.

Carthaginians did Carthage's leaders send an embassy to Rome to seek a peace treaty.

The Carthaginians included Regulus in their delegation because they hoped he might persuade the Romans to come to some agreement. Regulus, however, urged the Romans to continue the war, and the Senate followed his advice. When the Carthaginians returned to Africa, Regulus went with them as he had promised, even though a cruel fate awaited him.

What happened in Carthage is not known for certain, but grim tales of imprisonment and torture reached Rome. In the decades that followed, Regulus embodied Rome's ideals of courage and unswerving patriotic duty.

Quintus Fabius Maximus (active 216 B.C.) was nicknamed *Cunctator,* "the Delayer." Used derisively at first, the term later became a mark of honor.

In 217 B.C., the Carthaginian general Hannibal seemed unstoppable. He had crossed the Alps, defeated the Roman troops sent to stop him, and marched south into Italy's Campania region. Rome declared a national emergency and named Fabius dictator. Fabius had served as consul and general and was highly respected. Instead of confronting the wily Carthaginian on the battlefield, Fabius chose only to harass him. Keeping out of reach of the Carthaginian cavalry and advance troops, Fabius successfully prevented scouts from leaving Hannibal's camp and kept supplies from entering.

This strategy worked until the ingenious Carthaginian tied sticks and twigs to the horns of hundreds of oxen he had taken from neighboring farms. He then set fire to the dry sticks and forced the frightened creatures to head for the pass the Romans were watching. Taking advantage of the Romans' pre-

occupation with the "blazing woods," Hannibal quickly led his troops through a nearby unguarded pass and into southern Italy.

Those Romans who had questioned Fabius' delaying tactics now openly expressed their discontent; at the next consular elections they voted him out of office. In 216 B.C., the largest army Rome had ever raised prepared to meet Hannibal on the battlefield at Cannae, south of Rome. Even though his troops numbered thousands less than those of the Romans, Hannibal managed to surround and massacre his enemies.

The Romans now reconsidered Fabius' policies of observation and harassment and judged them the best method of handling Hannibal. They reelected Fabius consul, and in the years that followed he managed to retake several southern Italian towns from Hannibal. There was a new general, however—Publius Cornelius Scipio—who was proving his excellence on the battlefield and at gaining the ear of the Senate. Fabius argued vehemently, but in vain, against Scipio's plan for taking the Roman army to Africa and attacking Carthage. Fabius never learned of Scipio's victory over Hannibal in 202 B.C.; he had died the previous year.

Naevius (around 270–200 B.C.) was one of Rome's early epic poets and dramatists. Around 235 B.C., Naevius produced his first play. A plebeian by birth, he used his verse as a means of attacking Rome's upper class. One poem, for example, implied that Rome's well-known Metelli family were elected to high-ranking public positions by fate, not ability. Naevius was imprisoned for this accusation, but the confinement did little to curb his political attacks. Shortly thereafter, he was exiled from Rome for a similar offense.

Accounts tell of his death in Utica in North Africa.

With more than 35 plays, mostly comedies, attributed to his name, Naevius is credited with developing the genre called *fabulae praetextae* (serious plays), based on personalities and events in Roman history and legend. He also originated the *fabulae palliatae* (tales in Greek costume), comedies translated from the Greek and then adapted to the Roman stage. The celebrated comedies of the later Roman playwright Plautus, with their vivid characters and lively, colloquial language, clearly reflect Naevius' influence. Naevius' epic poem *Bellum Poenicum* (The Punic War) shows his genius and originality and strongly influenced Rome's renowned epic poet Virgil.

Ennius (239–169 B.C.) called himself a "man with three hearts." He considered himself a product of the three civilizations that merged in the Greek colony of Rudiae, his birthplace in southern Italy that came under Roman control. Ennius spoke Oscan, the native language of the area; Greek, the language in which he was educated; and Latin, the language of the army in which he served.

According to several accounts, the renowned hero of the Second Punic War, Scipio Africanus, so respected Ennius that he allowed the poet to be buried in the Scipio family's tomb. Interestingly, Scipio's archrival, Cato the Elder, had first brought Ennius to Rome in 204 B.C., after Ennius had served with Cato in Sardinia during the Second Punic War. Because of his friendship with such powerful men, Ennius was granted Roman citizenship.

Considered one of the foremost figures in early Roman literature, Ennius based his plays on translations of Greek originals, especially the tragedies of Euripides. Nevertheless, the few surviving fragments of his works reflect his originality and intensity. They also show clearly how Ennius adapted Latin meter to fit the Greek outline; incorporated figures of speech such as alliteration and assonance into the text; and replaced the easy flow of the Greek verse with a more formal style.

Ennius' best-known work is his *Annales*, a historical record of Rome from its beginnings to his own time. The *Annales* was the principal Roman epic until Virgil wrote the *Aeneid*, approximately 150 years later.

Cornelia (2nd century B.C.) was one of Rome's most respected personages. The daughter of Scipio Africanus (the general who defeated Hannibal), the mother of the Gracchi brothers (who fought for the rights of the people), and the mother-in-law of Scipio Aemilianus (who crushed Carthaginian opposition for the third and final time in Roman history), Cornelia was well versed in the political events of her day. When her husband, Tiberius Sempronius Gracchus, died in 154 B.C., she dedicated her life to running her household and raising her 12 children. She refused all proposals of marriage, including one from the ruler of Egypt.

Unfortunately, only two sons and a daughter survived to adulthood, but each became a distinguished citizen. Their education had been Cornelia's prime concern, for she herself enjoyed reading and other intellectual pursuits. Like the Scipios and others in their circle, she admired Greek culture.

Romans often told the story of how a boastful Roman lady once came to visit Cornelia. In the conversation that followed the lady spoke constantly of her expensive jewelry and other material possessions. Finally, she turned to

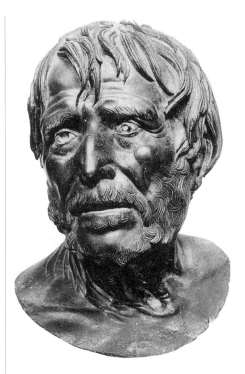

Historians and classicists agree that this bust represents an ancient poet, but which one? Found in a house at Herculaneum that had been buried during the A.D. 79 eruption of Mount Vesuvius, it was first identified as the Roman writer Seneca. Later, some theorized that it represented the Greek poet Hesiod. However, a new theory now suggests it is Ennius.

As a widowed mother, Cornelia (left) chose to devote her life to her children, instilling in them a sense of fairness, dignity, and patriotism that served to shape their lives. A German artist painted this dark-toned portrait of her in 1794.

Cornelia and asked to see what she owned. The unpretentious Cornelia hesitated for a moment and then, seeing her children entering the house, quietly pointed to her "jewels."

Scipio Aemilianus (around 185–129 B.C.) was born into one of Rome's best-known and most patriotic families. At age 17, Scipio accompanied his father to Greece and fought under him in the Third Macedonian War.

In 151 B.C., Scipio volunteered to serve in Spain. A series of defeats and disasters there had made all officers and soldiers wary of fighting in the area. Not so Scipio. His fearlessness and eagerness to accept the challenge soon convinced others to join him. That same year, he willingly accepted a Spanish chieftain's challenge to single combat and defeated his antagonist. He then scaled the wall surrounding the slain chieftain's city and led his troops to victory. For this heroic feat he won the prized *corona muralis* (mural crown), awarded to the Roman who first breached an enemy's wall.

In 148 B.C., Scipio returned to Rome from a peace mission in North Africa and stood for the office of aedile. Believing Scipio the only military commander capable of ending the Carthaginian threat, the Roman people convinced him to run for consul and elected him. Soon after, Scipio was on his way to Africa. Upon his arrival, he blockaded the city of Carthage, in part by constructing an enormous barrier across the entrance to the harbor. In the spring of 146 B.C., Scipio's troops finally entered Carthage and engaged in six days of bloody house-to-house fighting before crushing the defenders.

Back in Rome, Scipio was awarded a great triumph for his victory over Carthage and honored with the surname *Africanus,* just as his grandfather had been years earlier. To differentiate between the two, the Romans extended the title and called him Scipio Africanus Minor, or Scipio Africanus the Younger.

In 142 B.C., Scipio won election to the coveted office of censor. Following the example set years earlier by Cato the Elder, a statesman he very much admired, Scipio consistently tried to encourage the Romans to emulate their loyal and patriotic ancestors.

Difficulties in Spain soon led Scipio to a foreign battlefield again. He laid siege to the Spanish city of Numantia, which finally surrendered in 133 B.C.

The next crisis Rome faced was at home, as dissent over political and personal rights threatened to erupt into revolution. In the 130s B.C., the Gracchi brothers championed the cause of the people, but their revolutionary reforms created much turmoil. Scipio was in Spain at the time and therefore chose not to take sides, but upon his return he made it known that he was against the reforms urged by the Gracchi, even though his wife Sempronia was their sister.

The morning of the day Scipio was to deliver a speech explaining his position, he was found dead in his bedroom. The mystery of his death has never been resolved. Naturally, many of Scipio's contemporaries blamed Gaius Gracchus (Tiberius' brother), Sempronia, and even Cornelia (the mother of the Gracchi). Historians seem to agree, however, that he either committed suicide or died of natural causes.

Cinna (active 90–84 B.C.) was an aristocrat by birth but became a supporter and defender of the *populares,* or common people. After Sulla took Rome by force in 88 B.C. and drove the aging statesman and general Marius from power, Cinna became the unofficial leader of the *populares.*

That same year, Cinna won election to the consulship, and Sulla left Rome for Asia Minor to confront Mithridates, king of Pontus. Without Sulla to oppose him, Cinna immediately began to push for legislation to return power to the people. When Cinna resorted to armed force to accomplish these goals, his co-consul Gnaeus Octavius drove him from Rome.

Undeterred, Cinna rallied the support of the Italians with the promise of giving them full Roman rights and marched on Rome. When Marius, who had sought refuge in Africa, heard of Cinna's siege, he returned and joined forces with Cinna. Soon after, Marius and Cinna took control of Rome and began to massacre Sulla's supporters.

Recognized now as the leaders of Rome, Cinna and Marius ran for co-consul and were elected for the year 86 B.C. Seventeen days later, Marius died, and the power was Cinna's. He immediately pushed for a restoration of order, not by force but by new legislation, some of it quite revolutionary. For example, Cinna allowed debtors to settle their accounts by paying only 25 percent of what they owed. At the same time, he instituted a policy of "good money" to help correct the devaluation of currency that had occurred under previous governments. Cinna's efforts to return stability to Rome won the support of many. But he did make enemies and in 84 B.C. Cinna's troops mutinied and killed him.

BRITAIN

KENT

NORMANDY

BRITTANY

GAUL
(FRANCE)

•Alesia

Gergovia•

BELGIUM

Rhine River

GERMANY

HELVETIA
(SWITZERLAND)

TRANSALPINE
GAUL

A L P S

CISALPINE
GAUL

Rubicon
River

ILLYRICU

•Luca
(Lucca)

SPAIN

•Munda

Rome
•

I T A L Y

Adriatic
Sea

Tyrrhenian
Sea

M e d i t e r r a n e a n

AFRICA

| 0 | 200 | 400 | 600 kilometers |

| 0 | 200 | 400 | 600 miles |

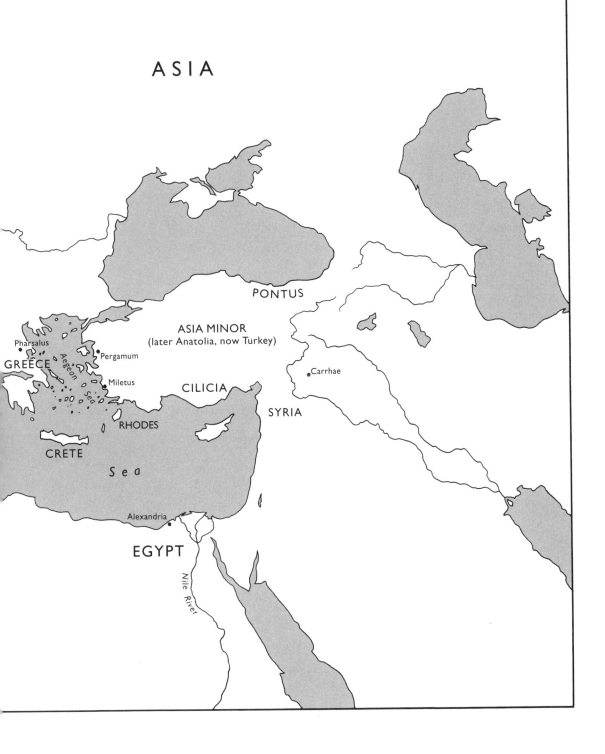

THE ROMAN WORLD UNDER JULIUS CAESAR
49 B.C. — 44 B.C.

ASIA

PONTUS

ASIA MINOR
(later Anatolia, now Turkey)

Pharsalus

Pergamum

GREECE

Aegean Sea

Miletus

CILICIA

Carrhae

SYRIA

RHODES

CRETE

Sea

Alexandria

EGYPT

Nile River

2 Prosperity and Power (73–30 B.C.)

 Rome's rise to power was relentless. By 78 B.C., almost every land bordering the northern Mediterranean Sea had pledged its allegiance to Rome. Italy had been the first, then Spain and southern France, followed by Greece, Macedonia, and much of Asia Minor (present-day Turkey). In North Africa, the people of Carthage and the land that roughly corresponds to present-day Tunisia also bowed to the laws of Rome. Peace was a way of life few Romans had experienced, and the doors to the Temple of Janus, the god of beginnings, remained open, a visible sign that the city was at war.

To be sure, Rome's successes brought prosperity and power to its leaders and people, but they also created problems that sometimes threatened to destroy the city itself. Class inequality—an issue that had plagued early Rome—continued to cause discontent among the poor, and disregard for the rights of noncitizens sowed the seeds of rebellion in the lands Rome governed.

While Rome's leaders were mostly patricians who traced their ancestry to the city's oldest and noblest families, a few men of less distinguished backgrounds—the renowned statesman and orator Marcus Tullius Cicero, for example—managed to climb the political ladder and achieve fame and power. In time, the constant threat of rebellion and civil strife forced Rome's leaders to extend, albeit gradually, greater political and personal rights to Rome's poorer inhabitants, then to provincials. Still, there were no sweeping reforms, and the extension of rights was both limited and selective.

Times continued to change, however, and by the middle of the first century B.C. leadership in Rome had become almost synonymous with popularity. Over the decades, power had shifted from patriots who fought for the glory of Rome to individuals who placed their own interests first. As a result, Romans often

IN THIS PART

SPARTACUS

CRASSUS

POMPEY

CAESAR

CICERO

ANTONY

CATULLUS

found themselves fighting fellow Romans. Tragic as the situation was, it was understandable, because Rome's policy makers had not adequately evaluated their laws to meet the growing demands of the provinces and their subjects.

Rome never sought to destroy the civilizations of its conquered peoples. As long as the provincials obeyed Rome's laws and paid their taxes, they were free to practice their traditional ways. Only those who openly opposed Rome and fomented rebellion were punished. For many Romans, especially those of the upper classes, it became the fashion to adopt Greek customs and ideas. In fact, many Romans considered the Greek way of life more refined than their own. At the same time, Rome exported its own way of life through its soldiers, who traversed the Mediterranean world.

Part 2 of *Ancient Romans* introduces several people whose personal goals of power and conquest changed the Roman world and set it on an irreversible path of conquest, power, and influence. Included also is Catullus, who played no part in Rome's military journey but whose influence on world literature continues to the present. Different as these men may be, all played an important role in the development of the Roman world.

Spartacus

GLADIATOR AND REBEL

Born in the lands to the east of Rome, Spartacus first served as a soldier in the Roman army and then became a bandit chieftain until he was caught and put on the block at a Roman slave auction. (No records explain why he left the army.) His build must have marked him as a gladiator, for he soon found himself training at Lentulus Batiates' gladiators' school in Capua, south of Rome. The Latin term *gladiator* was an appropriate one since the Romans had used their noun *gladius*, meaning "sword," to form it and most gladiators were slaves, condemned criminals, or prisoners of war who were forced to fight each other to the death for the amusement of the Roman public. A few gladiator-slaves even bought their freedom with presents given to them by admiring spectators. There were also freedmen who voluntarily chose to sign on as paid gladiators because they felt the potential rewards for success in the arena outweighed the dangers involved.

At Lentulus' school, prospective gladiators learned their trade with wooden practice swords. As a native of the East, Spartacus was most likely trained as a Thracian gladiator, which meant he used a round shield and curved sword in battle. This distinguished him from the gladiators known as *retiarii* (a fighter with a net), who wore very little clothing and fought only with a net and trident (a three-pronged spear). The Samnite (a fighter armed with the traditional weapons of the people from Samnium, an area in central Italy) gladiators were more heavily clad and armed with an oblong shield, a visored helmet, and a short sword. The Mirmillo's outfit closely resembled that of the Samnites, but its distinguishing mark was a fish crest on the helmet. There were many other classes of gladiators, but these four were the most common.

No records indicate how long Spartacus remained at Lentulus' school, but it is known that he escaped in 73 B.C. Approximately two hundred gladiators had planned to accompany him, but the conspiracy was discovered and only 70 or so managed to flee the school, using knives and roasting spits they had taken from the kitchen. As they stealthily made their way through the city, they happened upon a cart carrying weapons for gladiators to use in the arena. Quickly, they seized these arms and left Capua.

The Greek biographer Plutarch relates that the escapees first took refuge on a nearby mountain. (According to some sources, this was Mount Vesuvius, a volcano that had been dormant for many years but would erupt again in A.D. 79, wiping out the towns of Pompeii and Herculaneum.) When news of the breakout reached public officials, the praetor

This stone for a ring, dating to the 1st century A.D., shows a gladiator battling a lion. Most gladiators, like Spartacus, were slaves, but a few freedmen chose work as paid gladiators as a way to achieve glory.

Clodius marched against the rebels with an army of 3,000.

Clodius planned to starve Spartacus and his men into surrendering. First he laid siege to the mountain, then stationed special guards near the one narrow passage to the top. But no gladiator was about to yield his hard-won freedom easily. Noticing that many stout vines grew about the mountaintop, the rebels swiftly cut as many as they could and twisted them into rope ladders, which they used to descend the mountain so stealthily that the Roman sentries were unaware of what was happening. Then, just as swiftly, the ex-gladiators surrounded the Roman troops and seized their camp.

As news of such rebel successes spread, hundreds and then thousands of slaves escaped their masters and sought refuge with Spartacus. Joining him also were impoverished Romans and Italians who sought a better life.

Spartacus welcomed them all, but he knew the Romans would not allow his ragged band of ex-slaves the freedom to roam the countryside. He firmly believed that the only way to achieve freedom was to leave Italy, and he persuaded his fellow rebels to adopt this plan. Acknowledging Spartacus as their leader, the fugitives prepared to march north through Italy and across the Alps. There the group would disband, and each man would seek his native land and family.

However, as the ex-gladiators won additional victories over Roman troops, eventually crushing the armies of both consuls, many began to grow proud and arrogant. Spartacus warned that this would be their ruin, but his men grew increasingly unruly and began ravaging the countryside wherever they roamed. Since their numbers had swelled to approximately 90,000, they did significant damage and fear began to grip Rome.

The Senate, meanwhile, began addressing the revolt as a national crisis and appointed the praetor Crassus commander in chief of the war against Spartacus. Determined to carefully evaluate the situation before acting, Crassus sent two legions under a Lieutenant Mummius to watch and observe the enemy but not to engage in battle. For unknown reasons, Mummius disobeyed his orders and commanded his troops to attack. Many Romans were slain, and many more lost their

The valiant attempt of Spartacus to free himself and fellow gladiators from their Roman masters has captured the imagination of many artists and writers. In 1960, Universal Pictures produced a film starring Kirk Douglas as Spartacus that vividly recounted the ex-gladiator's near victory over the Romans.

weapons. Angered by the losses, Crassus assembled the surviving troops, separating into one group 500 of those who had first attacked. He then ordered every 10th man killed. Centuries earlier, Roman generals had used this method of punishment—known as decimation, from the Latin word *decem*, meaning 10—but no one had thought to revive it. The measure was effective: No Roman soldier considered disobeying future orders from Crassus.

Spartacus quickly recognized that Crassus was a far better strategist than his predecessors. Changing direction, he now advised his troops to proceed south to the toe of Italy and cross into Sicily. Slaves there had led successful battles against their masters, and Spartacus believed that these slaves would

revolt again if his troops were to join them.

Carefully plotting a route, he bypassed Crassus' troops and entered the region of Lucania. His next task was to secure ships for transport to Sicily. Knowing that pirates sailed freely in the waters around southern Italy, he found a number who agreed to ferry the rebels from Italy to Sicily for a price. But as soon as the pirates had Spartacus' money in their hands, they headed their vessels out to sea, leaving the bitterly disappointed rebels on shore.

Immediately, Spartacus rallied his troops and made for Rhegium, in the toe of Italy. Crassus followed and ordered his soldiers to erect a barrier across the slender isthmus separating the Italian mainland from the peninsula

> *"Ave, imperator, morituri te salutamus."*
> *(Hail, ruler, we who are about to die salute you.)*
>
> —traditional words uttered by gladiators before a fight

Spartacus

BORN

Date unknown
Probably Thrace

DIED

71 B.C.
Apulia, in southern Italy

PROFESSION

Gladiator turned rebel commander

ACCOMPLISHMENTS

Planned a successful escape from Lentulus' gladiator school; became leader of as many as 90,000 ex-slaves and others in a rebellion against the Romans; defeated several Roman armies before dying in battle

on which Rhegium was located. Spartacus could only watch as the Romans dug a 15-foot-wide ditch from one coast to the other and then built an enormous wall above it. As supplies began to run short, he was forced to act.

On a cold, stormy night, Spartacus ordered his men to collect trees, branches, and whatever else they might find and fill one area of the ditch. This done, he then marched a third of his troops across, with orders to head north. The others were to follow later.

Fearing an attack on Rome, Crassus assembled his eight legions (there were approximately 3,000 soldiers to a legion at this time) and prepared for battle. The fighting was extremely fierce, with neither side prepared to give ground. Finally, Spartacus' line gave way as the discipline, experience, and superior weaponry of the Roman troops proved overwhelming. The ex-gladiators continued to withstand the onslaught, however, and of the 12,300 rebels killed only two were found with wounds in their backs.

Realizing that defeat was imminent, Spartacus told the survivors to withdraw to the nearby mountains and regroup. At first this seemed the perfect strategy, especially when one of Crassus' officers rallied his men to pursue the rebels and walked into a rout. Then, emboldened by this victory, the rebels went back on the offensive and ignored Spartacus' order to withdraw.

Crassus was ready and waiting. Spartacus looked at the troops assembled before him and called for his horse. Drawing his sword, he killed the animal. If the rebels should win, he said, he would have many horses far better than this one, and if they lost he would have no need of a horse at all. With these words, he turned to the enemy and headed straight for Crassus. Unable to reach his intended victim, Spartacus grappled with everyone in his way until he stood alone, deserted by his troops but fighting to the end. Thus he enjoyed a warrior's death, in contrast to the fate of the 5,000 to 6,000 rebel captives crucified by Crassus' troops along the Appian Way, the road that led to Rome.

The 5,000 rebels who managed to escape slaughter or capture tried to make their way north to the Alps. Aware of the fugitives' escape route, troops returning from Spain under the command of Pompey intercepted the motley band and killed them all.

FURTHER READING

Ghnassia, Maurice. *Arena*. New York: Viking, 1969.

Koestler, Arthur. *The Gladiators*. New York: Macmillan, 1939.

Wiedemann, Thomas E. J. *Emperors and Gladiators*. New York: Routledge, 1992.

Crassus
(Marcus
Licinius Crassus)

POLITICAL FINANCIER

In 87 B.C., political affiliation could mean life or death in Rome, as a heated rivalry between the chief political leaders Marius and Sulla resulted in two waves of assassinations. Just months after Sulla's followers massacred hundreds of Marius' supporters, terror again gripped the city as Marius' followers murdered Sulla's people. A few prominent Romans managed to escape, among them Marcus Licinius Crassus, whose father and brother had been killed for supporting Sulla.

Knowing that his life was in danger, Crassus quickly slipped out of Rome with 3 friends and 10 servants. Their destination was Spain, where Crassus had lived when his father had served as propraetor (chief military magistrate). But Crassus had to use caution, because Marius' assassins were everywhere and no one was safe, even in Spain. After finding shelter in a large cave overlooking the Spanish seashore, Crassus did not even dare approach the owner of the land, his friend Vibius Pacianus, himself. Instead, he sent a servant with a message.

Well pleased to learn of Crassus' escape, Vibius ordered one of his slaves to leave a daily supply of food and other items that might make life in the cave a little more pleasant. Vibius promised the slave his freedom if he did as he was commanded without attempting to discover the identity of the fugitives. If he disobeyed, death would be his reward.

For eight months, Crassus lived this secluded life. Then, according to the Greek biographer Plutarch, news came that Cinna, Marius' successor, was dead. Crassus immediately came out of hiding and within a short time gathered a band of several thousand supporters. From these Crassus selected 2,500, bought some ships, and set sail for Africa. Once there, he joined his troops with those in the private army of the well-respected Roman Quintus Caecilius Metellus Pius. A disagreement between the two, however, caused Crassus to leave Africa with his troops, cross into Italy, and pledge allegiance to Sulla.

These were times for making money, and Crassus was a master at the trade. Raised as a member of the *optimates*, or upper class, he was well educated. His parents were not ostentatious, however, but had lived simply. After the political assassination of his father and brother, Crassus had married his sister-in-law, and the couple had had two sons.

Crassus was a friendly man who welcomed both friends and strangers to his house. A respected orator, he gladly defended all those who sought his counsel and expertise. Many people also came to Crassus seeking to borrow money. No one was denied or asked to pay interest, but Crassus knew the date each debt was due and always claimed his payment.

Yet there were Romans who criticized the manner in which Crassus made a considerable part of his fortune, even though it was impossible to call his methods illegal. By law, people whose names appeared on proscription lists (lists giving names of people condemned to die) lost all rights to their property and possessions. While some devious Romans contrived to have names added to the lists in order to acquire choice properties, Crassus does not appear to have used this tactic. Rather, he watched to see whose possessions would be for sale and promptly purchased those he desired. Usually, their price was far below the actual value. In fact, many properties had lost much of their value because they had been ransacked and damaged in the turmoil following the terrible struggles between Sulla's and Marius' forces.

Another of Crassus' schemes was to buy houses ravaged by fire. He knew well the areas in Rome most susceptible to fire and went quickly to the scene of any fire in order to offer the property owner a low sum for the now "worthless" structure. Pleased to be given any amount—household insurance did not exist at the time—the tearful owner accepted whatever Crassus offered. Once the transaction was complete, Crassus summoned his slaves, some 500 in number. Many accounts note that Crassus personally chose his slaves, preferring to choose from the prisoners of war those with architectural and building skills in their background, and trained them to perform a great variety of tasks.

After he received news of a fire, the first task was always to extinguish the fire, especially any smoldering embers. Since there was no fire department or fire hydrants, a fire could destroy a building before an owner could summon aid. For Crassus, however, extinguishing a fire was simple. Lining up his slaves, he organized a bucket brigade from the nearest water source

Caesar, Crassus, and Pompey may not have used a map, as this 19th-century drawing of their historic meeting suggests, but they did divide control of the Roman world among themselves.

to his newly purchased property. Mop-up and clean-up time followed, then all went to work repairing and renovating the structure. Within a short period of time, a "For Sale" sign would appear, with the asking price considerably higher than what Crassus had paid.

Although acknowledged as one of the richest men in Rome and accused by many of avarice, Crassus desired more than money. He wanted to be recognized for his military accomplishments and for his skill as a commander. What seemed to bother him especially was the praise and respect given Pompey, who was considerably younger. In the campaigns against Marius' supporters, Sulla had always favored Pompey, even addressing him as *Magnus*, meaning "Great."

To be sure, the personalities of the two were quite different. Crassus prided himself on being available to anyone seeking his advice or aid, whereas Pompey kept to himself and waited to be called to duty. Sulla and others also preferred Caesar to Crassus, but when Caesar asked to borrow money, Crassus readily agreed. In the years to come,

As an astute financier, Crassus made a fortune from wise investments and sales; when he lent his friends money, he did not charge interest but he collected his debts on time. This banker's sign reveals that professional moneylenders were also in business in Roman times.

the three men—Crassus, Pompey, and Caesar—would cast aside their many differences and form an alliance, each for his own gain. That triumvirate (from the Latin *tres viri*, meaning three men), however, was still in the future.

In 73 B.C. Crassus had just been elected to the office of praetor when Rome was plunged into a sudden crisis. Tens of thousands of slaves led by a former gladiator named Spartacus had escaped their masters and rebelled against Rome. Fearless fighters, the ex-slaves defeated every Roman army sent to capture them. Finally, the Senate turned to Crassus to put down the insurrection.

Eagerly, Crassus led his forces against the rebels. After harassing them in central Italy, Crassus followed them south and cornered them in the toe of Italy. To prevent their return north, he ordered a massive ditch and wall built across the peninsula. But Spartacus proved too wily for Crassus. He had his troops fill in a portion of the ditch and

led them across it on a stormy night. Still, Crassus was determined to defeat Spartacus, especially after he heard that Pompey was returning to Italy from Spain. Crassus did not want to share victory with his rival.

In 71 B.C., Crassus finally crushed the revolt. Spartacus was killed in the fighting, and on Crassus' orders, 6,000 rebel prisoners were crucified along the Appian Way leading to Rome. Five thousand of the rebels managed to escape capture, however, and were making their way north to the Alps and freedom when they were intercepted by Pompey. After annihilating them, Pompey claimed the final victory. Once again, Crassus felt slighted, especially when the Senate awarded Pompey a triumph for his victory over Marius' supporters in Spain and granted him just an *ovatio* (a second-rate triumph), because he had defeated only slaves.

Yet Crassus was not one to hold a grudge, and when Pompey ran for the office of consul he readily offered his assistance. Pompey accepted, and the two men were elected co-consuls for 70 B.C. Once in office, they immediately began rescinding many of the reforms enacted by the now-deceased Sulla. But their relationship grew steadily less cordial, and eventually their disagreements made passage of any significant legislation impossible.

While consul, Crassus hosted an enormous banquet at which 10,000 tables were set; and once he gave each Roman family a three-month supply of corn. This wooing of the people was becoming a common practice among politicians in Rome.

In 60 B.C., Crassus allied himself with Pompey and Caesar to form what was later called the First Triumvirate. Rebuffed by members of the Senate who feared their power and prestige, the three men had joined together, determined to attain their goals: Caesar wanted the consulship, Pompey land for his veterans, and Crassus wanted legislation that would further his own interests and those of the Roman tax collectors in Asia.

The alliance worked: Caesar became consul in 59 B.C. and quickly won passage of the measures sought by his partners. The following year, Caesar left for a five-year governorship of the province of Cisalpine Gaul (the area between the Apennine Mountains and the Alps), while Crassus and Pompey remained in Rome to manage affairs. Once again, differences surfaced, with Crassus determined to prevent Pompey from increasing his power base.

Caesar, meanwhile, devoted himself to his provincial duties but kept abreast of the situation in Rome. An ambitious man, he naturally worried about Pompey's increasing tendency to favor the Senate and saw it as harmful to his own interests. Caesar also knew he needed allies in Rome who would help him secure an extension of his five-year term in the province. Accordingly, in 56 B.C. he called a meeting of the triumvirate at Luca, close to the northern border of Italy. (By law, Caesar could not cross into Italy with his army without permission from the Senate.)

Despite their recent differences, the three again pledged to support each other. This time, however, the strategy was a little different: Crassus and Pompey were to run for consul for the year 55 B.C., following which each would be awarded an extended proconsulship—Pompey in Spain, Crassus in Syria. While co-consuls, Crassus and Pompey were to push through a bill granting Caesar an extension of his provincial rule.

Again the triumvirate succeeded, but this time there was greater opposition. Many Romans questioned the motives of the three and wondered why Crassus and Pompey wished to be co-consuls. Fearing a defeat at election time, the two allowed their followers to act without restraint. But after Pompey's men killed a representative of another candidate for the consulship, all opposition to their alliance ceased and Pompey and Crassus were elected.

Later that year, even before his term as consul had expired, the eager Crassus led his army eastward. He was so determined to win great victories and an attendant triumph that he paid no attention to the bad omens plaguing him along the way. When rough seas threatened to prevent his setting sail from the Italian town of Brundisium for Greece, he refused to accept the weather as a bad omen and ordered his captain to push off from the shore anyway. In the hours that followed, a great number of ships foundered and sank, but he disregarded this omen too.

When the first battles in the east brought easy victories, Crassus took them as proof that the omens were false. Even after he heard that an eagle, the Roman symbol on the military standard carried in front of each division, had turned its head backward, Crassus continued to order his army forward. Then, for some reason, he chose to return to Syria for the winter and not seek a major confrontation with the Parthians, as he had intended.

By spring the Parthians had devised a clever strategy. As Crassus marched along the Euphrates River, the Parthians convinced a local chief named Ariamnes to win the Roman's confidence and then lead him and his troops toward the open plain. Because Ariamnes had formerly gained the

Crassus

BORN
Around 115 B.C.
Place unknown

DIED
53 B.C.
Carrhae, northern Mesopotamia

PROFESSION
Financier, general, and statesman

ACCOMPLISHMENTS
Managed large amounts of property and money; suppressed the revolt of the ex-gladiator Spartacus; entered into a political alliance—the First Triumvirate—with Caesar and Pompey for control of the Roman world

> *"Men who devote much effort and time to building are their own undoers, and need no enemies."*
>
> —Crassus, quoted in Plutarch's *Lives*
> (around 1st century A.D.)

favor of Pompey, Crassus never suspected that he was in league with the Parthians. Crassus followed Ariamnes' advice and slowly maneuvered his troops away from the river to the plain, where Ariamnes left him. As the traveling became more difficult and there was no water supply in sight, the Romans realized that they had been tricked. Crassus, however, refused to consider defeat and prepared his troops for battle.

When the Parthians appeared, they did not look especially fearsome because they had covered their shining armor with animal skins. The Romans took heart, but when the Parthians removed the coverings, the brilliance of their weapons and the unnerving sound of their drums and bellowing animals shattered the Romans' spirit.

Just as Crassus' light-armed soldiers began their charge, a massive hail of arrows descended on them, forcing them to retreat. The Romans waited out the assault in square formation, with the light-armed troops huddled and protected by the heavy-armed soldiers. But their hope of regrouping once the Parthians had spent their arrows evaporated when they saw that a huge caravan of carts pulled by camels stood ready with more archers.

Crassus commanded his son Publius to take his troops and charge the Parthians. By drawing the enemy away from the plain, Crassus hoped to prevent them from encircling his soldiers.

Publius did as ordered, but again the Parthians outwitted the Romans. Pretending to retreat, they drew Publius' forces away from the main body of Romans and then turned on them fiercely, killing most of them, including Publius. Taking Publius' head as their prize, the Parthians stuck it on a spear point, rode up to Crassus' troops, and asked whose son this was, so brave a warrior fallen freshly on the field of war.

Horror and fear seized the surviving Romans. As they debated their course of action, Crassus opted to flee under cover of darkness and seek refuge in the nearby town of Carrhae. Because he had to move quickly, Crassus chose to leave his 4,000 wounded soldiers to the mercy of the enemy. With their supplies and morale desperately low, the Romans forced Crassus to reconsider his position and accept an invitation to meet with Parthian general Surena.

But, as Crassus suspected, the proposed meeting was a trap, and the Romans walked into an ambush. Plutarch estimated that 20,000 Romans, including Crassus, lost their lives. Ten thousand were taken prisoner, and another 10,000 managed to escape, eventually reaching Syria. As a token of his victory over the Romans, Surena sent Crassus' head to the king of Parthia.

FURTHER READING

Adock, Frank E. *Marcus Crassus, Millionaire*. Cambridge, England: Heffer, 1966.

Plutarch. *Plutarch's Lives*. Vol. 3. Translated by Bernadotte Perrin. Loeb Classical Library. Cambridge: Harvard University Press, 1968.

Ward, Allen M. *Marcus Crassus and the Late Roman Republic*. Columbia: University of Missouri Press, 1977.

Pompey
(Gnaeus Pompeius Magnus)

ROME'S ALEXANDER
THE GREAT

I ntrigue, civil war, and an assassination attempt all tested the courage and fortitude of the teenaged Gnaeus Pompeius (Pompey's official name at birth, the *Magnus* was an honorary title he later won). Socially and politically, Pompey's family belonged to the senatorial nobility. In 88 B.C., Pompey was 18 and a soldier in his father's army when civil strife erupted in Rome because of a struggle for dominance between Marius and Sulla. The *optimates*—members of the ruling class and supporters of Sulla—wanted Pompey's father, Pompeius Strabo, to lead the campaign against Marius. Strabo, however, wished to delay his reply until he could assess the situation and decide which course of action would gain him what he wanted most, a second consulship.

Strabo finally decided to aid the *populares*, who represented the common people and backed Marius. But even after making this decision, Strabo continued to vacillate. Upon learning that Strabo had set up camp and was planning to lead troops against him, Cinna hired assassins to set

The sculptor of this head of Pompey the Great, which was found in a tomb near Rome, captured the power and determination of his personality, combined with an air of aloofness.

Strabo's tent on fire. Cinna also bribed Lucius Terentius, one of Strabo's soldiers, to kill the young Pompey. Fortunately for Pompey, an informant told him of the conspiracy that evening at dinner. Showing nerves of steel, Pompey calmly continued eating and then retired to his tent. After arranging the bedclothes to look as if he were sleeping soundly, he crept out of the tent, gathered a few trusted soldiers, and ordered them to stand guard around his father's tent. Feeling somewhat relieved, Pompey returned to his own tent and waited, hidden in the shadows, until Terentius entered. When the traitor plunged his sword into what he believed was Pompey's body, Pompey burst into the tent and struck him down. The noise roused the soldiers nearby. Believing that the signal to mutiny had been given, they rushed forth, pledging their allegiance to Cinna.

Pompey confronted the troops and, with tears rolling down his cheeks, begged them not to desert his father. In desperation, he threw himself on the ground before the camp gates and announced that any who left had to trample on his body first. The soldiers immediately stopped their flight. Pompey was a man they trusted and respected and their admiration for him far outweighed their hatred and fear of his father. All but 800 soldiers now pledged their allegiance to Strabo and refused to join Cinna.

Cinna then sent an army against Strabo, and in the conflict that followed Pompey's father was killed. Almost immediately, Strabo's enemies brought Pompey to trial for embezzlement of public funds. Determined to prove his innocence, Pompey tracked down each theft and proved that one of his father's freed slaves had been responsible for all of them.

Strabo's enemies then accused Pompey of keeping hunting tackle and books that had been taken illegally

when his father had won the town of Asculum in central Italy in 89 B.C. Again Pompey acted swiftly, pleading that he had none of these items in his possession. This assertion was easily proved, because Cinna's guards had ransacked Pompey's house and taken everything.

Pompey's courage at the trial won him the respect of all who attended, including that of the judge, Antistius. Even before the trial was over, Antistius secretly offered Pompey his daughter, Antistia, in marriage. News of the engagement leaked out, and as Pompey exited the courtroom after being acquitted many of the onlookers began singing wedding songs. A few days later, Pompey married Antistia.

Rome was still in turmoil, but for the moment the civil strife seemed distant to Pompey. He had inherited his father's estates in Picenum, an area east of Rome and bordering the Adriatic Sea, as well as his father's *clientes*. The tradition of *clientes* had become important in republican Rome and would continue to be so in the decades that followed. Even though heirs inherited *clientes*, the latter were by right free individuals who pledged their loyalty to an influential Roman in return for protection and support. Because an important duty of *clientes* was to support their patron at election time, the number of *clientes* a Roman had was often the key to his political success.

Pompey's constant involvement in political affairs helped to mold his character, but he never became haughty or desirous of luxury. The Greek biographer Plutarch described him as gentle and dignified, with a degree of majesty in his character. He wore his hair combed back from his forehead in a bit of a wave, and the lines about his eyes made his face resemble the surviving portraits of Alexander the Great. In fact, many people even called him Alexander. In time, his accomplishments would rival those of the great Macedonian conqueror.

In 84 B.C., however, the 22-year-old Pompey was still deciding which faction in Rome to back. At first he allied himself with Cinna, but he soon realized that Cinna's associates distrusted him and he began to fear they would turn on him.

When news reached Rome in 83 B.C. that Sulla was returning with his troops to Italy, Pompey decided to pledge his allegiance to him—not as an individual but as a commander of an entire army.

Counting on the loyalty of the people in Picenum, Pompey began recruiting soldiers in the district. This was actually illegal, but the times were not normal, and Pompey's offense was ignored.

After defeating two armies loyal to Cinna, Pompey consolidated his position and then ventured out to meet the returning Sulla. This, the first meeting between the two men, proved to be a memorable occasion. As Pompey drew up his ranks in full battle attire and marched toward Sulla, the latter was so impressed that he dismounted. When Pompey hailed Sulla as *Imperator*, the title given a returning victorious general, Sulla, to everyone's surprise, returned Pompey's greeting and also saluted him as *Imperator*.

Sulla immediately commissioned his young ally to help bring all Italy under control. In the years that followed, Pompey proved himself an extremely capable leader and strategist. Seeing Pompey as a political asset, Sulla sought to strengthen their personal relationship. Following a custom practiced by many other leaders, Sulla offered the young general his stepdaughter Aemilia's hand in marriage. Pompey was still married to Antistia, but Sulla persuaded him to obtain a divorce.

The determined Sulla now considered Pompey his most capable military leader and ordered him to suppress revolts being led by opponents in Sicily and Africa. In 82 B.C., Pompey entered Sicily and crushed all resistance. The following year he sailed to Africa and, according to Plutarch, brought Numidia and parts of Libya under his control within a period of only 40 days. Believing that he had to deal forcefully with Sulla's enemies, Pompey ordered them all executed. To many Romans, this action seemed quite ruthless. Yet Pompey did show mercy on a number of occasions, especially when dealing with the Himeraeans in Sicily.

In that instance Sthenis, the leader of Himera, tried to dissuade Pompey from punishing the entire city. Sthenis argued that the only guilty party was the man who had persuaded the Himeraeans to oppose Sulla. When Pompey demanded to know the man's name, Sthenis gave his own. Impressed with such honesty, Pompey pardoned all the Himeraeans, including Sthenis.

Soon after, reports reached Pompey that his troops were willfully abusing civilians they encountered on their march across Sicily. So strongly was Pompey opposed to such conduct that he ordered the swords of these soldiers sealed in their scabbards and punished anyone who dared disobey his orders.

Yet Pompey could also be understanding of his soldiers' faults. On one occasion a few soldiers had, by chance, unearthed some treasure soon after arriving in Africa. As news of the discovery spread, the Romans began thinking that the Carthaginians might have buried their gold, silver, and other valuables in times of national emergency. Immediately, the soldiers fell to their knees and began turning the soil, acre after acre. Realizing that it was useless to try to stop them, Pompey let them continue and laughed at the sight of so many men digging frantically for nothing.

In Rome, Sulla was well pleased with Pompey's successes but wondered

Pompey

BORN
106 B.C.
Rome

DIED
48 B.C.
Pelusium, Egypt

PROFESSION
Statesman and general

ACCOMPLISHMENTS
Recovered Sicily and Africa from Marius; defeated Sertorius and won Spain for Sulla; intercepted the slaves fleeing Italy after Spartacus' defeat; rid the Mediterranean of pirates; defeated Mithridates in the East; made Tigranes, king of Armenia, a friend and ally of Rome; extended Roman control into Colchis on the Black Sea and surrounding areas; created the provinces of Bithynia-Pontus and Cilicia in Asia Minor; annexed Syria; made Judaea a dependent state; formed the First Triumvirate with Caesar and Crassus; pushed through reforms that restored the rights of tribunes; opposed Caesar's illegal entry into Italy with his army

In 55 B.C., Pompey erected the first permanent theater (in the center of this model) in Rome. Built of stone after the plans of one he had seen at Mytilene in Asia Minor, it seated at least 17,000 spectators.

about the allegiance of his soldiers. Times had changed, and soldiers were now beginning to show more loyalty to their general than to their country. To curtail Pompey's growing power, Sulla ordered him to send all but one legion back to Rome and to remain in Africa until a new commander arrived.

Angered by this order, Pompey's troops vowed not to return to Italy unless Pompey accompanied them. Since this meant rebellion, which Pompey did not want, he pleaded with them to follow orders. But even when he broke down and wept, the soldiers refused to obey Sulla's commands. They began to bend only after Pompey threatened sui-

cide. Several ancient sources claim that Pompey actually instigated this display as a way of persuading Sulla to rescind his order.

Whatever the truth may be, Sulla did in fact change his mind, allowing Pompey to enter Italy with his troops. As Pompey approached Rome, Sulla went out to meet him and addressed him as *Magnus*, "the Great." Pleased by this compliment, Pompey decided to ask for an even greater honor—a triumphal acknowledgment of his victories in Africa. This Sulla denied, claiming that awarding Pompey a triumph was illegal because by law only a general who had held the office of consul or praetor could be granted a triumph. Pompey had never held any major political office and was only an *eques*, or cavalryman.

Pompey objected vehemently to Sulla's decision. According to Plutarch, he boldly retorted that "more people worship the rising than the setting sun."

Sulla pondered that for a moment, uncertain whether he had heard correctly. He then looked around at the amazed onlookers and asked what Pompey had said. Pompey repeated his remark. This time Sulla understood. He was the setting sun whose career had peaked, while Pompey's ascent was just beginning. Unable to refute this assertion, Sulla turned to Pompey and said, "Let him triumph!"

Pompey had won, but his joy soon gave way to sadness when his wife, Aemilia, died in childbirth. Soon after the triumph, however, he married Mucia, a member of one of Rome's most distinguished families. Over the next three years, Mucia bore one daughter and two sons.

Politically, Pompey continued to support Sulla. But when Sulla died in 78 B.C., his co-consul, Marcus Aemilius Lepidus, began using his authority to revoke Sulla's policies. Pompey considered Lepidus' actions treasonous. Massing his army, Pompey drove Lepidus out of Italy the following year.

Secure in the knowledge that his soldiers would follow him anywhere, Pompey approached the Senate and offered to crush Quintus Sertorius, who had launched a rebellion in Spain and successfully defeated all efforts to subdue him. The Senate hesitated, fearful of Pompey's growing power, but finally dispatched him to Spain with the title of proconsul. For three years after Pompey's arrival there, Sertorius outmaneuvered every Roman army sent to conquer him. But, unfortunately for Sertorius, dissent within his ranks led one of his soldiers to turn traitor and assassinate him.

Sertorius' successor was no match for Pompey, and soon Spain was under Roman control again. Using his excellent administrative skills, Pompey began the task of reorganizing the province, resettling its inhabitants, and forming alliances with local leaders.

Then, late in 72 B.C., Pompey answered a summons from the Senate to return overland with his army to Italy. For more than a year, Rome had watched as thousands of slaves flocked to the rebel camp of a former gladiator named Spartacus. Fearing a full-scale war, Rome had commissioned Marcus Licinius Crassus to put down the revolt, which he did with brutal efficiency.

Approximately 5,000 slaves had managed to elude capture and were making their way toward the Alps when they met Pompey's returning army. Pompey annihilated the rebels without mercy and sent a report to the Senate, stating that Crassus had won the pitched battle but that he had ended the revolt.

The Senate granted Crassus an ovatio, a "second class" triumph—all that was allowed for a victory over slaves. By contrast, the senators awarded Pompey a triumph for his victories in Spain, even though he was still just an *eques* and had not fulfilled the necessary political requirements. Naturally, Crassus felt slighted. He had proceeded up the political ladder as the law required and won each honor in turn, while Pompey, who had never held a single major public office, was now preparing to celebrate a second triumph. As a result, relations between the two men became strained. However, by the next consular elections, Pompey and Crassus had resolved their differences and ran together. Opponents of Pompey's candidacy objected that he was still too young and had not held any of the prerequisite offices. But the Senate once again bowed to popular opinion and waived the usual requirements. In 70 B.C., Pompey assumed the consulship, with Crassus as his co-consul.

When Pompey's term as consul ended, he did not accept the customary proconsulship in a province but retired to private life. Meanwhile, pirates were overrunning the Mediterranean Sea, threatening commerce and travel. Headquartered in Cilicia on the coast of Asia Minor, the brigands had entered into an alliance with King Mithridates, who not only supported their efforts but even outfitted several of their ships. By 67 B.C., no one could sail the Mediterranean without paying a fee to the pirates or yielding to their wishes.

According to Plutarch, whenever the pirates captured a Roman, they would pretend to be afraid and beg the prisoner's pardon. They dressed the Roman in traditional Roman garb, claiming that they wished never to make such a mistake again. The pirates would then extend the ship's ladder and bid the captive go free, for that was his right as a Roman citizen. Because the vessel was in open water, the captive was compelled to step into a watery grave.

Realizing that Pompey might be the only Roman capable of defeating such a ruthless enemy, the Senate named him dictator, with the provision that he relinquish his powers once the crisis had passed. Pompey proceeded to divide the Mediterranean into sections, commanding each of his officers to patrol a particular area. Within 40 days, he had swept the pirates out of the western Mediterranean. The eastern part of this sea took a little longer—49 days, to be exact. Instead of executing the pirates, Pompey resettled them in sparsely populated areas. He reasoned that their presence would prevent foreign tribes from crossing into Roman lands. Pompey thus proved that he was not only a great military strategist but also a capable administrator.

True to his word, Pompey relinquished the title of dictator as the law required, but he remained in the East, visiting several cities purely as a tourist. In 66 B.C., the Senate ended Pompey's vacation when it appointed him commander in the East, with the task of defeating Mithridates and organizing Rome's provinces in Asia.

As always, Pompey eagerly accepted the challenge and immediately attacked the armies of Mithridates, whose strength had been considerably weakened by previous encounters with Roman forces. Pompey achieved rapid victory, but the wily Mithridates managed to escape capture. In 63 B.C., however, Mithridates committed suicide after his own son incited rebellion against him.

Pompey now turned his attention to other areas in the East. He concluded a treaty that made Tigranes, king of Armenia, a subject of Rome and then took control of Colchis on the Black Sea and of the lands south of the Caucasus Mountains. He organized two new Roman provinces—Bithynia-Pontus and Cilicia—took control of Syria, and settled Judaea. These deeds laid the foundation for Rome's eastern empire, which would survive for 500 years, flourishing long after Rome itself had fallen.

These were Pompey's glorious years. He returned to Italy with his army in 62 B.C. as the acknowledged military leader of the Roman world. He had fully earned the surname *Magnus* as well as the comparison with Alexander the Great.

In 61 B.C., soon after reentering Rome, the 45-year-old Pompey celebrated his third triumph. Never had the Romans seen such wealth and booty paraded in a triumph. There was Mithridates' throne, chariots adorned with silver and gold, exquisitely worked jewelry, and a solid-gold statue of Mithridates measuring twice his actual height. Among the prisoners were Mithridates' five sons and two daughters. However, the most widely anticipated event was the approach of Pompey himself in a chariot studded with gems and precious stones and drawn by four white horses.

The Roman political scene, however, was still plagued by intense intrigue and crafty deals. The *optimates* envied Pompey's power and popularity and opposed his every request. When Pompey realized that both Crassus and Gaius Julius Caesar also experienced the Senate's hostility, he saw these ambitious men as potentially valuable allies.

At about this time, Pompey divorced his wife, Mucia, for reasons that have never been explained. He now sought a wife who would bring him political advantage and found one in Caesar's daughter, Julia. As it turned out, he fell truly in love with Julia, and his devotion to her increased with the years. In 60 B.C., the wealthy Crassus joined Caesar and Pompey, and a powerful union was formed that greatly influenced events in Rome. Historians would refer to this alliance as the First Triumvirate.

When Caesar took up the post of proconsul in Cisalpine Gaul in 58 B.C., Pompey and Crassus remained in Rome. In 56 B.C., the powerful triumvirate met again at Luca, a city just inside the boundary line of Cisalpine Gaul, and drew a new political map.

Pompey and Crassus would run for the consulship for the year 55 B.C. Once in office, Crassus was to lead an army east against Parthia while Pompey remained in Rome, prepared to block any interference by groups hostile to the triumvirate. Following his year in office, Pompey would assume the governorship of Rome's resource-rich Spanish provinces but stay in Rome and rule through deputies. Caesar was to remain in Gaul for another five years.

All went according to plan until unexpected events intervened, beginning with the death of Julia, Caesar's daughter and Pompey's wife, in 54 B.C. The following year, Crassus was killed in battle. The triumvirate no longer existed.

Meanwhile, chaos threatened to engulf Rome as gangs supporting rival political factions roamed the streets, burning even the Senate house. Forced to act, the Senate reluctantly turned to Pompey and asked that he restore order to the capital. Pompey eagerly complied and regrouped his soldiers, scattered throughout Italy. After putting down the troublemakers, Pompey enacted several worthwhile measures designed to prevent further unrest.

One of Pompey's measures was to revamp the jury system to make trials fairer to defendants. He also decreed that electoral bribery was to be severely punished, and that public officials would have to wait five years between holding office in Rome and serving in

"Whenever I stamp my foot in any part of Italy, enough troops will rise up in an instant."

—Pompey, quoted in Plutarch's *Lives* (around 1st century A.D.)

a province. Because Caesar disagreed with many of Pompey's decrees, the relationship between the two became strained.

Pompey heightened the tension when he opposed Caesar's request to remain in Gaul with his army and at the same time run for the consulship. In 50 B.C., fearing that Caesar would attempt to seize power, the Senate asked Pompey to raise an army capable of counteracting any move by Caesar. That same year Pompey married the recently widowed Cornelia, daughter of Rome's most distinguished citizen, Caecilius Metellus Pius Scipio Nascia. He had little time to enjoy this new union. On January 7, 49 B.C., the Senate declared war on Caesar. Four days later, Caesar crossed the Rubicon River and advanced on Rome.

Recognizing that he was no match for Caesar as a military strategist, Pompey withdrew with his troops to southern Italy. He planned to cross into Greece and from there prevent food supplies from entering Italy, so that, starved into submission, Caesar would have to yield. But Caesar was a determined opponent, and his troops were in excellent shape after years of active duty in Gaul. Pompey's forces, on the other hand, had not fought in 12 years and lacked discipline.

Caesar's swift march across Italy caught Pompey by surprise, and he suddenly found himself being pursued into Greece. The two armies met on the plain of Pharsalus, in Thessaly, on August 9, 48 B.C. Caesar's force numbered 22,000, half the strength of Pompey's army.

After a long, hard fight, Caesar's seasoned soldiers gradually overwhelmed Pompey's troops. Managing to escape capture, Pompey fled to the island of Mitylene, where his new wife, Cornelia, and son awaited news of his victory. According to Plutarch, Pompey told his wife, "My dear Cornelia, you have experienced one season of a better fortune which may have given you unfounded hopes. . . . But we mortals are born to endure such events and to try fortune yet again, for it is possible to recover how we were, just as it was possible for us to fall from that happy state to this."

When Pompey learned that some of his troops had escaped and his navy was still intact, he set sail for Egypt with his wife and son and several warships and merchant vessels. He hoped to enlist the aid of Ptolemy, the boy-king whose father Pompey had once aided. Upon hearing that Ptolemy was at Pelusium engaged in battle against his sister Cleopatra, Pompey changed course and headed for that city. Ptolemy's advisors, meanwhile, debated whether to support Pompey or Caesar.

Because Pompey was close at hand, they decided to kill him, a deed they believed would merit Caesar's gratitude. They sent a small boat to meet Pompey's vessel and invited the Roman to come ashore. Suspecting nothing, Pompey accepted their invitation and entered the small craft with a few friends. Many on board Pompey's vessel questioned the wisdom of this move. But recognizing that there was no chance of escaping the Egyptian soldiers and fleet, they kept silent, lest their fears cause Pompey or themselves more harm.

When Pompey stood up to disembark, one of the Egyptians drew his sword and stabbed him from behind. Others joined in the attack. Drawing his outer clothes over his head, Pompey could only groan as the blows hit their mark. He was 58 years old, having celebrated his birthday the previous day.

After killing Pompey, the assassins cut off his head and threw his naked body overboard. But Pompey's freedman Philip, who had been with him at his death, waited until all had left the area. Slowly and reverently, he retrieved his master's body, washed it with sea water, and prepared to burn it on a funeral pyre. As he did so, an old Roman citizen who had once served under Pompey came by and offered his assistance in burying "the greatest of Roman generals."

When Caesar reached Egypt, Ptolemy's men sent him Pompey's head and signet ring, expecting praise and a reward. Bursting into tears, Caesar sentenced the assassins to death and ordered Pompey's ashes sent to Cornelia, who gave her husband's remains a proper burial at their country house near Alba.

FURTHER READING

Greenhalgh, Peter A. L. *Pompey, the Republican Prince*. Columbia: University of Missouri Press, 1981.

————. *Pompey, the Roman Alexander*. London, England: Weidenfeld & Nicolson, 1980.

Leach, John. *Pompey the Great*. Dover, N.H.: Croom Helm, 1978.

Plutarch. *Plutarch's Lives*. Vol. 5. Translated by Bernadotte Perrin. Loeb Classical Library. Cambridge: Harvard University Press, 1968.

Seager, Robin. *Pompey: A Political Biography*. Berkeley: University of California Press, 1979.

Caesar
(Gaius Julius
Caesar)

"I CAME, I SAW,
I CONQUERED"

A determined and forceful man, Julius Caesar was also somewhat vain. Sculptors honored his custom of combing his hair forward to cover the balding areas.

Friends, Romans, countrymen, lend me your ears;
I come to bury Caesar, not to praise him.
The evil that men do lives after them;
The good is oft interred with their bones;
So let it be with Caesar. The noble Brutus
Hath told you Caesar was ambitious. . .
Ambition should be made of sterner stuff.

For 400 years, actors in William Shakespeare's tragedy *Julius Caesar* have echoed Antony's words on stages around the world. And many have accepted the playwright's work as historically correct. Yet who was this Caesar whose life inspired one of the world's literary masterpieces? Did Mark Antony really deliver such a eulogy or were these Shakespeare's words? And why does Caesar's life and death continue to hold the world's attention?

Caesar traced his clan's name, Julius, to Iulus, the son of Rome's legendary hero Aeneas. According to Roman mythology, this connection gave Caesar a semidivine status because Aeneas's mother was Venus, the Roman goddess of love and beauty. The claim also made Caesar a member of one of Rome's noblest families. However, no member of the family had yet achieved great fame, wealth, or influence. In fact, one of Caesar's aunts had married the Roman statesman Marius, thereby aligning the family with the *populares* (political leaders who represented the Roman people), not the upper-class *optimates*.

Caesar seems to have chosen from an early age to have a political career. His lack of financial backing did not deter him; it only made him more resourceful. In 84 B.C., following the example of many politicians who used marriage as a means of advancing their careers, Caesar married Cornelia, the daughter of Cinna, Marius' political partner and successor.

Unfortunately for Caesar, the Marian forces were ousted in 83 B.C. by Sulla. Because of his close connection with the Marians, the 17-year-old Caesar was summoned to appear before Rome's new leader. Boldly, he refused to obey Sulla's command to divorce his wife. Then, after Sulla confiscated his own property and his wife's dowry, Caesar decided it best to leave Rome and seek refuge among the Sabines, northeast of the city. Rethinking his future, Caesar joined the military and served first in Asia Minor, then Cilicia. In 80 B.C. he was awarded the civic crown for heroic efforts in saving a fellow Roman.

Sulla's death in 78 B.C. brought Caesar back to Rome. Following the custom of the day, he began his political career as a prosecutor. Deciding that his speaking skills needed work, he set sail for the island of Rhodes to study oratory with the renowned Apollonius Molon. Sea travel had become increasingly dangerous because Rome had been expending its military power in civil wars and neglecting the task of protecting Romans from foreign enemies. As it happened, pirates roaming the Mediterranean seized the ship carrying Caesar to Rhodes.

Unperturbed by this unforeseen delay, Caesar arrogantly laughed at his captors when they set his ransom at 20 talents and boasted that they could easily get 50 for him. Taking him at his word, the pirates raised the ransom price and kept him prisoner.

Caesar proved no ordinary captive. According to the Greek biographer Plutarch, he immediately asserted himself and began dictating orders to his captors. When he wished to sleep, he told everyone to be quiet. When he wanted an audience for speeches he had written, he commanded them to listen. If any listener frowned or became distracted, he would threaten to kill him after he was freed.

For 38 days, Caesar entertained himself in this manner. Once the ransom money arrived, however, his carefree manner disappeared and he set sail for Miletus, a city in Asia Minor under Roman control. There he outfitted several ships and attacked his former captors, relying on speed, surprise, and determination, attributes he would draw upon repeatedly in decades to come.

Because Caesar held no political or military post, he decided to imprison the captured pirates at Pergamum while he waited for the Roman governor in the area to pass sentence. But when the governor delayed too long for his liking, Caesar ordered the pirates crucified—the very punishment he had threatened them with months earlier.

In 73 B.C., the 27-year-old Caesar returned to Rome and was elected mili-

Caesar

tary tribune. He then began pushing for legislation to undo Sulla's reforms. As in the past, Caesar aligned himself with the *populares*. Working with him was Pompey, another young Roman also proving himself a successful military and political leader. Around 68 B.C., Caesar was elected quaestor, the first step toward the coveted position of consul.

All Caesar's actions were calculated to maintain the support of the people. For example, while serving as aedile, in charge of public works, in 65 B.C., he spent tremendous sums of money on building projects and public entertainments such as gladiatorial combats. Not rich enough to fund such projects himself, Caesar resorted to borrowing—on many occasions from Rome's wealthy financier Crassus.

In 61 B.C., when Caesar's praetorship was over, he was assigned to the Roman province of Spain as propraetor. However, his debts were so high that his creditors refused to let him leave without making at least partial payment. Crassus willingly came to Caesar's aid and paid a quarter of the money owed. In Spain, Caesar carried out several successful military expeditions and soon was able to return to solvency, but he was not satisfied. Plutarch told how Caesar's companions found him in tears one day and asked why. Caesar answered, "I have done so little! Just think, Alexander the Great at my age was already a world conqueror." Fortune would, however, soon shine on Caesar, as it had on Alexander. The first major step was election to Rome's highest political office, the consulship.

When Caesar's enemies in the Senate began maneuvering to deny him the consulship, he turned to Pompey and Crassus. The three men made plans to control the Roman world together, each vowing to support the aims and objectives of the other two. History would call their alliance the First Triumvirate (from the Latin *tres*, "three," and *viri*, "men").

Caesar was not content to cement this alliance purely with verbal agreements. He married his daughter Julia to Pompey, while he himself wed Calpurnia, the daughter of Lucius Calpurnius Piso. (Piso followed Caesar as consul in 58 B.C.)

After defeating every attempt by the Senate to block his election, Caesar won the consulship and immediately pushed through legislation promoted by the triumvirate. Most important was the ruling that Caesar would next serve as proconsul in Cisalpine Gaul and Illyricum, not just for the normal one-year term but for five years. With this extended time he could expand his power base, recruit and train a well-disciplined army, enrich his coffers, and still be close to Italy. Just before Caesar left for his province in 58 B.C., the Senate added the province of Transalpine Gaul (the land beyond the Alps) when the official who was to have ruled the area died.

Once in Gaul, Caesar found that the tribes whose lands bordered his own province were often in conflict with one another. He saw this situation as a chance to intervene, win a victory, and add yet more territory to Rome's expanding world. By "helping" friendly Gallic tribes defeat unfriendly neighbors Caesar hoped to win control of all Gaul.

During his first term as proconsul, Caesar proved himself one of the world's greatest generals. Quick and decisive in his actions, he astutely analyzed his opponents' tactics, changing strategy to meet the occasion.

BORN
Around 100 B.C.
Rome

DIED
44 B.C.
Rome

PROFESSION
Statesman, general, writer

ACCOMPLISHMENTS
Conquered Gaul; commanded first Roman expedition into Britain; won allegiance of all Italy in 60 days; defeated Pompey in a civil war; established Cleopatra of Egypt as an ally and client of Rome; crushed all Pompeian resistance in Africa and Spain; became dictator for life in 44 B.C. and instituted numerous reforms

When the Helvetians mounted a surprise attack on the Romans, Caesar ordered his men to retreat until he felt they were in a position to regroup and fight. Plutarch relates that when a soldier then brought Caesar his horse, Caesar said, "When I have won the battle, I will use my horse for the chase, but for now let us fight the enemy," and marched forward on foot with his troops.

According to Plutarch, Caesar inspired his men to fight valiantly by distributing money and honors freely, not keeping everything for himself. He never avoided the front lines but showed his contempt for danger by eagerly entering the fray. Once, when 60,000 Nervii (a Belgian tribe) made a surprise attack on Caesar's troops and defeat seemed imminent, Caesar snatched a shield from one of his soldiers in the rear and rushed forward to oppose the enemy. Calling his officers by name and encouraging the troops, Caesar was able to turn the tide of battle.

According to the Roman biographer and historian Suetonius, Caesar was a tall, fair-complexioned man, rather full of face, with black, piercing eyes. Careful of his appearance, he kept his hair short and his face clean-shaven. As he began to go bald, he adopted the habit of brushing his hair forward. Although subject to occasional epileptic seizures, Caesar never used this weakness to avoid difficult situations but rather saw the battlefield as a form of treatment for his ailment. When traveling between camps, he often went by litter or in a chariot, dictating to a scribe. When Caesar did use his own horse, he rode rapidly. From childhood he had been an expert rider, learning to gallop with his hands behind his back.

This strict discipline governed Caesar's other habits as well. Plutarch wrote that once, upon dining at a friend's, Caesar was served a dish of asparagus sprinkled with sweet ointment instead of oil. Fully aware of what he was eating, Caesar showed no outward sign of distaste and reprimanded those dining with him for being so impolite as to criticize it. "It is rude enough not to eat what is set before you, but to criticize our host for his lack of etiquette shows your own lack of the same."

Caesar demonstrated fairness and empathy in dealing with his associates. When a fierce storm once forced Caesar and a group of companions to seek shelter in a poor man's house, Caesar noted that the tiny house could accommodate only one person. Without hesitation, Caesar ordered that a man in their party who was in poor health should go in, while he and the others would take shelter outdoors.

Caesar's years in Gaul were extremely active. He spent 58 B.C. subduing the Helvetians and stopping an advance of German troops under Ariovistus. The following year he defeated a fierce tribe known as the Belgae in northern Gaul. At the same time, troops under his subordinates conquered the areas known today as Normandy and Brittany.

Yet Caesar never forgot Rome and the political situation there. Aware that many Romans, including the well-known orator Cicero, opposed his aims and methods, Caesar knew he needed the continued support of Crassus and Pompey to extend his proconsulship in Gaul. However, when he learned that his two allies were feuding and that Pompey was beginning to question Caesar's ambitions, Caesar called a meeting of the triumvirate.

Forbidden by law from entering Italy with his troops and not wishing to go on his own, Caesar chose to hold the meeting in Luca, a town just inside the border of Cisalpine Gaul. Crassus came when summoned, but Pompey delayed at first in order to consider the situation. Caesar also invited Rome's senators, 120 of whom made the long journey. The most important meeting took place in April of 56 B.C. when the triumvirs put aside their differences and agreed on a plan of action.

Pompey and Crassus were to win a co-consulship for 55 B.C. Once in office, they were to push through legislation extending Caesar's provincial command for another five years. Crassus was to have Syria as his province for five years once he became proconsul, and Pompey was to have Spain for the same period. Under an additional provision, Pompey was to rule Spain, governing through representatives while he remained in Rome, controlling the political situation.

All went according to plan until 54 B.C. when Julia, Caesar's daughter and Pompey's wife, died in childbirth. With the strongest link between the two men gone, their differences became much more difficult to mend. And when Crassus died the following year fighting the Parthians, the triumvirate ceased to exist. Caesar continued to pursue his own goals, especially the complete conquest of Gaul. To make sure his exploits were reported accurately, he wrote an account of his campaigns titled *De Bello Gallico* (Concerning the Gallic War). Written in the third person, with Caesar as the observer and commentator, the work is clear, concise, and direct. Though it naturally favors Caesar and his decisions on the battlefield, there is little of propaganda about it.

Caesar was the first Roman to advance into Britain and his descriptions,

"Men readily believe what they want to believe."

— from *De Bello Gallico* (Concerning the Gallic War, 51 B.C.)

such as the one below, have proven invaluable to historians:

> Of all the Britons, the most civilized are those who live in Kent, which lies along the coast. Their customs differ little from those of the Gauls. The Britons who live in the interior do not sow grain, but live mostly on milk and meat and wear animal skins for clothes. All Britons dye their bodies with woad, a plant which gives their skin a bluish color, and are quite wild-looking in battle. They wear their hair long and shave every part of their body except their head and upper lip.

Caesar did not conquer Britain—his successors would do that—but he did establish a Roman presence there and, like Pompey in the East, he advanced the Roman army into previously unknown lands.

In 52 B.C., open rebellion almost cost Caesar his newly won territories. A Gallic chieftain named Vercingetorix stubbornly refused to pledge allegiance to Caesar and won the loyalty of many other Gallic tribes. Vercingetorix planned to drive a wedge between Caesar, then in winter quarters on the southern side of the Alps, and the rest of the Roman troops, encamped north of the Alps. To starve the Romans into surrendering, Vercingetorix asked his people to burn their houses, barns, farmlands, and pasturelands.

Responding to this threat, Caesar quickly mobilized his troops and met the enemy in battle. Changing tactics,

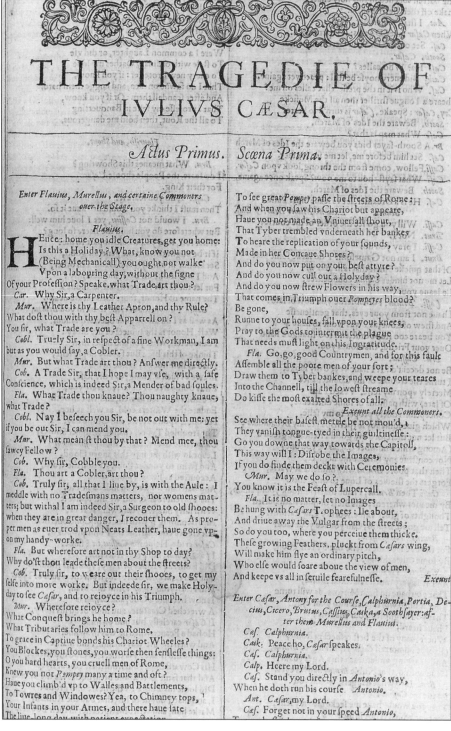

Known as the First Folio because of its format, this collected edition of William Shakespeare's works, including this tragedy based on the life of Julius Caesar, was published in 1623, seven years after Shakespeare's death.

as always, to counter those of his opponent, Caesar outmaneuvered the Gauls on several occasions. Even though the Gauls won a major encounter at Gergovia, they realized the weakness of their position and decided to fight next at Alesia, a hill town in central Gaul that they considered impregnable.

Acknowledging that Alesia could not be taken by force, Caesar turned to blockade and siege tactics. He did this so effectively that generals were to study the siege of Alesia for centuries to come.

As the siege progressed, Vercingetorix came to realize that there was no way out. Rather than allow his people to perish, he gave his fellow chieftains the option of surrendering him dead or alive to Caesar. When the Gauls sent this message to Caesar, he responded that he wanted Vercingetorix alive.

As Caesar stood before the Roman camp, Vercingetorix, dressed in full armor, rode toward his conqueror. When he reached the spot where Caesar stood, he dismounted, discarded his armor, and surrendered. Gaul was now Caesar's.

Back in Rome, meanwhile, Pompey had decided to ally himself with the *optimates* against Caesar. This was a critical step politically, because Pompey, as the only consul, was the sole ruler in Rome. By law, Caesar could not hold the consulship again until 48 B.C. and his provincial command was to end in February 49. This left 10 months when Caesar would be a private citizen, and he knew that his enemies were ready to imprison or kill him if he were to return to Rome.

To protect himself, Caesar planned to extend his command in Gaul through 49 B.C., but his enemies vowed to prevent this. Tensions increased as messages passed back and forth between the Senate, Pompey, and Caesar. When the Senate offered Pompey command of all the forces in Italy, Caesar agreed to resign his command if Pompey would do likewise. In a show of support for Pompey, the Senate voted on January 1, 49 B.C., to declare Caesar an enemy of Rome if he did not disband his army.

On January 10, Caesar chose the path of civil war and marched his army across the Rubicon River into Italy, exclaiming (in Plutarch's account) *"Alea jacta est!"* ("The die is cast!") As Caesar advanced on Rome, town after town pledged its allegiance to him. When reports of these events reached Rome, Pompey chose to leave the city and regroup his forces in Greece, where his support was stronger. With Pompey gone, Caesar was able to conquer Italy in only 60 days, without shedding a drop of blood.

Caesar had no immediate thought of pursuing Pompey beyond the Italian peninsula because Pompey's forces controlled the sea. Rather, he focused on consolidating his position by marching first to Spain, where he defeated commanders loyal to Pompey, then into southern Gaul, where he won more victories. In the midst of these campaigns, Caesar returned to Rome for 11 days and had himself proclaimed dictator. In this office he arranged for his election to the consulship the following year.

With his affairs in order, Caesar now felt ready to confront Pompey on land, not on the sea. On August 9, 48 B.C., the former allies clashed on the battlefield of Pharsalus in Greece. Caesar's soldiers, in peak condition from years of fighting in Gaul, completely outmaneuvered Pompey's troops. Forced to flee, Pompey escaped to Egypt, where the boy-king Ptolemy XIII had offered him his support. Ptolemy's advisors decided, however, that a dead Pompey was better than an angry Caesar and killed Pompey. When Caesar reached Egypt just days later, the advisors immediately offered him Pompey's head, hoping to receive his thanks. But Caesar's reaction was just the opposite. He looked at Pompey, his former ally and son-in-law, and cried. Instead of rewarding the assassins, he had them executed and arranged a fitting burial for one of Rome's great leaders.

Caesar then carefully analyzed the situation in Egypt, a land of great riches that was in the midst of civil war between Ptolemy and his sister Cleopatra. According to tradition, Caesar's decision about which side to support was determined by a dramatic incident that artists, writers, and filmmakers have elaborated upon over the centuries.

The 21-year-old Cleopatra, determined to be queen of Egypt, saw an alliance with Caesar as the way to reach her goal. However, Caesar was in the palace quarters in Alexandria surrounded by Ptolemy's supporters, who would arrest her if she tried to approach the Roman conqueror. Cleopatra reputedly ordered a trusted servant to roll her up in a rug and deliver this gift to Caesar.

Whether or not this charming ruse convinced Caesar to support Cleopatra, she apparently remained with Caesar in the palace while it was besieged by Ptolemy's forces. Finally, a Roman legion managed to reach the palace and, in the fierce fighting that followed, Caesar was forced to swim to safety. (One wall of the palace directly overlooked the harbor.) A few months later, other troops allied to Rome arrived and Caesar was able to defeat Ptolemy. He then proclaimed Cleopatra queen of Egypt and an ally of Rome. According to Plutarch, Cleopatra gave birth to a son, whom she named Caesarion after his father.

But Caesar felt he had dallied long enough in Egypt and his ambitious nature impelled him to leave. In 47 B.C., he marched north into Syria and fought a brief but decisive battle against Pharnaces in Pontus. His account of this victory was just as brief: *"Veni, vidi, vici."* ("I came, I saw, I conquered.")

Caesar then returned to Rome, had himself again proclaimed dictator, arranged to be elected consul for the following year, and left for Africa, where many of Pompey's former supporters had rallied behind Metellus Scipio, Pompey's father-in-law. Once again Roman fought Roman, and again Caesar prevailed. Plutarch wrote that once when a standard bearer was retreating in fear from the front lines, Caesar grabbed the man by the neck, forced him to turn around, and pointedly said, "Look, the enemy's that way!"

Back in Rome, Caesar celebrated four triumphs: Gaul, Egypt, Pontus, and Africa. The entire Mediterranean world now appeared to be his, until news reached the city that Pompey's sons and their supporters were rebelling in Spain. Immediately, Caesar set out for the West and crushed the opposition at Munda, Spain, in March 45 B.C. Now he could focus his energies on correcting the ills that, in his eyes, afflicted Rome's government.

First, in order to clarify and justify his actions, Caesar wrote a commentary on his war with Pompey. In the final year of his life, Caesar proved himself an extremely capable statesman. One of the first pieces of legislation he passed was an allotment of land to his soldiers. To accomplish this, Caesar established colonies in Italy and throughout the Roman world. In the centuries to come, these settlements would become beacons of Roman civilization, spreading Roman culture around the Mediterranean. Caesar also adopted a sweeping measure that effectively eliminated 25 percent of all debt. Rome's financiers were so confident in Caesar's leadership that the economy, which had stagnated during the civil war, began to revive.

Using the tremendous wealth he had accumulated from his victories, Caesar initiated an enormous building program. His projects included a new Forum; a temple dedicated to his legendary ancestor the goddess Venus; and the enormous Basilica Julia, where public business was conducted.

Then, realizing that there were problems with the Roman calendar, Caesar consulted the Alexandrian astronomer Sosigenes. The result was the Julian calendar, which allowed the great festivals to be celebrated at the proper season and allotted 365 days to a year, with an extra day added every four years as an adjustment. In Caesar's honor, the month of *Quintilis* was renamed *Iulius*—July, in the English-speaking world. Caesar's calendar has continued in use until the present, with only a few relatively minor changes.

Caesar's energy was boundless, as was his determination to continue revamping Rome politically, economically, and socially. But he had powerful enemies intent on thwarting his policies and winning more control for themselves. The soldiers were especially anxious, for they wanted the land they had been promised for their service. They resented Caesar's lenient treatment of former enemies, especially Romans who had opposed him. They may have been right: Gaius Cassius Longinus and Marcus Junius Brutus, the two principal conspirators against Caesar, were both former enemies Caesar had pardoned and rewarded.

The main rallying cry of the conspirators, who numbered about 60, was resistance to Caesar's autocratic ways. In Shakespeare's *Julius Caesar* (written around 1599 and based on an English translation of Plutarch), Mark Antony rails against Brutus for calling Caesar ambitious, yet he must have been to accomplish what he did. While Caesar refused an offer of kingship, he did accept the position of dictator for life in 44 B.C. This was too much for Brutus, who firmly believed in the republic. Like his ancestor Lucius Junius Brutus, who murdered Rome's last king and established the republic in 509 B.C., the later Brutus now conspired to kill the man who seemed to him to threaten the dissolution of the republic. No details of the conspiracy were ever leaked, despite the number of people involved—only the gods seemed intent on warning Caesar.

In early March 44 B.C., Caesar received several bad omens. One of the animals he sacrificed to the gods was found to have no heart. There were reports of strange noises at night and wild birds in the Forum. Caesar dismissed all these events as accidental and, on March 15—the Ides of March in the Roman calendar—proceeded to meet with the Senate as planned.

On his way, a soothsayer who earlier had warned Caesar about the Ides of March approached the dictator a second time. Refusing to show fear, Caesar turned to him and, according to Plutarch, said defiantly, "The Ides of March are come!" "Yes," replied the soothsayer, "but they are not passed." What thoughts went through Caesar's mind upon hearing this retort are not known, but when the subject of death had been mentioned at a dinner party the night before, the 56-year-old Caesar had been the first to answer the question about what type of death was best: "A sudden one."

On the Ides, the conspirators obliged him. As the Senate met, not in the Senate house as usual but in a building commissioned by Pompey, the conspirators surrounded Caesar and badgered him with questions. The signal to attack came when the conspirator Tillius took hold of Caesar's robe with both hands and pulled it from his neck. At this the other conspirators drew their daggers from beneath their robes and struck. Those not involved recoiled in shock, unable to speak or act. Caesar tried to parry the blows, but when Brutus raised his dagger to strike, Caesar covered his face and yielded, so great was his disappointment in a trusted friend. Whether by chance or not, Caesar's body fell against the statue of another former friend, Pompey.

News of the stabbing spread quickly across the city. At first, everyone rallied behind the conspirators. But when Caesar's will was read, announcing that he had left a considerable sum of money to each citizen of Rome, remorse and regret filled the people's hearts. Then, as the mangled corpse of their benefactor was carried through the Forum, cries condemning the assassins were heard everywhere. Once again, Caesar was the hero. His spirit was deified and the conspirators fled the city, to be hunted as criminals.

FURTHER READING

Bruns, Roger. *Julius Caesar*. New York: Chelsea House, 1987.

Caesar, Julius. *Gallic War*. Translated by H. J. Edwards. Loeb Classical Library. Cambridge: Harvard University Press, 1963.

Grant, Michael. *Julius Caesar*. New York: McGraw-Hill, 1969.

Plutarch. *Plutarch's Lives*. Vol. 7. Translated by Bernadotte Perrin. Loeb Classical Library. Cambridge: Harvard University Press, 1968.

Suetonius. *The Lives of the Caesars*. Translated by J. C. Rolfe. Loeb Classical Library. New York: Macmillan, 1914.

Cicero
(Marcus
Tullius Cicero)

"TO LIVE IS TO THINK"

hen the Romans hailed Cicero as the "father of his country" he was deeply proud of the honor, especially because he was a *novus homo* (new man), a term indicating that he was the first of his family to reach the Senate. This did not mean he was poor. On the contrary, his family was quite rich and lived in the prosperous town of Arpinum, south of Rome.

A firm believer in education, Cicero's father had sent Cicero and his brother to excellent schools—first in Rome, then in Greece, where the emphasis was on philosophy and rhetoric, the art of public speaking. According to the Greek biographer Plutarch, Cicero so excelled in his studies that the parents of fellow students eagerly visited the class just to watch the quick-witted youngster in action.

Cicero's studies ended abruptly in 89 B.C. when the Social War between Rome and its Italian allies threatened the survival of the republic. Cicero, just 17 at the outbreak of the war, served first under Pompey's father and then with Sulla. He had little taste for military life, and as soon as the war was over he returned to Rome to continue his studies. In 81 B.C., he began his public career as a lawyer.

A philosopher as well as a statesman, Cicero felt strongly that the ideals of the Roman republic should be preserved. For this reason, he opposed those who did not honor the traditional election system.

In 80 or 79 B.C., Cicero's defense of a Roman named Roscius won him immediate fame. Sulla ruled Rome at the time and one of his freed slaves, Chrysogonus, had purchased the estate of Roscius' father, whose execution Sulla had ordered. When Roscius publicly protested that the purchase price was too low, Sulla took the criticism as an insult and charged Roscius with murdering his own father. As a further affront, Sulla placed Chrysogonus in charge of the proceedings.

Refused representation by every lawyer he approached, Roscius took his case to Cicero. On the appointed day, Cicero appeared with his client in the open-air court of Rome, where crowds of onlookers had assembled to watch the proceedings. Swayed by Cicero's direct manner of presentation and arguments supported by convincing evidence, the jury acquitted Roscius.

Fearing that Sulla might take action against him, Cicero left Rome for Greece to further his studies. Upon his return, he began his climb up Rome's political ladder, serving first as quaestor in western Sicily in 75 B.C. Five years later, Cicero prosecuted Gaius Verres, the former Roman governor of Sicily, for exploiting Sicilians and Romans alike during his term in office. Defending Verres was Rome's most famous defense lawyer, Quintus Hortensius Hortalus. Verres hoped to prolong the case into 69 B.C., when he would be consul and, by law, exempt from prosecution. But Cicero quickly and with remarkable clarity presented witnesses and documentation to substantiate his charges. After the jury returned a guilty verdict against Verres, Cicero was acclaimed Rome's best lawyer, eclipsing Hortensius.

Cicero was also an excellent writer. Though he appears to have spoken extemporaneously in public, he rewrote his speeches and defenses several times before committing them to memory. Apparently, it was also his habit to rework passages he felt had been inadequate during delivery before publishing a speech.

One of Cicero's best-known defenses is his "Pro Archia"("In Defense of Archias"), delivered in 62 B.C. Archias, a Greek poet and tutor who had emigrated to Rome around 100 B.C., was charged with illegally assuming the privileges of Roman citizenship. At the end of the Social War in 89 B.C., Archias had been offered Roman citizenship if he would sign an official document within a 60-day period.

Unfortunately, the record files of the town where he had signed the official paper, Heraclea, had been destroyed by fire, and there was no copy to verify his claim of citizenship. Cicero willingly undertook the case. After covering the essential points, Cicero proceeded to speak about the merits of education and literature, extolling Archias' literary abilities. Cicero argued that any city or nation that considers itself civilized should want to claim as its citizens such a learned person and poet as Archias. He continued, saying that learning is by far one of the most important occupations: "The knowledge gained from studying nourishes youth, delights old age, adorns good times, offers refuge and solace in adversity, delights at home, does not impede outdoors, spends the night with us, travels with us, and goes to the country with us."

More than 50 of Cicero's defenses survive, with approximately the same number believed lost. Many of these speeches became models for future lawyers and are still studied in schools around the world. Cicero's style was clear and concise. To emphasize a point, he used rhetorical questions (queries that are posed to make a point, with no answer expected) and vivid figures of speech. He perfected the art of the periodic sentence, in which the essential point is delayed until the very end, producing a dramatic effect. These qualities were well illustrated in his *First Catilinian Oration*, delivered in 63 B.C.:

> For how long, Catiline, will you abuse our patience? For how long will your anger elude us?
> To what end will that unbridled audacity flaunt itself? . . .
> O times! O customs! The Senate knows all this, the consul sees it, yet he lives.

Lucius Catiline, a former praetor and governor of Africa, had become a bitter and dangerous man after being denied the consulship in 68 B.C. Three years later, he had been accused of plotting to murder the current consuls but had won acquittal. Despite his evil reputation, Catiline had many supporters because of his promise to abolish debts. Although many of Rome's debtors were victims of their own foolishness, a great number were merely casualties of the civil war between Marius and Sulla. All were desperate for relief. When he ran for consul against Cicero in 64 B.C., Catiline was given a good chance of winning. However, when Cicero purposely let his toga slip from his shoulder to show the armor underneath, his carefully calculated action reminded the voters of Catiline's past misdeeds and swung the election in Cicero's favor.

In retaliation, Catiline sent a group of henchmen to Cicero's house. Though claiming to be *clientes* (those who sought the protection of wealthy and distinguished Romans in return for political services), the men actually had orders to kill Cicero.

Forewarned, Cicero had locked his doors and admitted no one. Then he invoked his consular powers and called an emergency meeting of the Senate for the following day, November 8, 63 B.C.—not in the Senate chambers but in the Temple of Jupiter. It was there that Cicero delivered his thundering indictment of Catiline.

Catiline immediately addressed the assembled senators and begged them to disregard Cicero's accusations. But even as he reminded them of his noble ancestry and the many contributions of his relatives, the senators yelled, "Traitor!" "Enemy!" Roused to uncontrollable anger, Catiline rushed from the temple, threatening to destroy his enemies. He then headed north to Faesulae in Etruria, where his supporters had gathered under Gaius Manlius.

The Senate declared Catiline and Manlius public enemies and decreed that all their followers would be punished if they did not lay down their arms by a certain date. Fearing that Catiline might still sway the Senate or the Roman people to his cause, Cicero won approval to raise an army. His co-consul was to lead troops north against Catiline while he himself stood guard in Rome.

At this time, envoys from the Allobroges, a Gallic tribe north of Italy, were in Rome seeking financial aid. Learning that their request had been denied, one of Catiline's allies approached the envoys, offering to help them if they joined Catiline's conspiracy. Cicero learned of this meeting and persuaded the Allobroges to help him.

Following Cicero's plan, the Allobroges agreed to join Catiline, but only after receiving official letters signed by the leaders and giving details of the conspiracy. The conspirators delivered the letters and even offered to bring the Allobroges to Catiline. Cicero now sprang his trap. He ordered troops to intercept the envoys and the conspirators on their way north, arrest them, and search them for documents. The Allobroges were quickly released, but the conspirators and documents were held as proof of Catiline's treason.

After learning that a force of Catiline's men was preparing to free the arrested conspirators, Cicero posted troops throughout Rome. The following day, December 5, he called a meeting of the Senate to discuss what punishment should be decreed for those already in custody. Cato the Younger supported Cicero and spoke in favor of the death penalty, Julius Caesar against it. Convinced that Catiline had to be eliminated, Cicero proclaimed the death sentence for the five conspirators under arrest. Knowing that Roman law forbade a Roman's execution without a trial, Cicero took full responsibility for the sentence. However, in an attempt not to seem overcruel, he agreed to Caesar's request that the Senate not confiscate the conspirators' property. Fearing a return to civil war, all Rome supported Cicero.

Cicero was determined to act quickly. After ordering the executioners to perform their gruesome task, he spoke one word in a loud voice that rang out across the Forum, where a huge crowd had assembled—*"Vixerunt"* ("They did live"). The people shouted with joy at the news that the conspirators were dead, and in the days that followed hailed Cicero as the "father of his country."

In 60 B.C., the three most powerful Romans—Julius Caesar, Pompey, and Crassus—formed an alliance to control Rome and the Roman world. With each supporting the aims and ambitions of the others, not even the Senate could overrule them. The three invited Cicero to join them, but he declined, on the grounds that their actions were unconstitutional. The next year, Caesar invited Cicero to join him as an officer in Gaul. Again Cicero refused.

Cicero continued his neutral role undisturbed until 58 B.C., when Publius Clodius Pulcher became tribune. The two had been friends until Cicero testified against Clodius in 61 B.C. The previous December, Clodius had disguised himself as a woman and entered Caesar's house during the feast of the *Bona Dea,* the "Good Goddess." By law, only women were allowed to attend, but Clodius had made plans to meet with Pompeia, Caesar's wife. Clodius gave himself away when he spoke, however, and Caesar's servants sounded the alarm. At his trial, Clodius claimed that he had not been in Rome that day, but Cicero destroyed this alibi by testifying that he had seen Clodius in the city.

Clodius now sought revenge and charged that Cicero had acted illegally in 63 B.C. by executing the Catilinarian conspirators without a trial. Without waiting to be formally prosecuted, Cicero left Rome for Greece. Clodius then declared Cicero an exile, destroyed his house in Rome, and damaged his country villa in Tusculum.

Not everyone agreed with Clodius, but all feared his gangs of hooligans. Pompey, who had earlier refused to help Cicero, now realized how dangerous Clodius was and began working with the tribune Titus Annius Milo to recall Cicero. Because of their efforts, Cicero was recalled, and the Senate sent letters of thanks to the towns that had harbored him. The Senate also voted to rebuild Cicero's houses at public expense.

On August 4, 57 B.C., Cicero returned to Italy, landing at Brundisium in southern Italy. During his 16-month exile he had often despaired of his return, as the following excerpt from a letter to his brother reveals: "My brother, my brother, my brother . . . did you really fear that I did not wish to see

Cicero

BORN

106 B.C.
Arpinum, Italy

DIED

43 B.C.
Formiae, Italy

PROFESSION

Statesman, lawyer, writer, orator

ACCOMPLISHMENTS

Prosecuted Catiline and his conspirators for treason against the republic in 63 B.C.; became Rome's leading lawyer and orator; delivered 14 Philippics against Antony; wrote works on rhetoric, including *De Oratore* (Concerning Oratory); wrote several philosophical works, including *De Republica* (Concerning the Republic), *Tusculanarum Disputationum Libri* (Tusculan Disputations), *De Natura Deorum* (Concerning the Nature of the Gods), *De Senectute* (Concerning Old Age), *De Amicitia* (Concerning Friendship); prolific letter writer, more than 900 of which survive

you. . . . Rather, I did not want to be seen by you. You would have seen not your brother . . . the man you knew . . . but the image of a breathing corpse. . . . I should like that you look after Terentia [Cicero's wife] and write back to me about everything. Be strong, in so far as the situation allows."

Writing to Atticus, his close friend and the publisher of his writings, Cicero described the welcome he received when he returned to Rome: "The steps of the temple were crowded with the common people, who welcomed me with great applause; the same throngs, the same applause followed me to the Capitol, and there was an enormous crowd in the Forum and on the Capitol itself. . . . What I thought would be the most difficult part of my position to recover, my fame in the Forum, my reputation in the Senate, my influence with the *boni* [good people], I have regained far better than I had hoped."

This letter and the more than 900 others that have survived provide insights into Cicero as a friend, father, and husband. The letters also offer rare glimpses into everyday life in Rome during those turbulent times. The times were especially trying for Cicero, who believed strongly in the republic and feared the results of an alliance between Caesar, Pompey, and Crassus. In an attempt to weaken the ties among the three, Cicero took advantage of the strained relations between Pompey and Crassus and tried to widen the gap. Caesar, determined to keep the coalition intact, arranged for a meeting at Luca in 56 B.C. to renew the five-year-old alliance. Again the triumvirate asked Cicero to join them, but this time the pressure to do so was so great that Cicero agreed.

In the months that followed, the triumvirate used Cicero and his oratori-

cal ability to their own advantage, asking him to defend their friends against a variety of charges. Cicero confessed to Atticus that he felt shame when he knew the charges were justified and that his eloquent defense was the triumvirate's means of winning pardons for guilty people. Unable to continue in this role, Cicero decided to retire from public life.

But his retirement came to an end in 52 B.C. when Milo, the politician who had worked so hard for Cicero's recall from exile, killed Clodius. Asked to defend his friend, Cicero eagerly accepted the challenge. On the day of the hearing, Clodius' supporters crowded the court, jeering both Cicero and Milo. To prevent any trouble, soldiers had been placed on alert, but for some reason the tenseness of the situation disturbed Cicero. He lost his self-assurance and failed to win acquittal for Milo. Cicero later sent Milo, who then lived in exile in Massilia (present-day Marseilles, France), a reworked copy of his defense. In his reply, Milo warmly thanked Cicero for his efforts, adding that he was glad Cicero had not delivered the reworked speech, because then he never would have tasted the wonderful seafood in Massilia.

For Cicero, the political situation in Rome was deteriorating quite rapidly. Disillusioned by events, he withdrew from public life once again and spent his time writing. But events were moving quickly, and Cicero was too eloquent and persuasive a speaker, too well-known a Roman, to remain politically inactive for long. Men in power wanted the advantage of having the great orator as an ally.

In 51 B.C., Cicero reluctantly agreed to Pompey's request that he become governor of Cilicia in southern Asia Minor. For Cicero, who loved

Rome, this leave was almost a second exile. True to his nature, however, he conducted all provincial business with integrity and justice. When bandits threatened the safety of the province, Cicero put them down, a service for which he felt he deserved a triumph, but the Senate disagreed. Their refusal may have been justified, because Rome was now on the brink of civil war.

On January 10, 49 B.C., Caesar crossed into Italy from Cisalpine Gaul and declared war on Pompey. Cicero continued to support Pompey, whom he had always favored over Caesar. On January 17, he met with Pompey just outside Rome and agreed to supervise the recruitment of soldiers into Pompey's army in Campania, south of the city.

When Pompey left Rome in March, Cicero remained behind to reconsider whether Pompey or Caesar would best promote the ideals of the republic as he envisioned them. On March 28, Cicero met with Caesar, courageously stating his belief that Caesar should end this civil war and not pursue Pompey. Caesar paid no heed to the advice, but he did invite Cicero to join his cause. Cicero refused, then left to join Pompey in Greece.

Once there, he criticized Pompey's plans, just as he had Caesar's. In the decisive battle of Pharsalus in 48 B.C., when Caesar defeated Pompey, Cicero did not fight. After the battle, however, Caesar pardoned Cicero, who returned to Rome but not to politics. For Cicero, those days had ended. Once again he turned to writing—not about politics but about philosophy.

Despite his choice, Cicero wrote that life without politics was "just tolerable." In this state of mind, it was only natural that he chose as his models the Greek philosophers, especially the Stoics, who stressed indifference to both pleasurable and unpleasurable events and feelings. He disagreed with Epicureanism, the other major school of Greek thought, which taught that pleasure constituted the greatest happiness.

After his daughter Tullia died in childbirth in 45 B.C., Cicero devoted himself even more to philosophy. Yet even as he chose to retreat within himself, political events once again called him to the Forum. Hearing that Caesar had been assassinated, Cicero sprang to action. In a brief letter to Basilus, one of the conspirators, Cicero could barely contain his emotions: "I congratulate you, and rejoice for myself. I love you, and am looking after your interests. I wish to be respected by you, to be informed how you are and how everything is doing."

Cicero sincerely believed that with Caesar dead, the republic could thrive once again. He had not been a part of the conspiracy, nor was he even present when Caesar was killed, but he did speak publicly two days later, asking the Senate to grant the conspirators amnesty.

A month later, Cicero's joy was gone. He wrote his friend Atticus, "The tyrant is dead, but tyranny still lives." Antony now stood in Caesar's place, showing the same disregard for the principles of the republic. Cicero finally vented his anger in 14 orations against Antony, asking the Senate to declare him a public enemy. Known to history as the Philippic orations, these speeches infuriated Antony. Cicero did not care, for he had now chosen to support Caesar's great-nephew and adopted son, the young Octavius (later known as Augustus).

Octavius used Cicero for a time, recognizing the power of his influence, but had his own ambitions. He soon al-

lied himself with Antony and another general named Lepidus in what history calls the Second Triumvirate, an alliance that caused Cicero's downfall.

Each member of this triumvirate had enemies whom he wished killed and friends he wanted protected. Cicero's name appeared as a friend on Octavius' list but an enemy on Antony's. Cicero was not the only one in this situation, however, and a num-

According to tradition, the original *curia* (Senate House) was built by Rome's third legendary king, Tullus Hostilius, around 650 B.C. After it burned in a riot in 52 B.C., Julius Caesar built a new one in the same style nearby in 44 B.C. Simple and solid, its walls echoed with the voices of Cicero, Caesar, Antony, Augustus, and many other Roman leaders.

ber of bargains and concessions were made. Antony, however, refused to remove Cicero's name from his list. He could not forgive or forget the Philippics. Finally, Octavius yielded and agreed to hire assassins.

When reports of his impending murder reached Cicero at his country house in Tusculum, he decided it would be best to leave Italy for Greece. Since he lacked provisions, his brother Quintus, who was with him at the time, returned home to gather supplies. Unfortunately, a treacherous slave betrayed Quintus to the assassins, and he and his young son were murdered in Rome.

Cicero, meanwhile, had tried to put out to sea, but a storm blew up, forcing him and his companions to return to shore. While they rested at a small house that Cicero owned nearby, a crow flew through the bedroom window and began pecking at Cicero's face. The servants on duty forcefully led their master to his litter and began carrying him to the seashore. The crow, they argued, was an omen that an assassin was near. Soon after Cicero departed, an officer named Herennius broke into the house and found it deserted. After questioning all he could find, he finally learned that Cicero was en route to the seashore.

When Cicero heard someone running in his direction, he knew what had happened and ordered his slaves to set down his litter. Looking straight at his murderers, he stretched out his neck. Herennius immediately cut off Cicero's head with his sword. Obeying Antony's command, Herennius also cut off Cicero's hands, which had written the 14 Philippics. Back in Rome, Antony ordered Cicero's head and hands to be fastened to the *rostra* (the orators' platform) in the Forum.

Plutarch wrote that years later the Roman emperor Augustus once entered a room where his grandson was reading a work by Cicero. Fearing that his grandfather would be angry, the boy tried to hide the book beneath his clothes. Before he could do so, Augustus took the book from him, looked slowly through it, and then said, "My child, this was a learned man, and a lover of his country."

In the years that followed, Cicero's influence reached far beyond Rome. His writing became the accepted model of Latin style and vocabulary, and countless writers imitated and adapted his passages. In schools throughout the Western world, students—especially those studying philosophy and law—continue to read and analyze passages from his works.

FURTHER READING

Cicero. *De Republica*. Translated by Clinton Walker Keyes. Loeb Classical Library. Cambridge: Harvard University Press, 1928.

———. *Tusculan Disputations*. 2 vols. Translated by J. E. King. Loeb Classical Library. New York: Putnam, 1960.

Douglas, Alan E. *Cicero*. Oxford, England: Clarendon Press, 1968.

Haskell, H. J. *This Was Cicero*. New York: Fawcett, 1942.

Plutarch. *Plutarch's Lives*. Vol. 7. Translated by Bernadotte Perrin. Loeb Classical Library. Cambridge: Harvard University Press, 1968.

Rawson, Elizabeth. *Cicero: A Portrait*. Ithaca, N.Y.: Cornell University Press, 1975.

Stockton, David L. *Cicero: A Political Biography*. New York: Oxford University Press, 1971.

Mark Antony
(Marcus Antonius)

BORN LEADER

One of the most colorful personalities in Roman history, Mark Antony has captured the imagination of writers and actors through the centuries. Millions of students have memorized his eulogy of Julius Caesar as conceived by the English playwright William Shakespeare. Millions more have seen stage or screen recreations of Antony's romance with the Egyptian queen Cleopatra. However, few people know much more about this Roman who almost changed the course of history.

Born sometime between 83 and 81 B.C., Mark Antony seems to have spent his youth eating, drinking, and enjoying himself, all the while borrowing the funds to do so. These were not inherited traits, for his family had ample means and were well respected by Rome's leading citizens. Why Antony chose to befriend Romans of questionable character is not known.

According to the Greek historian Plutarch, Antony had a bold, masculine look that reminded people of portraits of Hercules, the mythical Greek hero. To make himself appear

A respected general, Mark Antony let his personal life interfere with his politics. For him, the result was disastrous—not only did he lose power but he also lost his life.

"It is well done, Eros, for you show your master how to do what you had not the heart to do yourself."

—Antony, quoted in Plutarch's *Lives* (around 1st century A.D.), reacting to the suicide of his servant Eros, after Eros kills himself rather than his master, as he was ordered to do

even more like Hercules, Antony adopted the habit of wearing his tunic bound low about his hips, with a sword at his side and a large outer cloak.

As his profession, Antony chose to pursue the two careers most commonly followed by males of his class and lineage—the military and politics. His friendly manner with his soldiers, his generosity, and his good humor won him many loyal supporters who, in a Rome increasingly controlled by force, would prove critical to his advancement.

Antony began his military career in 57 B.C., serving as a cavalry commander in Judaea and Egypt. Three years later, he left for Gaul to join the staff of his cousin Julius Caesar—an alliance that would shape the course of his life. With Caesar's help, Antony was elected in 51 B.C. to the quaestorship, the lowest of Rome's four high-ranking political offices. This position put him in charge of financial matters in Rome and made him eligible for the Senate.

Two years later, when Rome stood on the brink of civil war, Antony held the office of tribune. It was now his duty to protect the rights of the people against unjust actions by Roman officials. For this reason, Antony vetoed a motion before the Senate that deprived Caesar of his command and gave Pompey dictatorial powers. After repeated threats of bodily harm from Pompey's supporters, Antony and a companion

disguised themselves as slaves and fled north to join Caesar. They reached Caesar just after he had crossed the Rubicon River and declared war on Pompey.

Within 60 days of the crossing, Caesar was master of Italy and Pompey had fled to Greece. Caesar then headed for Spain to quell a revolt led by Pompey's supporters. Because turmoil still gripped Rome, Caesar knew he needed a capable military leader to take command of the city in his absence. He chose Antony.

Triumphant in Spain, Caesar returned to Rome and prepared to defeat Pompey. Antony accompanied him to Greece, where Caesar defeated Pompey's forces at Pharsalus in 48 B.C. Following this victory, Caesar praised Antony for his skillful handling of the army's left wing on the battlefield.

Determined not to return to Rome until Pompey was dead or a prisoner, Caesar headed east, leaving Antony in charge of Italy in the role of consul. This time, however, reports reached Caesar that Antony was drinking, abusing his power, and spending large amounts of money. Even more troublesome were the violent, armed gangs roaming the streets of Rome.

As usual, Caesar acted quickly. First he deposed Antony and had two other allies elected consuls for the remainder of 47 B.C. The following year Caesar held the consulship himself, not with Antony but with another military commander, Lepidus.

Perhaps because of this rebuff by Caesar, Antony began to change his wanton ways and become more responsible. Contributing to this change was his new wife, the strong-willed Fulvia. Her money also helped, considering Antony's continuing spendthrift ways.

Having both married for the third time, Antony and Fulvia were very devoted to each other and to each other's ambitions. In a determined effort, they strove to prove themselves loyal supporters of Caesar. Their strategy worked. When Caesar returned from Spain in 45 B.C., he chose Antony to share his carriage for part of the journey. The following year, when Caesar was elected consul for the fifth time, Antony was his co-consul.

But Caesar's days were numbered. According to Cicero, Antony had been approached about joining the conspiracy to assassinate Caesar but had never replied. Immediately following Caesar's murder on March 15, 44 B.C., Antony acted swiftly to usurp power for himself. It was he who gave the eulogy, read the will, and took possession of Caesar's property and papers. Antony's speech helped to turn the people against the conspirators and, instead of being acclaimed heroes, the conspirators were decried as traitors and had to flee Rome to save their lives.

Antony might have succeeded in dominating the Roman world if Caesar's great-nephew, Octavius (later called Augustus), had not asserted himself. In his will, Caesar had adopted Octavius as his son and named him, not Antony, as his heir. Caesar had also bequeathed to each Roman citizen a sum of money, a provision Antony refused to fulfill. Octavius, not about to yield to Antony, used his own money to honor the terms of Caesar's will, thereby endearing himself to the Roman people. The great orator Cicero encouraged Octavius to fight for his rights and delivered a series of 14 speeches attacking Antony.

In September of 44 B.C., Antony left Rome for Gaul. In the months that followed, several Roman armies were sent against him, but he defeated them all. Octavius, meanwhile, realizing that he did not have adequate backing militarily or in the Senate to win the power for himself, decided to form an alliance with Antony and another general, Lepidus.

In November 43 B.C., less than a year after Caesar's death, the new allies Antony, Lepidus, and Octavius met and formed the Second Triumvirate. Almost immediately, each of the three triumvirs drew up his own proscription list naming opponents he wished to eliminate. Thousands of Romans lost their lives in the terrible days that followed. When a friend of one triumvir appeared on the list of another the individual's fate was settled by bartering. When Cicero's name appeared on Antony's list, Octavius voiced his opposition, but Antony was so determined to rid himself of Cicero that Octavius yielded. So bitter were Antony's feelings against Cicero that when the orator's head and hands were brought to him, Antony ordered them nailed to the rostra in the Forum.

Yet even this wholesale slaughter was not sufficient to give the triumvirs control of the Roman world. As long as Caesar's assassins remained alive, the allegiance of the Roman people would be divided. Once again, civil war forced brother to fight brother and friend to fight friend. Leaving Lepidus in charge of Rome, Antony and Caesar headed east with their armies. In 42 B.C., at Philippi in Macedonia, Antony faced Cassius and Octavius confronted Brutus. In the fighting that followed, Octavius did little to distinguish himself, but Antony led a brilliant attack and routed Cassius' forces.

Days later, Octavius' troops overwhelmed those of Brutus and Brutus committed suicide rather than be taken prisoner. The Republican party and those who fought so valiantly to save it were dead. The triumvirate now ruled Rome. Militarily, the victory was Antony's, but Octavius, as Caesar's heir, was honored by all, especially since a decree had been passed deifying Julius Caesar. To the Romans, this meant that Octavius was the adopted son of a god.

The triumvirs now redivided the Roman world. Antony assumed control of the eastern provinces, Octavius of

Mark Antony

BORN
Between 83 B.C. and 81 B.C.
Place unknown

DIED
30 B.C.
Alexandria, Egypt

PROFESSION
General and statesman

ACCOMPLISHMENTS
Assumed leading role in Roman government after Julius Caesar's assassination; formed Second Triumvirate with Octavius and Lepidus; credited with victory over Caesar's assassins at Battle of Philippi; broke with Octavius and took control of the eastern Roman world

Elizabeth Taylor and Richard Burton appear in the 1963 film version of *Cleopatra.* The relationship between Antony and Cleopatra has been portrayed in countless novels, plays, and movies through the centuries. Always, the question arises: How would the course of history have changed had they won the battle against Octavius for control of the Roman world?

the western ones—except for Gaul, which also went to Antony. Lepidus seems to have fared poorly in this division. Historians believe that Antony and Octavius thought they had reason to suspect his loyalty and were waiting for him to prove himself before giving him control of Roman possessions in Africa.

Antony and Octavius then turned their efforts to restructuring the lands they governed. Antony set out for the East. One of the main items on his agenda concerned Cleopatra, the queen of Egypt. Antony had met her years earlier, when Roman forces had aided her father's troops on the battle-

field. Now he wanted to know why she had remained silent in the civil war and not supported the triumvirs.

In 42 B.C., Antony sent a message to Cleopatra asking that she meet him in Tarsus, in southeastern Asia Minor. Cleopatra accepted the invitation, but only on her terms. According to Plutarch, Cleopatra dressed herself as Venus, the Roman goddess of love and beauty, and sailed up the Cydnus River in a barge with a golden stern and purple sails (purple, the most expensive dye in ancient times, was a color reserved for royalty). Musicians played flutes and harps as rowers struck the water with silver oars. Young boys, dressed as Cupid (Venus' son, the god of love), stood alongside Cleopatra, who lay under a canopy of gold. Servant girls in the guise of sea nymphs steered the vessel and worked the ropes for the sail.

Sending a message to Antony that Venus had come to dine with Bacchus (the Roman god of wine and merriment), Cleopatra waited for the Roman general's reply. When Antony requested that Cleopatra join him, Cleopatra answered that it was more fitting for him to come dine with her. Antony obeyed.

Captivated by her charm, humor, and spirit, Antony returned with Cleopatra to Alexandria, Egypt, and spent the winter at the palace. Reports of Antony's relationship with the Egyptian queen quickly reached Rome. Decades later, Plutarch wrote how a friend of his grandfather had seen eight wild boars being roasted in the royal kitchens in Alexandria. When the visitor commented, "You must be expecting many guests," the cooks laughed and said no more than 12 were dining that day. The cooks then added that Antony always wanted his meal cooked exactly to his liking but never knew the time at which he would be ready to eat. To honor his wishes, the cooks had eight boars cooking so that each would be finished at a different time, one of which would surely match the time Antony decided to eat.

When Romans heard that Antony was spending money lavishly and had discarded his Roman garb for an eastern costume, many began to question his intentions. All the rumors ceased, however, when Antony suddenly reappeared in Rome.

Octavius, meanwhile, had experienced difficulty consolidating his rule in the West. Antony's wife, Fulvia, and his brother Lucius had rallied their supporters against him. Antony feigned ignorance of their activities but nevertheless returned to Rome to assess the situation.

Fulvia, apparently depressed by Antony's coldness, died in 40 B.C. Her death allowed Antony to mend his relationship with Octavius and he soon married Octavius' sister Octavia. However, there was still tension between the two allies. Neither Octavius nor the Roman people approved of Antony's relationship with Cleopatra, and the protests increased when it was revealed that Antony had fathered Cleopatra's newborn twins. By law, Antony could never marry Cleopatra because she was a foreigner, nor could any children by Cleopatra be considered his heirs.

In 37 B.C., Antony, Octavius, and Lepidus renewed their alliance for another five years, but the following year Octavius forced Lepidus into retirement. Octavius had greatly strengthened his position in the West after defeating all opposition. Militarily, Antony's position was also strong, but he needed a steady supply of funds to support his troops on land and sea and to pay his political and personal expenses. The latter had increased tremendously since Antony had reverted to the wild habits of his youth.

Antony knew that Egypt was the richest land in the Mediterranean world and that an alliance with Cleopatra would bring him needed funds. This may have influenced his decision to send his wife, Octavia, and their children back to Rome while he resumed his relationship with Cleopatra.

Antony still had the support of his troops, but the Roman people vehemently condemned his harsh treatment of Octavia and their children. In the months that followed, the breach between Antony and Octavius widened, especially after Octavius published what was supposed to be Antony's will. In this document (possibly a forgery), Antony asked to be buried in Alexandria and named as heirs his children by Cleopatra. The credibility of this document was enhanced when Antony officially divorced Octavia. It is not known whether he actually married Cleopatra, but rumors of a marriage circulated through the Mediterranean.

Octavius finally reached the breaking point, severing all ties with Antony and declaring war on Cleopatra. Antony was supremely confident, certain that his military genius and Cleopatra's funds would produce a smashing triumph over Octavius. He and Cleopatra spent the winter of 33-32 B.C. in Ephesus on the coast of Asia Minor, gathering their forces and preparing for battle.

In the spring of 32 B.C., Antony and Cleopatra began moving their troops to the western coast of Greece. Many Romans, including senators and public officials, had left Rome to join Antony, whom they considered the true ruler of Rome. Yet they wisely warned Antony against allying himself too closely with Cleopatra. Antony refused to heed their advice, arguing that without her resources he could not even go to war, much less win.

Despite Antony's confidence, things went badly right from the start. Octavius' trusted commander Agrippa crossed into western Greece with his forces and began capturing sites along the coast. When news of this reached Antony's camp, the morale and loyalty of his troops began to waver. Then, when Antony allowed Cleopatra to remain at his headquarters despite the urgings of his advisors to the contrary, many of his supporters wondered if Cleopatra actually ruled Antony. Some began to feel that a victory by Antony might actually be a defeat for Rome. In the days that followed, more and more soldiers deserted to Octavius' camp.

As Agrippa and Octavius closed in, Antony's supplies of food and water grew scarcer. His troops began to fall ill, and morale plunged still further. When Octavius cornered their fleet in the Gulf of Ambracia, Antony and Cleopatra tried to break through Octavius' lines and seek another, more favorable battleground. But when the opposing fleets clashed near the promontory of Actium on the morning of September 2, 31 B.C., Octavius' swift warships easily outmaneuvered his enemies' large, unwieldy vessels.

Cleopatra, with Antony's treasury in her possession, quickly ordered her 60 vessels to turn about and head for Egypt. When Antony saw purple sails heading south on the horizon, he knew they were Cleopatra's. (Sails were never set in battle, only in retreat.) He immediately ordered his sailors to withdraw from the battle and follow Cleopatra.

Unaware that their leader had deserted them, Antony's ground forces continued fighting. Even when reports spread of Antony's desertion, the loyal troops refused to believe them at first. When it finally became clear that their revered leader had betrayed them, they laid down their arms. Historically, the Battle of Actium decided the fate of the Roman world and left Octavius in total control.

But Antony still lived—as did Cleopatra. Determined to remain queen of Egypt, she had already begun rebuilding her treasury and killing off opponents. Antony, on the other hand, had lost much of his will to continue. After catching up with Cleopatra's escaping flagship and accepting her invitation to come aboard, he kept to himself. When they reached Egypt, he did not accompany Cleopatra to Alexandria.

Problems in Italy kept Octavius from pursuing his enemies immediately, but in 30 B.C. he set out for Egypt with his troops. Antony won the first battle in the Hippodrome at Alexandria and was so elated by his victory that he challenged Octavius to hand-to-hand combat. Octavius refused. Antony then offered to kill himself if Octavius would spare Cleopatra. Again Octavius refused.

On August 1, 30 B.C., the forces of Octavius and Antony faced each other for the last time. When Antony ordered his fleet to attack, the sailors immediately set to pulling on their oars, but as they approached the enemy they saluted Octavius instead of fighting. Antony's cavalry did the same. Only the foot soldiers, Antony's most loyal troops, offered battle, but they were quickly overwhelmed by Octavius' soldiers.

Plutarch wrote that Antony, dejected and alone, returned to Alexandria, berating Cleopatra for betraying him. Fearing his anger, Cleopatra left the palace with a few trusted companions and locked herself in the mausoleum already built to house her body after she died. She then sent a message to Antony that she had committed suicide.

Unable to face life without Cleopatra, Antony ordered a faithful

servant to kill him, but the servant killed himself instead. Antony then took his sword and plunged it into his own stomach. Bleeding but still alive, Antony begged those around to finish the task, but no one obeyed.

When news of Antony's deed reached Cleopatra, she asked her servants to bring Antony to her. When they did so, Cleopatra refused to open the door but sent down ropes and cords from the window and hoisted Antony up the side of the mausoleum. At the sight of Antony, love swept over her as she held him in her arms. Barely breathing, Antony sought to stop her crying and asked for a drink of wine. With his last breath, according to Plutarch, Antony urged that Cleopatra not pity him but rejoice in remembering his past happiness. He had been the most illustrious and powerful of all men, he said, and in the end he had not been conquered ignobly, for he was a Roman conquered by a Roman.

A guard at the mausoleum snatched Antony's bloodied sword and took it to Octavius, who was preparing to enter Alexandria. Determined to prevent Cleopatra from taking her life, Octavius took Cleopatra prisoner and ordered a proper funeral for his former ally and friend, Mark Antony.

FURTHER READING

Huzar, Eleanor Goltz. *Mark Antony: A Biography.* Minneapolis: University of Minnesota Press, 1978.

Plutarch. *Plutarch's Lives.* Vol. 9. Translated by Bernadotte Perrin. Loeb Classical Library. Cambridge: Harvard University Press, 1968.

Shakespeare, William. *Antony and Cleopatra.* Edited by Roma Gill. New York: Oxford University Press, 1997.

Catullus
(Gaius Valerius
Catullus)

PASSION IN POETRY

"Let us live and let us love," wrote the young Gaius Valerius Catullus soon after meeting Clodia, a woman 7 to 10 years his senior. Unfortunately for Catullus, Clodia's love for him was not as intense as his for her. Before their final parting, Catullus wrote poems dedicated to his Clodia that rank him among the world's greatest love poets.

Catullus was born about 84 B.C. to a wealthy and distinguished Roman family in Verona, a prosperous city in the Roman province of Cisalpine Gaul (literally, "Gaul this side of the Alps"). It is possible that Catullus may have met or seen Clodia while her husband served as provincial governor in 62 B.C. Soon afterward, Catullus left home and traveled to Rome with letters of introduction to high-ranking people who would encourage and guide him. Once there, he was so fascinated by the bustling metropolis that he made it his permanent residence.

The
Carmina
of
Caius Valerius Catullus

Now first completely Englished into Verse
and Prose, the Metrical Part by Capt.
Sir Richard F. Burton, K.C.M.G.,
F.R.G.S., etc., etc., etc., and the
Prose Portion, Introduction,
and Notes Explanatory
and Illustrative by
Leonard C.
Smithers

LONDON : MDCCCXCIIII : PRINTED FOR THE TRANS-
LATORS : IN ONE VOLUME : FOR PRIVATE SUB-
SCRIBERS ONLY

Catullus was a master at expressing his feelings in simple but direct language. Through the centuries, there have been many reprints of his works, including this 1894 edition from London.

> *"Everyone has his own faults; but we do not see the knap-sack which is on our own back."*
>
> —from Poem Number XXII, line 20 (1st century B.C.)

His love, Clodia, was a well-known figure in Roman society. She had married her cousin the politician Metellus Celer and was related by blood and marriage to Rome's leading families. According to several ancient sources, Clodia was the sister of Clodius, Cicero's archenemy, and a close friend of Julius Caesar's second wife, Pompeia. Little else is known about her except that she was exceedingly beautiful, had striking eyes, danced gracefully, and was exceptionally talented. When her husband died in 59 B.C., it was rumored that Clodia had poisoned him.

Charmed by Clodia's beauty but hesitant to approach her, Catullus sent her a poem explaining his silence. Because he felt it coarse to use her real name in his poems, he sought a poetic name that would be appropriate. Since Clodia enjoyed literature as Catullus did and was passionate by nature, he compared her to the renowned Greek lyric poetess Sappho, who came from the island of Lesbos in the Aegean Sea. Using this comparison, he coined the name Lesbia for his love.

Pleased with the young poet's expression of devotion, Clodia invited Catullus to her home. Soon after, he wrote a poem addressed to her pet sparrow that included a subtle mixture of passion and humor. In it he reflected upon the happiness of the tiny, thoughtless, imprisoned creature and the two thwarted, miserable human beings watching him. This was Catullus' way of expressing his burning passion by mocking the kisses given to the little bird, with whom he wished to exchange places.

Next came his cheerful lament after Clodia's bird died, filled with slang, pet names, and jokes, all of which he concealed with mock grief. Both poems were Catullus' means of approaching Clodia through a living being she loved.

Catullus continued to declare his love in poems, although very discreetly. Intoxicated with happiness, he wrote the words so often echoed by other love poets through the centuries:

> Let us live, my Lesbia, and let us love.
> And let us value the rumors of the
>   stern elders worth a penny.
> The suns are able to set and to return:
> But for us, once the brief light of day
>   sets,
> It is one perpetual night for sleeping.
> Give me 1,000 kisses, then 100.
> Then another 1,000, then 100.
> Then, when we have kissed many
>   thousands
> We will confuse the numbers, so that

Catullus

they will not know,
Nor will any evil person be able to
envy us
Because he will know how many
kisses.

At first, Catullus expressed only the beautiful side of the romance. But Clodia quickly tired of Catullus' fervor and began seeing some of Rome's most eligible men, as she had done in the past. When Catullus learned this, he attempted in his poems to recapture happier times. As Clodia's unfaithfulness became more pronounced, Catullus' verses hinted for the first time at quarrels and reconciliations, gave excuses for Lesbia's weaknesses, and pleaded with rivals not to pursue his beloved. Then, in an outburst of deep hurt and grief, he cried:

My love says she prefers to wed no
one
But me, not even if Jupiter himself
should ask,
She says this, but what a woman says
to her eager lover
Ought to be written on the wind and
the rapid wave.

Finally aware that Clodia no longer loved him, Catullus summed up his fierce conflict between passion and self-respect in his best-known poem:

I love and I hate, perhaps you ask why
I do this.
I do not know, but I feel it happening
and I am tormented.

Still, the repeated reconciliations and ruptures persisted and, while Catullus' love did not lessen, his hatred increased and the lyrical cry in his poems became one of the sharpest agony. In the spring of 57 B.C., realizing that Clodia had become an embarrassment to him personally, he finally found the

courage to repudiate her. Catullus finally broke with Clodia in 57 B.C., entering a period of depression and inactivity that ended only with his death three years later.

Literary critics have noted that it was Clodia who made Catullus and Clodia who ruined him—when he ceased to be a lover, he ceased to be a poet. Yet in the end, Clodia was Catullus' passport to undying fame.

Catullus' poems are unique in that they are direct personal expressions of his emotions. Like many Romans of the time, Catullus read, translated, and adapted the works of the Greeks. Unlike most ancient writers, however, he did not refer to mythological characters or the gods, drawing instead on his own knowledge of human nature. His ability to express reality, to let the reader experience the intensity of his emotions, was new to literature.

Catullus' poems often appeared to be spontaneous outbursts, but he mastered the art of using changes in meter to complement the feeling he was trying to convey. Though often called a lyric poet, Catullus did not fit the classic definition of this term. Traditionally, Greek and Latin lyric poets wrote verses that were meant to be sung. (The term *lyric* is derived from the Greek word *lyra*, the stringed instrument used to accompany poets reciting their works.) Catullus' poems were not written for the lyre, but they were certainly lyrical in the modern sense in that they expressed intense emotion.

Through the centuries, many great poets have translated and adapted Catullus' works, including his immediate successors Horace, Virgil, and Ovid. Other imitators include the Italian masters Dante Alighieri (1265–1321)

BORN
Around 84 B.C.
Verona, Cisalpine Gaul

DIED
Around 54 B.C.
Rome

PROFESSION
Poet

ACCOMPLISHMENTS
First Roman to write true love poetry; one of the most prominent of the 1st century B.C. writers; wrote 116 poems that survive, 25 on his love for Clodia;

and Petrarch (1304–74), the English writer Ben Jonson (1572–1637), and the French poet Jean-Antoine de Baïf (1532–89). In his play *Romeo and Juliet* William Shakespeare recalled Catullus' poem about Clodia's sparrow and had Romeo wish he were a bird so that Juliet might cherish him. But no poet ever felt passion more bitterly nor expressed it more vividly than Catullus himself.

Yet only 25 of the 116 poems credited to Catullus refer to Clodia. Most anthologies and literary texts focus on these 25, and the others usually receive only a brief mention. This is unfortunate, since many of them are excellent examples of Catullus' vividness of expression and his unusual ability to describe his inner feelings with depth and clarity. A fine example is Catullus' poem about the town of Sirmio (present-day Sirmione), where he owned property:

> O Sirmio, the jewel of almost islands
>   and islands. . .
> How happy, how pleased, I am to see
>   you. . . .
> Oh, what is more blessed than when,
>   with cares laid aside,
> The mind puts down its burden and
> Tired from work in other lands we
>   come home exhausted,
> And sleep on our longed-for bed.
> This alone makes up for such great
>   labor.
> Greetings, O wonderful Sirmio, and
>   rejoice in your master's joy. . . .

Catullus was not a historian, nor did he involve himself in the political wrangling that went on continually in Rome. His father had been a friend of Julius Caesar's and had entertained Caesar in his home. Perhaps Catullus even met Caesar when the latter was proconsul in Cisalpine Gaul, Catullus' homeland. Catullus did not like Caesar, however, and in one of his poems he bluntly stated his dislike of Caesar's actions in Gaul. Truthfulness was always one of his leading traits.

Of all the lines Catullus wrote, perhaps the most moving are those written to his brother, whose early death brought Catullus to a grave site in northwest Asia Minor:

> Through many nations and through
>   many seas I have come to these
>   wretched burial rites, O brother,
> So that I might give you the last rites
>   of death and may speak in vain to
>   your mute ashes,
> Because Fortune has taken you from
>   me—Alas, O poor brother, so un-
>   worthily taken from me
> Nevertheless, these rites which accord-
>   ing to ancient custom
> Are now performed as the sad duty at
>   your funeral rites,
> Accept them, drenched in your broth-
>   er's tears
> And forever, brother, hail and farewell.

FURTHER READING

Catullus, Tibullus, and Pervigilum Veneris. Translated by F. W. Cornish. Loeb Classical Library. New York: Macmillan, 1914.

Harrington, Karl P. *Catullus and His Influence.* Boston: Marshall Jones, 1923.

Martin, Charles. *Catullus.* New Haven, Yale University Press, 1992.

Quinn, Kenneth. *Catullus, an Interpretation.* New York: Barnes & Noble, 1973.

More Ancient Romans to Remember

Lucullus (**Lucius Licinius Lucullus**) (around 117–58/56 B.C.) aligned himself with Sulla and the *Optimates* early in his military and political career. In 82 B.C., when Rome's leaders sought to annex Bithynia, in Asia Minor, Rome's archenemy Mithridates VI, king of Pontus, marched into Bithynia. The Senate commissioned Lucullus, who was consul at the time, to lead an army against Mithridates.

In less than four years, Lucullus drove Mithridates out of Bithynia, then expelled him from his own homeland. However, able leadership and good military strategy were not enough to win Lucullus the support of his troops. He always kept his distance from his soldiers, considering them his inferiors. Morale among Lucullus' troops eventually deteriorated to such a point that they refused to fight on command.

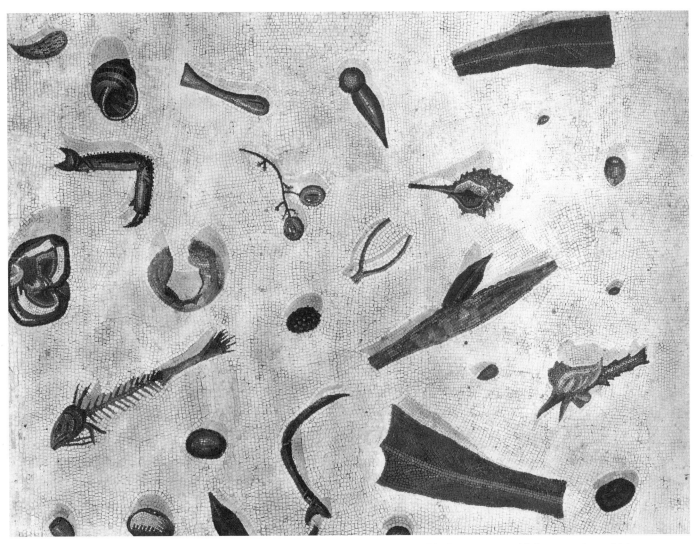

Lucullus, who appreciated good food and gave lavish banquets, may well have seen his floor strewn with items such as chicken heads and fish bones after a night of feasting. This mosaic floor, probably from the home of a well-to-do Roman, is especially creative in its depiction of an unswept floor littered with banquet leftovers.

Many of Lucullus' supporters in Rome were also growing dissatisfied with his policies. As a result, the Senate ordered Lucullus to yield his command to Pompey and return to Rome.

Once in Rome, Lucullus continued to involve himself in politics, but as the years passed he devoted himself more to personal pleasures. He loved food and gave lavish banquets. Lucullus also spent lavishly on his gardens. In the centuries that followed, the term *Lucullan* became a synonym for unrestrained luxury.

Lucullus also loved literature and was well-known as a patron of the arts. He freely opened his extensive library to anyone seriously interested in literature and philosophy.

Lepidus (Marcus Aemilius Lepidus)(died 13/12 B.C.) allied himself with Julius Caesar in the civil war between Caesar and Pompey. His military prowess and political astuteness soon won him Caesar's respect, and in 46 B.C. the two were co-consuls in Rome.

After Caesar's assassination in 44 B.C., Lepidus openly declared his support for Mark Antony against the conspirators. In return, Antony secured Lepidus' nomination to the powerful position of *pontifex maximus*, Rome's principal religious leader.

When Antony was forced to leave Italy and retreated to Gaul, Lepidus joined forces with him. The Senate then proclaimed Lepidus a public enemy. Soon afterward, Octavius (later known as Augustus) joined Antony and Lepidus, and the three formed the Second Triumvirate, with the intent of jointly ruling the Roman world.

In 42 B.C., Antony and Octavius left Lepidus in charge of affairs at Rome and marshaled their troops against Caesar's assassins at the battle of Philippi in Greece. Following their victory, Lepidus took charge of a Roman province in northwestern Africa where he remained until 36 B.C., when Octavius summoned him to Sicily to help put down opposition. Tired of his subordinate role in the triumvirate, Lepidus attempted to rouse his troops against Octavius. Much to his dismay, however, his soldiers deserted him for Octavius, who then forced Lepidus to retire from political life. Octavius did allow Lepidus to remain *pontifex maximus* until he died, in 13 or 12 B.C.

Catiline (Lucius Sergius Catilina) (around 108–62 B.C.) is one of the most maligned characters in Roman history. A member of one of Rome's oldest families, Catiline planned to run for the consulship after serving as propraetor in Africa from 67 B.C. to 66 B.C. According to Roman law, no public official could be prosecuted while in office, but upon his return to Rome, Catiline was accused of abuse of power. Because his case was still pending at the time of the consular elections, he became ineligible to run.

After finally being acquitted, Catiline sought election to the consulship in 64 B.C. Many of Rome's leading citizens and politicians, however, chose to back Cicero. Realizing that legal means would never win him public office, Catiline planned to stage an armed revolt against Rome.

Unknown to Catiline, spies within his camp were telling Cicero the details of the revolt. On October 21, 63 B.C., Cicero denounced Catiline in the Senate and charged him with treason. His eloquent speech so roused the senators that they passed a *senatus consultum ultimum*, an emergency decree authorizing Rome's officials to do whatever necessary to repress public enemies.

On the night of November 6, 63 B.C., Catiline and other leaders in his conspiracy plotted Cicero's death, but an informant foiled their attempt. On November 8, Cicero called an emergency meeting of the Senate. When he walked in to address the senators and saw Catiline, the audacity of the man so incensed Cicero that he denounced him as a public enemy, and sought direct action by the senators against this menace to Rome and the republic. Jeered when he attempted to address the Senate, Catiline left Rome to join his band north of the city.

Cicero knew he had to act quickly. After obtaining signed documents about the conspiracy, Cicero gave orders to arrest the five ringleaders still in Rome. Then, on December 5, Cicero argued before the Senate for the death penalty. Although he knew that by law every Roman citizen had the right to a trial, he did not wish to prolong the conspiracy and, with the Senate's approval, he ordered the five executed at once.

When Catiline learned of his associates' fate, he rallied his army and prepared to march north into Gaul. But forces sent by Cicero routed Catiline's troops. Recognizing that his cause was lost, Catiline committed suicide.

Cato the Younger (Marcius Porcius Cato) (95–46 B.C.) was the great-grandson of Cato the Elder. He gained a reputation for honesty and rigid morality quite early in his military and political career.

As the spokesman for the *optimates* (Rome's upper class), Cato opposed the coalition of Julius Caesar, Pompey, and Crassus. Cato's efforts to oppose the triumvirate and its policies, however,

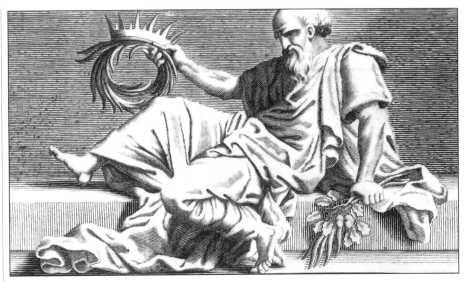

Respected as a poet and philosopher, Lucretius had an imagination and powers of description that have rarely been equaled by any poet, modern or ancient.

were unsuccessful, and after losing his bid for the consulship in 51 B.C. Cato chose to retire from politics.

When Caesar crossed the Rubicon River in January of 49 B.C. and declared war on Rome, Cato's energy quickly revived. Determined to stop Caesar, Cato backed Pompey.

After Pompey's defeat at Pharsalus in 48 B.C., Cato remained convinced that the best hope for the republic lay with Pompey's supporters. Therefore, he crossed to Africa and joined the pro-Pompey forces gathering there, then took the governorship of the city of Utica.

When news of Caesar's approaching troops reached Utica, Cato released all those who wished to escape Caesar's wrath and then opened the gates of the city.

Cato himself refused to surrender. After reading and rereading passages from the Greek philosopher Plato's work the *Phaedo*, which related the suicide of

the philosopher Socrates, Cato stabbed himself in the chest. As he fell forward, he knocked over an abacus. The noise brought those in the house rushing to his room. Finding him covered in blood and about to faint, they quickly bandaged his wound. When Cato revived and saw the bandages, he ripped them from his body and died shortly after, at the age of 49. In the years that followed, Cato's name became the rallying point for all those fighting for a return to republican ideals.

Lucretius (Titus Lucretius Carus) (around 94–55 B.C.) ranks as one of the world's great philosophical poets. His fame rests on one poem, *De Rerum Natura* (Concerning the Nature of Things), a philosophical, scientific, and didactic (instructional) work consisting of approximately 7,400 lines. The style of *De Rerum Natura* is basically epic in that Lucretius purposely used the dignified vocabulary and grand manner of expression characteristic of epic poetry.

THE
Workes of
Caius Crispus
Salustius

Contayning the Conspiracie of Cateline
The
Warre of Iugurth.
V. Bookes of Historicall
fragments.
II Orations to Cæsar
for the Institution of a
Comonwealth
And one against Cicero.

SPQR

SPQR

Cicero.

Cateline.

Cedant
arma
togæ.

Are to be sould
at the Eagle and
Child in Brittaines
Burse by Tho:

Vis expers
consilii
expers.

Sallust's account of Rome's near-disastrous conflicts with Jugurtha and Catiline, such as this edition of his work printed in 1629, has provided scholars with much information about this period in Roman history.

He also perfected the hexameter, the traditional meter used by epic poets.

Lucretius considered himself primarily a philosopher. Like the Greek philosopher Epicurus, he believed in a material universe that did not trace its origins to the gods but to atoms and an inexplicable scientific theory. Finding it impossible to believe that gods could act in the manner described in the Roman myths, Lucretius vehemently denounced religion.

According to Lucretius, science—not religion—should provide humans with comfort. He explained how the mechanical laws of nature and not the gods governed the world. Following the Greek philosophers who first proposed the theory of atoms, Lucretius believed that atoms were the origin of everything. He wrote that "nothing is ever born from nothing by divine intervention," and that "nothing ever returns to nothing." Rather, there is an infinite number of atoms, the combination of which determines what is created. Lucretius departed from his Greek predecessors by introducing the idea of free will into his theory, believing that the movement of atoms was not predetermined but in part spontaneous.

Complaining that the Latin language lacked the proper vocabulary to express his philosophical thoughts, Lucretius gave secondary meanings to commonly used words and even invented vocabulary whenever he felt it necessary. He also used figures of speech, old grammatical constructions, and a great variety of descriptive compound adjectives such as "forest-breaking winds" to render his lines more poetic and give them an epic grandeur.

Sallust (Gaius Crispius Sallustius) (around 86–35/34 B.C.) allied himself with Julius Caesar in 49 B.C. and was given command of a legion in the war against Pompey. Three years later, Caesar made Sallust governor of the Roman province of Africa Nova (present-day Algeria).

Upon his return to Rome, Sallust was charged with extortion and abuse of provincial power. His sumptuous gardens in Rome strongly suggested that he had amassed a great fortune by some means. Caesar intervened and Sallust was never brought to trial, but his political days were at an end. He now turned to writing history.

Drawing on his own experiences and other accounts of contemporary events, Sallust wrote *Bellum Catilinae* (Catiline's War). Because Sallust felt party strife was at the root of many of Rome's problems, he also wrote of the war between Rome and Jugurtha, the king of Numidia.

Although Sallust had a long writing career, his fame rests principally on these two works. Yet Sallust did not write without bias, nor was he a philosopher. In fact, his writings often reflected his resentment of the *optimates*. He was also guilty of geographical and chronological inaccuracies. But these are relatively minor criticisms when compared with the historical value of his works.

Brutus (Marcus Junius Brutus) (85–42 B.C.) is best known to history as one of the leaders of the conspiracy against Julius Caesar. A firm believer in the Roman republic, Brutus did not approve of Caesar's autocratic methods. To Cassius and those plotting to kill Caesar, Brutus was the perfect accomplice—the dictator's trusted friend and a man patriotically committed to the city's welfare.

Unfortunately for the conspirators, they had not anticipated Mark Antony's ability to sway the public, nor Octavius' increasing popularity. Fearing for their lives, Brutus and the other assassins had to flee Rome. Brutus sought refuge in Greece, where he rallied an army and became the acknowledged master of Greece and Macedonia.

In 42 B.C., at the Battle of Philippi in Greece, Brutus led the right wing of a combined army against Octavius' forces and routed them. The following day, Brutus positioned his troops in a spot the enemy would find difficult to attack. For 20 days the two armies watched and waited. Finally, the signal to attack was given. Brutus and the troops immediately near him fared well, but the rest of his army was quickly overwhelmed. Realizing that defeat was imminent and the republic was lost forever, Brutus escaped the battlefield with a few friends and hid in a nearby cave.

After considering the alternatives, Brutus took his sword and calmly asked his trusted attendant Strato to kill him. When he refused, Brutus pleaded with him until Strato took the sword, held it upright, and turned his face away while Brutus fell upon it. In the centuries that followed, Brutus came to epitomize the heroic patriot who gives his life in a futile attempt to save his country.

Nepos (Cornelius Nepos) (around 100–25 B.C.) was a Roman historian who wrote the first surviving biography in Latin. The few surviving texts of his works clearly prove that he was not a writer who searched out and analyzed details carefully. In fact, many passages show a carelessness and lack of unity. Because he wrote hastily, Nepos' manner was plain, simple, and colloquial.

Nepos' chief work was *De Viris Illustribus* (Concerning Outstanding Men), which included brief biographies of famous Romans and others, including Cato the Elder and the Carthaginian general Hannibal.

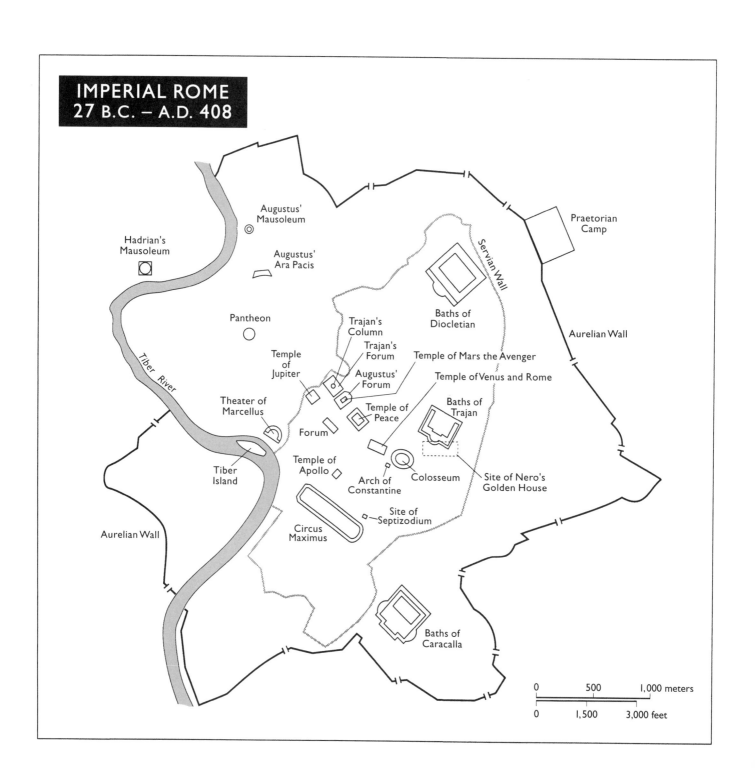

IMPERIAL ROME
27 B.C. – A.D. 408

Augustus' Mausoleum

Hadrian's Mausoleum

Praetorian Camp

Augustus' Ara Pacis

Servian Wall

Baths of Diocletian

Aurelian Wall

Pantheon

Trajan's Column

Trajan's Forum

Temple of Mars the Avenger

Temple of Jupiter

Augustus' Forum

Temple of Venus and Rome

Tiber River

Theater of Marcellus

Temple of Peace

Baths of Trajan

Forum

Tiber Island

Temple of Apollo

Arch of Constantine

Colosseum

Site of Nero's Golden House

Circus Maximus

Site of Septizodium

Aurelian Wall

Baths of Caracalla

0   500   1,000 meters

0   1,500   3,000 feet

3 An Empire Emerges (30 B.C.–A.D.37)

 In 509 B.C., rejoicing could be heard throughout Rome. The monarchy was gone, and Romans vowed that kings would never rule their land again. Rome had become a republic, governed by those elected by the people. For 400 years the republic stood, a testament to Roman pride and determination. But in the first century B.C., the political scene began to change. The consecutive dictatorships of Marius, Sulla, and Julius Caesar clearly reflected an emerging zest for power among individual Romans, which would prove fatal to the republic.

A new era began with Octavius (later called Augustus), the first leader since the days of kingship to inherit the power to rule Rome. The words *king* and *monarchy* were still anathema to the people, but Rome nevertheless became an empire with an emperor at its head.

The consequences of this change were felt immediately, in both the city of Rome and throughout the provinces. As money—in the form of tribute and taxes—poured into the state treasury, Romans strove to create a world-class civilization. The arts flourished as architects and writers sought to have their works equal Rome's political and military accomplishments.

Part 3 of *Ancient Romans* focuses on Romans who were directly responsible for designing and shaping life under the new empire, an empire whose influence has continued to the present day.

Augustus
(Gaius Octavius)

THE FIRST ROMAN EMPEROR

Named as heir in Julius Caesar's will, Gaius Octavius inherited the Roman world at the age of 18. Whether he would claim it—and whether he could hold it—were the questions being asked by citizens and provincials (those living in Rome's provinces) everywhere. In 44 B.C. neither Caesar's assassins nor his supporters considered the young Octavius a threat to their power. However, their underestimation of his drive and determination led to their downfall.

Octavius had been born in Velitrae, a town southeast of Rome, in 63 B.C., the same year Cicero foiled Catiline's attempt to take Rome by force. His parents were influential and rich. Octavius' father, the first in the family to attain the rank of senator, proved himself a capable administrator in the Roman province of Macedonia but died suddenly in 59 B.C. Octavius' mother, Atia, was the daughter of Julius Caesar's sister, Julia, a family tie that brought Octavius into close contact with Rome's rising leader. With no sons of his own, Caesar seems to have recognized his great-nephew's po-

Augustus brought a welcome peace to the Roman world. Revered and respected, he died a natural death, far different from that of his predecessor, Julius Caesar, and from many of those who would succeed him.

tential at an early age and favored the youth with special attention.

When Julia died, Caesar allowed 12-year-old Octavius to deliver the funeral oration. Four years later, Caesar asked Octavius to accompany him in a triumphal procession honoring his victories in Africa. The following year, Octavius accepted his great-uncle's invitation to join his military campaign in Spain, even though he was just recovering from a serious illness and Rome's enemies controlled the roads along which he had to travel. Caesar undoubtedly appreciated the boy's determination and drive.

After several decisive victories in Spain, Caesar began planning an offensive against the Dacians and Parthians to the East. Stopping first in Rome to attend to government matters, Caesar ordered Octavius and the army to continue their march east and wait for him in Illyria (present-day Albania). Octavius did as he was commanded, spending his free time studying Greek literature and military strategy. However, his studies were interrupted with the shattering announcement that his great-uncle had been assassinated.

After weighing his options, Octavius—now 18 years old—decided to return to Rome. But as he prepared to do so, a messenger arrived with news that Caesar's will named Octavius the dictator's adopted son and heir. Since there was no precedent for an heir to inherit power in Rome, Octavius knew he would encounter many obstacles if he continued now with his plan to return to Rome. Again Octavius had to make a choice. Despite opposition from his mother and stepfather, he resolved to seek his inheritance.

Mark Antony, Caesar's co-consul in 44 B.C. and a proven military leader, vehemently opposed Octavius' bid for power. Confident of widespread support among the military, Antony appropriated Caesar's papers and assets for himself and disregarded Caesar's bequest of

money to each Roman citizen. Rather than confront Antony, Octavius used his own funds to fulfill Caesar's wishes, thereby endearing himself to the people. The assassins were so concerned with protecting themselves from the anger of the people that they paid little heed to Octavius.

One Roman, however, saw the young heir as a potentially strong and effective leader. In the weeks that followed Caesar's assassination, the renowned statesman and orator Cicero openly supported Octavius over Antony and persuaded the Senate to do the same. As a result, armed conflict broke out between the Senate's forces and Antony's. To secure Octavius' support in the struggle, the Senate agreed to overlook his age and granted him the rank of senator. Months later, Rome's consuls died in battle and Octavius asked the Senate to ignore the rules a second time and name him consul. The senators complied almost immediately. They also officially recognized Octavius as Caesar's adopted son, granting him the use of his adopted father's name—Gaius Julius Caesar. However, historians always used the name Octavius when speaking of this period in his life.

Octavius soon proved himself far more ambitious than Cicero had imagined. As the young leader's power and influence increased, even the Senate began to fear that he might overrule their authority and thus sought ways to curb his power. Aware of this, Octavius turned to Antony, the man he had so recently opposed, seeking an alliance that he believed would advance his own interests. In the meantime, Antony had already joined forces with Lepidus, another influential Roman, and on November 27, 43 B.C., Octavius, Antony, and Lepidus formally united to restructure the government. Known collectively as the Second Triumvirate, the three men sought to consolidate their power by proscribing those individuals they considered their enemies. In the months that followed, more than 2,000 Romans (among them Cicero) lost their lives. Now only Caesar's assassins, who had left Italy and were rallying support in Greece and the East, remained as enemies.

Leaving Lepidus in charge of affairs in Italy, Octavius and Antony advanced into Greece at the head of their armies. In 42 B.C., on the plains of Philippi, the forces of the triumvirate routed Caesar's assassins. Octavius did not distinguish himself in battle, either because he was ill or, according to some sources, was unwilling to expose himself to danger. Nevertheless, according to a later account by the Roman historian Suetonius, Octavius showed little mercy toward the prisoners of war, although most were Romans, many from noble families. In fact, it was he who ordered the head of Brutus, the chief conspirator, returned to Rome and thrown at the feet of Julius Caesar's statue.

In 42 B.C., with all opposition defeated and the Roman world theirs, the members of the triumvirate met to divide the conquered lands among themselves. Antony took the East, Octavius the West, Lepidus parts of Spain, with the promise of Africa in the future. It was a settlement that foreshadowed conflict.

In Italy, Octavius' attempts to resettle returning soldiers on municipal lands brought criticism both from displaced landowners and soldiers who felt they deserved more than Octavius offered. As discontent spread, Antony's wife, Fulvia, and his brother Lucius sought to win the support of the malcontents and lead a revolt against Octavius. Their efforts failed, however, and Fulvia's subsequent death brought reconciliation between Antony and Octavius.

When a second rebellion threatened, led by Pompey's son Sextus, Octavius married Sextus' relative Scribo-

nia. Then, to further cement his political alliances and wrest Antony from his newly formed relationship with Cleopatra, the queen of Egypt, Octavius gave Antony his sister Octavia in marriage. At last a temporary peace settled on the Roman world.

A year later, Octavius divorced Scribonia—on the very day she gave birth to a daughter, Julia, according to some sources. Officially, Octavius spoke of mutual incompatibility, but in reality he had found a new love, Livia Drusilla, a member of one of Rome's leading families. In 38 B.C., Octavius married Livia, and he remained devoted to her until his death more than 50 years later, in A.D. 14.

Meanwhile, Sextus Pompeius continued to incite trouble, until finally full-scale war broke out in Sicily. Rallying to the aid of his colleague, Lepidus gathered his troops and crossed into Sicily. But his loyalty soon faltered as he thought of the rebuffs he had suffered under Octavius and Antony. Refusing to endure more insults, Lepidus sought control of the island, but Octavius acted quickly to subdue Lepidus, then ousted him from the triumvirate. Sextus remained a formidable adversary, however.

For eight years the two battled until Octavius' capable general Agrippa routed Sextus in a hard-won victory off the Sicilian coast in 36 B.C. Octavius and Antony now ruled the Roman world, but all was not well between the two. Politically, they had agreed that Octavius would rule the West and Antony the East, but reports reaching Rome spoke of Antony's disloyalty. And when Antony shipped Octavia and her children back to Rome so that he could renew his romance with Cleopatra, Octavius was furious, and so were the Roman people.

Determined to turn Rome decisively against Antony, Octavius ordered Antony's will opened and read publicly. Whether this was Antony's actual will or a forged one will probably never be known, but it certainly produced the effect Octavius wanted. The Romans were incensed to hear that Antony had named as his heirs his children by Cleopatra, which was illegal because they were not Roman citizens. In the power struggle that followed, Octavius persuaded the Senate to condemn Antony as a public enemy. Then, because he hesitated to declare war on a fellow Roman, Octavius declared war on Cleopatra instead.

In September 31 B.C., the forces of Octavius and Antony met in a great sea battle off the promontory of Actium in western Greece. Under the capable leadership of Agrippa, Octavius' forces emerged triumphant but failed to capture either Antony or Cleopatra. Soon after the start of the battle, Cleopatra realized that victory was impossible and turned her vessels toward Egypt. Seeing his lover in retreat, Antony deserted his men to accompany her.

Rallying his forces once again, Octavius set sail for Egypt. His arrival in Alexandria brought about the suicides of Antony and Cleopatra. As Octavius gazed at each body, he took compassion on them and decreed that they should be buried in the same tomb. Next he ordered Caesarion, allegedly Cleopatra's son by Julius Caesar, captured and killed, which ended any claim Caesarion might have made to Caesar's legacy. He spared Antony's children by Cleopatra, and raised them as his own.

The 37-year-old Octavius was now sole master of the Roman world, and determined to rule wisely. Aware that Egypt was the richest of Rome's possessions, he treated it with special care, even ordering workers to clean its irrigation canals so that the land would be more productive. In a sound political move, Octavius used the resources of Cleopatra's great treasury to pay the many veterans who had brought him victory. And while in Egypt, Octavius

reflected on the outstanding commanders who had preceded him, especially Alexander the Great, entombed in Alexandria. Wishing to gaze upon the features of the famed Macedonian, Octavius commanded that Alexander's corpse be removed from its shrine. Octavius placed a gold crown on the dead king's head, then scattered flowers over his body.

With affairs settled in the East, Octavius returned to Rome in 29 B.C. and celebrated a great triumph in honor of his military achievements. He then prepared to revamp the government and stabilize affairs throughout the Roman world. To mark the reign of the peace his policies had produced, Octavius ordered the doors of the Temple of Janus closed. For the Romans, Janus was the god of beginnings and was represented as a deity with two heads, one looking back, the other ahead. By tradition, the doors of Janus' temple were kept open in time of war as a symbol of the help he offered. The wars for Roman expansion had been so continuous that the temple doors had been closed only twice before Octavius' rule. The doors were opened again when conflicts erupted during his rule, but his pursuit of peace allowed him to close the temple on two additional occasions.

To give credence to his desire for peace, Octavius gradually reduced the number of Roman legions, from 60 or 70 to 28. He did not make military decisions completely on his own, however, but relied heavily on his trusted general Agrippa. In time, Octavius' rule became identified with the *Pax Romana*, or Roman Peace.

Communications were the key to Octavius' organizational plan for his dominions. He began work on a road system to unite Rome's provinces and connect the important cities within each province. Roman troops could now reach trouble spots quickly, and laws could be more easily disseminated.

Augustus

BORN

September 23, 63 B.C.
Velitrae, Italy

DIED

August 19, A.D. 14
Nola, Italy

PROFESSION

Roman emperor

ACCOMPLISHMENTS

Member of the Second Triumvirate with Antony and Lepidus; with Antony defeated Julius Caesar's assassins at Philippi; ruled western part of Roman world from 42 B.C. to 31 B.C.; sole ruler of Roman world from 30 B.C. to A.D. 14; consolidated and restructured the government of Rome and the provinces; ordered construction of many magnificent buildings in Rome and throughout the empire; established a system of roads connecting the provinces to Rome; set up Rome's first police force and fire brigade; revamped the Roman coinage

After Augustus' death, the record of his achievements was inscribed on bronze tablets and set up outside his mausoleum in Rome. The text was then replicated on public monuments throughout the empire. The original is lost, but this copy on the wall of the Temple of Rome and Augustus in Ankara, Turkey, is the best preserved.

By establishing a network of roads, Octavius also granted merchants ready access to markets around the Mediterranean. And to keep sea lanes clear of unfriendly vessels, Octavius established a fleet to patrol the Mediterranean.

Octavius knew that revolt, murder, and political assassination were always lurking where he might least expect them. He remembered well the fate of his great-uncle at the hands of trusted allies and was determined to avoid a similar fate. For more than 200 years, Roman generals had had their own personal bodyguard, or *cohors praetoria*—

praetorian cohort (from *praetorium*, the Latin word for area where the general's tent was pitched in a camp, and *cohors*, a unit in the Roman army). Octavius now established his own private force of nine cohorts, each numbering 500 infantrymen. Three cohorts he stationed within the city itself, the other six in neighboring towns. Known as the Praetorian Guard, these soldiers were Rome's elite corps, with members receiving higher rank and pay than those in the regular army.

Another concern was the Senate, which Octavius considered too large and unwieldy. He also objected to the bribery and illegal means many had used to secure their positions in it. To rectify the situation, Octavius asked the senators to suggest which of their number should remain and which dismissed. After carefully reviewing each name, Octavius chose those he wished to retain. When he appeared before the assembled senators to announce his decision, he reportedly had a sword and a steel breastplate concealed beneath his tunic and 10 burly senatorial allies at his side. Octavius permitted only one senator at a time to approach him, and each man was thoroughly searched. Octavius did not withdraw all the senatorial privileges of those he forced to resign: Each was still allowed to wear the senator's toga (the traditional male Roman garb, with a broad purple stripe as a sign of high rank), sit in specially assigned seats at public games, and attend Senate banquets.

The Romans welcomed Octavius' changes and the peace he had brought to their world. They showed their appreciation by electing him to successive consulships from 31 B.C. through 23 B.C. But Octavius knew well how fickle people could be. Therefore, he began encouraging his subjects to observe traditional Roman values, honoring the beliefs of Rome's earliest heroes. In a concerted effort to revive the old values, Octavius refurbished many of Rome's temples and revived ancient religious rites.

In January 27 B.C., Octavius offered to yield his control of Rome to the Senate and the Roman people. He did, however, have himself granted a 10-year governorship of Gaul (present-day France), Spain, and Syria, the three provinces where the greater part of his army was stationed. With foresight, Octavius shunned all honors and powers associated with royalty and contin-

ued to hold elections for Rome's chief magistrates. However, he used his *auctoritas* (prestige or authority) in such a way that everyone deferred the decision making to him. His methods proved highly effective. The Senate and people quickly dismissed his offer to surrender control of the government and openly acknowledged him as their leading citizen. They also granted him the honored title of *Augustus*, a term with religious connotations. This new title served to elevate Octavius above all Romans, indeed all humans. To emphasize this link with the gods even further, the senators decreed that the month known as *Sextilis* be renamed *Augustus*—a name that has remained unchanged through the centuries.

With the aid of such writers as Virgil, Livy, and Horace, Augustus promoted loyalty to Rome and its ideals. Legally, he was still dependent on the Senate and the people for the power to rule and enact legislation, but in reality the Roman world obeyed Augustus. In the East, where ruler worship was common, Augustus was openly honored as a deity. In the West, this belief was modified, with Augustus regarded as a mortal having a divine *genius* (spirit).

Acknowledging that he was not an outstanding military commander, Augustus wisely left military matters to his capable generals such as Agrippa. His primary concern was not expansion but security. He saw Rome's army mainly as a stabilizing force to maintain the empire's boundaries, repel enemy attacks, and take the offensive only when invading tribes refused to respect Rome's frontiers.

In 23 B.C., while personally directing a military campaign in Spain, Augustus became desperately ill. He had survived a serious ailment two years earlier, but this time death seemed imminent. Aware that many were ques-

tioning his ability to rule and hearing reports of conspiracies against his life, Augustus decided to step down as consul and grant himself a new position, *imperium maius* (greater power). This post was in fact more sweeping in its authority but not as visible to the public. Augustus also assumed the *tribunicia potestas* (tribune power), which made him the official advocate of the people and gave him the power to call meetings of the Senate.

Augustus recovered his health, but this brush with death convinced him to grant Agrippa additional powers so that, if necessary, the general could overrule the proconsuls in the provinces and maintain the allegiance of the empire's legions. Gradually, Augustus was assuming the role of dictator while at the same time maintaining the appearance of democracy.

In his effort to revive traditional Roman virtues, Augustus outlawed adultery, encouraged the Senate's passage of regulations aimed at reducing luxury, and granted special privileges to married couples. To help with administration, Augustus increased his staff, thereby creating the beginnings of the efficient civil service system that would be perfected by his successors. He also revamped the manner in which finances were handled, both in Rome and throughout the provinces. Another change that aided the economy was the widespread use of Roman coinage, especially gold and silver pieces. To ensure that the official currency would be uniform throughout the Roman world, Augustus ordered several mints built.

Realizing that his presence often spurred subordinates to action, Augustus traveled to many provinces to oversee the reorganization of government affairs. In 20 B.C. he visited Sicily and Greece, and in 16 B.C. he journeyed north to reorganize Gaul and formally establish its boundaries. After a stay of three to four years there, he returned to Rome. In 13 B.C., the Senate and the Roman people commemorated his achievements by erecting the *Ara Pacis* (Altar of Peace) in Rome, which is still standing today.

Except for another venture north in 9 B.C., to meet with German envoys, Augustus spent his remaining years in Rome. Determined that the empire he had so masterfully organized should not crumble at his death, Augustus thought about a successor. Augustus saw his only child, Julia, as the one individual who could give him an heir. After carefully reviewing the eligible suitors, Augustus chose his nephew Marcellus, but the lad died soon after the wedding. Augustus then turned to his trusted friend Agrippa, even though Agrippa was considerably older than Julia and happily married. Always the obedient commander, Agrippa yielded to Augustus' wishes, divorced his wife, and married Julia. In time, Julia bore two sons, Gaius Caesar and Lucius Caesar, both of whom Augustus adopted and brought up in his own house. Augustus also considered Livia's two sons from her former marriage, Tiberius and Drusus, as possible successors and entrusted them with important military commands.

With Agrippa's death in 12 B.C., Julia became a widow and Augustus lost one of his most trusted advisors and commanders. Because Tiberius had in the meantime proven himself a capable general, Augustus now arranged for him to marry Julia. But Tiberius objected because, like Agrippa, he too was already married and dearly loved his wife. When Augustus insisted, Tiberius obeyed, but his marriage to Julia was an unhappy one. When reports surfaced that Julia had been unfaithful, Augustus was forced to follow the law he himself had enacted: He banished Julia from Rome for five years

and forbade her to drink wine or enjoy any other luxury. He also denied her all male company without his permission. Augustus never forgave Julia and was so hurt by her improper conduct that he refused to let her see any visitors for a long time.

Other family misfortunes followed. Gaius Caesar died in A.D. 2 while commanding troops in the East. Two years later, Lucius Caesar died while on a similar assignment in the West. Augustus' choice of a successor now narrowed to Julia's third son, Agrippa Postumus, and his stepson Tiberius. (Tiberius' brother Drusus had died in 9 B.C. while invading Germany.) Almost immediately, Augustus recognized that Postumus was a poor choice and disinherited him for his coarse and violent behavior.

Only Tiberius remained—certainly not the one Augustus would have selected, but there was no other choice. To further ensure the continued rule of his family, Augustus required that Tiberius adopt his nephew, Drusus' son Germanicus, and then arranged for Germanicus to marry Julia's daughter, Agrippina the Elder.

Rome was now the Mediterranean's most powerful city, but for Augustus that was not enough. He wanted Rome to reflect its position in the world. And so, with the help of his advisors, Augustus ordered the construction of several enormous buildings. Visitors today can see the imposing remains of his Forum, the Theater of Marcellus, and the Temple of Mars the Avenger. According to Suetonius, Augustus once commented, "I found Rome a city of brick, and left it a city of marble."

Despite Augustus' supremacy, events did not always follow his plans. German tribes constantly harassed the Roman frontiers to the north, and in A.D. 9, the Germans under Arminius attacked the respected Roman general Varus and annihilated his three legions. Varus himself committed suicide rather than live with such a disgraceful defeat. According to ancient accounts, this disaster so affected the 71-year-old Augustus that he suffered a nervous breakdown, refusing to cut his hair or his beard and even dashing his head against a door, crying, "Quinctilius Varus, give me back my legions!" Finally, Augustus overcame his grief and renewed his interest in improving Roman life and government. Rome had become more crowded as people from surrounding areas sought a better life in the prosperous capital. Some of these newcomers were inevitably disappointed, and their discontent led to an increase in arson and other crimes. Augustus sought to remedy the situation by organizing the city's first police force and fire brigade.

Augustus was growing old, and he was tiring of the tremendous burden of ruling so vast an empire. He looked more and more to his stepson Tiberius for help. Early in A.D. 13, when the Senate formally renewed Augustus' powers for another 10 years, the senators granted Tiberius the same powers. In April, Augustus placed his will in the House of the Vestal Virgins at Rome. (The Vestals were priestesses who cared for the altar and temple of Vesta, the goddess of the hearth.) Included also were the complete records of the military and financial resources of the empire, as well as the *Res Gestae Divi Augusti* (The Deeds of the Divine Augustus).

In August A.D. 14, Augustus made a night journey by ship and caught a chill, which upset his stomach. A few days later, still feeling poorly, he journeyed to Naples and said goodbye to Tiberius, who was about to leave for Illyricum. With his ailment worsening, Augustus stopped at Nola on his way back to Rome. Aware that death was approaching, he sent messengers to recall Tiberius. After speaking with Tiberius in private for a long time, Augustus then removed himself from all government matters.

Suetonius recorded that on August 19, Augustus called for a mirror and had his hair combed. Then, turning to his friends who had assembled in his bedroom, he asked: "Have I played my part in this comedy of life well enough?" After a moment, he added, "If I have pleased you, please show your appreciation with a warm goodbye." He then dismissed his friends and turned to his wife Livia. Kissing her for the last time, he said, "Goodbye, Livia. Never forget our marriage!" He died later in the day.

As the news of Augustus' death spread across the Mediterranean World, people everywhere mourned his passing. As they had done with Julius Caesar, so now the senators voted to deify Augustus. In Velitrae, the small room in which Augustus supposedly had been born became a venerated site. No one was allowed to enter unless absolutely necessary, and then only after performing special purification rites. According to Suetonius, one of the house's later owners disregarded this prohibition and slept in the sacred room. That very night, some supernatural force hurled him from the bed, and the next morning he was found lying half dead by the door.

FURTHER READING

Holmes, T. Rice. *The Architect of the Roman Empire*. Oxford, England: Clarendon Press, 1928–31.

Suetonius. *The Lives of the Caesars*. Translated by J. C. Rolfe. Loeb Classical Library. New York: Macmillan, 1914.

Syme, Sir Ronald. *The Roman Revolution*. New York: Oxford University Press, 1960.

Walworth, Nancy. *Augustus Caesar*. New York: Chelsea House, 1989.

Agrippa (Marcus Vipsanius Agrippa)

A MAN OF ACTION

Wherever and whenever Octavius Caesar needed aid, there was Marcus Vipsanius Agrippa, ready to offer his services. In fact, Agrippa was directly responsible for Octavius' military and political success. He never claimed the honors or glory for himself but acted for the advancement of Rome and Octavius. His actions did not go unrewarded, however, for Octavius treated him with the respect he deserved.

Born sometime around 63 B.C. to parents who were most likely well-to-do, Agrippa was not mentioned by ancient writers until after Julius Caesar's assassination in 44 B.C. At that time, Agrippa was stationed with the Roman army in

Loyal and sincere, Agrippa was one of Augustus' most trusted generals and advisers. Even in matters regarding his personal family life, Agrippa readily deferred to Augustus' wishes.

Apollonia, in western Greece. Serving with him was Octavius, Julius Caesar's grandnephew. When news of the assassination reached Apollonia, dismay and confusion quickly overran the encampment.

Then came reports that were even more startling. In his will, Caesar had adopted Octavius as his son and named him his heir. But Octavius was only 18 and relatively inexperienced. Contemporary accounts report that Agrippa, himself only 19 or 20 at the time, was one of several who encouraged the young heir to claim his rights. Accepting their aid, Octavius raised a private army and marched to Rome. Agrippa went with him.

Agrippa quickly proved himself an able military commander and loyal subordinate. In 43 B.C., he led the prosecution against Cassius, one of Caesar's assassins, who had fled Rome and was gathering support in the East. Most likely, Agrippa held the important post of tribune at the time. In addition to Caesar's assassins, Octavius and Agrippa had to face Mark Antony, Caesar's close associate and the man who considered himself his rightful successor.

Within the year, two factions had formed: those who opposed Caesar's policies and those who vowed to continue them. The conspirators and many senators joined the first group, while Octavius and Antony reconciled their differences and allied themselves with another powerful Roman, named Lepidus, to form the Second Triumvirate.

In 41 B.C., Antony left Rome to consolidate the triumvirate's position in the East. Holding the high-ranking political post of consul was Antony's brother, Lucius. Determined to win control of Rome for his brother, Lucius allied himself with Antony's wife, Fulvia, and marched against Octavius.

Octavius immediately turned to Agrippa, who played an active role in the defeat of Lucius and his troops in 40 B.C. That same year, Agrippa held

the political office of *praetor urbanus*, with the responsibility of administering justice in Rome. His abilities were quickly tested when Antony returned to Italy and sought to oppose Octavius. A meeting between these powerful rivals took place at Brundisium, in southern Italy. Agrippa handled the negotiations and helped effect a reconciliation between the two men.

With their differences resolved, the triumvirs once again turned their efforts to bringing the Roman provinces under their control. By agreement, Antony was responsible for the East, Octavius for the West. Naturally, Octavius enlisted the aid of Agrippa, who spent the next two years fighting in Aquitania (present-day southwestern France) and along the Rhine River.

Proud of his successes but not desirous of public praise, Agrippa refused a triumph for his military achievements. He did not, however, refuse the office of consul, a position he held for the year 37 B.C. That same year he was party to another agreement between Octavius and Antony. Most likely as a result of these negotiations, Antony arranged for Agrippa to marry the daughter of Titus Atticus, a wealthy Roman.

Although the triumvirs were at peace with one another, trouble was brewing on the seas. Sextus Pompeius, the son of Caesar's old foe Pompey, had gradually increased his power base until he controlled virtually the entire Mediterranean. At various times Sextus had aligned himself with one or another of the triumvirs, but these relationships had been short-lived. By 39 B.C., Sextus had taken Sicily and imposed a blockade on Italy. Deprived of corn and other essential imports, Italy was in desperate straits. Finally, the triumvirs agreed to grant Sextus control of Sicily in return for his ending the blockade.

Shortly afterward, Octavius accused Sextus of breaking the agreement

Agrippa

BORN
Around 63 B.C.
In or near Rome

DIED
12 B.C.
Pannonia

PROFESSION
General and advisor to Augustus

ACCOMPLISHMENTS
Won significant military victories for Augustus, including Actium (31 B.C.); quelled numerous revolts throughout the empire; ordered the construction of many public buildings, including the first public baths in Rome, the Pantheon, and two aqueducts; ordered the cleaning of the sewers of Rome and improved the water supply

and sent forces against him. When Sextus emerged victorious, Octavius commissioned Agrippa to handle the situation. Agrippa stationed himself at Naples, south of Rome, and gave orders to turn neighboring Lake Avernus into a harbor for his fleet. Using it as his base, he led his ships into the Bay of Naples and south to Sicily, where in 36 B.C. he engaged Sextus in a decisive sea battle off Mylae. Agrippa's victory ended Sextus' bid for power and gave control of the Mediterranean to the triumvirs. In recognition of his outstanding service to Rome, Agrippa received an honorary golden crown.

No sooner was one victory complete, however, than trouble erupted in another area. Dalmatia, on the east coast of the Adriatic Sea, had caused problems over the years, so when the rebellious attitude of the inhabitants intensified in 35 B.C., Octavius sent Agrippa to quell the resistance. Agrippa performed with his usual efficiency and was back in Rome by 33 B.C. to take up the office of aedile, which gave him jurisdiction over all public buildings and projects.

Agrippa saw his new position as an opportunity to win the people over for Octavius. Thus he immediately set about cleaning the vast sewer system that ran throughout Rome, overhauling the aqueducts and channels that brought fresh water into the city, and beginning work on two new aqueducts.

Agrippa also ordered the construction of a granary to hold extra food supplies and paid considerable attention to the road system, realizing that good communication was essential to good government. In Gaul he established a network of roads that radiated from the central city of Lugdunum (present-day Lyon).

In 31 B.C., a crisis arose that threatened the very existence of the

Roman world. With Lepidus excluded from the triumvirate because he had tried to usurp power for himself, Antony and Octavius controlled the provinces. But Antony, who had chosen to ally himself with Cleopatra, the queen of Egypt, prepared for war against Octavius. Stationing himself on the west coast of Greece, the outer boundary of his half of the Roman world, Antony thought himself secure. But Antony did not know Agrippa.

Almost without Antony's knowledge, Agrippa led his fleet across the Adriatic Sea and then, in a series of carefully orchestrated maneuvers, defeated Antony's forces. Agrippa's victory enabled Octavius to become the sole ruler of the Roman world. When Antony escaped to Egypt and Octavius decided to pursue him, he left Agrippa and Maecenas, a patron of the arts, in charge of affairs in Rome.

In 28 B.C. and 27 B.C., Octavius and Agrippa shared the office of consul. As co-consul, Agrippa had a chance to continue and expand the projects he had implemented as aedile years earlier. From 27 B.C. to 25 B.C., Agrippa oversaw the construction of the temple known as the Pantheon. In the decades that followed, fire ravaged the temple twice before it was completely rebuilt by the Roman emperor Hadrian. Because Hadrian felt it dishonest to claim the Pantheon as his own creation, he ordered the original inscription bearing Agrippa's name to be copied onto the new building. Converted to a Christian church in the early 7th century A.D., the Pantheon survives as an enduring symbol of the grandeur that was once ancient Rome's.

Another building project to which Agrippa dedicated himself in the 20s B.C. was the construction of public baths, the first ever in Rome. In later years, public baths would become a standard feature in almost every Roman town throughout the empire. Open to everyone, the baths were a place where rich and poor, politically connected and virtually unknown, could mingle and converse. Politics, religion, philosophy, economics, and everyday gossip were discussed and debated there.

The two public bath complexes constructed by Agrippa—one abutted the Pantheon—were not as massive as those commissioned under future emperors, but they were extremely large structures, with hot rooms, cold rooms, exercise areas, a swimming pool, study areas, and even gardens. Because of the high temperature needed in some areas and the humidity required in others, new construction designs had to be devised using the domes and vaults that would later become the hallmark of Roman architecture.

Through the years, Agrippa amassed a great fortune. Although some of his wealth came from his first wife, most was due to his special position as second in command to Octavius, known to history as Augustus. Agrippa was a simple man and chose to spend much of his money on Rome, personally funding many of the public building projects he supervised over the years. In his will he left most of his property to Augustus, but he did make bequests to the Roman people.

When Augustus fell seriously ill in 23 B.C. and death seemed imminent, his thoughts naturally turned to a successor. Concerned that a power struggle might throw Rome into another civil war, Augustus handed Agrippa his signet ring as his way of saying that Agrippa should succeed him. At this time, Agrippa obeyed Augustus' command to divorce his wife and marry Augustus' daughter, Julia. With her he had three sons and two daughters.

Decades later, two of his grandsons—Caligula and Nero—became Roman emperors.

Augustus eventually recovered from his illness, and Agrippa continued as his unofficial second in command. He spent much of his time away from Italy subduing the Cantabri in Spain, establishing colonies for armed service veterans in the East, visiting King Herod in Judaea, and quelling a revolt on the Bosporus. When trouble erupted in the important Roman province of Pannonia (between the Alps and the Danube River) in 13 B.C., Agrippa headed north, intending to forestall a revolt. But he contracted a serious illness and died in March of 12 B.C. As a final tribute to his most faithful supporter, Augustus delivered the funeral oration himself and arranged for Agrippa's body to be buried in the mausoleum Augustus had prepared for himself.

As co-consul, Agrippa oversaw the construction of the temple known as the Pantheon. It was later rebuilt by the emperor Hadrian after a fire gutted it both inside and out.

FURTHER READING

Reinhold, Meyer. *Marcus Agrippa: A Biography.* Geneva, N.Y.: W. F. Humphrey, 1933.

Virgil (Publius Vergilius Maro)

POET OF THE EMPIRE

With thanks and admiration, Virgil and his fellow countrymen looked to Augustus as the bringer of peace to a war-torn world. In his poem, the *Aeneid*, Virgil addressed Augustus directly: "Remember, O Roman, to rule the people in the empire; this will be your duty: to impose the custom of peace, to spare the conquered, and to defeat the haughty."

Born on October 15, 70 B.C., at Andes, near the northern Italian city of Mantua, Virgil spent his early years far from Rome. Mantua and the surrounding area, extending from the Apennine Mountains to the Alps, formed part of the Roman province called Cisalpine Gaul. The area was quite Romanized, however. The rights of Roman citizenship were granted to its people shortly before Virgil's birth, and it was incorporated into Italy in 42 B.C.

By Rome's standards, Virgil's parents were not rich, but they lived comfortably, owned a villa and farm, and were able to give Virgil an excellent education, sending him first to neighboring Cremona, then to Mediolanum (present-day Milan), and finally to Rome to continue his study of rhetoric (the art of using words effectively). In Rome, Virgil joined the circle of the poet Catullus and began writing poetry himself. Virgil's father is believed to have begun life as a potter or day laborer before marrying his employer's daughter.

As a boy and a young man, Virgil lived through years of political turmoil, beginning with Caesar's bid for power in 49 B.C. and culminating in Augustus' defeat of Mark Antony at the Battle of Actium in 31 B.C. No accounts indicate that Virgil fought in any battles, but he did not escape the consequences of Rome's bloody civil wars.

In 41 B.C., the Second Triumvirate passed an expropriation bill that radically changed Virgil's life. Although each triumvir (Octavius, Mark Antony, and Lepidus) had his own agenda, each was also aware that the veterans of the recent conflict wanted immediate compensation for their services. Traditionally, this reward was a parcel of land, but because "free" land was becoming increasingly difficult to find in Italy, veterans' colonies were usually established instead, in the provinces. Antony disliked this policy and wanted Italian land for his soldiers. After some discussion, the triumvirs agreed to take land from Italian farmers and give it to returning soldiers. The farm belonging to Virgil's father was among the parcels of land selected.

Evicted from his farm and with no prospect of recouping his losses, Virgil's father headed south to Naples, where his 29-year-old son was studying philosophy and writing poetry. Accounts show that at this time Virgil owned a villa and a small parcel of land, both of which he seems to have inherited from a former teacher named Siro. Virgil welcomed his father; his poems from this period capture the sense of loss experienced by those displaced in Rome's political upheavals.

Between 42 and 37 B.C., Virgil composed the *Eclogues,* a collection of 10 pastoral poems focusing on the loves and lives of shepherds. Following the custom of the time, Virgil modeled his poems on those written by the Greek pastoral poets, especially Theocritus. Even the collection's title and the names of the characters in the poems are Greek, as is the setting—Arcadia, in southern Greece. But Virgil's *Eclogues* are an idealized version of country life in all times and places, portraying a world of joy, sunshine, bountiful crops, and contentment.

Virgil's poems contain many Italian elements, reflecting his deep love of the country and nature and the simple pleasures they afford. Any feelings of sorrow, anger, and resentment are muted, but Virgil did interweave references to contemporary events. In the *First Eclogue,* an evicted shepherd named Meliboeus envies the luck of Tityrus, who escaped eviction by appealing to the young god (a poetic reference to Augustus) in Rome. In actuality, Virgil appealed to Rome for the restoration of his father's land; he was apparently successful, but he could still empathize with those not so fortunate. The *Ninth Eclogue* focuses on two other evicted shepherds who tell of a third man who unsuccessfully attempted to save the entire district of Mantua from expropriation. This, too, may well have been a reference to Virgil's own situation.

The best known part of the collection is the *Fourth Eclogue,* later known as the *Messianic Eclogue.* Foretelling the birth of a boy who would herald a golden age, rid the world of sin, and bring peace, this poem inspired many differ-

Whether this "portrait" of Virgil is a true likeness or not is unknown. It appeared at the beginning of his *Second Eclogue* in an edition of his works dating to the late 4th or the 5th century A.D.

ent interpretations. Christians later considered it a prophecy of the coming of Jesus Christ, who was born approximately four decades after the eclogue was written. Historians believe, though, that Virgil actually had in mind the yet unborn child of Augustus' sister Octavia, who was married to Mark Antony.

Written in 40 B.C., this poem reflected the hopes that followed the reconciliation between Octavius and Antony. Later, after Augustus finally brought peace to the war-weary Roman world, many saw the *Fourth Eclogue* as a direct foreshadowing of Augustus' rule:

> Now from high heaven, a new generation is sent down. . . . Now, holy Lucina [the Roman goddess of childbirth] look favorably on that newborn boy, under whom the iron race [the worst race of humans] shall cease and the golden age shall rise over the whole world . . . for you, o boy . . . the she-goats shall return home unattended, with their udders swollen with

In Book Two of the *Aeneid,* Virgil tells how the Trojan prince Laocoön advised his fellow countrymen against bringing the great wooden horse within Troy's walls. Unfortunately, his advice was not heeded because the Trojans felt it was against the gods' wishes after they saw two snakes coil their bodies around Laocoön and kill him.

writers and lovers of literature now sought his company and advice.

Maecenas, one of Rome's greatest literary patrons and a trusted advisor of the emperor Augustus, recognized Virgil's potential and invited him to join his select circle of poets. As a result, Virgil came to know Rome's most promising literary figures and through them even met Augustus himself. Although granted a house in Rome, Virgil preferred his villa in Naples. Aware of the benefits of having a patron who paid the bills and allowed an author to devote his time to writing, Virgil introduced his poet friend Horace to Maecenas and won him acceptance to the circle.

Soon after Virgil completed the *Eclogues* in 37 B.C., he began work on his *Georgics,* a collection of four books dedicated to Maecenas. These extended poems, like the *Eclogues,* celebrated the joys and rewards of country living and pleaded for a return to the traditional agricultural life once practiced throughout Italy. Reviving and maintaining traditional Roman values was a key component of Augustus' governing policy and he must surely have welcomed Virgil's treatment of the subject.

In the second book of the *Georgics,* Virgil praised "a secure peace, a life unaware of how to cheat, and rich in its many resources; a leisurely retreat amid wide fields, caves, and living lakes, where the mooing of cattle and the content naps under the tree are present." He also used the *Georgics* to express his hatred of war and to lament the fact that most leaders preferred war to farming: "So many wars rage through the world, so many faces of crime; yet the plow merits no honor."

The *Eclogues* had won Virgil recognition and a patron; the *Georgics,* completed in 30 B.C., assured his fame. He spent seven years completing this work, which totaled 2,188 lines. Though some of that time had been taken up by study and reflection,

milk, and the herds shall not fear the great lions. . . . All lands shall bear all things . . . the ram himself . . . shall change his fleece into soft-glowing sea-purple, then to yellow saffron. . . . Look at how all things rejoice in the age to come! O let there then remain to me enough of life and breath to tell your deeds!

The *Eclogues* won Virgil the attention of Rome's literary community. Though he showed little inclination to enter into public life (perhaps in part because of poor health), numerous

Virgil's laborious method of composition had much to do with the long gap between his first and second major works. According to the Roman historian Suetonius, Virgil spent time every morning writing verses he had already conceived and reworked in his mind. He then used the rest of the day to revise them, cutting whatever he felt was extraneous.

Virgil's completion of the *Georgics* coincided with the end of the civil war between Augustus and Mark Antony. Augustus now ruled the Roman world, when the prospect of peace was the greatest it had been for decades. Virgil felt the time was now right to begin a project he had always had in mind—writing an epic poem.

The *Iliad* and the *Odyssey*, written by the Greek poet Homer, were still considered the supreme epic poems. Countless authors had imitated Homer's style and incorporated various episodes from his epics into their own works. Now Virgil sought to write an Italian epic, one that would reawaken national pride and rekindle in contemporary Romans the values of Rome's legendary heroes: loyalty, honesty, frugality, duty, and a love of family.

Naturally, the work would incorporate the stylistic elements of the Greek epic, but Virgil planned to write it in Latin and include Roman elements. As his theme, Virgil chose the Trojan hero Aeneas and his founding of the Italian settlement from which Rome eventually sprang.

By setting his tale in the past, Virgil could use prophecies to foretell the future glories that awaited the Roman people and their leaders. The poem would thus function on two levels. The first was the simple story of Aeneas escaping from Troy after the Trojan War—the subject of Homer's *Iliad*—and his journey across the Mediterranean Sea to a new home in Italy. The second level was Virgil's self-assigned mission to praise Rome, revive patriotism, and impart to Augustus the task of maintaining peace throughout the empire.

As a true epic hero, Virgil's Aeneas is single-minded in his devotion to the duty of founding a new homeland. Interacting with him on occasion were the mighty gods and goddesses of Mount Olympus, especially his mother Venus, the goddess of love and beauty. In Book Four, a violent storm shipwrecks Aeneas and his followers, tossing them upon the northern coast of Africa in present-day Tunisia, near the prosperous city of Carthage, ruled by the beautiful queen Dido. To ensure Aeneas' safety in this foreign land, Venus commanded her son Cupid, the god of love, to inflame Dido's heart with love for Aeneas. In the passages that follow, Virgil skillfully develops a love story that has become one of the most famous in world literature.

Aeneas finds refuge with Dido, but his love for her drives all thoughts of duty from his mind. Jupiter, the king of the gods, intervenes and sends Mercury, the messenger god, to visit Aeneas: "Go now, my son, call the winds and hasten along them on your wingèd feet. Speak to the Trojan Aeneas who lingers now in Carthage and does not even think of the cities granted him by fate. . . . Let him set sail. This is my command. Be you its messenger!"

This command leaves Aeneas torn between love and duty, but he finally makes the heart-wrenching decision to leave Carthage. Virgil's description of Aeneas' men preparing their vessels is one of literature's best-known similes: "Just as when ants, aware of the approaching winter, plunder a great pile of wheat and store it in their house, a black column [of ants] goes along the fields, as they carry their loot through the grass on the narrow path; one group pushes huge grains with their shoulders, another group organizes the troops and reprimands those who delay; the entire path seethes with work."

Virgil

BORN

70 B.C.
Andes, in Cisalpine Gaul

DIED

19 B.C.
Brundisium, Italy

PROFESSION

Poet

ACCOMPLISHMENTS

Wrote the *Eclogues*, 10 pastoral poems on the joys of country life; the *Georgics*, 4 books on farming, growing trees, raising cattle, and keeping bees; and the *Aeneid*, the national epic of Rome

> *"Fortune aids the daring."*
>
> —from the *Aeneid*
> (30–19 B.C.)

Desperate not to lose Aeneas, Dido begs him to stay or take her with him, but her pleas are in vain. Unable to face life without him, she retrieves his sword from the room they have shared and thrusts it into her breast. Of all the female characters in works by Roman authors, Dido is perhaps the most moving and the one who arouses the most sympathy. Virgil's audience would not have missed the parallel between Dido and Cleopatra, Mark Antony's lover, who committed suicide after Antony's defeat at the hands of Augustus.

In Book VI of the *Aeneid*, Virgil described Aeneas' visit to the underworld, where his dead father prophesies Rome's future glories. However, the most moving moment is no doubt the encounter between Aeneas and Dido, whose ghostly shade now inhabits the region set aside for those who died prematurely. With tears streaming down his cheeks, Aeneas attempts to explain his abrupt departure, but Dido does not listen and willfully walks away from him.

In Book VI, Virgil completes Aeneas' travels from Troy to Italy and begins to recount the great struggle—including many bloody battles—for control of what is to become his future homeland.

In 19 B.C., having spent 11 years writing and rewriting his epic poem, Virgil decided that another three years would be needed to complete the work. He was still somewhat of a recluse, remaining unmarried and devoting his life to his writing. As his health continued to be delicate, he finally decided that a trip abroad might help. Perhaps he also intended to visit areas of Greece mentioned in the poem so that he could improve upon his descriptions.

While in Greece, Virgil met Augustus, returning to Rome from a tour of the eastern provinces. Persuaded by the emperor to come back to Italy with him, Virgil fell ill on the way and died shortly after arriving in Brundisium.

Tradition says that he left orders with the executor of his will to burn the *Aeneid* should he die while away in Greece. In Virgil's opinion, the epic was unfinished and therefore unworthy of publication. But Augustus thought otherwise and sent the massive work to be published.

The *Aeneid* was an immediate success and became a standard text in the classrooms of the Roman world. A few decades later, the Roman teacher Quintilian suggested that Virgil's works, especially the *Aeneid*, become the basis of Rome's educational curriculum. In the centuries that followed, Virgil's work continued to be read and studied. The great Italian writer Dante Alighieri (1265–1321) made Virgil the guide in his famed *Divine Comedy*. The English poet John Milton (1608–74) modeled his epic work *Paradise Lost* on Virgil's *Aeneid*. Even today, Virgil continues to be studied in schools and colleges around the world, and writers paraphrase and adapt verses from his works.

Virgil's grave in Naples is a national landmark. (Virgil's body had been taken from Brundisium to Naples, the area he so loved, for burial.) Whether or not Virgil wrote the epitaph written on his tombstone is uncertain, but the words certainly are fitting: "Mantua bore me, the Calabrians took me, now Naples holds me: I have sung of cattle, fields, and leaders."

FURTHER READING

Virgil. *Virgil's Works: The Aeneid, Eclogues, and Georgics*. Translated by J. W. MacKail. New York: Modern Library, 1950.

———. *Virgil*. Translated by H. R. Fairclough. Loeb Classical Library. Cambridge: Harvard University Press, 1934–35.

Williams, Robert D. *The Aeneid*. Boston: Allen & Unwin, 1987.

Horace
(Quintus
Horatius Flaccus)

THE CONGENIAL POET

I am descended from a freedman, an ex-slave. . . . My father is responsible for what I am, my father who, though a poor man on a small farm, was unwilling to send me to school [in his hometown of Venusia] . . . but dared to take me as a boy to Rome to be taught those skills which any Roman senator would teach his own children. . . . For as long as I am sane, I shall never be ashamed of my father, nor shall I defend myself and apologize for my birth as so many do, saying that it was not their fault. [He lives simply] and my life is one free from the wretched burden of ambition."

In this direct and sincere language Horace described in his *Satires* his humble beginnings, of which he was actually quite proud. He had been born on December 8, 65 B.C., in the little town of Venusia in south-central Italy. Venusia lay south of Rome on the well-traveled Via Appia, or Appian Way, which connected Brundisium with Rome. His father, a thrifty and determined man, had once been a slave but had saved enough money to buy his freedom. He became an auctioneer's assistant (or a tax collector—there is some doubt on this issue) and in time purchased the small farm on which Horace was born. Of Horace's mother nothing is known.

Horace's father chose to devote his life to his son. Finding the schools in Venusia inadequate, he moved to Rome

Preferring not to write history or philosophical treatises, Horace chose to write about the more personal aspects of life, using his observations of situations and people as the basis of his poems.

Detrahit & pellem nitidus quâ quisque per ora
Ambulat; introrsum turpis. HORAT.

Q. HORATII FLACCI POEMATA.

Ex antiquis Codd. & certis Observationibus emendavit, variasque Scriptorum & Impressorum lectiones adjecit

ALEXANDER CUNINGAMIUS,

HAGAE COMITUM,
Apud THOMAM JONSONIUM,
M. DCC. XXI.

In the 1700s, Latin was a required course for secondary school students. Horace was always one of the Roman authors on the reading list.

and entrusted Horace's education to the well-respected grammarian Orbilius. Years later, Horace described his crotchety old teacher as *plagosum*, or "fond of flogging." The person truly responsible for molding Horace's character was his father, whose honesty, common sense, and sincere devotion Horace would revere and practice himself.

Sometime around 46 B.C., when Horace was about 20 years old, his father sent him to Athens to complete his education, an opportunity usually open only to sons of prominent Romans. Considered the world's center of learning, Athens introduced students to the Greek writers and philosophers. During Horace's stay, however, civil

strife in Rome was reaching a climax whose effects would soon reach even the privileged students in Athens.

Turmoil was not a new phenomenon in Rome. Civil war had marred the 80s B.C., and Julius Caesar's crossing of the Rubicon River in 49 B.C. threatened to do the same. In 48 B.C., Caesar won control of the Roman world by defeating his rival, Pompey, but many people distrusted Caesar's motives. Among them were Brutus and Cassius, whose professed goal was to keep Rome a republic, not a dictatorship subject to the will of one man. On March 15, 44 B.C., they acted in league with many of Rome's leading citizens and killed Caesar.

Contrary to their belief that the Roman people would support their actions, the assassins soon found themselves outcasts and were forced to flee Italy. Sometime around September 44 B.C., Brutus arrived in Athens. Here his ideals found enthusiastic backing, and many Roman students, including Horace, volunteered to join his army. It is not known how much military training Horace might have had, but he certainly had not been on the battlefield. Yet he, like many of the other students who embraced Brutus' cause, was elevated to the rank of officer. In fact, Horace held the honored post of a *tribunus militum*, or a senior officer of the legion (the Roman military unit).

Unfortunately, the military skills of these students did not match their zeal. At the Battle of Philippi, fought in November 42 B.C., the conspirators lost to the combined forces of the triumvirs—Octavius, Mark Antony, and Lepidus. Horace, having survived the battle, then considered his options. He still believed in the Roman republic, but he recognized that continued warfare would serve only to weaken and eventually ruin Rome. Thus, when Octavius granted a general amnesty to all who had supported the assassins, Horace accepted the offer and returned to Rome.

There he found that life had changed. The civil war was over, but sharp differences between the triumvirs continued to cause uneasiness and concern. In addition, Horace no longer had the support of his father, who had died while he was in Greece. Furthermore, the family farm in Venusia had been among those confiscated by the triumvirs, who had agreed to reward their victorious soldiers with land. With his options diminished, Horace took the few funds available to him and purchased one of 36 clerkships available in one of the government bureaus (either the quaestor's or treasurer's office).

Horace's salary was sufficient to cover his needs, and his duties were not extensive. In his free time he began to write poetry, specifically epodes (a form of lyric poetry in which a short line follows a longer one). By expressing his thoughts about life and philosophy in verse, Horace hoped to win favor with those who enjoyed poetry, thereby adding to his income. Around 39 B.C., a few of Horace's verses came to the attention of the aspiring young poet Virgil, five years his senior. Recognizing the merit of Horace's poetry, Virgil introduced him to Maecenas, a well-known patron of the arts. Four years later, in 35 B.C., in his first book of *Satires*, Horace wrote of this meeting with Maecenas:

> Chance did not throw me in your way. Rather, it was that greatest of men, Virgil . . . who told you who I was. Then, as I first came before you, speaking only a few words, one by one—childish bashfulness prevented me from speaking more . . . said plainly what I really was. You answered with a few words, as is your custom; I leave, and you call me back after nine months and order me to join the circle of your friends.

This volume was well received, especially by Maecenas, who gave Horace an estate some 39 miles northeast of Rome—the Sabine farm mentioned so often in his verses. In Book II of the *Satires*, Horace expressed his satisfaction with this gift:

> This was always in my wishes: a portion of land, not too large, with a garden, a fountain with a continual stream near my house, and a little woods beside. . . . I ask for nothing more.

In the same satire, Horace retold the story of the country mouse who so

Horace

BORN

December 65 B.C.
Venusia, in south-central Italy

DIED

November 27, 8 B.C.
Rome

PROFESSION

Poet

ACCOMPLISHMENTS

Published the first book of *Satires*, a collection of 10 informal "conversations," in 35 B.C.; around 30 B.C. published a collection of 17 poems entitled *Epodes* and a second book of eight *Satires*; in 23 B.C. published the *Odes*, a collection of 88 poems; between 20 and 19 B.C., published two books of *Epistles*; in 19 B.C. wrote the *Ars Poetica*, a guide for poets; and in 17 B.C. wrote the *Carmen Saeculare* to be sung at the centennial Secular Games

envied the luxurious lifestyle of his city friend that he forsook what he had for the city. All too soon, the dangers of city life made him realize the joys of what he had left: "I have no desire for a life like this, and so farewell; my wood and my cave, secure from surprises and with their simple ways, shall comfort me."

With the revenue his farm provided, Horace now could afford to devote himself completely to studying and writing. In the years that followed, he gratefully dedicated many of his poems to his patron Maecenas. Although Horace's circle of friends was expanding to include influential Romans such as Augustus, Agrippa, and the poet Tibullus, his personality did not change. Like Virgil, he never married, but he was not a recluse. Still, he was quite set in his ways and observed closely the advice he often gave: *"Carpe diem"* ("Take advantage of the day"). Well aware of his life of ease, Horace wrote that he had been a well-dressed, dark-haired youth whom others considered attractive. He then poked fun at himself for his altered appearance over the years, saying that "when you wish to laugh, look at me fat and sleek and well cared for, like a pig that belongs to Epicurus' flock." (Epicurus was a Greek philosopher who saw happiness and contentment as life's goals.)

Having studied the Greek masters, Horace—like his contemporaries—copied their thoughts and style. But he also demonstrated originality, especially in the *Satires*, which show that his style of writing was definitely Roman, not Greek. Horace was not the first to write in this style, but he is credited with bringing it to full maturity.

In the *Satires*, Horace focused mainly on ethical themes and morality, commenting on Rome's constant striving for riches and status and advising moderation in everything. Horace observed the weakness in human nature and the wickedness of people's actions, but instead of criticizing a specific individual he chose to condemn the fault. Moreover, he did not consider himself above reproach. In the *Satires*, as in all his works, he included vignettes that were autobiographical.

The style of the *Satires* is confidential, giving the reader the idea that he or she is sharing Horace's innermost thoughts:

> Anyone who slanders an absent friend, who does not defend a friend accused by another, who strives to raise loud laughs, and gain the reputation of being a funny person, who is able to feign things he has never seen, who is unable to keep a secret, he is a dangerous man: Oh Roman, beware of that individual! . . .

> No one is born without vices: however, that person is the best who possesses the least. When my dear friend weighs my good qualities against my bad ones, let him . . . turn the scale to the majority of the former (if indeed I do have a majority of good qualities), on this condition, that he shall be placed on the same scale.

Around 30 B.C., Horace published his *Epodes*, 17 poems quite different in tone from the *Satires*. Although they mocked many of the attitudes prevalent in Rome, ridiculing especially the social abuses of the time, the *Epodes* expressed Horace's deep love of the country and his distaste for war.

Six years later, when Horace was 42, he published three books of *Odes*. Written over a period of several years, these carefully wrought poems, 88 in all, reflect Horace's philosophy of life. They explore his favorite topics—love, nature, friends, wine, the simple life, and moderation in all things. As such, they were well received by Augustus, who sought to promote traditional values and instill in the Romans of his day the virtues that had made Rome great.

Through the centuries, the universal themes of the *Odes* have found countless admirers and imitators. Politicians, historians, and news reporters around the world have often borrowed Horace's description of Rome as the "ship of state" and used his phrase "the golden mean":

> Licinius, you will live more rightly by not always heading for the deep waters, nor by hugging too close the dangerous shore as you shun the stormy seas.
>
> Whoever chooses the golden mean is safe. . . . The lofty pine tree is more frequently shaken by winds, high towers fall with heavier ruin, and lightning strikes the tops of mountains.

By 13 B.C., Horace's literary career had peaked. He had become the poet laureate of the Roman world after Virgil's death in 19 B.C. Two years later, when Augustus called for the revival of the Secular Games (held every 100 or so years), he asked Horace to compose the *Carmen Saeculare* ("Secular Hymn") to be sung at the festivities. This was a great honor, because Augustus considered the games the religious confirmation of his rule.

But Horace was an independent man and first had to consider the nature of the assignment. Years earlier, when Augustus had asked Horace to be his private secretary, the poet had refused. His refusal had not harmed his relationship with the emperor, however, and may even have strengthened it. Horace never hid the fact that he was the son of an ex-slave, but he was not one to be told what to do. He agreed to write the *Carmen Saeculare* because he felt the games would help maintain the peace Augustus had brought to the world. Horace had not forgotten the republican sentiments of his youth, but he believed that peace was essential to the growth and well-being of any nation. For this reason he supported Augustus, even naming the emperor his heir. In turn, Augustus treated Horace with great praise and respect.

Though not a boastful man, Horace nevertheless considered his works important and hoped their worth would reach beyond his lifetime. In his epilogue to the three-volume edition of the *Odes* published in 23 B.C., he wrote:

> I have completed a monument more lasting than bronze, more lofty than the royal site of the pyramids, which neither the destructive rains, nor the blustery north wind, nor the passage of time is able to destroy. I shall not wholly die, and a great part of me shall escape the goddess of the underworld.

And he was right. After Horace's death on November 27, 8 B.C., his works became standard texts in the classrooms of the empire. Throughout the centuries, his works have inspired countless poets and writers. Hundreds of translations of his poems have been published, and more are certain to appear in the years to come.

FURTHER READING

Horace. *Odes and Epodes*. Translated by C. E. Bennett. Loeb Classical Library. Cambridge: Harvard University Press, 1914.

————. *Satires, Epistles, Ars Poetica*. Translated by H. R. Fairclough. Loeb Classical Library. Cambridge: Harvard University Press, 1966.

Noyes, Alfred. *Horace: A Portrait*. New York: Sheed & Ward, 1947.

Perret, Jacques. *Horace*. New York: New York University Press, 1964.

Livy
(Titus Livius)

"COURAGE IS THE MASK OF A SOLDIER"

S ince Rome's founding, in 753 B.C., the city's rulers had marched steadily toward world conquest, the world in the Romans' view being the lands surrounding the Mediterranean Sea. With the realization of this goal in the first century B.C., Romans paused to reflect on their glorious rise to power. Many felt a deep yearning to return to the past, to the strict value system and sincere patriotism expressed by Rome's early heroes and heroines, to a time when the city's welfare seemed more important than personal ambition. Many writers and politicians spoke of a steady decline in

An artist's interpretation of what Livy looked like adrons the top of this 1634 title page to an edition of Livy's history of Rome. Because few actual documents or portraits from ancient Rome have survived, later artists have had to rely on copies of the originals for their inspiration.

morals and widespread discontent among Rome's citizens and subjects.

The emperor Augustus spent much of his reign attempting to revive traditional values. Because he saw poets and writers as key to spreading his message, Augustus heavily patronized the arts. Assisting him was Rome's greatest patron of literature, Maecenas, who numbered among his protégés Virgil and Horace. Another writer who found favor with Augustus, but who never became a member of Maecenas' literary circle or of the literary world in Rome, was Titus Livius, known as Livy.

Almost nothing is known about the private life of this writer who became one of Rome's greatest historians. His birthdate is given variously as 64 B.C. and 59 B.C. His birthplace is more certain—Patavium (present-day Padua) in northern Italy. Like Rome, Patavium traced its founding to the fall of the ancient city of Troy.

The founder of Patavium was said to have been a Trojan named Antenor, who had left Troy with Aeneas, the legendary founder of Rome. Through the centuries, the citizens of Patavium had always taken great pride in their illustrious beginnings. They were a very conservative people, firm believers in honesty, devotion to duty, courage, and self-restraint. Even as moral decline settled on much of the Roman world, the Patavians preserved their centuries-old values. In the civil war between Pompey and Julius Caesar they had supported Pompey because they believed in republicanism and condemned dictatorship.

Livy inherited the value system of his fellow Patavians, but his family background is a mystery. His writings show that he was well educated, strongly suggesting that his parents were well-to-do. (Patavium was a prosperous town, close to the Adriatic seacoast and a center of trade.) However, Patavium's support of Pompey had caused its citizens much suffering and perhaps prevented Livy from completing his studies in Greece, as was the custom among upper-class Romans. It does not appear that Livy ever served in the army or took an active part in politics. He did marry and raise a family, however, as accounts mention a son and a son-in-law.

Sometime around 30 B.C., Livy moved to Rome, not for status or economic opportunity but to write the history of his beloved nation. To do so, he needed access to source material that existed only in Rome. Unfortunately for posterity, Livy was content with secondary sources and did not feel the need to use original documents. Livy carefully assessed various reports on an event and chose the one he felt most reliable.

Augustus found Livy's work especially appealing, as did many of Livy's contemporaries. Gradually, his fame spread across the empire. The statesman Pliny the Younger told of a Spaniard who once traveled to Rome to see the wonders of the capital. As he was walking about the city, he met a Roman who pointed to another man, saying that he was the historian Livy. As the story goes, the Spaniard looked at the historian with reverence and then made immediate plans to return to Spain, reckoning that there were no greater sights to be seen.

For approximately 40 years, from the time he entered Rome until his death in A.D. 17, Livy devoted himself to writing his massive history. Titled *Ab Urbe Condita* (From the Founding of the City), it consisted of 142 books, covering events from the time of Aeneas to the death of Drusus (younger brother of the emperor Tiberius) in 9 B.C. Of the original work, 35 books have survived, Books I–X and XXI–XLV. A few additional fragments also survive, but the rest is known mainly from summaries made during the 1st century A.D. and later.

"It is easy at any moment you please to give up possession of a great fortune; to make and prepare it is difficult and arduous."

—from *Ab Urbe Condita* (From the Founding of the City, Book 24, section 22)

This 15th-century French translation of part of Livy's *Ab Urbe Condita* was the first major translation of Livy into French (Livy himself is shown writing at left). The ancient Romans did not use commas or periods, nor did they capitalize proper nouns, but later editors added punctuation marks to help readers.

In his introduction to *Ab Urbe Condita*, Livy clearly states the purpose of his work:

Whether or not what I shall do is worth the trouble, if I trace the history of the Roman people from the founding of the city, I am not quite sure. . . . However, it will please me to have contributed to the achievements of a people who are the best in the world. . . . The task is a great undertaking since it reaches back more than 700 years. . . . In my opinion, everyone should carefully consider what the life and customs of our ancestors were, how the empire was acquired and then increased. Everyone should then consider how, with morals and discipline declining from what they once were, they sunk more and more and then began to fall headlong, until the present times, in which we can endure neither our vices nor their remedies. It is exactly this which is especially healthy and profitable in the study of history, that you look at every type of conduct . . . that you then select for yourself and your country, what you wish to imitate . . . and what you wish to avoid.

In the pages that followed, Livy continued his emphasis on moral character and the qualities that led to good citizenship and produced true patriots. Sometimes his own patriotism led to a bias against Rome's enemies—not a spiteful one but a bias driven solely by his love of Rome. Throughout his work, Livy concentrated heavily on vividly representing his characters, whose traits and ambitions he believed controlled events. History was to him a reflection of these individuals and should be understood as such.

Livy's emphasis differed from that of his predecessors in that he focused more on realism and tone. He used short sentences to portray action scenes. But when quoting or paraphrasing speeches of great orators or works of political significance, he used long sentences and compound words to convey the gravity of the moment. This was new to Latin history writing.

The so-called golden age of Latin literature, of which Cicero had been the master, was passing, and a new literary period—later writers would call it the Silver Age—was beginning. The variety of styles and expressions found in Livy reflect this change, as does his lack of symmetry and his use of parallel constructions. Yet his elevated manner of describing a scene and his vivid imagination are characteristic of the Golden Age. Livy's language and use of stylistic constructions, however, are much simpler than those used by Cicero.

In Book I, Livy recounted the legendary battle between two sets of triplets fought during the reign of Rome's third king to settle the war between the Romans and their neighbors the Albans. Whichever side won would take possession of the other's lands. In

Livy's masterful description of this scene, one can sense both the intense excitement and the underlying anxiety of events, as well as the author's deeply felt patriotism:

> The triplets take their arms . . . and advance onto the battlefield, between the two lines of battle. . . . The signal is given and the triplets . . . rush forward with their dangerous weapons. . . . Then . . . the quick brandishing of arms and weapons on both sides and wounds and blood now come into view. Two Romans fall lifeless, one upon the other. All three Albans are wounded. . . . By chance, [the Roman] is uninjured. And, although alone he is by no means equal to his three opponents, yet he is confident against each singly. In order to separate their attack, the Roman begins running, reasoning that each of the Curiatii will follow as his wound allows. . . . Looking back, [the Roman] sees the Curiatii following him, at great intervals from each other, and notes that one of them is not too far distant. With great fury, he turns. . . . Having killed the first enemy, the victorious Horatius now seeks the second battle. . . . And so, he kills the second foe . . . and looks confidently to a third battle. The other, dragging his body exhausted from the wound and the running . . . meets his enemy. . . . The victorious Roman shouts, "I have given two Curiatii to the shades of my brothers; the third I will give to the cause of this war." . . . He then thrusts his sword into the throat of his opponent, who can barely support himself on his shield. . . . The tombs still stand in the place where each fell, the two Roman tombs in one place, nearer to Alba, the three Alban tombs closer to Rome, but in the same spot where each battle was fought.

FURTHER READING

Livy. 13 vols. Translated by B. O. Foster, et al. Loeb Classical Library. Cambridge: Harvard University Press, 1940.

Livy

BORN

59 B.C. or 64 B.C.
Patavium (Padua), Italy

DIED

A.D. 17
Patavium (Padua), Italy

PROFESSION

Historian

ACCOMPLISHMENTS

Wrote *Ab Urbe Condita*, a history of Rome in 142 books that covered the period from the city's founding to 9 B.C.

Ovid
(Publius
Ovidius Naso)

"LET ME BE ETERNAL"

antua rejoices in Virgil; Verona in Catullus; I shall be called the glory of the people of Peligni." So wrote the Roman poet Ovid in his first series of published poems, the *Amores* (Loves). Yet Ovid was not like Virgil or Catullus. He saw life as a gift to be enjoyed and did not have the patriotic idealism and fervor that characterized Virgil's works. Nor did he allow himself to experience the intense passion and emotion that brought such sorrow and agony to Catullus.

Nevertheless, even at this early age, Ovid was correct in assessing the merit of his verses, for, like Virgil and Catullus, he too would be acclaimed one of Rome's greatest poets. His poetry is characterized by the ease with which the words flow, the directness of the statement, and the focus on himself. As a result of the third characteristic, we know much about Ovid the man, for in a later collection of poems titled *Tristia* (Laments) he wrote the story of his life.

Born in 43 B.C., in Sulmo (present-day Sulmona), a small mountain town east of Rome that originally had been the territory of the Peligni (a people in central Italy), Publius Ovidius Naso traced his lineage to an old and respected family in the area. His father was quite wealthy and eager to see his two sons (Ovid's brother Lucius was one year his senior) educated in a manner that would prepare them for distinguished careers in government. Thus, when Ovid was 12 and his brother 13, their father took the boys to Rome and arranged for them to have the best teachers available. Special emphasis was given to rhetoric, since the law and politics of the time demanded that an individual be able to speak well extemporaneously.

Ovid disliked the legal training he was forced to take and the rigid arguments he had to study and deliver. Instead, he preferred to make a name for himself by writing poetry, as he clearly stated in one of his early poems: "What you seek [that is, a career in law or the military] is work that dies; for me eternal fame is sought, so that I shall be sung about in all the world." Ovid's father strongly opposed his son's interest in poetry, because he felt that a literary career would lead only to poverty. However, after Lucius died at the early age of 20, Ovid's father's objections seem to have mellowed. Ovid continued his studies, completing them, as was customary for men of his social class, with a trip to Greece and Asia Minor. Ovid also spent a year in Sicily.

These travels proved invaluable later when the impressions of what he saw and heard were reflected in his verses. But, in the late 20s B.C., Ovid had not yet devoted himself to poetry. Dutiful to his father's wishes, he held several minor judicial posts and argued some cases, without much enthusiasm. Studiousness and devotion to duty were not part of Ovid's nature. His real interest lay in verse and in living and loving. As he wrote: "Let the past and ancient customs please others. I congratulate myself that I was born now, for this age is suited to my tastes."

There was much in Rome that pleased Ovid, especially the amusements of the pleasure-seeking young aristocrats. He knew that the emperor Augustus was trying to revive traditional values and rein in morals, but he chose not to listen. Let Virgil and Horace promote such values in their works; he would not. Even the circle of friends in which they moved was different. The great patron of the arts Maecenas, who encouraged Virgil and Horace, did not invite Ovid into his group, and perhaps Ovid would not have accepted had he been asked. Instead, Ovid belonged to another literary circle, under the patronage of Marcus Valerius Messala.

By the time Ovid was 30, he had married three times and been divorced twice. His third wife, a member of a distinguished noble family, brought him both social status and much happiness. Their marriage lasted until his death at the age of 60.

It was during the 20s B.C., the years of his first two marriages, that he wrote the *Amores*, three books of love poems dedicated to a woman named Corinna, a fictitious name. The real Corinna has never been discovered, and Ovid's professions of love never ring true in the way those of Catullus do. For the latter, love was real and could bring intense pleasure or excruciating pain. For Ovid, love was fanciful and passing, nothing over which anyone should become too distressed. When compared to Catullus' exquisite lines expressing his love and hate for Clodia, Ovid's lines sound insincere, almost as if he is a third party speaking, not one of the lovers involved:

"I will hate, if I am able: if not, unwillingly I will love: The bull does not love his yoke, yet it has what it hates."

In the *Ars Amatoria* (The Art of Love), published around 1 B.C., Ovid continued to express his feelings on the subject of love, telling his readers how to use seduction and intrigue to win another's affection. He claimed that his advice came from personal experience and that Rome abounded with opportunities for those who wished to find love: the theater, the circus, even nightly feasts in private homes were all perfect "battlefields" and "hunting grounds" for would-be lovers. In Book I of the *Ars Amatoria* he wrote, "As many stars as are in the sky, so many girls does Rome have." In his worldly wisdom, he advised, "Be lovable so that you will be loved."

Ovid followed the *Ars Amatoria* with *Remedia Amoris* (The Remedy of Love), in which he discussed a variety of ways in which a person could stifle love. Although Augustus did not react officially to these poems, he surely cannot have approved of them. Perhaps the emperor chose to focus on the other works Ovid was writing—the *Heroides*, the *Fasti*, and the *Metamorphoses*.

The *Heroides* (Heroines) purports to be a collection of letters written by legendary and mythological women to their absent or faithless lovers or husbands. Included is one from Queen Dido of Carthage in northern Africa to Aeneas, whose settlement in Italy led to the foundation of Rome:

> I write and there is a Trojan sword on my lap: and the tears flow down my cheeks onto the unsheathed sword, which soon shall be bathed with blood instead of tears. . . This inscription will be on the marble of my tombstone:
> "Aeneas provided both the cause of death and the sword.
> Dido, with her own hand, killed herself."

The sculptor who fashioned this statue of Ovid sometime in the Middle Ages chose to picture him more as a scholar than as the lover of life that Ovid always said he was.

OVID'S INVECTIVE or CURSE AGAINST IBIS,

Faithfully and familiarly Tranflated into Englifh Verfe.

And the Hiftories therein contained, being in number two hundred and fifty (at the leaft) briefly explained, one by one; With Natural, Moral, Poetical, Political, Mathematical, and fome few Theological Applications.

Whereunto is prefixed a double INDEX: One of the Proper Names herein mentioned; Another of the Common Heads from thence deduced.

Both pleafant and profitable for each fort, Sex and Age, and very ufeful for Grammar Schools.

By *John Jones* M. A. Teacher of a private School in the City of HEREFORD.

Ῥᾴδιον ἔςι μωμεῖᾰϑαι, ἤ ιμμεῖϑαι.

Carpere vel noli noftra, vel ede tua.

In his poem titled *Ibis,* written shortly after his banishment from Rome, Ovid cursed an unknown friend who had proved himself false. This 1667 edition notes that Ovid's work is "pleasant and profitable for each sort, Sex, and Age, and very useful for Grammar Schools."

Of all Ovid's works, the *Fasti* (Festivals) is the most nationalistic. Perhaps it was designed to win him Augustus' favor. Divided into 12 books, of which only 6 have survived, the *Fasti* presents a month-by-month account of Rome's religious festivals, their origins, and the rituals connected with them.

The best known of all Ovid's works, and the one on which his fame rests, is the *Metamorphoses* (Changes), a collection of myths and legends divided into 15 books. Although the topics are quite diverse, there is an underlying unity in that every story refers in some way to a change of form. In the tale of the maiden Daphne, for instance, the sun god Apollo falls in love with the beautiful Daphne and pursues her relentlessly. Desperate to escape, Daphne prays for help and is turned into a laurel tree. In the tale of Midas, the greedy king who asked that everything he touched be turned to gold, Midas realizes the foolishness of his wish when he has only gold to eat and drink. To rid himself of what has now become a curse, Midas washes himself in the waters of the Pactolus River. The ancients used this legend to explain the gold-bearing sands the river produced.

The *Metamorphoses* begins with the creation of the world and ends with the death and deification of Julius Caesar, which allows for the final metamorphosis of the work: from the chaos of civil wars to the peace Augustus ushers into the world. Most of the stories are from Greek mythology, but a few trace their origin to the Near East. Still present, however, are Ovid's wittiness and zest for life. The reader is carried on a wave of energy from tale to tale as Ovid paints a vivid picture of each scene he describes. His poetic skill links the episodes together to form a unit that runs smoothly from passage to passage. Not surprisingly, countless authors in following centuries borrowed and adapted individual legends from Ovid's *Metamorphoses*.

Even a cursory reading of a passage from the *Metamorphoses* reveals Ovid's keen imagination and ability to describe a particular situation. And so, despite its great length—approximately 12,000 verses—the text never becomes boring. An example of Ovid's high

Ovid

BORN

March 20, 43 B.C.
Sulmo (Sulmona), Italy

DIED

A.D. 17
Tomis, on the Black Sea

PROFESSION

Poet

ACCOMPLISHMENTS

Wrote a variety of poems, many of which focus on love and advice to lovers: *Amores* (Loves), *Ars Amatoria* (The Art of Love), *Remedia Amoris* (The Remedy of Love), *Heroides* (Heroines), *Fasti* (Festivals), *Metamorphoses* (Changes), and *Tristia* (Sorrows); wrote several other works, including a tragedy entitled *Medea*

"Either carry it through or do not try at all."

—from *Ars Amatoria* (around 1 B.C.)

spirits is his description of the one-eyed giant Polyphemus, who seeks to win the love of a beautiful maiden named Galatea: "And now Polyphemus, to please [Galatea] you tend to your appearance and comb your shaggy hair with a rake and cut your rough beard with a sickle."

By A.D. 8, the *Metamorphoses* was ready for a publisher. Several passages were already in circulation and had won enthusiastic reviews, but there were still a few revisions Ovid wanted to make. He believed this was his best work and pointedly ended the poem with the following lines:

> And so I have created a work which neither the wrath of Jupiter nor fire nor the sword nor consuming old age is able to destroy. When that final day shall come . . . let me be eternal and go above the lofty stars . . . and through all the centuries I shall live.

Ovid's moment of glory was short-lived, however; in that same year, fate dashed him from the pinnacle of fame to the depths of despair. A summons from Augustus reached Ovid while he was on the island of Elba, east of Italy in the Tyrrhenian Sea. Returning immediately to Rome, he proceeded at once to the emperor's quarters and met with him privately. Exactly what transpired has been debated for centuries, but the result was Ovid's immediate banishment to the dreary town of Tomis, a Roman outpost on the Black Sea.

On various occasions, Ovid gave two reasons for his punishment—the *Ars Amatoria* and an "error." Why Augustus chose to banish him for a book that had been written years earlier is not certain, and Ovid never explained

what the error was. It remains one of the best-kept secrets in literary history. Many have speculated, however, that Ovid personally insulted Augustus in some way or that he became too friendly with Augustus' daughter Julia and was blamed by Augustus for encouraging immoral behavior in her.

Despite numerous pleas from Ovid and other well-known Romans to rescind the order expelling Ovid, Augustus never did. However, he did not impose *exilium* (exile) on Ovid, stopping at a decree of *relegatio*: this meant that, while Ovid had to live in Tomis, he could retain his Roman citizenship, his property, and his money. To protect his interests, Ovid's wife remained in Rome. The devoted couple were never again to see each other.

At first, Ovid could barely endure life in Tomis, which was still subject to raids by neighboring tribes. He must have bristled when told that even he was expected to stand duty as part of the home guard. The region's brutally cold winters and constant snowfalls were far different from Rome's temperate weather, and there were few opportunities to attend cultural events or mingle with cultured people.

As a result, Ovid devoted much of his time to writing. Even though Augustus had banned his books from the public shelves at home, he knew that his friends would circulate any new verses he might send them. Ovid's first work from exile, titled *Tristia* (Sorrows), spoke in vivid and descriptive language of the hardships he was being forced to endure: "Snow falls . . . and the first snow has not yet melted when another storm comes, and the snow from a storm two years earlier is often

БАСНЬ VII.
Похищеніе Прозерпины.

A favorite subject with artists are the stories in Ovid's *Metamorphoses*. In this Russian translation, the illustrator has chosen the moment when Pluto, the god of the underworld, seizes Proserpina to make her his queen. (The Russian caption reads "the abduction of Proserpina.")

found on the ground in some places." An unsuccessful plea to be recalled, the *Tristia* included an autobiographical sketch that contains a moving description of Ovid's last hours in Rome:

> When the very sad image of that night
>   comes to mind
> The last time I was in the city,
> When I remember the night on which
>   I left so much behind
> A tear glides down from my eyes.

However, as the years passed and Augustus showed no sign of rescinding his order, Ovid gradually began to acclimate himself to his new surroundings. He even learned the native language, Getic, and composed some poetry in it, none of which has survived. The people of Tomis welcomed him and even showed him great honors, for which he was grateful, but his heart belonged to Rome. Ancient accounts cite this as a possible reason for the fact that the works he composed in Tomis did not equal in spontaneity or imagination his earlier verses. To be sure, Ovid's works had a lasting effect on Roman literature. Neither stiff nor correct in the manner of the Greek poets the Romans had so insistently mirrored, they possessed a vigor and charm that marked the beginning of a new literary style.

FURTHER READING

Ovid. *Ovid.* 6 vols. Translated by Grant Showerman. Loeb Classical Library. Cambridge: Harvard University Press, 1977.

———. *The Love Poems.* Translated by A. D. Melville. New York: Oxford University Press, 1990.

———. *Metamorphoses.* Translated by A. D. Melville. New York: Oxford University Press, 1987.

———. *Sorrows of an Exile.* Translated by A. D. Melville. New York: Oxford University Press, 1995.

Rand, Edward K. *Ovid and His Influence.* Boston: Marshall Jones, 1925.

Tiberius
(Tiberius
Claudius Nero)

UNHAPPY EMPEROR

If this sculpted head of Tiberius is as realistic in form as so many of the Roman statues were, then the emperor's outer countenance certainly did not reflect his many disappointments.

F ate did not treat Tiberius kindly, and the misfortunes that plagued him from infancy through adulthood naturally affected his personality and temperament.

Descended from Rome's oldest and most noble families, Tiberius Claudius Nero was born in November 42 B.C., just weeks after the Battle of Philippi, in which Octavius (later called Augustus) and Antony defeated the assassins of Julius Caesar. Sharing the joy of victory was Tiberius' father, a former naval commander under Caesar.

Unfortunately, the joy was short-lived. Less than a year later, the threat of civil war once again hung over Rome. Antony was still in the East, attending to administrative matters. Octavius was in Italy, attempting to consolidate his position there. In Rome, Antony's brother Lucius had been elected consul for the year 41 B.C. Anxious to advance Antony's interests, Lucius openly opposed Octavius, and early in 40 B.C. the two met on the battlefield. This time it was Tiberius' father who experienced the agony of defeat, for he had chosen to support Lucius. In the agreement that followed, the elder Tiberius was the only public official who chose not to surrender to Octavius.

After escaping south with his wife, Livia Drusilla, and the young Tiberius, Tiberius' father lived the life of a fugitive, first in Naples, then in Sicily, and finally in Greece. According to the Roman historian Suetonius, on one occasion the young Tiberius' cries almost betrayed his parents' whereabouts when they were being pursued by their enemies. Another time, Livia used the cover of darkness to flee the Greek city of Sparta. Holding her son tightly in her arms, she was running into the woods just beyond the city when a sudden forest fire broke out, scorching her hair and robe.

When Antony and Octavius finally agreed to settle their differences, the elder Tiberius returned to Rome with his pregnant wife and three-year-old son under a general amnesty granted Antony's supporters. In Rome, Livia's beauty quickly caught the attention of Octavius, who immediately divorced his own wife and asked Tiberius to divorce Livia. Although Tiberius had stood up for himself in the past, in this situation he seems to have had no alternative but to do as Octavius commanded.

According to the divorce terms, Tiberius had custody of young Tiberius and of the child Livia was carrying. A few years later, when Tiberius died, the two children came to live with their mother and stepfather Octavius, the most powerful man in Rome. Life now changed radically for the young Tiberius. Considering his stepson a possible successor to himself, Octavius entrusted him with various official and religious duties. In fact, Tiberius was only nine years old when Octavius assigned him his first public task—the eulogy at his father's funeral from the Rostra in the Roman Forum. Other civic and religious responsibilities followed. On many of these occasions, his brother Drusus

and his stepcousin Marcellus, the son of Octavius' sister, accompanied him. Octavius saw all three boys as possible successors and raised them in a manner that would prepare them for such a position of responsibility and duty. The one female member of this elite group of Roman youngsters was Julia, Octavius' daughter by a previous wife.

The year 31 B.C. marked a turning point in the history of the Roman empire and in Tiberius' life. After Antony's defeat at Actium, Octavius ruled Rome's lands from east to west and a welcome calm, the so-called *Pax Romana* (Roman peace), settled over the Roman world. To celebrate Octavius' victory at Actium, the Senate awarded him a triumph. As his companions in the procession, Octavius chose Tiberius and Marcellus.

Certainly, Tiberius must have impressed all those who watched the triumphal procession. According to Suetonius, he was strong, well built, of above-average height, and exceedingly well proportioned. His complexion was pale and his face handsome, though he suffered from occasional acne. As was the fashion in his family, he wore his hair long in back so that it covered his neck. Suetonius continued his description of the future emperor with the observation that he was left-handed and that he could poke a hole through an apple with his finger. Tiberius said little, but when he did he spoke very slowly and with deliberate movements of his fingers.

Octavius did not like Tiberius' mannerisms, but his concern for the future welfare of Rome far outweighed such dislikes and, when he set out for Gaul and Spain in 27 B.C., he took Tiberius and Marcellus with him. Tiberius at 15 was still too young to be in the field, but he did learn much about daily routine at military camp sites.

Upon returning to Rome, Octavius (known now as Augustus) officially made known his preference for Marcellus by giving him his daughter, Julia, in marriage. Marcellus' death two years later ended Augustus' immediate prospects for a grandson to designate as heir. So he soon arranged a second marriage for Julia, this time to his most trusted general, Agrippa.

Tiberius, meanwhile, had found his own happiness. More fortunate than most Romans of his class who had to marry for political reasons, Tiberius loved his wife, the beautiful Vipsania Agrippina, daughter of Agrippa. In the years that followed, Tiberius fathered a son, whom he named Drusus after his beloved brother.

Tiberius began spending less and less time in Rome, for Augustus had recognized his military ability and kept sending him on a variety of missions. Tiberius' first major assignment was in the East, where at the young age of 22 he won great fame by recovering the Roman military standards that the Parthians had taken when they defeated the Roman legions under Crassus decades earlier. Other assignments took him to the Alps, Pannonia (on the Adriatic Sea), and Germany. Everywhere he met success, both on the battlefield and in camp, for his soldiers admired and respected him.

At home, however, fate did not treat him so kindly. In 12 B.C., Agrippa died, leaving Augustus' daughter Julia a widow. Upon the command of Augustus, Tiberius was forced to divorce his beloved Vipsania, who was pregnant with their second child, and marry Julia. Just as his father had obeyed Augustus' command to divorce his wife years earlier, so now Tiberius did not dispute this order. But his heart was broken, and accounts relate that sometime later Tiberius saw Vipsania on a street in Rome and followed her, weeping.

Personal tragedy again struck Tiberius in 9 B.C., when a messenger brought news that his brother, Drusus, who was campaigning in Germany, had fallen from his horse and broken a leg. Tiberius immediately mounted his horse and rode night and day until he reached his brother's bedside. When Drusus died shortly afterward, Tiberius led the funeral procession back to Rome, walking the entire way on foot.

For Tiberius, Rome was becoming a place to escape from, not enjoy. Julia, who had a reputation for faithlessness, soon found others she preferred to Tiberius. By law, Tiberius could divorce Julia if he could prove her adultery. But Julia was the emperor's daughter, and Augustus certainly would not act kindly toward anyone who denounced her. Furthermore, Augustus seems to have been completely unaware of his daughter's wanton ways.

Therefore, Tiberius chose the one option open to him—military service far from Rome. Augustus welcomed Tiberius' decision because he was a proven commander and the empire needed such leaders. In the years that followed, Augustus no longer treated Tiberius as his successor, but he did go on rewarding him with honors. In 6 B.C., for example, he granted Tiberius the powers of tribune for a five-year period.

This last honor does not seem to have meant much to Tiberius, who that same year chose to retire completely from political and military life, saying that he wanted a rest. He set sail for Rhodes, an island in the Aegean Sea that he had visited and enjoyed years earlier. There he lived a quiet life, seeking no honors or special treatment.

In 2 B.C., news reached Tiberius that Augustus had banished Julia from Rome and formally approved a divorce. Rumor said that Tiberius' mother, Livia, had been instrumental in securing proof of her daughter-in-law's unfaithfulness and had presented it to Augustus. By law, Julia should have been executed, but Augustus could not bring himself to order such a drastic

Tiberius

BORN

November 16, 42 B.C.
Rome or Fundi, Italy

DIED

March 16, A.D. 37
Misenum, Italy

PROFESSION

Roman emperor

ACCOMPLISHMENTS

Led many successful military campaigns in Asia Minor, Pannonia, and Germany; second in command of the Roman Empire from A.D. 4 until Augustus' death in A.D. 14; ruler of the Roman Empire from A.D. 14 until his death in A.D. 37; greatly increased the public treasury; kept Rome's government stable and prosperous

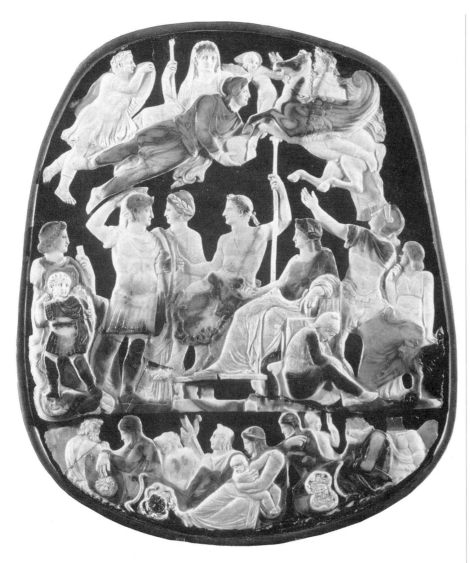

The so-called *Grand Camée de France* (Great Cameo of France) is a large carved gemstone made in Rome, most likely around A.D. 20. The scene at top shows the deified Augustus watching over his family; Tiberius is seated in the center, and Livia is seated to his left. The figures in the bottom section represent barbarians, whom the Caesars had defeated and then kept under control.

Tiberius, however, and continued to favor Julia's sons Gaius and Lucius. But Augustus disliked Julia's third son, Postumus, and sent him into exile with his mother.

Finally, in A.D. 2, Augustus relented and recalled Tiberius, stipulating that he was to take no part in politics. That same year, Lucius died while on his way to Spain, leaving Gaius the main contender. Then, in A.D. 4, news reached Rome that Gaius had been killed while fighting in Asia Minor. Augustus now found that all his designated successors were dead or, as in the case of Postumus, disowned. Only Tiberius remained. Soon after Gaius' death, Augustus adopted Tiberius as his son, thereby officially recognizing him as his successor. But his feelings for Tiberius had not changed. It was said that soon after adopting Tiberius, Augustus remarked, "I do this for the sake of the state."

Yet Augustus did show some concern for his successor's welfare, publicly recognizing him as the one Roman capable of governing the vast empire. In one of his letters to Tiberius, Augustus wrote: "Good-bye, my very dear Tiberius, and the best of luck go with you in your battles on my behalf. . . . If anything goes wrong with you, I shall never smile again!"

When Augustus died in A.D. 14, Tiberius was slow to accept the official role of emperor, noting that the task of ruling was an incredibly burdensome one and that he had already spent most of his life working on behalf of the nation. Finally, on September 17, a month after Augustus' death, Tiberius agreed to become Rome's second emperor, the third Caesar to rule Rome.

A conservative emperor, Tiberius remained loyal to the policies established by Augustus and followed his advice not to expand the empire beyond the Euphrates River in the east and the Rhine River in the west. Preferring negotiations to warfare, Tiberius spent his

punishment and chose instead to confine her to the tiny island of Pandataria in the Tyrrhenian Sea. Tiberius welcomed the news, and when his five-year term as tribune expired, he requested that he be allowed to return to Rome to visit his family. Although Tiberius' withdrawal from Rome had been voluntary, Augustus now chose to accept it as permanent and denied the request.

This rebuff had dire consequences for Tiberius, who became known as the Exile. The public held him in disrespect, and many of the statues erected in his honor were overturned. The situation became so serious that Tiberius withdrew almost completely from public life and sent urgent pleas to Livia for help. Augustus remained set against

time consolidating the provinces and making sure that each was run smoothly. Revolts were immediately quelled. To provide provincials with a greater sense of political stability, Tiberius extended the one-year term traditionally granted provincial officials.

Believing free speech to be the test of a free country, Tiberius did not condemn those who chose to slander his person or spread false rumors—but he detested flatterers. While accepting the supreme power for himself, Tiberius allowed senators and public officials to exercise their own authority and make judgments concerning the welfare of the empire. Moreover, he consistently refused to accept honors for himself or allow temples to be dedicated in his name.

In matters of finance Tiberius was extremely frugal, leaving the treasury 20 times larger upon his death than at the time of his accession. Suetonius wrote that Tiberius cut expenses for public entertainment as one means of lowering costs. To accomplish this he lowered the pay for actors, limited the number of gladiatorial combats during a festival, and reduced the number of games held annually.

Believing food prices to be too high, he set a restriction on the amount of food that could be sold in shops and set a limit on the prices for the food. He even banned pastries as a wasteful expenditure. According to Suetonius, food left over from a dinner party during Tiberius' reign would be served to the next day's guests. Tiberius even ordered that, if half a boar was sufficient to feed the assembled guests, then only half would be served. To those who argued that the provinces should pay more taxes and tribute to Rome, he replied, "A good shepherd shears his flock, he does not flay them."

During his first two years in office Tiberius did not leave Rome, and after that he rarely went farther than a few towns away. He never remarried

"Let them hate me, as long as they approve my conduct."

—Tiberius, quoted in Suetonius' *The Lives of the Caesars* (A.D. 120)

and continued to hold Julia in great contempt, refusing to rescind her banishment decree. He even changed Augustus' order giving her freedom of movement on her island, confining her instead to the house in which she lived, and banned all visitors. So intense was his anger against Julia that he discontinued the allowance Augustus had established for her; within months after Augustus' death, Julia died of malnutrition.

But even Julia's death did not bring Tiberius out of his shell. For one thing, he was beginning to distrust those around him. Suspicious by nature, he sought to insulate himself against potential enemies. There was never a lack of courtiers willing to tell the emperor of possible conspiracies. As the months passed, Tiberius paid more attention to these *delatores*, or informers. Not all were honest or patriotic, and many Romans were convicted on the word of an informer who sought only a share of the convicted person's property. A terrible fear gripped the upper classes of Rome and those closely connected with Tiberius as each wondered who would be next on the list.

Well aware that death might come at any time, Tiberius sought to prepare an heir who could shoulder the tremendous burden of governing the empire. For years succession had been a moot point, because Tiberius had adopted his nephew Germanicus in A.D. 4 on instructions from Augustus. Then, when Germanicus died—either from natural causes or, as was rumored, from poison—Tiberius turned to his biological son, Drusus. But in A.D. 23,

Drusus was found dead, another alleged victim of poisoning.

Suspicious as Tiberius was, he did not suspect the one man he had come to trust—Sejanus. Years earlier, Tiberius had named Sejanus commander of the Praetorian Guard. Originally organized as the bodyguard for Roman generals, the Guard had become a permanent unit under Augustus, who increased its number and stationed three units near the city and six more in towns within easy marching distance of Rome. Recognizing the Guard as a great advantage in an emergency, Tiberius ordered all nine sections to be stationed just outside the walls of the city. As a result, the commander of the Guard had the military might to take over the city.

Tiberius most likely recognized Sejanus' potential power but saw him only as a loyal subordinate. He gradually yielded more of the public decision making to Sejanus. In A.D. 26, when he was 67 years old, Tiberius left Rome for Campania, south of Rome. Soon after, he set sail for the tiny island of Capri, just off the west coast of Italy. For him this was the perfect place to escape the world, because it had only two accessible harbors. Once there, Tiberius seemed to forget the cares of the empire. During his absence, rumors began to circulate about his activities, and detractors told malicious tales about him. Some reports went so far as to claim that his mind had become disordered.

Whether or not he was concerned about the rumors, Tiberius refused to return to Rome and instead relied completely on Sejanus to handle the affairs of the empire. In A.D. 31, Tiberius chose Sejanus as his co-consul and named Macro, another trusted officer, commander of the Guard. Tiberius also granted Sejanus permission to marry Livilla, the widow of his son Drusus. Before long, Tiberius learned that Sejanus was abusing his powers and that he had conspired with Livilla years earlier to poison Drusus.

Once convinced of Sejanus' disloyalty, Tiberius acted quickly. He did not return to Rome but instead wrote a letter accusing Sejanus of treason and calling for his execution. He then had the letter smuggled into the Senate, so that Sejanus and his agents could not intercept it. The senators, who detested and feared Sejanus, gladly complied with the emperor's wishes, and Sejanus met his fate at the hands of the executioner.

The years that followed this incident were quite unpleasant for Tiberius' associates. As his fear of assassination increased, he considered everyone a suspect. Daily, the list of *delatores* grew, as did the number of executions. A desire for relief spread throughout Rome and Italy, but there was still the question of who would succeed Tiberius. Originally, Germanicus' three sons had been the prime contenders, but Sejanus had eliminated two, leaving only Gaius, later known as Caligula. Having little choice, Tiberius adopted Gaius as his son and successor.

In the spring of A.D. 37, Tiberius made one of his occasional visits to the mainland. According to Suetonius, as he rode along the Appian Way toward Rome, he stopped to feed his pet snake. Stunned when he found the snake dead, half-eaten by a swarm of ants, Tiberius immediately ordered his group to turn back to Campania. Recognizing the snake's death as an omen, a soothsayer who was with Tiberius warned, "Beware the power of the mob!"

Soon after, Tiberius fell ill, but he refused to admit that his condition was serious and entered a local javelin contest. After twisting his side with the force of a throw, he then aggravated his condition by sitting in a draft while still perspiring. Refusing to accept medical advice, Tiberius continued to attend banquets and participate in the festivities. His intent was to make his way slowly back to the safety of Capri and recover his health, but bad weather and increasing bouts of illness prevented his sailing.

As Tiberius lay dying, rumors circulated that a slow-working poison given him by Gaius was wasting away his body. To be sure, Gaius was eager to become emperor and had the support of the Praetorian Guard, but whether he resorted to murder is a question that has remained unanswered.

At the time of his death, Tiberius was 77 years old and had ruled the Roman Empire for almost 23 years. In his will he named Gaius and his own grandson Tiberius Gemellus as co-heirs, with the right of survival. The precedent for succession was clear, and the Caesars were to remain Rome's ruling family.

FURTHER READING

Marsh, Frank B. *The Reign of Tiberius*. New York: Oxford University Press, 1931.

Mason, Ernst. *Tiberius*. New York: Ballantine, 1960.

Seager, Robin. *Tiberius*. Berkeley: University of California Press, 1972.

Suetonius. *The Lives of the Caesars*. Translated by J. C. Rolfe. Loeb Classical Library. New York: Macmillan, 1914.

Tacitus. *Annales*. Translated by John Jackson. Loeb Classical Library. Cambridge: Harvard University Press, 1963.

Livia
(Livia Drusilla)

FIRST LADY OF ROME

Wife of Rome's first emperor, mother of its second, and grandmother of its fourth, Livia knew well the intrigue that plagued the city's politics. An influential, determined woman, Livia naturally had enemies, but she won respect from all classes of society for her moral character and devotion to her family.

Born in 58 B.C., Livia traced her ancestry to the ancient and powerful Claudian family, which proudly claimed de-

A strong-willed and determined woman, Livia quickly adapted herself to the role of "first lady." Augustus often sought her advice when deliberating matters of state.

Little remains today of Livia and Augustus' house in Rome. After suffering considerable damage when fire destroyed much of Rome in A.D., it was rebuilt and survived even the invasions by northern tribes. But in the late 1700s, an owner of the property began selling even the bricks and stone to a stone cutter. The house is a protected historic site today, and archaeologists are working to discover more about the lives of one of Rome's most famous couples.

scent from the 4th-century B.C. censor Appius Claudius the Blind, who introduced legislation that gave more civil rights to the lower classes of Rome. In more recent times, members of her family had held the rank of consul and of dictator and had celebrated three triumphs. With such connections, it was only natural that Livia would develop into a patriotic young woman who placed the highest value on the nation and the traditional values that had made it great.

Sometime in the 40s B.C., Livia married Tiberius Claudius Nero, also a descendant of the Claudian family. She soon gave birth to a son, the future emperor Tiberius. Livia's husband was considerably older than she, as was cus-

tomary in ancient Rome, because most upper-class marriages were arranged. This practice was considered the best way to preserve and further a family's social and political position.

The 40s, however, saw many aspiring political and military careers dashed. In 42 B.C., the Second Triumvirate—Octavius (later Augustus), Mark Antony, and Lepidus—defeated the assassins of Julius Caesar in a decisive battle at Philippi, in Greece. The victory marked the end of a bitter civil war between the two factions, but for Tiberius and Livia their difficulties were just beginning.

Livia's father had committed suicide after learning that the triumvirs had condemned him for siding with the opposition. Now, after Philippi, her own life was in danger. As the tension between Octavius and Antony increased, Tiberius chose to align himself with Antony's brother Lucius against Octavius. When Lucius lost, Tiberius fled with Livia and their infant son to Sicily and then to Greece. The experience must have been quite harrowing for Livia especially, who was only 18 or 19 years old.

After months of living as fugitives, Tiberius and Livia welcomed the peace agreement between Octavius and Antony. When Antony headed back to Rome, Tiberius and his family marched with him. Livia, now pregnant with her second child, found that her trials were far from over. Before long, her beauty and character came to the attention of Octavius. Eager to have such a woman as his bride, he divorced his wife (who was also pregnant) and forced Tiberius to do the same. The young Tiberius was given into the care of his father, as was the infant Drusus when he was born, four months after Livia married Octavius.

How Livia felt about this radical change in her life is not known. What is certain is that she remained faithful to Octavius throughout their marriage, which lasted from 38 B.C. until his death in A.D. 14. His last words to her were, "Good-bye, Livia. Never forget our marriage!"

That marriage had been long and eventful. Some five years after her marriage to Augustus, her first husband died and the two children of that marriage, Tiberius and Drusus, were entrusted to Livia and Augustus. Although Augustus had hoped to have children with Livia, their marriage was childless. But this did not diminish his affection for her. Rather, he valued her advice and often sought her counsel in matters concerning the empire. Once, according to contemporary accounts, Augustus pardoned a conspirator named Cinna Magnus because of Livia's insistence that he do so.

Praised for her frugality, dignity, and intelligence, Livia oversaw the running of Augustus' home with a fairness and thoroughness that won her the admiration of the Roman people. Like her husband, she shunned extravagance and luxury. According to Suetonius, Livia and Augustus lived for more than 40 years in an unpretentious house on Rome's Palatine Hill. Despite his high office, Augustus wore togas (the official robe worn by Roman citizens) that had been woven only by Livia's servants or others under her supervision.

As the years passed and Augustus became more and more concerned with who should succeed him, so too did Livia. On this matter, however, they differed. Livia openly favored her son Tiberius, while Augustus preferred first his sister's son, Marcellus, and then his grandsons, Gaius and Lucius. Livia re-alized she should not be too insistent regarding the heir, because political assassination was becoming a useful tool in Rome. But she continued to promote Tiberius, at least until 6 B.C., when he chose voluntarily to leave Rome and live on the island of Rhodes.

Livia must certainly have believed that one of the reasons for this decision was his unhappy marriage to Augustus' daughter, Julia. Augustus had forced Tiberius to divorce his beloved wife Livia and marry Julia. The couple had never cared for one another, however, and Julia was now openly unfaithful.

Roman law called for the execution of any wife who committed adultery, but few Romans would dare to declare the emperor's daughter an adultress. It is uncertain whether Livia actually obtained proof of Julia's adultery and presented it to Augustus, but somehow he finally was made aware of Julia's conduct and was forced to act. Augustus banished Julia to the small island of Pandataria, which allowed Tiberius to divorce her.

The question of who would succeed Augustus remained, with Livia continuing to work on her son's behalf. When three potential rivals—Augustus' nephew Marcellus and Julia's sons Gaius and Lucius—died under mysterious circumstances, Livia came under suspicion, but nothing was ever proved. In A.D. 4, Augustus adopted Tiberius and Agrippa Postumus, Julia's youngest son. Livia's dream had now almost become a reality. Only Postumus posed a threat to that dream, but after Augustus banished him for improper conduct in A.D. 7, Tiberius was recognized as Augustus' immediate successor. Shortly after Augustus' death, in A.D. 14, a soldier following orders killed Postumus. Livia's name was immediately linked with the murder, but no proof ever sur-

Livia

BORN
58 B.C.
Probably Rome

DIED
A.D. 29
Rome

PROFESSION
Wife of Rome's first emperor (Augustus), mother of Rome's second (Tiberius), and grandmother of Rome's fourth (Claudius)

ACCOMPLISHMENTS
Lent an air of dignity to Rome in a period when morals were rapidly declining; functioned as an important political partner of Augustus

faced. Tiberius now became emperor of Rome.

Tiberius appreciated his mother's concern for him but had no desire to be her subordinate. He had witnessed the growth of her influence over Augustus as the years passed and was determined that the same would not happen to him.

There were other powerful women in Rome who exerted their influence at many levels, chief among them Antonia, the wife of Tiberius' brother Drusus. Well respected for her upright character and beloved by the Roman people, Antonia was also close to Tiberius, but she was not domineering.

Livia, on the other hand, was used to power. For decades her ideas had been valued. She saw herself as the matriarch and expected to be treated as such. Though Tiberius did consult her on many occasions and followed her advice, he complained that she wished to be co-ruler with him. For this reason, he avoided long and frequent meetings with his mother and repeatedly warned her not to interfere too openly in the affairs of state. Once, when he learned that Livia had gone to the scene of a raging fire near Rome's Temple of Vesta and placed herself in charge of the situation, just as she would have if Augustus had been alive, Tiberius was furious.

In the months that followed, tension between mother and son intensified until, on one occasion, Tiberius openly quarreled with Livia in public. For quite some time, Livia had been pestering him to add a particular name to the jury list. After repeatedly ignoring her requests, Tiberius finally agreed to do so, but on the condition that the words "forced upon the emperor by his mother" be written next to the name.

Livia was so incensed by this insult that she produced some old letters by Augustus in which he commented on Tiberius' dour and stubborn nature. Some accounts of this incident claim that Tiberius was so angered by this act that he chose to leave Rome forever and make his permanent home on Capri.

Despite her difficulties with Tiberius, Livia continued to be honored by the people. She regularly welcomed senators and other distinguished Romans to her house and discussed government matters with them. When she died in A.D. 29, all Rome mourned her passing. Tiberius did not even attend her funeral.

In death as in life, Livia was mindful of her role as "first lady of Rome" and left generous bequests to the people. But Tiberius refused to execute her will or to allow her to be deified. Tiberius' successor, Gaius, who had known Livia well and recognized her great contributions to the welfare of the empire, finally fulfilled the terms of her will. Years later, Livia's grandson Claudius, Rome's fourth emperor, submitted to the senate a law deifying the spirit of his renowned grandmother.

FURTHER READING

Balsdon, J. P. V. D. *Roman Women: Their History and Habits.* Westport, Conn.: Greenwood, 1962.

Ferrero, Guglielmo. *The Women of the Caesars.* New York: Putnam, 1925.

Lefkowitz, Mary R., and Maureen B. Fant, eds. *Women in Greece and Rome.* Toronto: Samuel-Stevens, 1977.

Lefkowitz, Mary R., and Maureen B. Fant, eds. *Women's Life in Greece and Rome.* Baltimore: Johns Hopkins University Press, 1982.

More Ancient Romans to Remember

Maecenas (Gaius Maecenas) (about 70–8 B.C.) is renowned throughout the world of literature for his patronage particularly of the literary giants Virgil and Horace. His great wealth allowed him to support and encourage those whose writings he felt had exceptional merit and would promote the traditional ideals and values of the Roman Empire. Maecenas was one of Augustus' most trusted advisors and he was responsible for effecting a reconciliation between Augustus and Mark Antony in 40 B.C. Gradually but steadily, Maecenas' power and prestige increased until he shared the unofficial position of being second in command with Agrippa.

Maecenas never held public office, but when Augustus was fighting in the East between 36 and 33 B.C., he was in charge of affairs in Rome. He took charge again between 31 and 29 B.C.

Maecenas' home life was not as rewarding as his public life, especially after his beautiful but insolent wife, Terentia, tired of him. To make matters worse, her brother was implicated in a conspiracy to assassinate Augustus but managed to avoid capture when Maecenas told Terentia that the plot had been uncovered. Soon after, there evolved a noticeable difference in the relationship between Augustus and Maecenas. Whether Augustus was angry because Maecenas had allowed his brother-in-law to escape or whether he was in fact having an affair with Terentia will never be known. Maecenas, however, continued to support Augustus. In his will, he left his magnificent home and gardens on Rome's Esquiline Hill to the emperor.

Tibullus (Albius Tibullus) (around 55 B.C.–19 B.C.) was the second of Rome's great elegiac poets. (The works of Gallus, the first, have not survived.) Tibullus served in the military under Messala Corvinus. This friendship proved rewarding for Tibullus because Messala, upon his return to Rome, established his own literary circle. Unlike the members of Maecenas' coterie, Messala and his associates did not promote the policies and beliefs of the emperor Augustus. Tibullus, for example, never mentioned Augustus in his poetry. Nor did he celebrate devotion to duty and fighting for the glory of Rome. Instead, his poems explore the emotions and sorrows aroused by love.

Tibullus' poems—which comprise four books known as the *Corpus Tibullianum*—reflect his quiet and unassuming character as well as his preference for the country and the simple life. His smoothly flowing lines idealize the countryside and mix tenderness with an elegant refinement that raises his poetry above that of his contemporaries.

ELEGIES

BOOK I

I

'Twas Cynthia with her eyes first caused me
    pain,
Unused, before, one burning pang to feel;
Then Love cast down my looks of proud dis-
    dain,
And pressed my neck with unrelenting heel.

3

Following the accepted practice, Propertius made up a fictitious name to which he could address his love poems. Thus, through the ages, his love has been known as Cynthia. What her real name was, we still do not know.

Tibullus won great praise from his contemporaries. The following lines provide a brief example of his style: "You alone are pleasing to me and, except for you, no girl in Rome is beautiful to my eyes. Would that you were able to seem beautiful only to me and displeasing to all others. For only then will I be safe."

Propertius (Sextus Propertius) (around 50 B.C.– after 16 B.C.) is regarded by many as the greatest of Rome's elegiac poets. He enjoyed a comfortable existence until the 40s B.C. when his father died, and then his family's property was endangered when Octavius and Antony confiscated large parcels of land for the benefit of their soldiers. More fortunate than many landholders who lost all their land, Propertius' family retained a considerable portion. Determined that these changed circumstances should not affect her son's future, Propertius' mother took him to Rome to complete his education.

When he came of age, Propertius fell deeply in love with a Roman woman whose beauty and charm inspired him to write a series of poems in her honor. Because so many of the poems in his first book of poems (he wrote four in all) refer to Cynthia and his feelings for her, the book was entitled *Cynthia*.

When Maecenas, the noted literary patron of the Augustan age, came to read *Cynthia*, he was impressed and invited Propertius to join his literary circle. Propertius' second book of verse also contained many poems about Cynthia. In it he often accuses her of being fickle and of not returning his love. Although Propertius wrote on other topics and in a variety of styles, he was unable to do so successfully until after his rejection of Cynthia. The following excerpts illustrate his poetic skill:

Why do you ask "Why?" Love does not have any why.
Love does not know how to yield to great wealth.
To be sure, no one who is insane with love can see.

Vitruvius (Marcus Vitruvius Pollio) (1st century B.C.) is best known as the author of *De Architectura* (Concerning Architecture), a work comprising 10 books and written as a guide for Rome's architects. Vitruvius preferred the Greek architectural style and devoted much of his writing to buildings influenced by this style. In fact, various passages imply that he did not approve of the new designs of the late 1st century B.C., which departed from Greek models toward a more elaborate style meant to reflect the grandeur of Rome. *De Architectura* is of considerable importance, being the only ancient source that provides theoretical information about construction at the time. Included are such topics as city planning, the choice of a proper site, materials used in building, descriptions of public and private buildings, and the techniques of creating and maintaining a city water supply. In the following passage from Book VI, Vitruvius explains why climate should determine the style of a house:

One style of house appears to be appropriate to build in Egypt, another in Spain, still another in Rome. This is due to

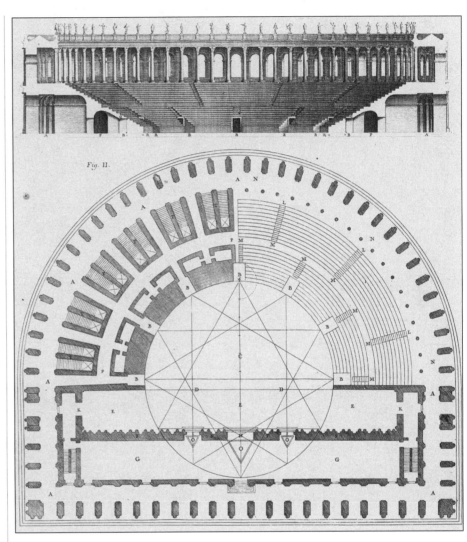

Fig. II.

the fact that one part of the earth lies directly under the sun's course, another is far distant from the sun, and still another lies midway between these two. . . . In the north, houses should be roofed over completely and sheltered as much as possible, with a warm exposure. But, in southern countries that suffer from the sun's heat, houses ought to be built more in the open and facing the north or northeast.

Germanicus (Germanicus Caesar) (15 B.C.–A.D. 19) was the son of the emperor Tiberius' beloved brother,

Vitruvius began Chapter 6 of his book on architecture with the words, "The plan of the theater itself is to be constructed as follows." He then proceeded to describe, in detail, his design for a Roman theater.

Germanicus was next in line to succeed Tiberius as emperor of Rome when death, either from natural causes or by poison, struck at age 49.

Drusus. In A.D. 4, the emperor Augustus adopted Germanicus' uncle Tiberius and ordered Tiberius to adopt Germanicus. The purpose of these adoptions was to create a line of succession: Tiberius was to follow Augustus, Germanicus to follow Tiberius.

Augustus then arranged for a political marriage between Germanicus and his granddaughter Agrippina (known as Agrippina the Elder). Their son Gaius became Rome's third emperor, and their daughter, Agrippina the Younger, was the mother of Rome's fifth emperor.

After his adoption by Tiberius, Germanicus' career accelerated and he quickly proved himself an excellent general who inspired confidence and loyalty among his troops. When Augustus died in A.D. 14, Germanicus' troops refused to recognize Tiberius as the new emperor. For them, Germanicus was the only choice, but Germanicus convinced them to pledge their allegiance to Tiberius.

In A.D. 18, Tiberius commissioned Germanicus to assume supreme command of all the eastern provinces except Syria, which had been given to

Gnaeus Calpurnius Piso. Once in the East, Germanicus found it difficult to work with Piso on many matters.

Piso finally left the region in A.D. 19 and shortly thereafter Germanicus was stricken by a mysterious incurable ailment.

When the widowed Agrippina returned to Rome, she was invited to place her husband's ashes in Augustus' mausoleum. Tiberius, meanwhile, was unable to conceal the hatred he felt for Germanicus and Agrippina and, in A.D. 29 or 30, banished her to the island of Pandataria, where she died in A.D. 33, probably of voluntary starvation.

Sejanus (Lucius Aelius Sejanus) (died A.D. 31) became Rome's second in command after winning the confidence of the emperor Tiberius. Under Augustus, Sejanus' father became commander of the Praetorian Guard, the personal bodyguard of the emperor. When Tiberius succeeded Augustus in A.D. 14, he made Sejanus co-commander with his father, and then sole commander of the Praetorian Guard.

With each successive year, Sejanus increased his influence over Tiberius and even began to plot against possible successors to the emperor. No charges, however, were ever made.

Desirous of more power, Sejanus began suggesting that Tiberius retire to Capri. Tiberius welcomed the advice and, in A.D. 27, left Rome for the island, never to return. With the emperor gone, Sejanus moved to consolidate his position.

But Sejanus had not reckoned with Antonia, the quiet but much respected widow of Tiberius' brother, Drusus. She had repeatedly warned Tiberius to beware of Sejanus, and by A.D. 31 he finally understood that she was right.

Acting through Macro, a trusted Praetorian officer, Tiberius sent a letter to the Senate denouncing Sejanus and accusing him of conspiring against the empire. The senators acted immediately, ordering Sejanus' arrest and execution.

Phaedrus (Gaius Julius Phaedrus) (around 15 B.C.–A.D. 50) was a slave of the emperor Augustus. A native of Macedonia or Thrace, Phaedrus was encouraged to study the Greek and Roman writers and learn Latin. Impressed with Phaedrus' literary ability, Augustus granted him his freedom.

Phaedrus devoted himself entirely to writing fables, unlike most other writers, who used fables as only one element in their works. Phaedrus based his stories to a great extent on those written by the Greek fabulist Aesop, but he amplified the originals with personal experiences and jokes. Phaedrus considered his tales worthy of immortal fame and prided himself on his ability to keep them concise and brief. Following Aesop's example, Phaedrus' characters were animals whose actions were meant to teach a moral lesson. The following fable is titled "The Frog's Complaint."

> Once upon a time, when the sun wished to marry, the frogs raised a shout to the skies. Moved by this noisy clamor, Jupiter, the king of the gods, asked the reason for the complaining. A certain inhabitant of the pond explained, "Now, one sun dries up all the lakes and forces the wretched frogs to die on the dry sand. What will happen if the sun has children?"

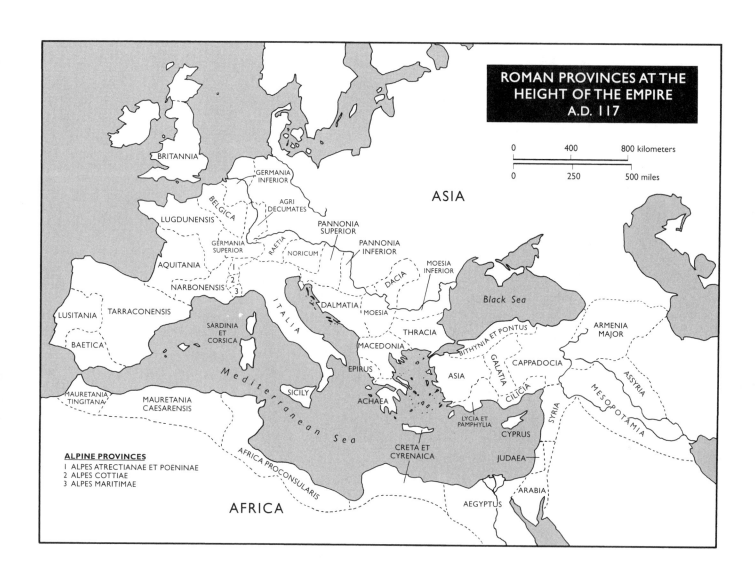

ROMAN PROVINCES AT THE
HEIGHT OF THE EMPIRE
A.D. 117

0   400   800 kilometers

0   250   500 miles

ASIA

BRITANNIA

GERMANIA
INFERIOR

BELGICA

AGRI
DECUMATES

LUGDUNENSIS

PANNONIA
SUPERIOR

GERMANIA
SUPERIOR

RAETIA

NORICUM

PANNONIA
INFERIOR

AQUITANIA

MOESIA
INFERIOR

2

1

NARBONENSIS

3

DACIA

Black Sea

ARMENIA
MAJOR

DALMATIA

LUSITANIA

TARRACONENSIS

ITALIA

SARDINIA
ET
CORSICA

MOESIA

THRACIA

BITHYNIA ET PONTUS

ASSYRIA

BAETICA

MACEDONIA

GALATIA

CAPPADOCIA

MESOPOTAMIA

EPIRUS

ASIA

CILICIA

MAURETANIA
TINGITANA

SICILY

Mediterranean

ACHAEA

SYRIA

MAURETANIA
CAESARENSIS

Sea

LYCIA ET
PAMPHYLIA

CYPRUS

CRETA ET
CYRENAICA

JUDAEA

ALPINE PROVINCES
1 ALPES ATRECTIANAE ET POENINAE
2 ALPES COTTIAE
3 ALPES MARITIMAE

AFRICA PROCONSULARIS

ARABIA

AFRICA

AEGYPTUS

4 The Empire Expands (A.D. 37–98)

Tiberius had followed Augustus as emperor, but his tone and style did not command the respect and trust that Augustus' had. And Rome became increasingly uneasy as each successor of Tiberius assumed power. Constant political intrigue heightened the tension, and the threat of civil war was always in the air.

Still, the empire rested on powerful foundations. Strong frontier defenses gave Rome's subjects a sense of security and stability as they grew wealthy from increased trade with the provinces of the Mediterranean world and the peoples beyond Rome's boundaries.

Part 4 of *Ancient Romans* focuses on Roman emperors who succeeded in expanding the limits of the empire's rule beyond the boundaries established by Augustus, and on writers whose verses mirrored a nation and a people who considered this expansion a sign of success, even though their internal affairs were showing signs of decay.

Claudius (Tiberius Claudius Nero Germanicus)

DEDICATED TO DUTY

W hen members of the Praetorian Guard murdered the hated emperor Caligula in A.D.41, Rome stood at a crossroads. The Senate saw Caligula's death as a perfect opportunity to return Rome to the days of the republic. But the Praetorians favored the new direction Rome had taken, since the continuation of the empire ensured their pay and importance. Both sides knew that the winner in this struggle would be the one who took the most decisive action. While the senators debated, the Guard recognized Caligula's uncle, Tiberius Claudius Nero Germanicus, as the new emperor and threw their power behind him. The fourth Caesar now ruled Rome.

Roman artists were known for the realistic quality of their work. This head of Claudius is a good example: its sculptor clearly saw the emperor as an anxious and, at times, hesitant man.

Claudius

"I decide in favor of the party which has told the truth."

—Claudius, quoted in Suetonius' *The Lives of the Caesars* (around A.D. 120)

BORN

August 1, 10 B.C.
Lugdunum, Gaul

DIED

October 13, A.D. 54
Rome

PROFESSION

Roman emperor

ACCOMPLISHMENTS

Wrote a history of Rome and other works; added the provinces of Britannia, Mauretania, and Thrace to the Roman Empire; ordered a new harbor built at Ostia, Rome's port city; encouraged senators, knights, and public officials to fulfill their duties and responsibilities

To many, Claudius was the least likely candidate to head the Roman Empire. He was around 50 years old and had never held a military post or even trained as a soldier. Until Caligula made him his co-consul in A.D. 37, Claudius had taken no active part in government matters or held any elective office. However, he was the only surviving adult male of the Julian and Claudian families, the families of the Caesars.

According to the Roman historian Suetonius, when Claudius heard the reports of Caligula's murder he naturally feared for his own life. With no time to flee the palace, he looked desperately for a safe hiding place. Thinking the door curtains of a nearby balcony a perfect refuge, he ran behind them. But an observant guardsman saw a pair of feet sticking out from beneath the bottom edge of the curtains and seized Claudius, thinking he was an intruder or a spy. The guard then recognized Claudius and led him to the guards' quarters just outside the city walls.

On January 25, just one day after Caligula's murder, the Praetorian Guard pledged their allegiance to Claudius. Aware that it could not defeat the powerful guard, the Senate did the same. And so it was that the man considered the least likely to succeed now ruled the Mediterranean world. Yet Claudius took his new responsibilities very seriously, even though he knew exactly how his relatives and others felt about him.

As a young boy, Claudius had endured the scorn of all who knew him, including his grandmother Livia and even his mother, Antonia, who called him a monster. Claudius was only a year old when his father Drusus died after falling from a horse during a military campaign in Gaul (present-day France). He was a sickly child who walked awkwardly and had mannerisms that most considered offensive. According to Suetonius, he laughed uncontrollably and had the terrible tendency to slobber at the mouth and develop a runny nose when he became angry. Suetonius also wrote that Claudius stammered when he spoke and had a nervous tic that caused his head to twitch. Even as he grew into a tall, well-built, handsome young man, these traits persisted. When he became emperor, his constant bouts of illness suddenly came to an end, but he still suffered from stomach pains that were sometimes so severe that he considered suicide.

How to treat the young Claudius had always been a delicate matter. Augustus once wrote to Livia: "I have spoken with Tiberius about what is to be done with your grandson Claudius at the coming Games of Mars. . . . The question is whether he is—shall I say?—sane. . . . If not, the Roman people (who enjoy ridiculing abnormal behavior) must not be given a chance to laugh at him and, at the same time, at us." To avoid such a possibility, Augustus made it very clear that he was unwilling to grant Claudius any responsibility. In A.D. 12, Augustus and Tiberius thus came to a joint decision that Claudius was to be excluded from

Although Tiberius sought to erase all memory of his mother, Livia, Claudius was determined to honor his grandmother. In A.D. 43, as a thanksgiving offering to the gods for her safe recovery from an illness 21 years earlier, he dedicated a monument to her in Rome. One of the reliefs on the monument showed figures making a sacrifice in front of the Temple of the Great Mother.

all public activities. Privately they encouraged his love of history and his desire to write.

Unfortunately, none of Claudius' works survive, but it was well known that the Augustan historian Livy recognized his literary talents and encouraged him to write. In addition to a history of Rome, Claudius also wrote an autobiography, 20 books on Etruscan history, eight on the Carthaginians, a small book on playing dice, and an essay on the Roman alphabet, which included a suggestion to add three letters. Later, after Claudius became emperor, he incorporated these three letters into the Latin alphabet, but the Romans discontinued their use after his death.

Among Claudius' first decrees as emperor was a general amnesty for all who had opposed Caligula. He did, however, exclude a few of the colonels and centurions most directly involved in the conspiracy. Claudius then granted his grandmother Livia divine honors, a move her son Tiberius had adamantly rejected. For himself he

sought no special privileges and refused the title *Imperator* (Commander), because he was well aware that he had never led an army nor seen active duty.

Although most senators resigned themselves to accepting Claudius as the new emperor, a handful resolved to return Rome to a republican form of government. In A.D. 42, Scribonius, the governor of the Roman province of Dalmatia on the Adriatic Sea, rebelled against Claudius. Supported by a group of senators, Scribonius seemed certain to win. Then, just five days after the revolt broke out, soldiers assigned to placing garlands on the eagles attached to the military standards that were carried before each marching unit found it impossible to keep the garlands in place. When they also found that they could not lift their standards into position they panicked, thinking the gods disapproved of their part in the conspiracy, and they refused to fight.

Despite the brevity of the rebellion, Claudius now believed he was in constant danger. Aware that many senators had supported the conspiracy, Claudius developed a distrust for the Senate that he was never able to overcome. At the same time, Claudius' relationship with the *equites* (the class just below the senators) was becoming more cordial, and he promoted legislation to offer the *equites* new opportunities. Still, Claudius did not trust the *equites* completely, and a growing number of foiled conspiracies and assassination attempts only made him more suspicious. Despite stepped-up security measures and a series of treason trials, he began to share the fear of assassination that had so tormented Tiberius.

Unlike Tiberius, however, Claudius did not withdraw from public life. Rather, he continued to participate actively in every phase of government, enacting decrees and implementing policies he considered in Rome's best interests. He also began to rely more on his wife and individual freedmen for advice.

When Claudius became emperor in A.D. 41, he was married to his third wife, Valeria Messalina, the grandniece of Augustus. His children by his first wife had died in infancy, and his only surviving child was a daughter by his second wife. With Messalina, Claudius fathered two more children: a daughter, Octavia, who later married Nero (Rome's fourth emperor), and a son, Germanicus (later called Britannicus). Messalina quickly won Claudius' confidence but did not become involved politically during the first years of their marriage.

In A.D. 43, Claudius ordered the invasion of Britain, the first such command since Julius Caesar had invaded the island in 55 and 54 B.C. Claudius' actions came after the British threatened revenge for a Senate refusal to return certain deserters. Claudius himself accompanied the troops, but he fought no battles and remained on the island only a few months. Soon after, Britannia was annexed as Rome's newest province, with Camulodunum (present-day Colchester) its capital.

Unlike his predecessors Augustus and Tiberius, who believed in consolidation rather than expansion, Claudius was ready to increase the number of provinces under Rome's control. Mauretania, in North Africa, and Thrace, on the northern coast of the Aegean, followed Britannia as new Roman provinces. Accompanying this expansion came several changes in government policy. Although Claudius did not favor granting citizenship to every Roman subject, he did grant those rights to several groups in the provinces. For this he was severely criticized by those who held that only Romans should rule the empire and that such an extension of rights would weaken Rome.

During Claudius' rule several people from the western provinces rose through the political ranks to become Roman consuls. The Gauls especially gained Claudius' favor and won increased privileges under the changed rules. Claudius believed that well-organized cities were the key to a province's welfare and accordingly granted special privileges to several strategically located towns.

Claudius also established colonies of veterans in outlying districts, where they might act as a deterrent to hostile neighbors. Yet he was very careful not to let his provincial policies anger the powerful Parthians to the east or Germans to the north. Like his predecessors, his goal was to maintain peace with Rome's neighbors.

The administration of justice was one duty that Claudius enjoyed. As the years passed, he devoted himself more and more to judicial matters, serving as judge at the senatorial courts as well as his own imperial court. Suetonius reports that his decisions were quite unpredictable, especially since he often fell asleep in the middle of a case. Yet Claudius did act wisely and justly on many occasions, although at other times his judgments appeared thoughtless and hasty. The fate of a man found guilty of forgery provides one example of the emperor's erratic behavior. When the crowd attending the trial heard the guilty verdict, they shouted: "He ought to have his hands cut off!" Immediately, and with little thought for the consequences, Claudius summoned an executioner to act on the suggestion.

In another matter, when a Greek was brought to trial for illegally claiming rights of Roman citizenship, there arose the question as to what he should wear during his trial: the toga of Roman citizenship, or the mantle worn by Greeks. Claudius ordered the man to wear the toga when he was being defended and the mantle when accused.

While Claudius preferred rendering judgments to administering government affairs, he did maintain a watchful eye on all matters under his control, especially the proper upkeep of Rome itself. When a terrible fire ravaged one area of the city, he summoned help from other city districts. He even recruited firefighters and paid them himself for their services.

Claudius also turned his attention to the construction of public works and ordered a new harbor built at Ostia, Rome's port city, which would ensure the steady arrival of necessary supplies from the provinces. To provide enough water for the ever-increasing population of Rome, Claudius ordered the completion of an aqueduct begun by Caligula and oversaw the building of a new one.

Over the years, Claudius' most trusted associates were not the senators or knights but rather his freedmen (former slaves who had been freed by their masters or who had saved enough money to buy their freedom), who were well educated and of Greek or Hellenistic background. The most influential freedmen were Narcissus and Pallas, whose power almost equaled that of Claudius.

Messalina's influence on Claudius grew steadily until many Romans believed that she and the freedmen really ruled the empire. In A.D. 48, however, Messalina abused her position by conspiring against Claudius with her lover Gaius Silius. In open defiance of her husband, Messalina and Silius were joined in a marriage ceremony while Claudius was at Ostia, overseeing the progress of the new harbor. Ever loyal

to his master, Narcissus reported this outrage to Claudius. Stunned and disoriented, Claudius ordered the immediate execution of the two lovers. Narcissus now enjoyed the complete trust of his emperor—but not for long.

When Claudius decided to marry again, he chose his brother Germanicus' daughter Agrippina, 15 years his junior. Known to history as Agrippina the Younger, she was also the great-granddaughter of Augustus. Helping to arrange the marriage was Pallas, Claudius' freedman and finance minister as well as a friend and the personal advisor of Agrippina. In the months that followed, Narcissus gradually lost his influence with the emperor and was forced by Agrippina to commit suicide.

Agrippina soon proved to be even more domineering than Messalina. Claudius, who was aging, had turned his thoughts to choosing a successor. His son Britannicus was the most likely candidate, but Agrippina had other ideas. She favored Nero, her own son by a previous marriage, and was determined to see him emperor. In A.D. 50, Agrippina finally convinced Claudius to adopt the 13-year-old Nero and name him Britannicus' guardian.

When Claudius died suddenly in A.D. 54 and Nero succeeded to the throne, it was widely rumored that the cause of death was a dish of poisoned mushrooms given him by Agrippina. The allegation was never proved.

Soon after Claudius' death, the Roman Senate voted to deify him, the first emperor to be so honored since Augustus.

FURTHER READING

Levick, Barbara. *Claudius*. New Haven: Yale University Press, 1990.

Suetonius. *The Lives of the Caesars*. Translated by J. C. Rolfe. Loeb Classical Library. New York: Macmillan, 1914.

Nero
(Lucius Domitius Ahenobarbus)

THE SINGING EMPEROR

W hen Claudius died in A.D. 54 and Nero found himself emperor of Rome at the age of 16, it was only the latest in a series of unexpected events in his life. At the center of all these events was his mother, the strong-willed Agrippina the Younger. When Nero was only two years old, his uncle, the emperor Caligula, had banished Agrippina to the island of Pandataria and allowed Nero to live with his aunt Domitia Lepida. After Nero's father, Gnaeus Domitius Ahenobarbus, died the following year, the young boy's situation grew steadily worse until finally Caligula decided to claim Nero's inheritance for himself.

But the following year assassins took Caligula's life, and Claudius came to power. Claudius recalled Agrippina and restored Nero's inheritance to him. Once in Rome, Agrippina devoted herself to her son and provided him with an excellent education.

In A.D. 49, Claudius had his wife Messalina executed for adultery and unseemly conduct, married Agrippina—and Nero suddenly found himself the emperor's stepson. Agrippina now aimed to have her son declared Rome's next emperor. She convinced Claudius to adopt Nero, who, as a

Accounts of Nero's reign have so focused on the cruelty he inflicted and condoned that many of the good measures passed while Seneca and Burrus advised him are forgotten.

The illustrator of this 17th-century reconstruction of a scene in the *Circus* seemed determined to include every sort of gladiatorial activity. There are men on horseback, unarmed wrestlers, gladiators fighting wild animals, and gladiators fighting singly and in groups. For the Romans, however, the *Circus* was a U-shaped building for chariot racing (a sport that Nero loved), not gladiators. Chariots would race around the *spina* or barrier in the middle. (The illustrator here, however, included no chariots.)

result, became the designated heir in place of Britannicus, Claudius' son from a previous marriage.

Four years later, in A.D. 54, Claudius died suddenly, possibly the victim of poison administered by Agrippina. Almost immediately, the Praetorian Guard hailed Nero the new emperor and took him to their camp to address the troops. Aware of the power of the guard, the senators had little choice but to accept Nero's accession. Helping Agrippina realize her ambitions was Sextus Afranius Burrus, the commander of the guard.

By law, Nero was too young to rule the vast empire. He needed a regent, someone to advise him and make the necessary decisions. Naturally, Agrippina designated herself to fill that role. At first, Nero seemed only too willing to agree to his mother's wishes. When the first coins of Nero's rule appeared, the front side showed Agrippina facing

Nero, with Agrippina's head on the right, the position of honor. Her name and title as regent appeared on the front, while Nero's name was on the reverse.

Agrippina's dominance did not last long. Burrus had become increasingly influential in political circles, together with the respected Stoic philosopher Seneca, whom Agrippina had brought to the palace to be her son's tutor. The two men disliked Agrippina's overbearing personality and began encouraging Nero to make decisions on his own.

In A.D. 56 Agrippina was forced to retire from politics, and Burrus and Seneca became the two most powerful figures in the Roman empire. Under their guidance, Nero ruled quite responsibly, declaring that he planned to model his rule on that of the revered Augustus. He abolished the secret treason trials Claudius had conducted as a way of eliminating threats to his person and rule, causing many leading citizens to live in constant fear of condemnation for some petty, unjust cause. Nero also attacked corruption and ended the flagrant abuse of power exercised by favored freedmen. As Nero granted the Senate more and more authority, the mutual distrust that had developed under Claudius gradually eased.

Unlike Claudius who had devoted much of his time to deciding legal cases, Nero preferred to rule only on those matters brought to the imperial court. The rest he left to the assigned judges. Nor did he make quick decisions, but, according to Suetonius, deferred his judgment to the day after the case was heard so that he might study and review the arguments and the law involved.

According to ancient accounts, Nero disliked unnecessary bloodshed and forbade the killing of gladiators and condemned criminals in the arena. To ensure the observance of these and other laws, Nero imposed strict penalties which were regularly enforced. Nero also considered slaves in his legislation and granted them the right to file a civil complaint against an unfair master.

Yet, as the years passed, Burrus and Seneca devoted ever more energy to ruling Rome and Nero looked for ways to spend his free time. His greatest enjoyments were music and the theater. He showed an increasing preference for anything Greek, from literature to hairstyles, and even began wearing Greek-style clothing instead of the Roman toga.

The historian Suetonius relates that in the months following his accession, Nero called Terpnus, the greatest lyre player of the time, to the palace and asked him to perform. Soon after, Nero began studying the lyre himself. During singing exercises, he would lie on his back with a slab of lead on his chest, a drill the ancients believed helped strengthen a singer's voice. He

refused to eat apples and other foods said to harm the vocal chords. On certain days he abstained from eating bread; on others he ate only chives in oil, a combination that was supposed to benefit the voice.

Agrippina strongly disapproved of her son's new interests and voiced her opinions openly. When Nero heard of these remarks, he resolved to rid himself of his mother forever. According to the historian Tacitus, he tried to kill her by providing her with a defective boat, but when the vessel sank Agrippina managed to swim to shore. Nero, however, was not to be deterred and he hired an assassin to complete the task.

Three years later, in A.D. 62, Nero arranged to have his wife, Octavia, killed. Their marriage had been purely a political arrangement; Octavia was the daughter of Claudius. Nero's desire to be free of Octavia intensified after he met Poppaea Sabina, the beautiful young wife of the Roman senator Marcus Salvius Otho. Unfortunately for Nero, Poppaea died soon after he married her.

Nero's growing readiness to shed blood was due in part to the loss of Burrus' and Seneca's steadying influence. Burrus had died in A.D. 62; Seneca, aware that his ability to sway Nero would be crippled without Burrus' aid, retired from political service. Seneca also disliked Nero's new advisor, Tigellinus, who seemed to encourage the emperor's every vice. The most horrifying of these was Nero's habit of donning a disguise and prowling the streets at night, looting stores and murdering innocent men on their way home.

Gradually, Nero forgot his government responsibilities and immersed himself in a life of pleasure. Sometime around A.D. 59 or 60, he played the lyre for the first time before an audience. In the years that followed, he began performing before larger and larger groups. Because he enjoyed

Nero

BORN
December 15, A.D. 37
Antium, Italy

DIED
June 9, A.D. 68
Rome

PROFESSIONS
Roman emperor

ACCOMPLISHMENTS
Patronized the arts; rebuilt Rome after a disastrous fire; fostered peace throughout the empire; concluded a lasting agreement concerning Armenia; crushed a revolt by Queen Boudicca in Britain

"Hidden talents count for nothing."

—Nero, quoted in Suetonius' *The Lives of the Caesars* (around A.D. 120)

writing poetry, he often composed his own lyrics. He began racing chariots, a sport that had always fascinated him.

Nero also performed a wide variety of roles in the theater. According to Suetonius, he forbade any spectator from leaving the theater during his performances. Because of this decree, pregnant women sometimes had to give birth right in the theater, and men who could not stand the boredom any longer often escaped over the rear wall.

In July A.D. 64, a fire broke out in the Circus Maximus (where the chariot races were held) area and, fanned by the wind, spread across Rome. The fire raged for six days and did catastrophic damage to the city. At the time, Nero was at his palace in Antium. He immediately rushed back to the city, allowed his gardens to be used as temporary relief shelters, ordered extra food shipped in, and even reduced the cost of corn to help those devastated by the disaster. But few Romans gave him credit for these efforts, believing that Nero himself had started the fire. Everyone knew that Nero had been planning to expand his palace but had found it difficult to do so because of buildings crowding around it. The Romans reasoned that the easiest way for Nero to gain the space he needed seemed to be to burn whatever stood in the way. As their anger grew, the Romans even charged that Nero was playing the lyre and singing while the city burned. Eventually, this untruth was accepted as fact and entered many historical accounts.

Whether or not Nero actually set the fire, the ancient accounts differ in their opinion on this matter, it gave him the opportunity to begin work on his *Domus Aurea* (Golden House). When it became known that the emperor's new palace would cover one-third of the city, the people expressed

such resentment that Nero decided to put the blame for the fire on the members of a new religious group known as Christians. He then ordered the arrest and execution of all those who professed their belief in Christianity. This brutal action set a precedent followed by several later emperors.

Having diverted the anger of the public, Nero turned again to his *Domus Aurea*. According to Suetonius, the entrance hall was large enough to hold a 120-foot-high statue of Nero, and the mile-long main corridor was lined with stately columns. To complement his ideas of grandeur and give the effect of a city within his palace walls, Nero ordered a series of buildings constructed around an enormous pool. Certain areas of the house Nero ordered overlaid with gold and studded with precious stones. For the lavishly decorated dining rooms, he directed that the ceilings be made of carved ivory panels that could be opened to allow flowers or perfume from hidden sprinklers to descend upon the guests. Sea water flowed from the taps in the bathing areas. Upon the palace's completion, Nero joyfully cried, "Now, I can finally live like a human being!"

The *Domus Aurea* was not Nero's only extravagance. Believing his funds to be limitless, Nero commissioned the construction of other lavish buildings, including an enormous covered bath surrounded by columns near the Bay of Naples. Nero also spent vast sums on his personal effects, never wanting to wear the same clothes twice. Nero ruled that only he, as emperor, had the privilege of wearing clothes dyed purple. Purple dye, which was expensive and difficult to obtain in quantity, was used chiefly by royalty and high-ranking dignitaries.

Such extravagances quickly exhausted the public treasury, and Nero had to seek other ways of raising money. He took back gifts he had awarded to Greek cities, seized the property of those he believed guilty of failing to show him proper gratitude, and depreciated the coinage system, lowering the value of the coins then used as currency. Suetonius quotes Nero's order to a new public official: "You know what I need! Let's make sure that nobody is left with anything."

Despite Nero's irresponsibility and lack of attention to the needs of the empire, his rule was largely peaceful. Revolts did erupt here and there, but none resulted in the loss of territory. One of the most violent was a rebellion led by the British Queen Boudicca in A.D. 60, which resulted in a wholesale slaughter of Romans and Roman sympathizers before it was put down. In the East, a potentially destructive war with the Armenians was avoided by a treaty in which Rome recognized Tiridates as king of an independent Armenia, in return for Tiridates' agreement to respect Rome's interests in the region.

The agreement with Tiridates and the defeat of Boudicca were major achievements, but the deteriorating situation in Rome had effects throughout the empire. Romans of all classes now questioned Nero's right to remain emperor. In his attempt to curb unrest, Nero revived the detested treason law and many Romans lost their lives to his whims.

There were many reported plots hatched against Nero, the most serious being a conspiracy headed by Gaius Calpurnius Piso. The details are sketchy, but Tacitus claimed that the conspirators included senators, knights, soldiers, and philosophers. When Nero called upon one conspirator, Subrius Flavus, to explain his actions, Flavus said, "Because I hated you. For as long as you deserved my respect, I was as loyal as any of your soldiers. I started to hate you after you murdered your mother and your wife and became a charioteer, an actor, and an arsonist." For some reason, Nero did not punish all the conspirators, but among those who died were Seneca and the poet Lucan. In the months that followed, Nero eliminated several army chiefs, including the respected Corbulo, who had skillfully negotiated a treaty with the Armenians.

In A.D. 66, Nero traveled to Greece, whose civilization and culture he so admired. As a gift to the nation and all it represented, he gave the Greeks their "freedom," that is, the right not to pay taxes to Rome. He also entered every athletic and dramatic contest being staged. His hosts made sure that he always won. Accounts tell of his gaining more than 1,800 prizes, including first prize for a chariot race in which he fell off his chariot.

Nero's enjoyment was cut short by a sudden summons from Helius, one of the freedmen Nero had left in charge of affairs at Rome. In the 15 months Nero had been away, conditions at home had steadily worsened. Amid great fanfare, Nero re-entered Rome in January A.D. 68. But he soon left for Neapolis (present-day Naples), whose Greek atmosphere he preferred. Nero seemed oblivious to the fact that Rome was seething with hatred for him, and when news reached him that Roman troops in Gaul had revolted, he continued watching the athletic contests at a gymnasium and refused to consider the matter for eight days.

When Nero finally returned to Rome, he made light of the growing crisis and immersed himself in experiments with new types of musical instruments. Then in March a new crisis erupted: Spain's provincial governor, Servius Sulpicius Galba, withdrew his allegiance from Nero and declared himself the new emperor of Rome. This time Nero reacted—he fell down in a faint. And when messengers arrived with reports of unrest among Rome's troops in the East, the situation became extremely critical.

The Senate decided to act on its own and ordered that Nero be killed according to ancient custom. Upon asking what this meant, Nero was told that he would be stripped naked, have his head placed in a wooden form of a yoke, and whipped. Nero refused to endure such an ignominious death, but he had few alternatives. Deserted by the Praetorian Guard, his trusty freedmen, and even his personal bodyguard, Nero saw escape from the city as his only chance for safety. With the few companions who had remained faithful to him, he fled toward the outskirts of the city. As he did so, he supposedly cried, "Ah! What an artist perishes with me!" Before he had gone very far, the sound of horses' hooves along the road told him that his arrest was imminent. With the aid of his secretary, he took a dagger and stabbed himself in the throat.

FURTHER READING

Grant, Michael. *Nero*. London: Weidenfeld & Nicolson, 1970.

Powers, Elizabeth. *Nero*. New York: Chelsea House, 1988.

Sienkiewicz, Henryk. *Quo Vadis?* Translated by Jeremiah Curtin. New York: Heritage, 1960.

Suetonius. *The Lives of the Caesars*. Translated by J. C. Rolfe. Loeb Classical Library. New York: Macmillan, 1914.

Warmington, Brian H. *Nero, Reality and Legend*. New York: Norton, 1969.

Weigall, Arthur E. P. B. *Nero, the Singing Emperor of Rome*. New York: Putnam, 1930.

Agrippina the Younger (Agrippina Minor)

A DETERMINED WOMAN

ew Romans could boast of a more distinguished lineage than Agrippina the Younger. And few knew as well as she how politics and political favoritism controlled life in Rome. Her father was Germanicus, the stepson and, later, adopted son of the emperor Augustus. Her mother was the granddaughter of Augustus who became known to history as Agrippina the Elder.

Born in A.D. 15 in Germany, where her father had been sent to command the Roman legions stationed there, Agrippina had a happy childhood. But political maneuverings and jealousy quickly disrupted her family's life after Germanicus died from a brief, unexplained illness in A.D. 19. As suspicion grew that Germanicus had been poisoned, the emperor Tiberius became the prime suspect. Calm was soon restored, but relations between Germanicus' widow and Tiberius remained strained. Tiberius even refused to grant Agrippina the Elder permission to remarry, and in A.D. 29 he banished her to the island of Pandataria, where she died of starvation in A.D. 33.

Naturally, these tumultuous events affected Agrippina the Younger, who was only 14 at the time of her mother's banishment. She did not accompany her mother into exile, because she was required elsewhere—in A.D. 28, she had married a grandnephew of Augustus, Gnaeus Domitius Ahenobarbus. That she was only 13 was not unusual, for it was customary for Romans, especially those in the upper classes, to arrange suitable marriages for their young daughters.

In A.D. 37, Agrippina gave birth to a son. Named for his father, this boy would later be granted the name Nero and become Rome's fifth emperor. In the same year, Agrippina's brother Gaius (known later as Caligula) succeeded Tiberius as emperor of Rome. For two years all went well. Then Caligula was needed in Germany to crush a conspiracy launched to dethrone him. After learning that Agrippina was involved in the plot to wrest control of the empire from him and give it to Marcus Aemilius Lepidus, her close friend, Caligula banished Agrippina to the island of Pandataria and confiscated her property. Leaving her son Nero in the care of his aunt, Agrippina set sail for the same island where her mother had perished only a few years earlier.

But Agrippina was not destined to suffer the same fate. In January A.D. 41, assassins ended Caligula's rule and Agrippina's uncle Claudius was hailed Rome's fourth emperor. Soon after his accession, Claudius allowed Agrippina to return to Rome and Nero. Records show that she married a Roman named Passienus Crispus. When he died unexpect-

The figures carved on this gemstone from Rome that dates to about A.D. 48 or 49 are most likely Claudius and his wife, Agrippina the Younger. Facing them on the left are Germanicus and his wife, Agrippina the Elder.

Agrippina the Younger

BORN

A.D. 15
Ara Ubiorum, Germany

DIED

A.D. 59
Near Naples

PROFESSION

Wife of emperor Claudius, mother of emperor Nero; regent for Nero

ACCOMPLISHMENTS

Advised her husband Claudius on political matters; after Claudius' death acted as regent for her 16-year-old son Nero, who was too young to rule; first woman to wield such power in Rome

edly, in A.D. 49, there were rumors that he had been poisoned. Whether or not Agrippina killed her husband, she did marry Claudius that same year. Then, when Claudius adopted Nero the following year and favored Nero as successor over his own son Britannicus, many Romans became convinced that Agrippina was plotting the demise of yet another husband.

Agrippina began to exercise greater and greater control over Claudius and public affairs. Yielding to her wishes, Claudius recalled the philosopher Seneca from exile and Agrippina immediately employed him as a tutor for Nero. Then, in an attempt to consolidate her power, Agrippina shifted Claudius' loyalty from his trusted freedman Narcissus to another named Burrus. Agrippina distrusted Narcissus because he had opposed her marriage to Claudius. Burrus, on the other hand, not only favored Agrippina but was also a close friend of Seneca's.

In October A.D. 54, Claudius suddenly died, possibly from eating a dish of poisoned mushrooms. Suspicion naturally fell on Agrippina, but nothing came of accusations against her because the Praetorian Guard immediately hailed Nero as the new emperor. Aware of the guard's power, the Senate had no choice but to ratify their declaration. Agrippina was now the mother of Rome's fifth emperor. Because Nero was only 16, she assumed the role of regent.

Agrippina welcomed her new responsibilities almost as if she had prepared for them all her life. The first coins issued under Nero's rule bore the profiles of Agrippina and Nero. Agrippina, however, was given more prominence because her name and titles were on the front of the coin, while those of Nero were on the reverse.

> *"It was I who made you emperor."*
>
> —Agrippina speaking to Nero, quoted in *The History of Rome* by Dio Cassius (A.D. 150–235)

Agrippina was extremely influential in political matters and regularly listened to all discussions of public business, often from behind a specially hung curtain so that her presence would not be noticed. Reports soon circulated that she was once again ruthlessly eliminating all potential rivals. But Nero soon began to assert himself, and when a second set of coins was issued, only a year after the first, they had his own name and titles on the front. Before long, Agrippina's likeness disappeared altogether from the coins, and Nero even moved her out of the imperial palace and into her own house. But Agrippina still had the support of many Romans, who honored her as the daughter of the beloved Germanicus.

Not one to be intimidated, Agrippina openly expressed her dislike of Nero's preference for Greek customs and the theater and criticized his mistress, Poppaea Sabina. When these remarks were reported to Nero, he deprived Agrippina of her honors and then had people sue and publicly mock her constantly. Agrippina would not be silenced, however, and let it be known that she was prepared to oppose Nero openly. As a result, Nero saw murder as his only course. The Roman historian Suetonius wrote that Nero tried three times to poison his mother but, aware of his intentions, Agrippina protected herself by taking an antidote before eating. Nero then rigged a device in her bedroom that would cause the ceiling panels to fall on her while she slept. This attempt would have succeeded if one of those involved had not decided to warn Agrippina.

Increasingly desperate to be rid of his mother, Nero invited Agrippina to his home near the Bay of Naples. This time he sent her out in a boat specially designed to sink once it reached open water. But again the resourceful Agrippina outmaneuvered her son, freeing herself from the sinking vessel and swimming to shore.

Nero now abandoned all pretense and, in A.D. 59, when Agrippina was 44 years old, had his mother put to the sword by one of her freedmen. Afterward he circulated the story that Agrippina had been involved in a plot on his life. Nero then sent the same message in an official report to the Senate. The latter agreed with his actions since, according to Roman law, death was the punishment prescribed for treason. Despite concern that Agrippina's supporters might organize a revolt, nothing materialized.

FURTHER READING

Balsdon, J. P. V. D. *Roman Women: Their History and Habits*. Westport, Conn.: Greenwood, 1962.

Bauman, Richard A. *Women and Politics in Ancient Rome*. New York: Routledge, 1992.

Seneca
(Lucius Annaeus Seneca)

"A LIFE WITHOUT PURPOSE IS EMPTY"

S eneca had always hoped to avoid being forced by the emperor to choose suicide or death by execution. But political events had not followed his wishes and, as life ebbed from his body, he sought strength in the family values instilled in him as a youth—patience and fortitude.

Seneca was born sometime around 4 B.C., in the prosperous southern Spanish city of Córdoba. His family, wealthy and respected, belonged to the class known as the *equites*. Seneca's father was a well-known rhetorician (a teacher of the art of speaking); his mother, Helvia, was also well educated and highly regarded in the community. The names of Seneca's two brothers have also entered the history books: Gallio, who presided over the trial of the Christian apostle Paul in about A.D. 52, and Marcus Annaeus Mela, who fathered the famed writer Lucan.

Seneca spent his early years in Spain, then accompanied his aunt to Rome, where he studied rhetoric, grammar, and other subjects. His parents moved to Rome during Seneca's school years, and their connections won him entry into Rome's highest circles. As was the custom for boys of

Best known today for his philosophical writings, Seneca was also a money-lender, an imperial tutor, a playwright, and an influential palace adviser.

his class and upbringing, Seneca practiced at the law courts, but the subject that interested him most was philosophy.

Seneca had been plagued with poor health since early childhood. Sometime in the late A.D. 20s, his physical condition deteriorated to such an extent that he left Rome to spend time in the hot climate of Egypt, where Gaius Galerius, his aunt's husband, was stationed as governor. In A.D. 31, Seneca returned to Rome after Galerius' tour of duty was over.

Again he entered the law courts, this time to begin his career as an advocate and politician. Under the emperor Caligula, Seneca gained the office of quaestor, but the unpredictable Caligula was grievously offended when he saw that Seneca's writings and legal arguments were winning him fame. Caligula began to deride Seneca as a "mere textbook orator." There were rumors that Caligula even ordered Seneca killed but rescinded the command after being convinced that Seneca was so sickly that he would soon die of natural causes.

Seneca would find life even more difficult under Caligula's successor, Claudius. In A.D. 41, Claudius banished Seneca to the island of Corsica on charges of committing adultery with Julia Livilla, Caligula's sister and Claudius' niece. Whether Seneca was actually guilty is unknown, but many sources blame his exile on Claudius' wife, Messalina, whose jealous hatred of Julia was well known. According to the historian Suetonius, Seneca never had an opportunity to defend himself against the vague charges.

Seneca's eight lonely years on Corsica were a severe punishment for a man who enjoyed culture and the bustling activity of a metropolis. However, he tried to accept his fate calmly, devoting much of his time to studying and writing. In an essay entitled "Consolation to Helvia," Seneca attempted to cheer his mother and convince her that exile was quite tolerable. In fact, passages from several of his writings indicate that he longed to be recalled to Rome.

Fortunately for Seneca, events in Rome eventually worked in his favor. In A.D. 48, when Claudius learned that Messalina was plotting against him, he convicted her of treason and ordered her killed. The following year, Claudius married his niece, the willful Agrippina. She thought Seneca would be the perfect tutor for Nero, her son by a previous marriage, and convinced Claudius to recall the man he had exiled eight years earlier.

At that point life changed radically for Seneca. He returned to Rome, reentered politics, and married Pompeia Paulina, a young woman of wealth and influence. Despite the great difference in their ages, the marriage—unlike many of the time—was one of mutual respect and love. Yet, it was his new position as tutor to Agrippina's son that gradually made Seneca one of the most powerful men in Rome.

The early 50s witnessed a steady increase in Agrippina's influence until it seemed that she had become the real power in Rome. Advising her were two trusted allies, Seneca and Burrus, the head of the Praetorian Guard. When Claudius died suddenly in A.D. 54 and the 16-year-old Nero succeeded him, Seneca and Burrus made many of the day-to-day decisions affecting the government of Rome and its provinces.

For five years, Nero willingly followed the advice of Seneca and Burrus. Agrippina remained a force, but Nero resented her overbearing personality

Seneca

and wished to be free of her. Seneca and Burrus well understood this power struggle and allowed Nero to gradually force his mother out of politics. In the years that followed, they reversed some of the laws established by Nero's predecessors. They greatly reduced the number of treason trials and openly discouraged the idea of accusing someone of treason just to confiscate his property. They tried to enforce rules that would provide for more humane treatment of slaves and allowed the Senate to once again play a major role in the government.

After Rome's legions quelled a revolt led by Queen Boudicca in Britain, Seneca and Burrus won passage of new and fairer laws to govern the area. They also brought about a settlement with Parthia over the status of Armenia, achieving peaceful relations in an area long afflicted with war. Historians have come to refer to these years of achievement as the *Quinquennium Neronis* (the five-year period of Nero, or the golden age of Nero).

It is not known whether Seneca played a part in Nero's murder of Agrippina, but he did write the letter that Nero sent to the Senate in defense of his actions. However, Seneca found it increasingly difficult to curb Nero's inclination toward crime and vice. Burrus' death in A.D. 62 effectively brought an end to Seneca's influence as others, including the freedman Tigellinus, soon won Nero's confidence. Unfortunately, these men did not concern themselves with the welfare of the empire but sought instead to enrich themselves.

Eventually, it became clear that Nero envied Seneca's wealth. The emperor had run up enormous debts and had confiscated the property of a number of Romans to replenish his capital. Seneca also learned that Nero's new

advisors were encouraging the emperor to rid himself of his tutor and govern on his own. They spoke disapprovingly of Seneca's vast gardens and villas, noting that they were more magnificent than those of the emperor.

Sensing that his days were numbered, Seneca approached Nero, requested permission to retire from public service, and offered to give the emperor all his possessions. With little hesitation Nero approved Seneca's retirement, but he refused to accept the gift of his property. Seneca was not to be fooled, however. Aware that his position was precarious, he withdrew from the city, traveled about southern Italy, and rarely entertained or visited with people. Seneca wrote nine "closet" tragedies, that is, plays which were meant to be read, not performed. He also wrote essays about natural history and composed many letters to his friend Lucilius. Ultimately, Seneca's fame has rested on his writings rather than his achievements as Nero's advisor.

Ironically, Seneca never considered literature his main occupation. It is Seneca's philosophical essays that have been adopted and adapted through the centuries.

For three years, Seneca avoided Nero's wrath, but in A.D. 65, Seneca was linked with an unsuccessful conspiracy led by Gaius Calpurnius Piso. Whether the charge was true or false, it gave Nero an excuse to get rid of his former tutor. Before long, an imperial messenger arrived at Seneca's villa, four miles outside Rome, and handed him a message from Nero. Seneca remained calm as he read that he had only two options—execution or suicide. He chose the latter. When several friends who were with him at the time began to weep, Seneca reminded them of the lessons of philosophy, especially the

BORN
Around 4 B.C.
Córdoba, Spain

DIED
A.D. 65
Near Rome

PROFESSION
Statesman, philosopher, playwright

ACCOMPLISHMENTS
Adviser to the emperor Nero for five years; promoted legislation to liberalize Roman policies and promote peace in the provinces; wrote nine tragedies, a variety of philosophical essays, and numerous letters expressing his moral sentiments

> "No one cares how well he lives, but how long. Yet for all it is possible to affect how well he lives, but to no one for how long."
>
> —from *Epistulae Morales* (Moral Letters, around A.D. 56)

philosophy of the Stoics. The latter believed the wise person should live in harmony with nature through reason, thereby remaining unmoved by passion or reason.

Unwilling to let her husband die alone or to survive without him, Seneca's wife vowed to share his fate. With the same instrument, they opened the veins on both their arms. According to the Roman historian Tacitus, Seneca did not want his wife to see the great pain he was suffering and ordered Paulina taken to her room. When Nero heard what she had done, he immediately dispatched a messenger with orders to bind up her wounds and nurse her back to health. Paulina did survive, but only for a few years. She never regained her health and, according to ancient accounts, her coloring remained a ghostly white.

Though Nero had found it easy to end Seneca's life, he found it impossible to control his influence. In fact, many later emperors would find great consolation reading Seneca. And, as Christianity spread across the Roman world, Christian writers and teachers drew upon Seneca's essays. During the Middle Ages, his moral essays were widely read and adapted. European writers in the 16th century, especially in France and England, modeled their plays on his tragedies. In fact, many of his ideas seem as relevant today as they did when Seneca first set them down.

In one of his letters to Lucilius, Seneca counseled against using travel as a cure for unhappiness:

> You may cross the vast sea, yet your faults will follow you wherever you travel. Do you ask why your flight does not help you? It is because you flee with yourself. You must lay aside the burdens of the spirit, for until you do, no place will please you.

In his *Essay on Providence*, Seneca advised on the proper attitude toward the difficulties experienced in life:

> To be prosperous at all times and to live without any mental upsets is to remain ignorant of one half of nature. You may be a worthy individual, but how should I know that if Fate grants you no chance to prove your courage? No individual can know himself without a trial. . . . Misfortune is an opportunity for courage. The recruit turns pale at the thought of being wounded; the veteran who knows that he has often won the victory after losing blood looks boldly at his wound.

In another letter to Lucilius, Seneca spoke of the equality between slaves and masters:

> It pleases me to hear that you live on friendly terms with your slaves. This is only proper for a wise and well-educated man like yourself. Yet, people will say, "They are slaves." Nay, rather . . . they are fellow slaves if you consider the facts. . . . Show me a person who is not a slave, for one individual is a slave to his passions, another to greed, another to ambition. All humans are slaves to fear.

Finally, in an essay entitled *Concerning the Tranquility of the Spirit*, Seneca urged his readers to participate in life and strive to improve it:

> No one is more worthy of contempt than an old person who has no accomplishments but age to prove that he has lived for a long time.

FURTHER READING

Costa, Charles D. N. *Seneca*. Boston: Routledge & Kegan Paul, 1974.

Seneca. *Epistulae Morales*. 3 vols. Translated by Richard M. Gummere. Loeb Classical Library. New York: Putnam, 1917.

————. *Moral Essays*. 3 vols. Translated by John W. Basore. Loeb Classical Library. Cambridge: Harvard University Press, 1951.

————. *Tragedies*. 3 vols. Translated by Frank J. Miller. Loeb Classical Library. New York: Putnam, 1917.

Vespasian
(Titus Flavius Vespasianus)

"THE MULE DRIVER"

After the emperor Nero committed suicide on June 9, A.D. 68, Rome endured a tumultuous year in which three different men claimed the title of emperor. Galba, the first, was assassinated by Marcus Salvius Otho, who was defeated in battle by the general Vitellius. Then Vitellius faced a challenge from Vespasian, who had the support of the Roman legions in Egypt, Judaea, and the northern provinces. Also supporting Vespasian were Gaius Lucinius Mucianus, the Roman governor of Syria, and Tiberius Julius Alexander, prefect of the Roman troops in Egypt. Though these were formidable opponents, Vitellius was not prepared

Vespasian was the first Roman ruler who could not trace his lineage to the city's old aristocratic families. Yet his hard-headedness and experience made him a strong leader.

To recover from the excesses of Nero's reign, Vespasian raised existing taxes and created a variety of new ones. Here provincials are shown giving their coins (there was no paper money) to the tax collector.

to surrender his position without a fight; he and Vespasian prepared their troops for action.

At this time Vespasian was 60 years old. He had had much military and political experience, but his ancestry did not equal that of previous emperors or of others who might contend for the title. His family belonged to the *equites*, the social class ranking just below senators. Only two of his relatives had achieved any prominence: an uncle who had served in the Senate and an older brother, Sabinus, who had been a senator and had also held the post of prefect of Rome under Nero and Vitellius. Vespasian hoped that Sabinus might persuade Vitellius to step aside without a battle.

But Sabinus never got the chance to try. Marcus Antonius Primus, the Roman commander of Pannonia (a region north of Italy), disregarded orders to wait for Mucianus and marched his troops into Italy. After defeating Vitellius' forces at the Second Battle of Bedriacum, Primus entered Rome on December 20. Both Vitellius and Sabinus died in battle at Bedriacum. Primus' personal ambitions were cut short when Mucianus arrived in Rome

with his 20,000 soldiers and took control of the elite Praetorian Guard.

On December 21, the Senate officially named Vespasian emperor, while he was still in Egypt. He had originally gone there to try to prevent Egypt's grain from reaching Rome, thereby starving Vitellius and those under him into submission. But with Vitellius now dead and Rome under the control of his generals, Vespasian headed west at a deliberate pace. He took some 9 or 10 months to reach the capital, giving himself time to prepare his agenda for the revitalization of the empire. His previous experience in the military and politics all served him well.

Vespasian's first career appointment had been as an army officer in Thrace. This position was followed by a quaestorship in the province of Crete and Cyrenaica. Continuing his move up the political ladder, Vespasian gained a praetorship under the emperor Caligula. Aware that friendship with the emperor was key to political and military advancement, Vespasian quickly sought to align himself with Caligula's successor Claudius. This strategy worked and, in A.D. 43, Vespasian found himself commanding the left wing of the Roman army as it advanced into Britain.

According to the Roman historian Suetonius, Vespasian distinguished himself in this campaign, fighting in 30 battles, defeating two fierce tribes, and capturing more than 20 towns as well as the island of Vectis (the Isle of Wight). For his brave and courageous leadership Claudius (who had also participated in the invasion) granted Vespasian triumphal decorations, two priesthoods (official appointments awarded to members of the upper class), and, in A.D. 51, a consulship. But Claudius' sudden death in A.D. 54 brought a temporary end to Vespasian's advancing career.

For almost 10 years, Vespasian lived quietly with his wife, Flavia

Domitilla, who like himself lacked noble ancestry. The two loved each other dearly and had three children: Titus, Domitian, and Domitilla (a daughter who died young and was later deified).

Finally, in A.D. 63, Vespasian received the proconsulship of Africa, where he governed with great justice and dignity. The people, however, did not always appreciate his determination to be fair and proper. Nor did they agree completely with his preference for a simple and unpretentious lifestyle. On one occasion, they even pelted him with turnips. No one, however, ever charged that his frugality was a ruse to enrich himself. In fact, when Vespasian returned to Rome, he was so poor that he had to mortgage his assets to his brother and become a trader in mules. Because of this occupation he gained the nickname Mule Driver.

In A.D. 66, Nero requested that Vespasian accompany him to Greece and attend the many dramatic performances he planned to give. Vespasian agreed, but soon after incurred the emperor's wrath when he either left the room or fell asleep during one of Nero's recitals. Apparently the emperor forgave Vespasian the following year, for he named him commander of the legions sent to crush a Jewish revolt in Judaea. Nero and his advisors soon congratulated themselves on their foresight when reports reached Rome that Vespasian had won two major victories, captured almost the entire area (except for the city of Jerusalem), and still remained loyal to his emperor. But when Vespasian learned of Nero's suicide, he immediately ordered his troops to stop fighting and sent his son Titus to extend his congratulations to the new emperor, Galba. But before Titus could reach Rome, Galba was dead. As Otho and Vitellius now began to vie for control, Vespasian began to feel that he was as qualified as anyone else to be emperor.

Years earlier, Vespasian had learned that before his mother gave birth to each of her three children a certain oak tree that was sacred to Mars had produced three shoots that predicted each child's future. The first shoot was quite thin and withered quickly, just like the infant Domitilla, who died before she celebrated her first birthday. The second was strong and healthy, like Vespasian's brother Sabinus. The third shoot was even more robust, almost a tree in itself—a sure sign that the third child, Vespasian, would have the gift of leadership.

Soon after becoming emperor, Vespasian publicized this and other omens that had foreshadowed his rise to power. Well aware that his background did not match that of previous emperors, he did not attempt to conceal it but proudly referred instead to his humble beginnings.

Nor did Vespasian seek public honors. Proof of this came when he was granted a triumph for his victories in Judaea and became so weary as the procession slowly made its way to the center of the city that he exclaimed, "What an old fool I was to ask for a triumph, as if I owed this honor to my ancestors or that it was always one of my ambitions. Alas, it serves me right that I am now so bored!"

But Vespasian found little time to be bored once he assumed control. According to Suetonius, he awoke before daylight to handle his private correspondence and official reports. Next he admitted friends and received their greetings while he dressed. After attending to new business, he took a drive and then had an afternoon nap. Finally, he took a bath and went to dinner, which was the time when his close associates would ask for favors, because the emperor always seemed to be in a good mood.

Helping Vespasian get through the rigorous daily schedule was his son Titus, who returned to Rome after

Vespasian

BORN
A.D. 9
Reate, Italy

DIED
A.D. 79
Reate, Italy

PROFESSION
Roman emperor

ACCOMPLISHMENTS
Ended devastating civil wars for control of the empire after Nero's death and brought peace to the Roman world; crushed Jewish revolt in Judaea; annexed northern England, pacified Wales, and invaded Scotland; revitalized the empire and replenished the public treasury; extended the rights of citizenship beyond Italy; revamped the Senate and the *equites* class, introducing more Italians and provincials; rebuilt the burned temple on the Capitoline Hill; built the Temple of Peace; began construction of the Colosseum

> *"Alas, I think I am becoming a god."*
>
> —Vespasian on his deathbed, quoted in Suetonius' *The Lives of the Caesars* (A.D. 120)

capturing Jerusalem. Vespasian saw himself as the first of a ruling dynasty, with Titus and then his second son, Domitian, succeeding him.

Not everyone agreed with Vespasian's idea of a hereditary monarchy, however, but only a few openly objected. Ever since the banishment of the kings in 509 B.C., the Romans had vehemently opposed the idea of a monarchy. Now, in the 1st century A.D., there were those who thought having a strong central leader was the only way to forestall revolts and the disintegration of the empire. Vespasian himself certainly believed this; his autocratic rule not only consolidated the power of the emperor but also strengthened the ties that bound the empire into a unit.

As the years passed, Vespasian did not tire of governing or abdicate his powers to others, as several of his predecessors had done, but continued to work for the good of the empire. And although he never was overly concerned with official titles, he did assume the name Caesar Vespasianus Augustus to link himself with his predecessors. Because he was a descendant of the Flavian family—not a Julian or a Claudian, like previous emperors—he and his sons became known to history as the Flavian emperors.

One of Vespasian's most pressing concerns was the condition of the treasury, now depleted because of Nero's extravagances and the civil wars that followed his suicide. Vespasian realized that drastic means were called for to produce new revenues. Accordingly, he raised the existing taxes and created a variety of new ones, rescinded the tax exemptions that had been granted certain cities, and reclaimed public land. These measures soon had the treasury collecting more than it was paying out.

Vespasian used some of the surplus money to fund several building projects in Rome. He ordered the restoration of the temple on the Capitoline Hill, which had been ravaged by fire during the recent civil strife, and even carried away the first basketful of rubble himself. He granted the ownership of collapsed buildings and those destroyed by fire to anyone who wished to renovate them, if the original owners did not claim them. To commemorate the peace and prosperity he was bringing to the empire, Vespasian commissioned the building of a great Temple of Peace near the Forum. And he sent workers to refurbish Nero's gardens, then opened them to the public. At the same time, he organized the building of an enormous amphitheater on the site of Nero's swimming pool. So massive was this structure that it was still not completed at the time of Vespasian's death. Known at first as the Flavian Amphitheater, it was later called the Colosseum, a derivative of the Greek word *kolossos*, meaning "gigantic." Today its massive ruins are among Rome's greatest tourist attractions.

A strict disciplinarian, Vespasian discharged or punished soldiers who caused problems in the communities they served. On one occasion, Vespasian received a request for a special shoe allowance from the soldiers acting as the fire brigade for the area just south of Rome. "No," the emperor replied, "and, in the future, you may go barefoot!" According to Suetonius, the firefighters took his words literally and never again wore shoes.

Vespasian also sought to correct the unfair manner in which his predecessors had treated the senators and the *equites*, hundreds of whom had been executed on false charges of treason. After reviving the office of censor, as Claudius had done years earlier, Vespasian then "censored" those senators and *equites* he deemed unworthy of the privileged rank. Next he added new members, chosen not only from among worthy Romans in the city but also from throughout Italy and the provinces. In this way the two groups became more representative of the entire empire. Vespasian also extended the rights of Roman citizenship to communities beyond Italy. Just as Gaul was Romanized under Claudius, now Vespasian Romanized Spain. The heritage of this adoption of Roman customs is still evident in both lands today.

Well acquainted with the provinces and Rome's boundaries, Vespasian sought to bring stability to problem areas. One of the most significant foreign developments of his reign took place in Britain with the annexation of northern England, the pacification of Wales, and the invasion of Scotland under the general Agricola. A few decades later, the Roman historian Tacitus wrote that Vespasian was the only emperor who had become better as the years passed. To commemorate the achievement of order throughout the empire, Vespasian had the word *pax* (peace) inscribed on much of the coinage minted during his reign.

As the years passed and he approached his 70th birthday, the emperor relied more and more on his son Titus. Despite his advancing age, he was still energetic and healthy. According to Suetonius, Vespasian was squarely built, with strong, well-proportioned arms and legs. He never took any type of medicine but did enjoy regular massages. Once a month, he fasted for a day.

In A.D. 79, while visiting south of Rome, Vespasian caught a slight fever. He quickly hurried back to Rome and then to his summer estate near Reate, where he took a cold bath. But instead of getting better, he felt worse. Refusing to accept that he was ill, he continued his daily schedule, attending to his duties as usual. When a wave of dizziness overwhelmed him, he struggled to remain standing, muttering that an "emperor should die on his feet." He then collapsed into the arms of his attendants and died.

The succession to the throne went smoothly, with Titus assuming the role of emperor first, followed by his brother Domitian, thereby fulfilling more of the many omens in which Vespasian had believed. In a dream Vespasian had once seen a scale perfectly balanced, with the emperor Claudius and his adopted son Nero sitting on one side and he and his two sons on the other. The prophecy proved correct, because both families ruled the Roman world for the same number of years.

FURTHER READING

Greenhalgh, P. A. L. *The Year of the Four Emperors*. New York: Barnes & Noble, 1975.

Suetonius. *The Lives of the Caesars*. Translated by J. C. Rolfe. Loeb Classical Library. New York: Macmillan, 1914.

Wellesley, Kenneth. *The Long Year: A.D. 69*. Boulder, Colo.: Westview, 1975.

Domitian
(Titus Flavius
Domitianus)

MASTER AND GOD

As a child, Domitian learned firsthand how political intrigue and jealousy could favor or ruin an entire family. Born on October 24, A.D. 51, Domitian spent his early years in poverty. Life became especially difficult after his father's friend, the freedman Narcissus, lost his position as close advisor to the emperor Claudius. Soon afterward, the family's situation worsened when Domitian's father, the future emperor Vespasian, became a political outcast and was relieved of all duties and responsibilities.

The family's fortunes changed dramatically in the late 60s A.D., when Claudius' successor, Nero, assigned Vespasian the important task of crushing a Jewish revolt in Judaea. In A.D. 67, Vespasian set out for the East with Domitian's older brother, Titus, leaving Domitian in Rome. Then came Nero's suicide in A.D. 68 and a bitter struggle for command. First Galba, then Otho claimed the right to rule, but both were soon killed, and a third general, Vitellius, became emperor. His days, however, were also numbered, as troops supporting Vespasian immediately advanced on Rome.

With Domitian in Rome was his uncle Sabinus (Vespasian's older brother), who had held the position of prefect under Nero and Otho. When pro-Vespasian troops under Primus invaded Rome, the Vitellian forces naturally turned against Sabinus, who took refuge with Domitian in the ancient temple on the Capitoline Hill. Sabinus died in the ensuing battle as Vitellius' soldiers stormed the Capitol and set fire to the temple. Domitian managed to escape by concealing himself in the caretaker's quarters. The next morning, pretending to be a follower of Isis, an Egyptian earth goddess worshiped by many Romans, Domitian fled across the Tiber River and was given a hiding place by a friend's mother.

After learning that Primus' troops had claimed victory and taken possession of the city, Domitian returned to Rome, where the pro-Vespasian troops hailed him as emperor. This title was purely honorary, however; the real leader in Vespasian's absence was his trusted friend Mucianus. Still, for the 18-year-old Domitian, the sudden popularity and power were a welcome change, however brief.

Although Vespasian made it very clear that both his sons were to succeed him, he was unwilling to entrust Domitian with much responsibility. Domitian was still young, and Vespasian was concerned about his judgment and rebellious nature. On the other hand, Vespasian considered Titus his co-ruler and treated him accordingly.

Naturally, Domitian resented his father's attitude and envied his brother. When Vespasian died in A.D. 79, Domitian was 28 and eager to prove himself. Upon learning that his father's will named Titus the sole immediate successor, Domitian angrily charged that "someone" had tampered with his father's will. To substantiate this charge he referred to an earlier decree in which Vespasian had named the two brothers co-rulers. No one doubted that Domitian was accusing his brother: Titus was a master of penmanship and often boasted that he could imitate anyone's handwriting.

Domitian's anger and jealousy did not have to smolder long. Little more than two years after taking office, Titus lay dead and the Senate was confirming Domitian's claim to the empire. There were rumors that Domitian had hastened his brother's death, but nobody was ever able to prove the charge. Most accounts of Domitian's 15-year rule, especially those by Pliny the Younger and Tacitus, depict him as cruel and autocratic. (Suetonius took a more favorable view.) Yet, for all the criticism leveled at Domitian, he did serve the empire well. He aroused criticism mainly because he did not always abide by his own laws. But the vices often associated with Domitian became pronounced only in the latter part of his rule.

During the first years, Domitian sought to stem corruption and other evils he felt were damaging to the empire. He faulted his predecessors for not enforcing the laws they passed governing public morals. Under Domitian, if a juror was found guilty of taking a bribe, not only he but all those who had served with him were punished. He carefully chose as provincial governors men with reputations for honesty and sincerity, dismissing any whose actions made them unfit to rule. His taxes were heavy, but he tried to ensure that no one was unduly taxed or cheated.

Domitian knew that a balanced budget was the key to continued prosperity, but as the years passed this became increasingly difficult for him. The military had always been a drain on the

treasury, but it became an even greater burden after Domitian increased military pay by more than 30 percent in A.D. 84. He had originally planned to cut the military establishment, but when he realized that such a move would expose Rome's frontiers to invasion, he dismissed the idea.

Although relatively inexperienced in military matters when he became emperor, Domitian went out with his troops on many occasions and spent more time with them than his predecessors had. His primary aim was to strengthen the existing boundaries of the empire. He was especially successful in setting up a line of defense along the Rhine and Danube rivers. In A.D.

Often criticized for his extravagance and tyrannical rule, Domitian did, however, serve the empire well by strengthening Rome's boundaries and defeating neighboring tribes.

83, Domitian personally led his soldiers in a successful battle against the Chatti, who occupied the area between the upper Rhine and upper Danube and had for decades posed a constant threat to Rome. His battles against the powerful Dacians were not as successful. However, he did win an honorable peace and returned to Rome in A.D. 89 to celebrate a triumph.

Domitian faced a crisis in A.D. 89, when the Roman governor of upper Germany, Lucius Antonius Saturninus, rebelled and proclaimed himself Rome's new emperor. Domitian took immediate action, ordering Roman troops stationed in Spain to march to Germany. Meanwhile, he gathered his own troops and headed north. Nature was on his side. Unexpectedly warm weather caused the Rhine to thaw, and additional forces on whom Saturninus had depended were unable to cross and join his troops. As a result, the revolt faltered.

Following this incident, Domitian became increasingly concerned that other conspiracies might form. To counter such a possibility, he ordered the execution of many men involved in Saturninus' conspiracy, and he also reinstated the hated law of *maiestas* (treason). As the years passed, Domitian used this law to eliminate any he considered traitors.

A group that especially felt Domitian's wrath was the so-called philosophers. Many were senators who strongly opposed Domitian's autocratic rule. On two separate occasions, Domitian banned them as a group and ordered several killed. Following the example of his predecessors, Domitian then confiscated their property. Because his debts were accumulating faster than he could pay them, rumors spread that the executions were merely an excuse to increase his revenues.

Domitian's increasing debt did not, however, stop him from spending. His building program continued to be a great drain on the public treasury. Around Rome alone, he ordered the construction of a new Forum (later known as the Forum Nervae), a house on the Palatine Hill, an enormous country house just south of the city, a concert hall, and two temples dedicated to Jupiter, the king of the gods.

Domitian's expenditures were also increased by the magnificent public games he hosted. In addition to the traditional chariot races he staged full-scale battles and a sea fight in the Flavian Amphitheater (later called the Colosseum). His nighttime gladiatorial shows, illuminated by torchlight, won him great favor with the Roman people—both men and women participated in these bloody spectacles—as did his distribution on three separate occasions of three gold coins to each Roman.

Though Domitian was winning the favor of the common people, he was steadily alienating the upper classes. After A.D. 93, many prominent Romans began referring to his rule as the Reign of Terror. As time passed, Domitian's clothing became more and more extravagant and he insisted on being addressed as *dominus et deus* (master and god). This angered many Romans, who did not customarily consider any living person a god.

As tensions increased, the senators found themselves increasingly the object of the emperor's wrath, especially after he appointed himself censor for life. Other emperors had assumed the office, but only for a specified period of time. Domitian, however, was determined to have complete control of the Senate. As censor, he could legally pass judgment on each senator, remove those he considered unworthy, and enroll new senators who were more to his liking.

Finally, several high-ranking officials, two praetorian commanders, and the emperor's wife, Domitia, quietly formed a conspiracy to rid Rome of the man they now detested and feared. Their loyalty to each other was such that no one ever suspected a plot until after the deed was done, and no one ever knew exactly how many people were involved. Domitian himself, though unusually agitated on the fateful day, apparently never suspected that a conspiracy was brewing in his own palace.

Domitian's agitation arose from his firm belief in omens. According to ancient sources, astrologers had once told him that certain signs predicted his death on September 18, A.D. 96, at the age of 44. The omens even gave the time of his death, the fifth hour (just before noon, in the Roman system of telling time).

Early on the morning of the 18th, Domitian scratched a wart on his face until it bled, saying, "I hope this is all the blood the omen requires." Later he asked his freedmen who were in attendance, "What time is it?" Unknown to him, the freedmen were co-conspirators; knowing about the omen, they lied and said it was the sixth hour. A look of joy spread across Domitian's face and he went to take a bath.

As Domitian was bathing, his chief attendant, Parthenius, announced that a man had called on urgent business and would not leave until Domitian spoke with him. Believing that all was well, Domitian dismissed his attendants and hurried to his bedroom.

The details of what followed are sketchy. According to Suetonius, the visitor was Stephanus, a servant employed by Domitian's niece. Stephanus' arm, supposedly injured days before, was wrapped in woolen bandages that actually concealed a dagger. When he entered Domitian's bedroom, Stephanus gave the emperor a document containing proof of a conspiracy. As Domitian read the paper, Stephanus pulled out his dagger and stabbed the emperor in the groin.

Domitian was a strong man, and despite his wound he wrestled Stephanus to the ground. At this point other conspirators burst into the room and stabbed the emperor seven times.

Upon hearing of Domitian's assassination, the Senate rejoiced and did not even mount an effort to find the murderers, but immediately conferred the imperial powers on a respected statesman named Marcus Cocceius Nerva. The Roman people accepted the news with indifference, but the army, especially the Praetorians, remained loyal to their commander-in-chief and demanded that the conspirators be arrested and executed. They were so insistent that Nerva found himself forced to answer their demand and allowed them to kill Domitian's assassins. No honors, however, were granted Domitian's corpse; public undertakers were called to take it away. Suetonius wrote that Domitian's old nurse, Phyllis, cremated the body and then secretly took the ashes to the Temple of the Flavians, where she mixed them with those of Domitian's niece Julia, for whom she had also cared years earlier.

FURTHER READING

Suetonius. *The Lives of the Caesars.* Translated by J. C. Rolfe. Loeb Classical Library. New York: Macmillan, 1914.

Domitian

BORN

October 24, A.D. 51
Rome

DIED

September 18, A.D. 96
Rome

PROFESSION

Roman emperor

ACCOMPLISHMENTS

Strengthened Rome's boundary line along the Rhine and Danube rivers; conquered the tribes of the Chatti there; concluded a peace treaty with the king of Dacia; built two temples to Jupiter, a new Forum, a concert hall, a grand house on the Palatine Hill, and a country house south of Rome; enacted laws aimed at reviving traditional morality

Martial (Marcus Valerius Martialis)

MASTER OF THE EPIGRAM

When he was in his 50s, Martial wrote, "My foolish parents taught me poetry / But what was grammar and rhetoric to me?" This early training nevertheless shaped his life and allowed him to become one of Rome's most celebrated poets. When he composed these lines, Martial may well have been thinking about how little compensation he had received for his work. But he never regretted his choice of profession, for as he said, "Despite all the compliments, what profit is there in my verses? Yet, even if there is no profit, my poems give me joy."

Martial earned his fame in Rome but was a provincial by birth. Home was the Spanish town of Bilbilis, perched high above the rushing Salo River, whose waters were used in making the town's chief export, iron. His parents certainly were not rich, but they believed firmly in education and used their limited resources to provide the young Martial

Uncovered in Pompeii, Italy, this wall painting shows the god of merriment and wine, Bacchus—himself shaped like a bunch of grapes—at the foot of Mount Vesuvius. Martial described the scene after the eruption in his *Epigrams*: "This is Vesuvius, shaded yesterday with green vines.... Now all lies drowned in fire and grey ash."

with a good foundation in grammar and rhetoric, the art of speaking. Sometime around A.D. 64, when he was in his early 20s, Martial left Spain for Rome.

Once in the capital, Martial followed the accepted custom of attaching himself as a "client" to a distinguished family. This centuries-old practice required a client to support his patron's endeavors in both political and private life. In return, a patron was obliged to assist his clients financially and offer protection when needed. Naturally, Martial chose as his patrons fellow Spaniards who were well-to-do and politically prominent—in his case the statesman and philosopher Seneca and the poet Lucan (Seneca's nephew). Unfortunately for Martial, these relationships were short-lived.

A year after his arrival in Rome, the ill-fated conspiracy of Gaius Calpurnius Piso against the emperor Nero was uncovered and crushed. Among those accused of being co-conspirators were Seneca and Lucan. Although their guilt was never proved, they were convicted and sentenced to death. What happened to Martial after the loss of his patrons is not known, but it seems certain that he continued to write and may even have pleaded some cases in the law courts. However, for the next 15 years no accounts mention his name. Even Martial himself seems to have chosen to forget the years from A.D. 65 to 80, for he never referred to them in his poems.

In A.D. 80, Martial published a small book of poems entitled *Liber Spectaculorum* (Book of Spectacles) to commemorate the completion of Rome's great amphitheater, the Colosseum. Gradually, his verse brought him recognition and some financial reward. But the latter must have been quite small, since he complained in one verse that "I live up three flights of stairs and high ones." In Rome's intense summer heat, he may well have

longed to trade his stuffy little apartment for the open countryside of his homeland. Yet he did not return but persevered with his writing. Records show that by A.D. 84, Martial owned a small farm at Nomentum, 14 miles northeast of Rome. Whether he bought it himself or was given it is not known, but it certainly provided him with a welcome respite.

In the years that followed, Martial gained several honors, including the so-called "right of three children," which exempted fathers of three or more children from certain responsibilities. (This honor derived from a measure enacted by the emperor Augustus in an attempt to reverse the declining birthrate among Roman citizens.) It is not known whether Martial was ever married, and most sources agree that he never fathered any children. By granting him this privilege anyway, the emperors Titus and Domitian showed that they considered him worthy of special recognition.

Another imperial honor granted Martial was that of a military tribuneship. This position as a senior officer in Rome's army raised Martial to the rank of *equites*, the class of knights just below senators in social and political standing. After being in office for six months, Martial was allowed the special privilege of relinquishing his duties while, at the same time retaining the rights of an *eques* for the rest of his life. Martial's financial situation also improved, because at some point he moved from his cramped third-floor quarters to his own house on Rome's Quirinal Hill.

Well aware of the power and fickleness of haughty emperors, Martial knew that praise was an effective way of winning their patronage. Therefore he inserted into many of his poems phrases that literary critics have since labeled excessive use of flattery. In fact, some of these lines are so affected as to border on the artificial. But times were

Martial

BORN

Around A.D. 40
Bilbilis, Spain

DIED

A.D. 103 or 104
Bilbilis, Spain

PROFESSION

Poet

ACCOMPLISHMENTS

Wrote his first book of poems, *Liber Spectaculorum*, in A.D. 80, in commemoration of the opening of the Colosseum in Rome; wrote approximately 1,500 epigrams, divided later into 14 books known as the *Epigrammaton Libri*

> "Let sweet harmony forever preside over their home
> And let mutual love guide the well-matched couple;
> May she love him when time has touched his hair
> And he, when she is old, still think her fair."

—from *Epigrammaton Libri* (written between A.D. 86 and 101)

difficult, and death or disgrace often visited those who failed to show proper respect for the emperor. Martial, lacking any hereditary income and living only on what his verses could produce, did what he had to in order to survive.

Domitian's successors did not favor flatterers, however, and Martial changed the tone of his verse accordingly. There were other changes also. The vulgarity that had marked so many of his earlier poems now became more infrequent. At times, he had used very graphic language, and even when he only implied some obscene situation he still managed to express himself in an explicit manner. In later centuries, many of these poems were censored or omitted from anthologies.

In the years that followed the publication of *Liber Spectaculorum*, Martial published an additional 14 books of poems. His reputation established, Martial now counted among his friends the leading literary figures of the time, including Pliny the Younger, Juvenal, and Quintilian. However, his writings differed greatly from the works of these writers. Martial knew his limits and recognized that he was best at poems that were short and to the point. The uneven quality of his work is perhaps due to the fact that he wrote so many poems in an effort to make enough money to live decently.

Martial's most important contribution to literature is his perfection of the epigram, a short poem with a witty or satirical point—or, as the colloquial phrase defines it, a short poem with a sting in its tail.

Martial was a keen observer of the life around him, and everything he saw was a potential subject for his poetry. For example, graffiti was just as common in Rome as in modern cities, and Martial made clear his feelings about it:

> I wonder, wall, that you have not fallen in ruins
> You who have borne the boring words of so many scribblers.

In another epigram, he laughed at a man who managed to win a daily invitation to dinner:

> Philo swears that he has never eaten dinner at home, and this is so.
> He eats not at all whenever no one invites him.

At times, Martial seemed to have no patience with people and saw through their lies and excuses:

> You say you will live tomorrow, you always say tomorrow, Postumus,
> Tell me, Postumus, when does that tomorrow come?

Another poem, written as an epitaph for a little girl named Erotion, shows a serious side to his personality as he gave expression to his sorrow and empathized with her parents:

> She would have completed her sixth cold winter,
> If only she had not lived six days too few. . . .
> Do not be heavy on her, o earth, for she was not heavy on you.

Sometime around A.D. 100, Martial decided to return home. He must have been short of funds once again, because Pliny the Younger provided him with the money for the journey. Over the years, Martial had often spoken of home and included occasional references to his native land in his poems. He described himself as a typical Spaniard with bristly hair, a heavy beard, and hairy legs. In the months that followed his return, he clearly expressed his joy in a poem addressed to Juvenal:

> Perhaps, my Juvenal, your feet
> May walk along some noisy Roman street, . . .
> While I, after many years in Rome,
> Have once again my Spanish home.
> Bilbilis, rich in steel and gold,
> Makes me a countryman as of old.

Never again did Martial return to Rome. He remained in Bilbilis in a country house that a wealthy patroness named Marcella seems to have given him. In A.D. 103, he published his last book of poems and died soon after. The following year, Pliny the Younger wrote: "I hear that Valerius Martial has died and I am sorely grieved. He was a man of genius, and subtle sharp intelligence. . . . Perhaps his poems will not last, but he wrote as if they would."

FURTHER READING

Martial. 2 vols. Translated by W. C. A. Ker and revised by E. H. Warmington. Loeb Classical Library. Cambridge: Harvard University Press, 1968.

Tacitus (Publius, or Gaius, Cornelius Tacitus)

CHRONICLER OF ROME

Begun by Vespasian, increased by Titus, and advanced by Domitian." That is how the historian Tacitus described his official career under Rome's three Flavian emperors. Although no definite information is known about his family background or early life, most accounts cite the year A.D. 55 or 56 as the most probable time of his birth, which took place either in northern Italy or southern Gaul. His parents must have been fairly prosperous, because he received a good education. He learned quickly and proved himself an excellent public speaker at an early age.

A lover of history and of Rome, Tacitus focused his works on the events and people of his own age. Clear and descriptive, his words present a vivid picture of these turbulent years.

THE FIRST BOOKE OF THE ANNALES OF
CORNELIVS TACITVS.

The Proeme of Tacitus, *containing the forme of gouernment vntill* Auguftus *time : with the fubiect of this worke.*

THE citie of Rome was in the beginning gouerned by Kings. Libertie and the Confulfhip *L. Brutus* brought in. The Dictators were chofen but for a time : the *Decemuiri* paffed not two yeeres : neither had the Confularie authoritie of the Tribunes of the foldiers any long continuance : nor *Cinna*, nor *Sillaes* dominion : *Pompey* and *Craffus* quickly yeelded to *Caefars* forces : *Lepidus* and *Antonie* to *Auguftus* ; who entitling himfelfe by the name of Prince, brought vnder his obedience the whole Romane ftate, wearied and weakened with ciuill diforders. But as well the profperous, as vnprofperous fucceffes of the ancient Commonwealth, excellent writers haue recorded: neither wanted there woorthie & fingular wits, to deliuer *Auguftus* exploits; vntill they were by the ouerfwarming of flatterers vtterly difcouraged. *Tiberius, Caius, Claudius* and *Neroes* actions, they yet liuing and flourifhing, were falfly fet downe, for feare ; and after their death, through frefh hatred, as corruptly as before. Whereupon I intend to deliuer fome few things done in *Auguftus* later times : then *Neroes* raigne, and other occurrents as they fell out, without paffion or partialitie, as being free from motiues of both.

1. The meanes by which Auguftus *came to the empire : and whom he chofe to fucceed.*

AFter that *Brutus* and *Caffius* were flaine, and no armes now publikely borne ; *Pompey* defeated in Sicilie ; *Lepidus* difarmed ; *Antonie* killed ; and no chiefe leader of *Iulius Caefars* faction left, but onely *Auguftus* : he would no longer be called *Triumuir*, but in fhew contented with the dignitie of a Tribune to defend the people, bearing himfelfe as Conful : after he had wound into the fauour of the foldier by giftes ; of the people by prouifion of fuftenance ; and of all in generall with the fweetenes of eafe and repofe ; by little and little taking vpon him, he drew to himfelfe the affaires of Senate ; the dutie of magiftrates and lawes, without contradiction of any : the ftowteft by war or profcriptions alreadie fpent, and the reft of the nobilitie, by how much the more feruiceable, by fo much the more bettered in wealth, and aduanced in honors : feeing their preferment to growe by new gouernment, did rather choofe the prefent eftate with fecuritie, than ftriue to recouer their olde with danger. That forme of gouernment the prouinces difliked not, as miftrufting the Senates and peoples regiment by reafon of noble mens factions ; couetoufnes of magiftrates : the lawes affoording no fecuritie, being fwaied hither

A i   and

Historians through the centuries have read reprints and translations of Tacitus' works, including the *Annales,* to learn more about the Roman Empire in the 1st century A.D.

cessor Titus, Tacitus advanced from quaestor to aedile to praetor, and held a religious post under Domitian. From A.D. 89 to 93, Tacitus appears to have left Rome, most likely to hold a senior post in one of the provinces. His return to Rome in A.D. 93 coincided with the beginning of the so-called Reign of Terror, which ended with Domitian's death in A.D. 96.

These were difficult times for anyone who had achieved distinction, belonged to the senatorial class, or had money and influence. Informers were everywhere, eager to report to the emperor whatever they heard, whether it was true or false. Tacitus' reputation as an orator, lawyer, and honest politician was well established, but he had to take care not to arouse the emperor's animosity. Therefore, although he detested Domitian's actions and manner of governing, he kept silent about the abuses and injustices he saw. Many have criticized Tacitus for this, but he was taking the necessary steps to ensure his survival.

Under Domitian's successor, Nerva, Tacitus completed his climb up the political ladder and attained the office of consul, Rome's highest office apart from that of emperor. Nerva also chose Tacitus to give the funeral oration for Verginius Rufus, a general who twice refused the title of emperor after the death of Nero in A.D. 68, deferring first to Galba, then to Otho.

Under Trajan, the emperor who followed Nerva, Tacitus continued in his role as one of Rome's best public speakers and lawyers. One of his most important actions occurred in A.D. 100, when he and Pliny the Younger successfully prosecuted Marius Priscus for extortion during his proconsulship in Africa. In the years that followed, Tacitus continued to be active politically, serving as proconsul in A.D. 112–13, possibly in Asia Minor. In the end, Tacitus is remembered not for his honesty as a politician, his ability as an or-

Under Vespasian, Tacitus held several minor political posts as well as the office of military tribune. In A.D. 77 or 78, he married the daughter of Agricola, one of the emperor's most trusted generals. Then, under Vespasian's suc-

"The worst kind of enemies—flatterers."

—from *Agricola* (A.D. 98)

Tacitus

BORN
Around A.D. 55
Northern Italy or southern Gaul

DIED
After A.D. 115
Place unknown; perhaps Rome

PROFESSION
Orator, statesman, historian

ACCOMPLISHMENTS
Wrote several histories: *Agricola*, a biography of the Roman conqueror and governor of Britain; *Germania*, about the geography, tribes, people, and customs of Germany; *Dialogus de Oratoribus* (Dialogue about Orators), on the art of public speaking; *Historiae*, an account of the years A.D. 69–96; *Annales*, an account of the years A.D. 14–68

ator, or his reputation as a lawyer. Rather, his fame rested on his historical accounts of the Roman empire and the times in which he lived. Tacitus considered Nerva's accession the beginning of "a blessed age," a time when he could freely express his views about his country and his fellow Romans.

As Tacitus turned his attention more to writing and less to the practice of law, he planned an ambitious series of historical accounts that would cover events from Augustus to Trajan. One of his first pieces was the *Agricola*, a biography of his illustrious father-in-law. Published in A.D. 98, it focused on Agricola's role as conqueror and governor of Britain and included passages describing the geography and climate of the island. Of great importance to historians are the paragraphs dealing with provincial administration; the details Tacitus provided have greatly helped future generations understand how Rome's provincial system worked.

Regarded as an excellent example of biographical writing, *Agricola* immortalized its subject, portraying him to all future generations as a capable general and administrator as well as a patriotic but modest Roman citizen. In stark contrast to this description are the passages about Domitian, which clearly reflect the bitterness Tacitus felt when he remembered the horrors of his rule.

Tacitus' next work was the *Germania*, which focused on the geography of Germany and the customs, dress, religious practices, and daily habits of the people. He often wrote in vivid detail, as when he described the tall men of the north, with their "fierce, sky-blue eyes, and red hair." Even today, *Germania* remains an important historical record, even though Tacitus never seems to have visited the area and based his writings solely on research and accounts by others.

In the *Germania*, as in the *Agricola*, Tacitus' style and treatment of the subject are unique. His admiration for many aspects of German life led him to contrast the simple, wholesome values of these people with the immoral ways of Romans: "There is no one in Germany who smiles at evil behavior. Nor is it considered proper or stylish to corrupt or to be corrupted." Tacitus left no doubt in the reader's mind that he believed the opposite was true in Rome, a supposedly more advanced civilization.

Tacitus also wrote a piece entitled *Dialogus de Oratoribus*, which discusses the art of public speaking and compares oratory with poetry. For Tacitus, oratory had reached its height decades earlier under Cicero. In his admiration of the master orator, Tacitus seems to have imitated Cicero's sentence structure wherever possible. According to Tacitus, the autocratic rule of the emperors had stifled the orator's inspiration and led public speakers to reiterate memorized phrases instead of creatively developing their own.

Although Tacitus' comments did little to change the teaching of oratory, his contemporaries found them of great merit and praised them highly. In the end, however, his acclaim as a writer rested not on these early works but on his narrative accounts of Rome's history. First came *Historiae*, a collection of 12 or 14 books that focused on events from A.D. 69, when Galba became emperor, to the year A.D. 96, when Domitian died. From various references in the text it is clear that Tacitus sent passages of *Historiae* to his friend Pliny the Younger for revision. Pliny also supplied Tacitus with details about various events, including the eruption of Mount Vesuvius in A.D. 79. Unfortunately, only Books 1 through 4 and a section of Book 5, covering the beginning of Vespasian's rule, have survived.

Historiae clearly illustrates how Tacitus' style developed and matured. There is nothing artificial, no pat phrases, no long, involved sentences like those used by Cicero. Tacitus' manner of presentation is much more to the point. His tone is often pessimistic, especially when describing the events of the 1st century A.D. In Book 1 of *Historiae* he wrote, "The period which I am entering is one rich in disasters, terrible in battles, torn apart by civil discord—savage even in peace."

Tacitus finds cause for optimism only when contemplating the better side of human nature:

> This period was not so barren of courage that it did not produce some good examples. Mothers accompanied their children in flight; wives followed their husbands into exile; relatives were daring; sons-in-law steadfast, slaves loyal even when faced with torture.

After completing *Historiae,* sometime between A.D. 105 and 109, Tacitus turned his attention to the years immediately preceding A.D. 69. Known as the *Annales* (Annals), this later work focused on the period from the death of Augustus in A.D. 14 to the death of Nero in A.D. 68. As with the *Historiae,* many of these 16 or 18 books have not survived. Enough, however, remains to establish that this was indeed Tacitus' masterpiece.

For source material, Tacitus read the works of his predecessors, including accounts by historians of minor impor-

tance. He also spent time reading the official records of the Senate, the *acta diurna* (literally, daily acts, a daily journal with all the news the government chose to make public), and personal memoirs, such as those of Agrippina the Younger and the Roman general Corbulo.

From Tacitus' comments it seems clear that he consulted a variety of sources whenever he was unsure about a particular historical point. If several sources agreed, he chose that opinion as the true one. If his "experts" did not mention an incident, he considered it hearsay or rumor and omitted it. When his sources differed in their opinion, he recorded their differences.

Yet for all his research and adherence to fact, Tacitus was not unbiased. Though he was not one to repeat rumors, his account of Tiberius' rule clearly reflects his intense dislike of the man. Tacitus strove to paint a vivid picture of each subject, whether a person or an event. Because he wanted his portrait to be realistic, he chose his material carefully and used dramatic language wherever desirable. To make a point, he condensed his sentences so that key words would stand out. He also varied his phrasing, depending upon the intent of the passage he was writing. All these characteristics made his works masterpieces of style.

FURTHER READING

Benario, Herbert W. *An Introduction to Tacitus.* Athens: University of Georgia Press, 1975.

Mellor, Ronald. *Tacitus.* New York: Routledge, 1993.

Mendell, Clarence W. *Tacitus, the Man and His Work.* New Haven: Yale University Press, 1957.

Tacitus. *The Histories and the Annals.* 4 vols. Translated by Clifford H. Moore and John Jackson. Loeb Classical Library. Cambridge: Harvard University Press, 1962.

Pliny the Younger (Gaius Plinius Caecilius Secundus)

"EXPERIENCE, THAT EXCELLENT TEACHER"

I thought that I would perish with everyone and that everything would perish along with wretched me," wrote Pliny to his friend the historian Tacitus, after the latter had asked for more information about the tragic eruption of Mount Vesuvius some 24 years earlier. Even after so much time had passed, the thought of that disaster still made Pliny cringe. He had been only 18 years old at the time and was living with his uncle, Pliny the Elder, at Misenum, across the bay from Vesuvius.

Pliny loved his uncle dearly, but the change from his home in northern Italy to his uncle's had been a difficult adjustment. Pliny's parents had been influential, well-to-do citizens of Comum (present-day Como), where Pliny was born in A.D. 61 or 62. But the death of Pliny's father in A.D. 76 abruptly changed the boy's life; according to Roman law, young Pliny was still a minor, and his care was to be entrusted to male guardians. Accepting this responsibility were his

This statue of Pliny the Younger, which dates back to the Middle Ages, is part of a cathedral in Como, Italy. The sculptor must have thought it only fitting that the famed ancient patron of Como should have his own seat from which he might gaze out at the city he so loved.

mother's brother, Pliny the Elder, and a family friend, Verginius Rufus.

A learned man and an acclaimed writer, Pliny the Elder eagerly undertook the education of his nephew and fostered in him a love of learning. After he adopted the youth as his son and heir, the younger Pliny became known as Plinius Secundus, or Pliny the Younger.

In August A.D. 79, Pliny's life at Misenum was rudely interrupted when Mount Vesuvius, a long-dormant volcano, began sending tremors across the land. Accustomed to feeling the earth shake beneath their feet on occasion, the inhabitants of the area at first felt no alarm and continued about their daily business. As commander of the small Roman fleet stationed at Misenum, Pliny the Elder kept himself informed about the situation, especially since his boats might be needed to evacuate the area. Pliny the Younger's letter to Tacitus 24 years later clearly describes what happened next:

> Around one in the afternoon on August 23rd, my mother, who was with us at Misenum, called my uncle's attention to a large and unusual cloud formation. . . . We could not tell from which mountain the cloud was rising—only later did we realize that it was from Mount Vesuvius. In shape and appearance it resembled a pine tree and each gust of air seemed to separate parts of the cloud from its long "trunk." . . . Because my uncle was a scholar and a very curious individual, he was eager to inspect this phenomenon at close range and ordered a small vessel readied. He asked if I wished to accompany him, but I declined as I had still some [of his own] homework assignments to complete.

Pliny then told how his uncle calmly assessed the situation and decided to take a nap before continuing his investigation. When the ash and pumice continued to fall, his companions awakened him and pleaded with him to escape. As they headed back to the shore, with pillows tied on their heads for protection, the odor of sulfur overcame Pliny the Elder's weak lungs and he was unable to continue. Two days later, when friends returned for the body, they found it intact and without a bruise, almost as if he had died in his sleep.

Having answered Tacitus' request for the details of his uncle's death, Pliny ended his letter. Soon afterward, he received a second request from the historian, asking for information about what had happened at Misenum. This time he wrote of his own experience:

> That night the tremors became so violent that everything seemed to move or be moved. My mother burst into my room, just as I was rising. We sat down in the courtyard of the house. I hesitate whether I should call it courage or lack of experience, but I called for a book by Livy and began to read and take notes on the material. Soon, however, it seemed best to leave town for the buildings were shaking about us.

Pliny continued his description of the scene, noting how the panic-stricken crowds followed first one person, then another, thinking that someone else's plan was better than their own. When a huge cloud covered the lands and the sea, Pliny's mother begged him to flee without her, saying that her age and poor health would slow him down. But Pliny ignored her pleas, gently took her hand, and guided her steps.

As the ash fell and a dense mist threatened to engulf them from behind, Pliny advised, "Let us turn aside for a moment until we see that we will not be trampled by the onrushing crowd." As they did so, a dark, suffocating night engulfed them.

By daybreak, the nightmare was over. But for the second time in three years, Pliny had lost a father. This time, however, he was 18 and no longer a minor. In fact, he was a very rich young man, having inherited both his father's and his uncle's estates, each of which was considerable. Therefore, honoring the custom for Romans of his social standing, Pliny made plans to follow a senatorial career.

By the time he turned 19, Pliny was pleading cases in the law courts and gaining a reputation for effective argument. In the years that followed, he won renown in the civil courts, especially the political one, where extortion cases against provincial officials were tried.

Politically he also advanced quite rapidly, beginning with minor posts and then, as he met the age requirements, advancing to quaestor, tribune, and praetor. In A.D. 100 he achieved the consulship, the highest office (apart from emperor) that a Roman could attain. He also served for six months to a year in the military, a prerequisite for any candidate for public office. Pliny's tour of duty, however, was one of staff service with a legion stationed in Syria, not on the battlefield.

Pliny's mild manner and devotion to duty won him the respect of each succeeding emperor. His great wealth naturally brought him to the attention of Domitian, whose debts were enormous and who used a variety of ways, many illegal, to increase his own funds. Pliny well understood the situation and never openly criticized policies of which he disapproved. He accepted the duties of each office he held under Domitian and won praise for his service. But he kept himself apart from political intrigue, refusing to become involved in cases that might conflict with his other duties.

Pliny did, however, prosecute a friend of Domitian's for extortion in the province of Baetica in Spain. Pliny's assistant in the prosecution, Senecio, paid with his life for what Domitian called disloyalty. Pliny just barely escaped the same fate, for a signed document naming Pliny as a traitor was found on Domitian's desk after the emperor's murder.

Nerva, Domitian's successor, was well acquainted with Pliny's ability to manage money and chose Pliny to head the state treasury. Then under Trajan, Nerva's successor, Pliny's advancement continued. From A.D. 104 to 106, Pliny was put in charge of Rome's public works, an important position since it involved management of the sewer system, the efficiency of which was necessary to Rome's survival as a capital city. An honest, upright, and conscientious official, Pliny proved himself the perfect candidate for an assignment in the troublesome province of Bithynia, where corruption had drastically depleted the provincial treasury. The dates of his tenure there were most likely A.D.111–113. Pliny must have died soon after, for there is no mention of his holding any other public office and his letter writing ceased.

> *"Pain has its limits, apprehension none."*
>
> —from Pliny's letter to Macrinus, Book VIII, Letter XVII

Almost 400 of Pliny's letters have survived, and they have earned him undying literary fame. They were originally organized into 10 books. The first nine, on personal topics, were published between A.D. 100 and 109. The tenth book included 121 letters to Trajan about events in Bithynia and gave Trajan's replies.

Because Pliny intended to publish his letters, he always carefully reviewed and edited each one, then later selected only those that he felt were worthy of publication. As a result, the letters do not have the spontaneous or emotional quality usually found in personal letters. They do, however, provide a wonderful insight into Pliny's life and times. Unlike his friend Tacitus, who was quite pessimistic about life under the emperors, Pliny was optimistic and cheerful.

To be sure, Pliny's life had been an easy one with few cares or concerns. His greatest disappointment was that his marriages (two are documented, and there may have been a third one as well) had produced no heirs to whom he could leave his name. He loved his wife Calpurnia and wrote of his concern and affection when she was in Campania convalescing from an illness: "I fear everything, I imagine everything . . . and I think especially of what I dread most. Therefore, I sincerely ask that you put my fear to rest by writing one or two letters every day. I will feel happier while I read them and then begin to be afraid again as soon as I shall have read them."

In his letters to Trajan, all of which were direct and to the point, Pliny asked the emperor for advice whenever he was unsure about what course of action he should take. The question of how to deal with the growing numbers of Christians was an espe-cially difficult one for Pliny. From Bithynia he wrote the emperor:

It is my custom, master, to refer to you all matters about which I have any doubts. I have never interfered in any investigations concerning Christians. Therefore, I do not know what the customary punishment is or how they should be questioned. I have given considerable thought to this matter. . . . In the meantime, I have acted as follows with those Christians who have been sent to me. I have asked whether they were Christians. Those who say yes, I ask a second and a third time. . . . Those who continue to say they are Christians, I order taken to prison. If any of these are Romans, I note that they should be sent to Rome for trial. [Roman law granted every Roman citizen the right to a trial in Rome.]

That Trajan agreed completely with Pliny's actions is evident from the emperor's reply, which Pliny included in his book: "My dear Pliny, you acted as you should have in investigating the cases of those who were brought to you as Christians."

Not all Pliny's letters, however, focused on business or family matters. Pliny wrote to many people on a great variety of subjects. He always devoted each letter to a single topic, as when he wrote to his friend Calvisius to express his contempt for the games in the Circus Maximus:

The past few days I have spent quietly with my writing tablets and little books. "How," you ask, "could you do this in the city?" Yes, there was the circus, which does not interest me in the slightest. There is never anything new or different. I marvel that so many thousands of men wish to see again and again horses running and men standing in chariots. Yet, if they were attracted by the speed of certain horses or the skill of a particular driver, there might be some reason for their interest. But no, now they favor this team, now that team.

Unlike other fields of literature, in which the Romans imitated their Greek predecessors, letter writing was a uniquely Roman pursuit. For the Greeks, who traditionally lived in small communities and traveled only on occasion, the idea of writing to someone you might see that very day seemed pointless. By Pliny's time, however, there was an extensive and well-maintained system of communication across the Roman empire. Mail traveled fairly rapidly, and it was the only way families and friends could stay in touch with those serving or living in distant provinces.

Letter writing among the Romans was, however, confined to the upper classes. The majority of Romans did not have the leisure time to write or the means to do so, for it was costly to send a letter. Furthermore, few ordinary citizens traveled far from their hometowns, so there was no reason for friends and relatives to write them letters. For the well-to-do, on the other hand, letter writing became the fashion, and Pliny developed it into an art form. Because of this, the scenes he describes generally concern the lives of those with influence and wealth, not the poor and uneducated.

While the law courts, politics, and letter writing were Pliny's main interests, he had other pursuits as well. His great wealth allowed him to be a philanthropist, and in fact he gave great sums of money to his hometown of Comum. A firm believer in education, Pliny gave money to pay teachers in the town, built a library, established an endowment fund, and contributed one-third of the funds needed to maintain a school for the town's children. In his will he also provided for public baths and set up a fund to support his freedmen.

If Pliny had been told that his life and writings would be topics of study centuries after his death, he would certainly have been delighted, judging by a letter he once wrote to his friend Maximus:

I have never experienced greater pleasure than in a recent conversation with Cornelius Tacitus who told me about sitting with a Roman *eques* at the last circus games. After talking about a variety of topics, the *eques* had asked, "Are you an Italian or a provincial?" Tacitus answered, "You know me surely from my writings." To which the *eques* replied, "Are you Tacitus or Pliny?"

FURTHER READING

Bulwer-Lytton, Sir Edward G. E. *The Last Days of Pompeii.* New York: Dodd, Mead, 1946.

Connolly, Peter. *Pompeii.* New York: Oxford University Press, 1994. Deiss, Joseph Jay. *The Town of Hercules* [Pompeii]. Malibu, Calif.: J. Paul Getty Museum, 1995.

Pliny. *Letters, Panegyricus.* 2 vols. Translated by Betty Radice. Loeb Classical Library. Cambridge: Harvard University Press, 1969.

Pliny the Younger

BORN
A.D. 61 or 62
Comum, Italy

DIED
After A.D. 113
Perhaps in Bithynia

PROFESSIONS
Letter writer, lawyer, public administrator

ACCOMPLISHMENTS
Successfully prosecuted the Roman governor of Africa and officials in Spain on extortion charges; administered the military and state treasuries; corrected abuses by Roman officials in Bithynia; wrote, edited, and published hundreds of letters on private and public matters

More Ancient Romans to Remember

Caligula (Gaius Caesar) (A.D. 12–41), the fourth of the "Twelve Caesars," spent much time as a child in Germany with his father, Germanicus, Tiberius' adopted son and the commander of the Roman troops in that area. The soldiers gave him his nickname Caligula ("little boots") because he was always walking around in a small pair of boots. In the years that followed, political intrigue resulted

This youthful bust of Caligula gives little indication of the ruthless tyrant that he was to become as emperor.

in the deaths of his father and his two older brothers.

At Tiberius' death in A.D. 37, only two heirs to the throne still lived, Caligula and another grandson, Tiberius Gemellus—both of whom Tiberius had named as co-heirs in his will.

Then in a political maneuver, the Senate declared Tiberius' will invalid and Caligula was named sole heir. Everywhere the Roman public rejoiced, because the son of Germanicus, the man they had admired and loved, was now emperor.

Seven months after taking office, however, Caligula fell seriously ill. Although his body recovered, his mind did not, according to surviving sources.

According to contemporary sources, Caligula began to act like a madman, with no one immune to his cruelty. In addition, Caligula used the money Tiberius had accumulated in the public treasury to entertain himself and the people with games and theatrical performances. As the funds dwindled, Caligula looked for new ways to finance his extravagances, including confiscation of property and extortion.

Even the provinces suffered, especially when Caligula marched north into Gaul and mercilessly plundered the inhabitants.

By A.D. 41, Romans had had enough of Caligula. On January 24, as he sat in the theater during the Palatine Games, a few friends persuaded him to take a walk. At some point during this outing, the tribune of the Praetorian Guard raised his sword and struck the first blow. Others quickly followed his example. Within minutes, the tyrant was dead.

Arria Major (died A.D. 42) was unfailing in her devotion to her family. At one point both her husband, Caecina Paetus, and her son fell gravely ill at the same time. When the son died, Arria feared that the terrible news might kill her husband, so she chose not to tell him. Only after Paetus had fully recovered did she tell him of their great loss.

The ultimate proof of Arria's devotion came a few years later. In A.D. 42, Paetus was serving in the Roman province of Illyricum when he joined a former consul, Lucius Scribonius, in a plot against the emperor Claudius. When the conspiracy failed, Paetus was among those arrested and recalled to Rome. Arria was not allowed to accompany her husband. Undeterred, she hired a private boat, crossed the Adriatic Sea, and reached Rome when Paetus did.

Found guilty of treason, Paetus was allowed to choose his manner of death: suicide or execution. Arria knew Paetus would choose suicide as the noblest route, so she resolved to share his fate. Alone with him for the last time, she took a dagger and plunged it into her breast. She then handed the weapon to her husband, saying, "Paetus, it does not hurt." He then followed her example.

Lucan (Marcus Annaeus Lucanus) (A.D. 39–65) was born in Spain, but emigrated at an early age to Rome. In the years that followed, his uncle Seneca, an advisor to the emperor Nero, oversaw his education and showed Nero some of the young man's writings. Impressed by Lucan's talent, Nero included him in the inner circle of palace associates.

In A.D. 60, at the age of 21, Lucan won a prize for a poem in praise of Nero. Two or three years later, Lucan published the first three books of his epic *Pharsalia*. Nero, however, jealously guarded his own reputation as a poet and detested all who might rival him. When Lucan's genius became a threat to the emperor's self-esteem, he decreed that Lucan could no longer give public readings.

Furious at such unfair treatment, Lucan turned against Nero and joined the conspiracy of Piso in A.D. 65. After Piso's attempt failed and the 26-year-old Lucan was given a choice between execution and suicide, he chose the latter. As the blood poured from his self-inflicted wound, Lucan recited lines he had written about a soldier bleeding to death: "His tears were blood . . . his perspiration flows red, and every limb is drenched from the flowing veins. Thus is the whole body one wound."

Lucan's reputation rests on the bursts of energy, imagination, and directness found throughout his work. Unfortunately, little of his poetry has survived except for 10 books of the *Bellum Civile* (Civil War), which focused on the conflict between Julius Caesar and Pompey in the 40s B.C. Written in epic style on the model of Virgil's *Aeneid*, it contains several powerful passages.

Petronius (Gaius Petronius Arbiter) (died A.D. 46) spent his days sleeping and his nights working or enjoying himself—at least according to Tacitus, who also said of Petronius, "Energy is often the basis of success, but idleness made Petronius. . . . Yet, as governor of the province of Bithynia he showed himself a capable administrator. Then, returning to his old habits, he accepted Nero's invitation to join his small inner circle of friends and became the emperor's *elegantiae arbiter* [director of elegance]."

Aware that Tigellinus, Nero's chief of staff, was plotting his ruin, Petronius took his own life. Petronius' major work, the *Satyricon*, presents a vivid portrait of fun-loving Rome in the 1st century A.D. "Trimalchio's Dinner," one of its most famous episodes, tells of a vulgar but extremely rich freedman named Trimalchio who hosts a dinner for several friends and acquaintances. When he invites his guests to tell stories, each tries to outdo the others with obscene tales and absurd adventures.

Trimalchio interrupts the fun and asks a guest named Niceros, to tell of his adventure. Niceros shocks the other guests with a tale of a companion who, while walking by a cemetery one evening, "suddenly stopped, looked to the sky, and before I could react, turned into a wolf. Then, pointing his 'muzzle' toward the moon, he let out an ear-piercing howl and fled into the woods."

Because Petronius used the *sermo plebeius* (the language spoken by the common people) in recounting this tale, it is one of the few surviving records of colloquial Latin from the period. Furthermore, unlike most Latin works, which focus more on narrative than on character, Petronius' Trimalchio is a memorable individual and one of the great comic characters in literature.

Galba (Servius Sulpicius Galba), (around 3 B.C.–A.D. 69) the seventh of the "Twelve Caesars" to rule Rome, traced his ancestry to some of Rome's most noble citizens. After serving as proconsul in Africa in A.D. 45, Galba chose to retire from public life, but in A.D. 60 the emperor Nero offered him a governorship in Spain, where Galba served for eight years. According to the historian Suetonius, in A.D. 68 Galba intercepted a secret message from Nero ordering his assassination. So when Roman officials in nearby provinces proposed that he join them in a plot to rid the empire of Nero's tyranny, Galba readily agreed.

When Nero committed suicide, Roman troops throughout the provinces, as well as the powerful Praetorian Guard, hailed Galba as the new emperor. Although no relation to the Caesars, Galba took the name of Servius Galba Caesar Augustus and began marching slowly toward Rome. Once in power he proved to be a cruel ruler. On January 2, A.D. 69, the Roman army in Germany proclaimed the general Vitellius emperor. Before long the Praetorian Guard declared their allegiance to another rival, Marcus Salvius Otho, who promptly ordered that the 72-year-old Galba be put to death.

Otho (Marcus Salvius Otho) (A.D. 32–69) was only 37 when he eliminated Galba and became emperor of Rome, but he had already experienced the dangers of political life. More than 10 years earlier, the emperor Nero had fallen in love with Otho's wife, Poppaea Sabina, and forced Otho to divorce Poppaea so that he might marry her. Nero then sent Otho to govern the distant Roman province of Lusitania (Portugal and western Spain).

Otho remained in Spain until Nero's death in A.D. 68. When Otho then heard that Galba was prepared to declare himself emperor, Otho pledged his support to Galba. He felt deeply betrayed the following year when Galba named Piso Licinianus as his successor.

In league with the Praetorian Guard, Otho had Galba assassinated. But Otho's position proved to be as shaky as the hated Galba's because the troops in Germany continued to back their commander, Vitellius, for the imperial throne.

In March A.D. 69, Vitellius' troops defeated Otho's near Cremona in northern Italy. Soon after, Otho committed suicide. His reign lasted only 95 days.

Vitellius (Aulus Vitellius) (A.D. 15–69) was governor of lower Germany when his troops proclaimed him emperor on January 2, A.D. 69. Vitellius had begun his march south to Rome when he learned that Marcus Salvius Otho had also been proclaimed emperor. Civil war was now inevitable, and on April 19 Vitellius' troops defeated Otho's, leading to Otho's suicide.

Vitellius reached Rome with his troops in July and soon revealed that he was incompetent and unfit to rule. Roman troops in the East, who had initially backed Vitellius, began hailing the general Vespasian as emperor. In the fall, a pro-Vespasian commander from the Danube region, Primus, marched on Rome and defeated Vitellius' forces at Cremona. On December 20, Vespasian's forces invaded the city. Realizing that all was lost, Vitellius hid in an empty house belonging to his wife. His enemies found him, dragged him out, and put him to death.

Titus (Titus Flavius Vespasianus) (A.D. 39–81) accompanied his father, Vespasian, to the East in A.D. 67 to help quell a Jewish revolt that threatened Rome's authority in the area. Within two years, the entire area (except for Jerusalem) had fallen under Roman control. Called to assume the emperorship in Rome in A.D. 69, Vespasian left Titus to take Jerusalem, which he did in May A.D. 70. Titus then returned to Rome to celebrate a joint triumph with his father. To commemorate his victory in Jerusalem, Titus later commissioned the building of the Arch of Titus.

As emperor, Titus continued his father's building projects and ordered the completion of the Flavian Amphitheater (known today as the Colosseum). The original structure covered approximately five acres; its walls were nearly 160 feet high and it had an estimated seating capacity of 50,000.

Suetonius wrote that Titus was a kind-hearted ruler. At dinner one evening Titus is said to have remarked, "My friends, I have wasted a day" after realizing he had let the day pass without doing anyone a favor.

Unfortunately for Titus, disaster struck three times during his brief rule. The first calamity occurred in A.D. 79, when Mount Vesuvius erupted and buried several surrounding towns, in-

Sometime after A.D. 81, the Romans erected an arch to Titus, commemorating his capture of Jerusalem 11 years earlier. Relief panels decorating the arch show Roman soldiers carrying the spoils of war as they march in the emperor's triumphal procession.

cluding Pompeii, Herculaneum, and Stabiae. The following year a devastating fire burned for three days and three nights, destroying much of Rome. That same year, one of the worst plagues ever to afflict Rome broke out. After each disaster, Titus immediately appropriated funds for relief work, even stripping his own country homes to help refurnish the temples and public buildings.

Suddenly, on September 13, A.D. 81—after a reign of only two years, two months, and 20 days—Titus died, at the age of 41. All Rome mourned his passing and, according to Suetonius, the empire lost the "love and darling of the human race."

Agricola (Gnaeus Julius Agricola) (A.D. 40–93) was appointed governor of Britain in A.D. 71 by the emperor Vespasian. The latter did so in appreciation for Agricola's support in the civil war that had brought Vespasian to power in A.D. 69. Agricola continued to hold this post under Vespasian's sons, Titus and Domitian.

An extremely capable general, Agricola gradually extended Rome's boundaries farther into northern England and conquered areas in Wales and the island of Mona (present-day Anglesey). To protect the northern frontier he advanced into Scotland as far as the highlands and established military outposts in strategic areas across the territory. Agricola also managed to circumnavigate the island of Britain, a feat that Roman historians noted with great admiration. Agricola's greatest accomplishments, however, and those for which he is most remembered, were his Romanization of Britain and his wise consolidation of the island's economy.

According to Tacitus, who married Agricola's daughter in A.D. 78, Agricola was a master military strategist and capable administrator as well as a loyal, honest, and modest Roman citizen.

Nerva (Marcus Cocceius Nerva) (around A.D. 30–98) became emperor in A.D. 96 on the same day that Domitian was assassinated. Whether or not he was involved in the conspiracy is uncertain, but the Senate recognized Nerva as the perfect choice, because he was a fellow senator and had opposed Domitian's autocratic rule.

Approximately 65 years old at the time of his accession, Nerva had been consul with Vespasian in A.D. 71 and with Domitian in A.D. 90. A peaceful and just individual, Nerva won the respect of his peers, but he was not strong enough to oppose the Praetorian Guard, who had remained faithful to Domitian. He yielded to their demands that he arrest and condemn the principal conspirators in the emperor's death.

After just 17 months in office, Nerva died suddenly on January 25, A.D. 98. The first of the so-called five good emperors, he wisely provided for a successor by adopting Trajan, the commander of Roman troops in Germany.

Statius (Publius Papinius Statius) (A.D. 45–96) is considered a principal epic and lyric poet of what is often referred to as the silver age of Latin literature. Statius completed one epic work, entitled *Thebaid*, which focused on the legendary struggle for control of the ancient Greek city of Thebes. His second work, *Achilleid*, centered on the great Greek hero Achilles but ended abruptly, perhaps cut short by the poet's death. Using the master epic poet Virgil as his model, Statius wrote verses that exhibit power, dramatic suspense, and colorful descriptions.

Statius' continuous use of hyperbole and his exaggerated flattery of Domitian have caused many to criticize his work. In his defense, Statius was living in difficult times, when a phrase or passage misread or misinterpreted could result in condemnation and the death sentence.

Statius' 32-poem collection entitled *Silvae* celebrates life's enjoyments and has provided historians with reliable accounts of the wealthy class of *libertini* (freedmen) under Domitian's rule. His most famous poem is *Ode to Sleep*, which ends: "Come, Sleep, I ask you not to pour complete wings on my eyes—let the happier people pray for this—touch me with the last part of the branch—that is enough—or cross lightly on tiptoe."

Pliny the Elder (Gaius Plinius Secundus) (A.D. 23 or 24–79) began his military career at about the age of 23, serving with the Roman legions in Germany. While in Germany, Pliny began writing a history of Roman military campaigns in the area.

Returning to Rome in A.D. 57 or 58, Pliny spent the next few years in retirement, possibly because he disliked the new emperor, Nero. With Nero's death and Vespasian's accession, Pliny once again entered political life. For a time he served in Germany with the future emperor Titus. Writing, however, continued to occupy much of his free time, for he had begun his great work the *Natural History*. Of all his writings only this has survived.

In A.D. 79, Pliny held the post of commander of the fleet at Misenum, a small port town on the Bay of Naples. When reports reached him on August 23 of an unusual cloud formation across the bay to the east, Pliny decided to investigate personally. In the hours that followed, Pliny found it increasingly difficult to breathe and collapsed.

The 37 books of his *Natural History* gradually were accepted as the leading authority on scientific matters, and his facts went unchallenged until 1492, when an Italian named Niccolò Leoniceno disputed them. Other scientists soon followed his lead. Historically, however, the *Natural History* is an important literary work and provides an invaluable insight into the scientific world of the 1st century A.D.

SCOTLAND

IRELAND

WALES

ENGLAND

MONA
(ANGLESEY)

VECTIS
(ISLE OF WIGHT)

Rhine River

Ara
Ubiorum •

Trier •

GERMANY

Danube River

GAUL
(FRANCE)

Vindo
(Vien

Lugdunum •

Lake
Garda

Frigidu
River

GALLAECIA

Aquae Sextiae

Po River

Nicaea •

Sal

Numantia •

Massilia
(Marseilles)

CORSICA

ELBA

Tiber River

SPAIN

Bilbilis

Salo River

Rome •

Pollentia •

PANDATARIA •

Cordoba •

SARDINIA

Bay of
Naples

CAPRI

BAETICA

Pillars of Hercules
(Strait of Gibraltar)

Mediterranean

Himera

Mylae

SICILY

Carthage •

Syracuse •

AFRICA NOVA
(ALGERIA)

NUMIDIA

Thamugadi •

Thapsus •

Lepcis Magna •

AFRICA

| 0 | 200 | 400 | 600 kilometers |

| 0 | 200 | 400 | 600 miles |

THE WORLD OF ANCIENT ROME
390 B.C. – A.D. 410

ASIA

Sarmizagethusa

Sirmium

COLCHIS   Caucasus Mts.   Caspian Sea

Tomis   Black Sea

SCYTHIA

Naissus

Serdica
(Sofia)
Dyracchium   Bosporus

Pydna   Thessalonica   Byzantium (later Constantinople;
Apollonia   Philippi   now Istanbul)

Thermopylae   Troy   Nicomedia
Delphi   Chaeronea   LESBOS   ASIA MINOR
Actium   Thebes   Mitylene   Tigris River   PARTHIA

ARCADIA   Ephesus   Faustinopolis   Carrhae
Gulf of   ANDROS   Tarsus   Issus
Ambracia   Athens   Antioch   Euphrates River
Sparta   BOEOTIA   Orontes River   Palmyra   Ctesiphon
RHODES   Palmyra

CRETE   CYPRUS   Damascus
Sea   PHOENICIA   Tyre   LEBANON

Jerusalem
JUDAEA   JORDAN

Alexandria
Pelusium   Petra

LIBYA   Persian
Gulf

EGYPT   ARABIA

Nile River

Red Sea

Syene
(Aswan)

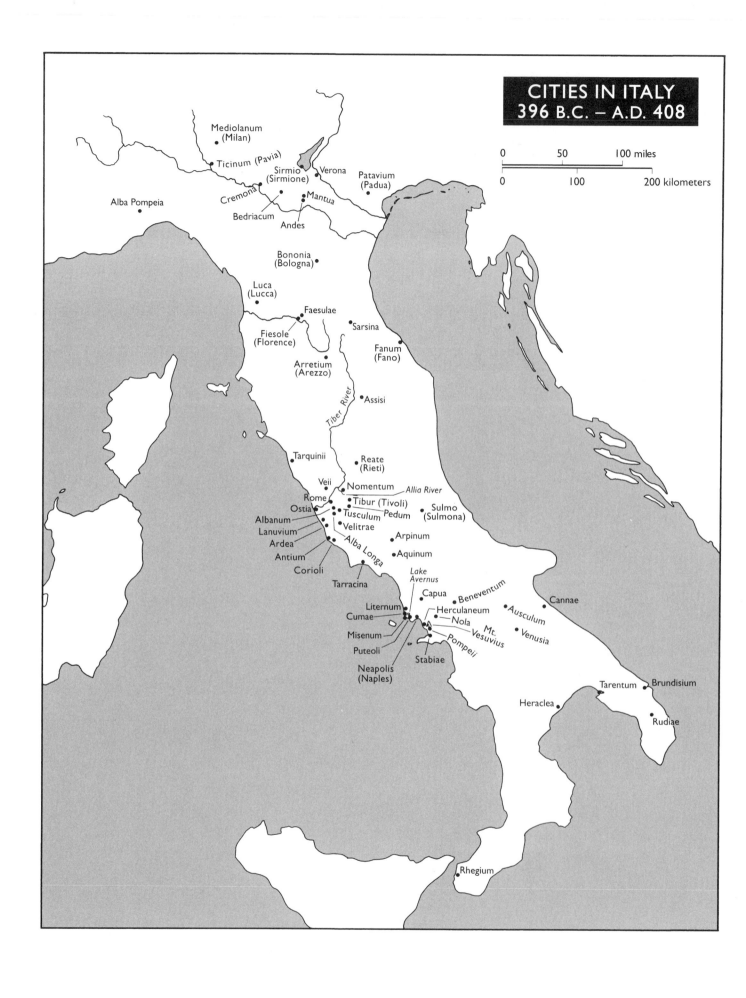

**CITIES IN ITALY
396 B.C. – A.D. 408**

Mediolanum (Milan)
Ticinum (Pavia)
Sirmio (Sirmione)
Verona
Patavium (Padua)
Alba Pompeia
Cremona
Mantua
Bedriacum
Andes
Bononia (Bologna)
Luca (Lucca)
Faesulae
Sarsina
Fiesole (Florence)
Fanum (Fano)
Arretium (Arezzo)
Tiber River
Assisi
Tarquinii
Reate (Rieti)
Veii
Nomentum
Allia River
Rome
Tibur (Tivoli)
Ostia
Tusculum
Pedum
Sulmo (Sulmona)
Albanum
Velitrae
Lanuvium
Arpinum
Ardea
Alba Longa
Aquinum
Antium
Corioli
Tarracina
Lake Avernus
Capua
Beneventum
Ausculum
Cannae
Liternum
Herculaneum
Cumae
Nola
Misenum
Mt. Vesuvius
Venusia
Puteoli
Pompeii
Neapolis (Naples)
Stabiae
Tarentum
Brundisium
Heraclea
Rudiae
Rhegium

0   50   100 miles
0   100   200 kilometers

5 Preserving the Roman World (A.D. 98–410)

 Nerva had been the first of the five so-called good emperors to rule Rome, and although his reign was short it served to temper the instability and sense of insecurity that had settled on the Roman world. With Trajan's accession after Nerva's death in A.D. 98, Rome again became a stabilizing and respected world power. Prosperity returned, and Rome's treasury filled once more. While some leaders continued to focus on expansion, others sought to consolidate and strengthen Rome's existing boundaries, trade routes, and government policies.

Complementing this emphasis on restoring confidence in Rome's power were several building programs. Emperors constructed a number of colossal monuments to reflect Rome's greatness as well as their own authoritative role in the empire.

Part 5 of *Ancient Romans,* like Part 1, spans several centuries. There the similarity ends. Whereas Part 1 ends with Rome's relentless rise to world supremacy, Part 5 ends with what is generally termed the fall of Rome. But this "fall" involves only the collapse of the western Roman Empire with its capital at Rome. The glory of the eastern Roman Empire, focused on its capital of Constantinople (now Istanbul), was just beginning.

Part 5 centers on people who sought to preserve the Roman Empire and to maintain the ideals and traditions that had allowed it to become one of the world's greatest nations.

Trajan
(Marcus Ulpius
Traianus)

"THE BEST LEADER"

rajan paid little heed to Augustus' advice to keep the empire's boundaries at the Rhine and Euphrates rivers. His army was well disciplined, its soldiers ready to follow his every command. Why, he reasoned, should mighty Rome stop at these rivers when victory on the battlefield seemed to come so easily? Trajan no doubt thought of a previous world conqueror, Alexander the Great, and his victorious march to India. Perhaps he, Trajan, could do the same. However, when Trajan reached the Persian Gulf in A.D. 115, the first and only Roman general ever to do so, tradition indicates that he broke down and wept. Now 62, Trajan felt that he was too old to complete the strenuous march to India. Yet he was not displeased with himself, for his life had been a full one.

Born in A.D. 53, in the southern Spanish town of Baetica, Trajan came from a well-to-do Roman family who preferred the military to academic studies. As a result, Trajan spent much of his youth at military outposts with his father. Around A.D. 75, when his father was the provincial governor of Syria, Trajan held the post there of military tribune (a senior officer of the legion). In the years that followed, Trajan moved up the political ladder, holding the offices of quaestor, aedile, and praetor. Around the year A.D. 89, he received command of a legion, with orders to crush Saturninus' attempt to overthrow the emperor Domitian by fomenting a revolt in his province of Upper Germany. But the revolt ended before Trajan could reach Germany.

In the years that followed, the emperor Domitian became increasingly suspicious of those about him and ordered many people killed. Trajan managed to escape his wrath and even won his favor. In the year A.D. 91 Domitian granted

Commissioned during Trajan's reign, this relief was one of several that honored the emperor's institution of the *alimenta,* a social-welfare program for poor children. Trajan is shown, at left, addressing the people from the Temple of the Deified Julius Caesar and, at right, seated with a figure representing Italy standing by his outstretched arm.

Trajan the honored position of consul, Rome's most prestigious office next to emperor.

When assassins killed Domitian in A.D. 96, Trajan was serving as the governor of Upper Germany. Domitian's successor, Nerva, aware of Trajan's skill as a military commander and his ability to get along with the Senate, officially adopted him as his son and designated him to be his successor. Three months later, Trajan learned that Nerva had died and the Senate was proclaiming him Rome's new emperor.

The transfer of power was smooth and immediate, with no objections to Trajan's being an "outsider," that is, a Roman from the provinces. But Trajan was not anxious to proceed to Rome. He remained in Germany for almost a year, inspecting and strengthening the empire's borders along the Rhine and Danube rivers.

Trajan did, however, address his imperial duties and issued several decrees from his post in Germany. Among the first was the deification of Nerva and the discharge (or execution, according to some sources) of the Praetorian Guards who had forced Nerva to kill Domitian's assassins. Then, contrary to accepted practice, Trajan granted his soldiers only half the cash gifts normally given by a new emperor. (This was an economic measure designed to keep the public treasury out of debt.) Surprisingly, the military did not revolt or even complain—a marked testament to their respect for Trajan.

Once in Rome, Trajan continued to implement the administrative changes he felt were necessary. Well aware that the senators wished a return to the policies of the republic, when the Senate had been an active governing body, Trajan made it a practice to consult individual senators and hold informal group meetings. He also called for secret ballots in the Senate, believing this would grant each senator the freedom to act as he felt

"Anonymous accusations are the worst examples of our times and are not of our rule."

—Trajan, in a letter written to Pliny the Younger (between A.D. 111 and 113)

appropriate. Because Trajan allowed more provincials into the Senate, this body began to focus less on Rome itself and respond more to the needs of the entire empire. The great majority of senators welcomed the respect Trajan gave them and served him well in return, even though they knew he alone had the final decision on all matters.

After settling affairs with the Senate, Trajan turned to the people. Following the example set by several of his predecessors, he gave cash donations to the citizens. He also revamped the welfare system, redefining the criteria that determined who was poor and increasing the number of those eligible for free grain. Aware that his predecessors had consistently raised taxes and that the provinces had had to struggle to pay their share, Trajan cut taxes and decreased the amount of gold that cities normally sent to a new emperor.

To curtail corruption and other abuses in the provinces, Trajan carefully chose those whom he promoted to the rank of governor. To provinces where previous Roman magistrates had caused problems, Trajan sent special administrators to investigate and correct the situation. One such administrator was Pliny the Younger, whom Trajan assigned to Bithynia, on the northern coast of Asia Minor. From Pliny's letters to the emperor during his two years in the province we have learned that Trajan, not the provincial governors, was the one in charge. Per-

To commemorate his victory over the Dacians, Trajan ordered a column some 100 feet in height erected in his Forum at Rome. Scenes of battles, Dacian and Roman campsites, and soldiers marching through Dacia were carved in a spiral design over the entire length of the column.

haps the best-known correspondence between the two involves Pliny's questioning of Trajan on how to handle the Christians. Trajan's reply shows that he was opposed to hasty action and did not believe in condemning anyone for their beliefs as long as they did not interfere with Roman policy. It also reveals that Trajan sought to maintain peace whenever possible.

Trajan's best-known decree affected the growing numbers of poor children in the cities throughout Italy. Aware that these youngsters had no resources or possibilities of education, he established a public fund, known as the *alimenta* (food), to provide for their needs. While some sources maintain that Trajan's predecessor, Nerva, was the one who actually implemented the *alimenta*, most agree that it was Trajan's idea.

Though his policies and personality made him extremely popular, Trajan still worried about treason and rebellion. To counteract any budding conspiracy or discontent, Trajan created a new bodyguard of carefully chosen mounted soldiers. Mostly Germans and Pannonians (people who lived in part of present-day Hungary and Yugoslavia), this group numbered 500 at first, then 1,000. On the whole, however, Trajan adhered firmly to the belief that a true Roman emperor should not be a *dominus* (master) but a *princeps* (leader). The Romans agreed with Trajan's assessment and awarded him the prestigious title of *Optimus Princeps*, the "best leader."

Trajan's main goal as emperor was always to strengthen the empire, mainly through extending its borders and conquering those tribes that constantly harassed Roman outposts. In A.D. 101–102 he invaded Dacia (present-day Romania), capturing its capital and forcing Decebalus, its king, to accept

Trajan

BORN

September A.D. 53
Baetica, Spain

DIED

August 8, A.D. 117
Selinus, Asia Minor

PROFESSION

General and emperor

ACCOMPLISHMENTS

Established public funds for the support of poor children; lowered taxes; increased the number of people eligible for free grain; conquered Dacia; extended the empire's eastern boundaries to include Arabia; conquered Parthia and placed a pro-Roman ruler on the throne; inaugurated a massive building program that included roads, bridges, the Forum of Trajan, Trajan's Column, public baths, and an aqueduct

Rome's peace terms. Under the agreement, Decebalus was to support Rome and its allies and render them whatever assistance they needed.

In A.D. 105, Decebalus violated this agreement, laying siege to the Roman garrisons in Dacia and attacking the neighboring Iazyges, who were allies of Rome. Once again, Trajan led his army north and invaded Dacia. After freeing the garrisons, he marched across a great bridge his architect, Apollodorus of Damascus, had built over the Danube River and retook Dacia's capital. Refusing to become a prisoner, Decebalus committed suicide.

Gold and silver from the rich Dacian mines soon began pouring into Rome's treasury, allowing Trajan to embark on an extensive building program. From the beginning of his rule, he had spent money on urgently needed repairs to roads, harbors, and public buildings. Now, with the added revenue, he could really employ the talents of Apollodorus.

To commemorate his victory over Dacia, Trajan ordered the building of a monument that still stands today and is known as Trajan's Column. Around the base, sculptors carved great mounds of captured weapons. Spiraling upward around the 100-foot column are 155 scenes depicting in chronological order Trajan's campaigns in Dacia. The remarkably detailed carving presents a vivid portrait of the ancients—their armor and weapons, their distinctive facial features, the towns and fortresses under siege, the tortures and cruelties inflicted by both sides, and the Dacian countryside. Trajan is depicted in many scenes, making sacrifices to the gods, addressing his soldiers, receiving envoys, and finally accepting the surrender of the Dacians. (Originally, a statue of Trajan stood atop the column, but in 1588 it was replaced by one of the Christian saint Peter.) The identity of the architect of Trajan's Column is unknown, but many scholars credit Apollodorus with its design.

Trajan's Column rose majestically above a splendid new forum, the Forum of Trajan. As a testament to the emperor's military skills, a statue of Trajan on horseback stood in a porticoed square in the center of the Forum. To make room for streets, shops, and warehouses, the lower slopes of the Capitoline and Quirinal hills were cut back. Also incorporated into the design of the Forum area were libraries, with countless Greek and Latin books, and a temple.

To the north of the Forum were the Markets of Trajan, with a central hall 84 feet long and 30 feet wide that housed 150 stores and businesses—an early prototype of the modern shopping mall. Even more majestic were Trajan's public baths, the largest yet built in Rome, where intricate mechanisms regulated the temperature of air and water. To bring in the necessary water, Trajan commissioned Apollodorus to design a new aqueduct. Its completion came only two days after the opening of the baths.

Trajan did not confine his public works program to Rome. He inaugurated similar projects across Italy and in the provinces, although none of those were as extensive. He also focused considerable attention on building a great network of roads and bridges throughout the empire. And at Thamugadi in Numidia, Trajan founded a colony for former soldiers, the ruins of which provide an excellent idea of life in a provincial city.

Romans and provincials everywhere appreciated Trajan's efforts, especially because he did not increase taxes or seek other burdensome ways to raise the needed money. According to the

Roman historian Dio Cassius, Trajan envied no one and honored and praised all whom he considered good. He himself was slow to anger and paid little attention to lies and slander. A tall, well-built man whose hair turned gray prematurely, Trajan visited the homes of fellow citizens, at times without a guard, and enjoyed a pleasant time with them.

The Dacian campaign was the chief military achievement of Trajan's rule. The triumph awarded him for this success was the most magnificent ever held in Rome. Tradition says that the games celebrating Trajan's victory lasted 123 days, that 11,000 animals were slaughtered in the arena, and that 10,000 gladiators fought to the death.

However, Trajan's military achievements did not end with the conquest of Dacia. In A.D. 106, he turned his attention to the East, creating the province of Arabia to secure the land bordering the eastern Mediterranean Sea. Four years later, the Parthians began to threaten Roman interests in the region, deposing the pro-Roman king of neighboring Armenia and installing their own puppet ruler. The Romans did not react immediately, but in 114 Trajan himself led the troops into Armenia and captured the area. The following year, the Romans advanced into Parthia and took its capital city of Ctesiphon.

Buoyed by these seemingly easy victories, Trajan continued his advance and marched to the Persian Gulf, but at this point he sadly abandoned his dream of becoming a world conqueror on the scale of Alexander. He was not ready to retire as a general, however, and led a second expedition into Parthia in A.D. 116. Even this conquest failed to subdue the Parthians for long, and Trajan finally had to recognize that the borders of the empire were extended so far in the East that Rome's armies could not hope to patrol them effectively.

Frustrated in his ambitions and feeling unwell, Trajan made preparations to return home. He soon fell ill, and in August A.D.117 the 64-year-old emperor died at Selinus on the southern coast of Asia Minor. His beloved wife, Plotina, was at his side.

Trajan's ashes were carried to Rome and buried with great ceremony in the base of his triumphal column. While the Roman world mourned Trajan's death, the question of succession was on everyone's mind. With no children of his own, Trajan had supposedly announced on his deathbed that he had adopted Hadrian, the Roman general in charge of the eastern provinces. But not everyone agreed with this choice, and some even rumored that Plotina, not Trajan, had appointed Hadrian. Whatever the case, the Senate voted Hadrian Trajan's successor.

As the decades passed, Romans and provincials throughout the Mediterranean world fondly remembered Trajan's rule and agreed with the inscriptions on his coins that spoke of happiness, justice, security, and prosperity. Two hundred years later, Romans would still consider this period the height of the empire, and the historian Eutropius would write that every emperor should wish to be *felicior Augusto, melior Traino* (happier than Augustus, better than Trajan).

FURTHER READING

Lepper, F. A. *Trajan's Parthian War*. New York: Oxford University Press, 1948.

Rossi, Lino. *Trajan's Column and the Dacian Wars*. Ithaca, N.Y.: Cornell University Press, 1971.

Hadrian
(Publius Aelius Hadrianus)

THE TRAVELING EMPEROR

When Hadrian was nine years old his father died and he was adopted by distant relatives, the emperor Trajan and his wife, Plotina, who had no children of their own. According to the provisions in Hadrian's father's will, both Trajan and Attianus were to be the youngster's guardians and advisors. A native of Baetica in southern Spain, like the emperor, Attianus quickly won Trajan's respect and became a chief officer in his Praetorian Guard. After Trajan's death, Attianus was instrumental in making certain that Hadrian was recognized as the heir and rightful successor.

Young Hadrian received an admirable education with the best Greek and Roman tutors and was groomed for a leading role in Roman affairs. Over the ensuing years, he accompanied Trajan on the battlefield against the Dacians, commanded legions, and governed the province of Lower Pannonia.

In A.D. 108, when he was 32, Hadrian gained the prestigious office of consul. Four years later he became the chief Roman official in Athens. Nomination to this post was a great honor and Hadrian welcomed the opportunity to spend time in the city whose customs, literature, and art he loved. But military needs soon called Hadrian from the peaceful atmosphere of Athens to Syria. In the East he extended the empire's boundaries into Parthia and served as commander of the legions in Syria, a key military post.

For Hadrian, hunting a wild boar provided relaxation and a respite from the daily pressures of ruling the empire.

The Pantheon, built in the early 1st century A.D. and then rebuilt by Hadrian approximately 100 years later, stands today as a symbol of "eternal Rome." Within its walls, emperors, kings, queens, and prime ministers have worked, worshiped, and made plans for the future of the city. This photograph was taken in 1883.

The sequence of events that led to Hadrian's elevation to emperor in 117 is a matter of conjecture, because ancient sources have little to say about it. Trajan seems to have died on August 8. Hadrian learned of the death the next day, but only on August 11 was it announced that the emperor was dead and that he had adopted Hadrian on his deathbed. The army did not question the report and immediately hailed Hadrian as Rome's new emperor. The Senate also gave its official approval, despite grumbling by some senators that others were just as qualified for the position. But all the official seals and proclamations could not squelch rumors that Plotina, Trajan's wife, had fabricated the story that the dying Trajan personally chose Hadrian to succeed him.

Hadrian, a cautious man, decided to consolidate his position in the East be-fore proceeding to Rome. Believing that Trajan's conquests in Parthia, Armenia, and Mesopotamia would be a continuous drain on Rome's military and financial resources, Hadrian ordered his generals to pull their soldiers back to the Euphrates River. (The emperor Augustus had advised his successors to keep the Euphrates as the empire's eastern boundary, but Trajan had refused to listen.) A number of senators still endorsed Trajan's desire for expansion and bitterly opposed Hadrian's "retreat."

In Rome, Hadrian's old mentor Attianus, commander of the Praetorian Guard, took action to quell any dangerous dissent in the Senate. As a result, four senators, all of whom had held the office of consul, were charged with conspiracy and executed. Although Hadrian claimed he was not responsible for the killings, his relationship with the Senate suffered.

In the summer of 118, approximately a year after Trajan's death, Hadrian arrived in Rome. To win the support of the people, he increased the amount of public funding offered by the state, held magnificent gladiator shows, granted Italian cities a dispensation from sending the customary accession gifts, increased the *alimenta* (food) system Trajan had established to help poor children, and cancelled all debts owed to the state dating from the past 15 years. Hadrian also concerned himself with the legal system and commissioned the well-known African jurist Julianus to collect and compile the various laws and regulations that the praetors had issued over the years. Julianus' work greatly benefited the poor by listing their rights in a public document.

In the interest of fair treatment for all his subjects, Hadrian implemented many other measures. Masters who tortured or killed their slaves were liable to be punished. Roman fathers, who by tradition had held the right of life or death over their families, now found their authority curtailed. Helping Hadrian decide the many legal problems presented to him was a newly appointed board of legal advisors.

After spending three years in Rome attending to administrative duties, Hadrian left to inspect the empire personally. He wanted to see for himself the needs of his subjects so that he could propose laws and programs that would benefit the people in each province. For him the empire was not a collection of conquered areas subject to the whims of an absentee ruler but a commonwealth composed of individual provinces. He therefore thought that personal visits were necessary to maintain good relations between subjects and ruler and to discourage corruption and unfair business practices.

Hadrian strongly encouraged each province to retain and honor its own national identity. To emphasize his feelings on this matter he commissioned the minting of a series of coins, each honoring a province or area. The principal figure on the coins was a woman dressed in the native costume of the province she was representing. In her hand was an appropriate symbol; for example, coins honoring Greece included an image representative of the Olympic games.

Hadrian was a strong-minded man not easily swayed by anyone else's opinion. He accepted conspiracies and threats as a part of life as emperor and refused to invoke the law of treason (which said that anyone found guilty of conspiring against the state must be executed). Nor did he ever resort to employing informers. Even in his appearance he was an individualist—the first emperor to grow a beard, a precedent his successors followed.

In 121, Hadrian set out for Gaul and Germany. The following year found him in Britain, carefully inspecting the northern defense system. Here Rome had two separate problems. Not only did Roman soldiers have to guard against invasion from the unconquered north but even in the south there were tribes that refused to accept Roman rule. To afford better protection for his troops, Hadrian commissioned the building of a great wall, approximately 80 miles long, from Wallsend-on-Tyne on the east coast to Bowness-on-Solway on the west. Constructed of stone in the east and turf in the west, the wall reached a height of 15 feet and a width of 20 feet in some areas. Several gates provided passage through the wall, while strategically located forts and towers allowed Roman soldiers to patrol the border safely. As an added precaution against invaders, the soldiers dug a V-shaped ditch away from the base of the wall. Today visitors from around the world walk along Hadrian's Wall, where 15,000 Roman soldiers once stood guard. The surrounding area has become an

Hadrian

BORN

January 24, A.D. 76
Baetica (southern Spain) or Rome

DIED

July 10, A.D. 138
Baiae, Italy

PROFESSION

General and emperor

ACCOMPLISHMENTS

Maintained peace in most of the Roman world for 21 years; re-established Rome's eastern border at the Euphrates River; ordered the building of Hadrian's Wall in northern England; ordered a compilation of the edicts and laws passed by the praetors; reorganized and strengthened the military; rebuilt the Pantheon and commissioned the building of other temples; ordered the building of an enormous private villa at Tibur and a massive tomb for himself in Rome

archaeological treasure house for research on that historical period.

Because families of the soldiers stationed in this remote region often chose to accompany their loved ones, settlements gradually cropped up along the wall. Eventually, as the threat of war passed, the settlements attracted many new residents. Trade increased, and with it the economic prosperity of the settlements. For Hadrian the settlements were an even greater deterrent to war than the fortifications; he encouraged their growth not only in Britain but in other frontier areas as well. He then began to assign troops permanently to an area, further encouraging the growth of new settlements. Naturally, this change affected the soldiers, who now began performing nonmilitary as well as traditional service duties. A troop's responsibilities expanded to include the escorting of grain supplies, quarrying stone, guarding cattle, and the like. As the decades passed, these settlements played a key role in the Romanization of the local people.

Hadrian did not remain in Britain to see the completion of his wall, which took until 126, but continued to inspect the outposts of the empire. Everywhere, the troops warmly welcomed their commander in chief. They respected his insistence on strict discipline and appreciated his eagerness to understand life from their viewpoint. To do this, Hadrian ate, slept, and lived in the soldiers' barracks, not in luxurious commanders' quarters.

In 123, Hadrian sailed east across the Mediterranean to Asia Minor. After settling some difficulties that had arisen between the Parthians and Romans, he turned west again, first to Athens, then home to Rome in 125. But his stay in the capital was relatively short. In the year 128, Hadrian set sail for North Africa, then returned to his beloved Athens. His preference for Greek literature, art, and philosophy won him the nickname of "the little Greek."

Hadrian soon left Greece for the Middle East, where he visited Syria, Arabia, and Egypt, finally returning to Rome around 132. Peace and prosperity continued to reign over the empire, and Hadrian saw himself as a second Augustus, responsible for maintaining world peace and ushering in Rome's second golden age.

But in 134 serious problems in Judaea brought Hadrian to the battlefield. Objecting to the establishment of a Roman temple and colony in Jerusalem, the Jews under Bar Kokhba (also known as Bar Koziba) had revolted in 132, taking the city in a surprise attack and annihilating the Roman garrison stationed there. Unwilling to tolerate any group that did not wish to be part of the empire or observe its laws, Hadrian gathered an army, marched east, and retook Jerusalem. Determined to avoid further confrontations, he forbade all Jews from entering the city. Then, with peace established, Hadrian returned to Rome.

His many years of travel and the heavy burden of ruling the empire were now beginning to weigh on Hadrian. Almost 60 years of age, he chose to devote his time to the pursuits that had always interested him: building and writing.

One of Hadrian's first projects was to rebuild the Pantheon, a temple dedicated to all the gods. Built between 27 and 25 B.C. by Augustus' friend Agrippa, the Pantheon lay in ruins after a fire that raced through it during Trajan's rule. Hadrian and his architect saw this as the perfect opportunity to try a new design that would reflect the might of the empire it represented. The entrance would be the traditional rectangular portico with three rows of columns, but the temple area would be round and its roof an immense dome, reaching up almost 142 feet. To light the massive interior there would be a

28-foot central opening in the dome, allowing the sun's rays to enter.

Still standing today, the rebuilt Pantheon is a leading symbol of Rome's grandeur. After the fall of the western empire, it became a Christian church, then a fortress, and is now a national monument where Italy's kings and great artists, such as Raphael, are buried. Though the Pantheon is the best known of Hadrian's temples, others include the Temple of Venus and Rome and the Temple of Trajan.

For his own enjoyment, Hadrian set about constructing an enormous villa on the hilly slopes of Tibur (modern Tivoli) on the outskirts of Rome. As with the Pantheon and other building projects, Hadrian worked together with his architects and engineers in creating and developing designs. For 10 years, from 125 to 135, workers labored on his villa. Covering approximately seven square miles, the complex included baths, sculpture gardens, outdoor dining areas, libraries, theaters, and pavilions. Each building represented a site or structure that Hadrian had admired on his travels—such as the celebrated Painted Porch of Athens, where the philosopher Socrates had taught—so that Hadrian could "revisit" all these places without the hazards and difficulties of real travel. Housed in these buildings were the art objects Hadrian had carefully collected during his travels. In this way he created what might be considered one of the greatest private museums in the ancient world. Even today, visitors to his estate continue to marvel at the beauty and majesty of his design.

As the years passed, Hadrian began to think about his impending death and the choice of a successor. As a young man, he had married Trajan's grandniece Vibia Sabina, but their marriage had been childless. In 136, Hadrian adopted a senator named Lucius Ceionius Commodus as his son and heir. Why Hadrian chose this particular man is uncertain, especially because Commodus disdained hard work. When Commodus died, Hadrian chose more wisely and adopted a well-respected senator named Antoninus. But choosing a successor just for himself was not enough for Hadrian. Determined to extend his power and influence long beyond his death, Hadrian made Antoninus adopt 18-year-old Marcus Aurelius as his own son and successor. In the years that followed, these proved to be beneficial decisions.

While selecting his heirs, Hadrian was also overseeing the completion of his tomb. Modeled on the structure built to house the body of Augustus, Hadrian's tomb was an enormous round building, approximately 230 feet in diameter, set on a square base. A series of attached columns graced the marble exterior. A cone-shaped marble dome surrounded by cypress trees crowned the massive structure.

When Hadrian died, in July 138, his tomb was still incomplete. Not until the following year did the new emperor, Antoninus, place Hadrian's remains in their proper burial chamber. For approximately the next 200 years, Hadrian's tomb became the official resting place for Rome's emperors. By the end of the 6th century it had become a fortress. Now known as the Castel Sant'Angelo (Castle of the Blessed Angel), it is a military museum and has become a popular tourist attraction.

FURTHER READING

Boatwright, Mary Taliaferro. *Hadrian and the City of Rome.* Princeton, N.J.: Princeton University Press, 1987.

Breeze, David J., and Brian Dobson. *Hadrian's Wall.* London: Allen Lane, 1976.

MacDonald, William L. *Hadrian's Villa and Its Legacy.* New Haven, Conn.: Yale University Press, 1995.

Juvenal (Decimus Junius Juvenalis)

MASTER SATIRIST

"W"hat shall I do in Rome? I cannot lie." So wrote Juvenal in A.D. 100. Nor was this his only negative remark about the empire's capital city. Further on in the same work he had the character Umbricius say:

> Since there is no place in Rome for honest skills, no rewards for work, since today my means is less than it was yesterday and tomorrow will wear away something from the little that remains, I propose to leave my country.

Born between A.D. 55 and 60 in Aquinum, just south of Rome, Juvenal came from a well-to-do family and entered

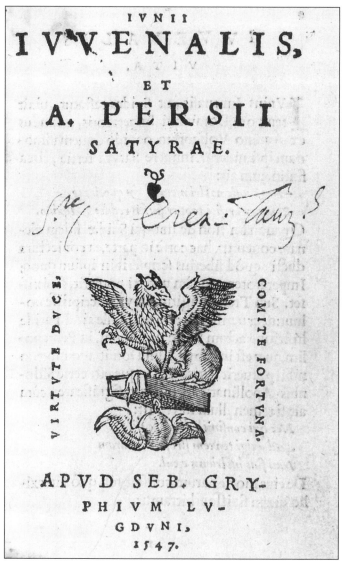

The popular satirist Aulus Persius died in A.D. 62, when Juvenal, who would become Rome's most famous satirist, was a young child. In later centuries, reprints of their works were often combined in one volume of satires.

"No one suddenly becomes a very bad man."

—from *Satire II* (between A.D. 100 and 110)

Juvenal

BORN
Between A.D. 55 and 60
Aquinum, Italy

DIED
After A.D. 127
Place unknown

PROFESSION
Satirist

ACCOMPLISHMENTS
Perfected the style of writing known as satire; wrote 16 satires, divided into five books arranged in order of publication

military service as a young man. When he was passed over for a promotion, he expressed his disappointment in satires (literary works in dialogue, verse, and poetry that use ridicule and good humor to expose vices, abuses, and the the like). Because Domitian, the emperor at the time, did not allow public dissent or ridicule, Juvenal's sarcasm was considered unpatriotic and close to treason. Ancient sources imply that Juvenal's ridicule of a palace favorite in one of his satires resulted in his being banished from Rome.

This punishment apparently made Juvenal even more bitter. By law, a banished person lost his property and possessions, and Juvenal was penniless when he returned to Rome after Domitian's death in A.D. 96. To survive, Juvenal turned to writing, depending on rich patrons to subsidize him. Fortunately for him, his contemporaries enjoyed his work; in time, he was able to purchase a home in Rome and a small country house in neighboring Tibur. The milder tone of his later works reflects both his acceptance of life and his improved circumstances. Even in this phase, however, he was far from an optimist.

Juvenal's portrayal of Roman life shows its worst side, emphasizing everything he saw that was unjust, immoral, and degenerate. Each of his satires centers around a particular theme.

In *Satire I,* Juvenal stated almost angrily that crime, free spending, and all other evils had reached such heights in Rome that it was impossible not to write satire. "If you wish to be anyone of importance," he wrote, "dare to commit a crime that merits prison as a punishment. . . . Today money is the most sacred of the deities, although as yet, it does not have a temple."

Corruption was ever on Juvenal's mind, as was the lack of respect shown to teachers and writers. Everyone made demands on their knowledge and expected perfection, then complained about paying for these services. No one, however, hesitated to give great sums to sports heroes. In *Satire VII,* Juvenal exclaimed, "It would take 100 lawyers to earn what one driver in the chariot races makes" and "What is a teacher's pay, except perhaps some cheap wine or a ham?" For Juvenal, the days when teaching was an admired profession had long since passed. He offered the following advice in the final lines of the satire: "Schoolmasters, when the year comes to an end, accept for your efforts the piece of gold which spectators demand for a jockey who has won one race!"

Often titled "The Vanity of Human Wishes," *Satire X* is perhaps Juvenal's best-known work. Asserting that most humans desire what is unimportant, Juvenal examined each of these desires and showed how it often caused pain and discontent. He began by stating that "few people are able to distinguish true blessings from misfortune." So many, he wrote, wished to be kings and command armies, ignoring the fate of men such as Crassus and Pompey, both of whom died as a result

Clearly thinking of what she should next write on her tablet, this young girl from Pompeii certainly was not the frivolous type Juvenal enjoyed satirizing in his works. She does, however, exhibit the fine clothes of a wealthy Roman, and Juvenal did comment on the vanity of such Roman women.

of their ambitions: "Few kings go to the underworld without a wound or murder and few tyrants die a bloodless death."

Juvenal noted that people prayed to the gods for long life—"but old age is filled with how many evils and deformities! Just look at the ugly face of old age so unlike its former self, the misshapen hide that serves as skin, the hanging cheeks and great wrinkles." As for good looks, "One young man may be handsomer than another, but in old age all look alike—their voices become as shaky as their limbs, their heads are bald, and their noses drip as when they were children."

Juvenal then advised his readers to let the gods choose what would be best for each person and what would be good for Rome:

> You, however, should pray for a sound mind in a sound body, for a strong spirit that has no fear of death and

considers the length of life one of Nature's gifts, that can endure whatever work should come to it, that does not know anger, and that desires nothing. . . . The only path to a life of peace is through virtue.

Juvenal's satires may have cut too deep for the comfort of his fellow Romans. Of all his contemporaries, only the epigrammatist Martial mentioned him in writing and remarked on his eloquence. In the decades following Juvenal's death, no Roman writer even referred to him. As the centuries passed, however, he came into his own. Christian writers agreed with his description of Rome as a city of evil and included references to his works in their books. As interest in Juvenal grew, so too did the demand for publication of his satires. Sometime before 400, an edition of the satires was published; it soon became popular reading and had increasing influence over the centuries.

Later writers looked to Juvenal as the master of satire and freely imitated his works. The 18th-century English writer Samuel Johnson, for example, modeled his satire "London" on Juvenal's portraits of Rome. Today many commonly used proverbs and phrases trace their roots to Juvenal's 16 satires. In addition to "a sound mind in a sound body," other examples are "bread and circuses" and "Who will guard the guards themselves?"

FURTHER READING

Highet, Gilbert. *Juvenal the Satirist*. New York: Oxford University Press, 1954.

Juvenal. *The Satires*. Translated by Niall Rudd. New York: Oxford University Press, 1992.

Juvenal and Persius. Translated by G. G. Ramsay. Loeb Classical Library. New York: Putnam, 1918.

Marcus Aurelius (Marcus Annius Verus)

PHILOSOPHER-EMPEROR

N
othing but the best" seems an apt phrase to describe Marcus Aurelius' childhood and youth. His family was one of the most distinguished in 2nd-century Rome, and the year Marcus was born—A.D. 121—his grandfather held the prestigious office of consul. One of Marcus' aunts was the sister of Antoninus Pius, who would follow Hadrian as emperor, and his mother's family owned a prosperous tile factory outside Rome, the revenue from which had helped make them one of the city's richest families.

Marcus must have had an engaging personality as a child, for he quickly won the attention and respect of Hadrian, who ruled from A.D. 117 to 138. Hadrian nicknamed young Marcus *Verissimus* (most genuine, or most real) and appointed him a special priest at age eight. In the years that followed, Hadrian arranged for Marcus to receive the best education possible in Rome.

The question of succession was important to Hadrian, especially because he had no sons of his own. In 136, he chose a high-ranking Roman named Lucius Ceionius Commodus and engaged Marcus to Commodus' daughter. But when Commodus died suddenly two years later, Hadrian was forced to seek another Roman who would rule the empire responsibly and well. Aware that his last days were near, Hadrian decided that the best way to ensure the future tranquility of the empire was to choose not one but a series of successors. As his immediate heir Hadrian chose Marcus' uncle Antoninus Pius. He then ordered Antoninus to adopt two heirs to succeed him. One was 17-year-old Marcus, the other Commodus' son, seven-year-old Lucius Verus.

After Hadrian's death in July 138, Antoninus quietly and smoothly assumed the role of emperor. In the weeks that followed, he ended Marcus' engagement to Commodus' daughter and betrothed him to his own daughter, later known as Faustina the Younger. For the next 23 years Marcus remained the emperor-in-training.

Antoninus surely welcomed the assistance, for the burden of governing so vast an empire was a weighty one. Just two years after assuming his new role, Antoninus honored the young Marcus by naming him co-consul. In 145, Marcus married Faustina, and a year later his father-in-law granted him some of the special powers and rights held by emperors.

During these formative years, Marcus wrote often to his teacher, the well-respected Fronto. These letters, never intended for publication, reveal much about the development of Marcus' personality. They show clearly that Marcus' interest switched from rhetoric (the art of public speaking) to

Granted a triumph for his successful defense of the empire against invading foreign tribes, the emperor Marcus Aurelius approaches the Roman Forum in his triumphal chariot.

obtain through reason. For Marcus, Stoicism put life into perspective and dictated his actions in the years that followed.

When Antoninus died in March 161, there was no question of who was to succeed him. But Marcus was not about to accept the title of emperor for himself alone. He had never forgotten Hadrian's long-term plan and now insisted that his brother by adoption, Lucius Verus, be declared co-emperor with him.

And so, for the first time in Roman history, there were two official emperors. The only precedent involved the office of consul. For almost 500 years the consulship had been the highest office in Rome, with two consuls elected annually. However, with the rise first of dictators and then of emperors, the consulship had gradually become more of an honorary post.

Even though both emperors officially shared equal powers, the experienced Marcus quickly became the senior emperor, with most official business directed to him. To strengthen his ties with Lucius Verus, Marcus announced the engagement of his eldest daughter, 11-year-old Annia Lucilla, to the 30-year-old Verus.

Among the first measures taken by the new emperors was to increase the *alimenta* (a public allowance given poor children). They also made provisions to lighten the tax burdens imposed on Rome's less privileged classes.

Many challenges awaited Marcus and Lucius Verus. Residents along the empire's borders were restless, and increasing reports of invasions and rebellions forced the emperors to leave Rome and re-establish peace in the provinces. The same year they acceded to power, Rome's old enemy the Parthians overran Armenia, invaded the Roman province of Syria, and defeated two Roman armies.

In February 162, Marcus dispatched Lucius with a great army to

philosophy. This did not please Fronto, who taught oratory and rhetoric, but Marcus was tired of learning and repeating arguments for the courtroom and public debate. In 146, he chose to devote the free moments he had to studying Stoicism, a philosophy founded by a Greek named Zeno around in the late fourth century B.C. According to the Stoics, wise men are not influenced or governed by passion and emotion but are instead able to remain indifferent to the world about them. They follow only virtue, which they

rout the Parthians. The offensive was spearheaded by two local commanders, Statius Priscus and Avidius Cassius. By 164, Priscus had wrested control of Armenia from the Parthians; two years later, Cassius marched into Mesopotamia and claimed the region for Rome. Once again, Rome's borders extended beyond the Euphrates River.

These triumphs held a heavy price, though, because the returning soldiers brought a deadly plague back from the East, outbreaks of which ravaged the Roman world for 15 years, claiming thousands of victims. Centuries later, historians would consider this plague one of the prime factors that contributed to the decline of the empire.

The plague was not Marcus' only concern. The very year the Romans achieved victory in the East, German tribes overran the empire's northern boundaries and poured across the Danube River. Again Marcus sent Verus out, but this time he also accompanied the troops. As the Romans marched to crush the enemy, several German tribes evaded the oncoming legions and invaded northern Italy. The situation was very tense, especially since the plague had caused a shortage of soldiers, but Marcus and Verus managed to defeat the Germans and free Italy.

Once again, however, sorrow followed victory when Verus suddenly died in 169, leaving Marcus the sole emperor of the Roman world. Then, in 175, he was confronted by a serious challenge when Avidius Cassius, the general who had led Rome's troops to victory in Mesopotamia, proclaimed himself emperor. Some sources say that he acted only upon hearing erroneously that Marcus had died; others claim that he spread the rumor himself. Given his military record, Cassius easily won the support of his soldiers and several eastern provinces, including Egypt. Recognizing the possibility of a coup, Marcus prepared to march against Cassius.

However, when Cassius' troops learned that Marcus was alive and on his way, they turned on their treacherous leader and killed him.

Marcus decided to visit the East anyway, so that he could personally inspect conditions and bring a sense of stability to the area. His wife, Faustina, traveled with him. When she died in Asia Minor, possibly from complications of pregnancy, Marcus was deeply grieved. He ordered the town where she died, Halala, renamed Faustinopolis in her honor and had the Senate deify her.

Marcus returned to Rome late in 176 but then spent three years battling the German tribes while his son Commodus, to whom Marcus had granted all imperial rights, managed affairs in Rome. After defeating the powerful Marcomanni and Quadi, Marcus allowed both German tribes to keep their lands, because he considered vacant land useless. Furthermore, he envisioned a time when the Germans would be Romanized and fully integrated into the empire.

Marcus was never to achieve this goal. In March 180, while still in the north, he fell seriously ill. Aware that he might not survive, he sent for his son Commodus. In the days that followed, physicians tried various remedies in a futile attempt to reverse Marcus' decline. On March 17, the last of the so-called five good emperors died.

In his aim to make the empire more secure, Marcus had spent much of his 19-year rule on the battlefield, even though he preferred peace to war and mediation to fighting. Historians attribute no scandals or tyrannical acts to his rule. In regard to the treatment of Christians, Marcus did not order or condone persecutions such as Nero had, but observed the same policy set by Trajan and practiced by Hadrian—condemning Christians only when they refused to worship Roman gods and

Marcus Aurelius

BORN

April 26, A.D. 121
Rome

DIED

March 17, A.D. 180
Vindobona or Sirmium in Pannonia

PROFESSION

Roman emperor

ACCOMPLISHMENTS

Defeated the Parthians; retook Armenia; extended Rome's eastern boundaries beyond the Euphrates River and into Mesopotamia; led two successful campaigns against the Germans to defeat the Marcomanni and Quadi; wrote extended philosophical reflections later published as *Meditations*

> *"As for life, it is a battle and a journey in a strange land."*
>
> —from *Meditations*, Book II (2nd century A.D.)

abide by Rome's rules. But in 177, events in Lugdunum, Gaul (now Lyon, France), led to a terrible persecution during which many Christians died. The recent plague, frontier battles, and economic difficulties had frustrated the population, for whom the local Christians became the scapegoats. Marcus did not initiate the persecution, but neither did he order it stopped. Nor did he ever mention his feelings toward Christians in his writings.

Rather, the focus of Marcus' written works centered on his Stoic beliefs. After his death, someone collected his writings into 12 books and published them. Known as the *Meditations* because they are Marcus' personal thoughts about life, they have brought him immortal fame—certainly more glory than his accomplishments as emperor. In fact, the *Meditations* is the most famous book ever published by a reigning monarch.

Marcus never intended the *Meditations* to be published; they were private thoughts he wrote down (in Greek) when he was alone, often after retiring to his tent while on campaign. The first book differs in that it gives thanks to his family, friends, teachers, and the gods. Probably written shortly before his death, it provides an introduction to the personal reflections that follow.

Marcus frequently elevated the spiritual aspects of life over the material world: "Before it is too late, try to see that you have within yourself something higher and more godlike than the mere instincts which move your emotions and work you like a puppet!" Marcus did not believe in an afterlife and even doubted the value of earthly fame: "Short then is each person's life and small the tiny corner of the earth on which he lives, and brief too is even the longest survival of one's name among posterity."

Accordingly, Marcus did not rejoice in his victories, nor dwell on his accomplishments. The only explicit reference to his military accomplishments comes in Book 10, when he mentions the Sarmatian people who lived along the Danube River: "A spider is proud when he snags a fly, a person when he snares a rabbit . . . another bears, and others Sarmatians. But, if you question their motives, aren't they all bandits?" Although one of the most powerful men in the world, Marcus saw himself and the Roman Empire as a small, almost insignificant part of something far more vast: "Asia and Europe are corners of the universe and every sea is a drop in the universe. Every second of time is just a point in eternity." On another occasion he wrote, "I have a city and a fatherland. As Marcus, I am a Roman; as a man, I am a citizen of the universe."

For centuries, visitors to Rome's Capitoline Hill could see in the area's magnificent square a regal statue of Marcus Aurelius sitting on his horse with his right arm outstretched. Accounts tell us that the raised right hoof of the horse may have rested on the sculpted image of a vanquished foe, which has long since disappeared. In the late 20th century, the harmful effects of pollution forced the government to remove the statue to the neighboring Capitoline Museum.

FURTHER READING

Birley, Anthony R. *Marcus Aurelius.* Boston: Little, Brown, 1966.

———. *Marcus Aurelius, A Biography.* New Haven: Yale University Press, 1987.

Farquharson, Arthur S. L. *Marcus Aurelius, His Life and His World.* New York: William Salloch, 1951.

Marcus Aurelius. *The Meditations.* Translated by A. S. L. Farquharson. New York: Oxford University Press, 1991.

Septimius Severus

A MILITARY MONARCH

On December 31, A.D. 192, the Roman emperor Commodus, the dissolute son of the great Marcus Aurelius, was strangled to death by a wrestler. A general named Pertinax, the son of a freed slave, became the new emperor, but he soon offended the Praetorian Guard and was murdered by a guardsman. With no direct successor in line to follow Pertinax, the Praetorian Guard offered the throne to the highest bidder. Two influential Romans accepted the challenge, and Didius Julianus' offer of 25,000 *sestertii* (a coin denomination) per soldier won him the post. Whether Rome would survive this sequence of events was in doubt, for turmoil reigned and civil war threatened.

Septimius Severus was one of the major actors in this unfolding drama. As governor of Pannonia (an area encompassing part of present-day Austria, Slovenia, and Hungary) and commander of the largest army stationed on the Danube River, Severus was one of Rome's most powerful generals. Since A.D. 173, when he first became a senator, Severus had worked his way slowly up the political and military ladder. His legions believed he was the man to rule Rome, and on April 13, 193, they proclaimed him emperor. Severus accepted their loyalty and marched on Rome, prepared, as he clear-

Decorating the arch erected in honor of Septimius' family in Lepcis Magna in modern Libya is a scene showing the emperor clasping the hand of his son and successor Caracalla. Between them stands Septimius' other son, Geta. Watching the proceedings is Julia Domna (second from the left), Septimius' wife.

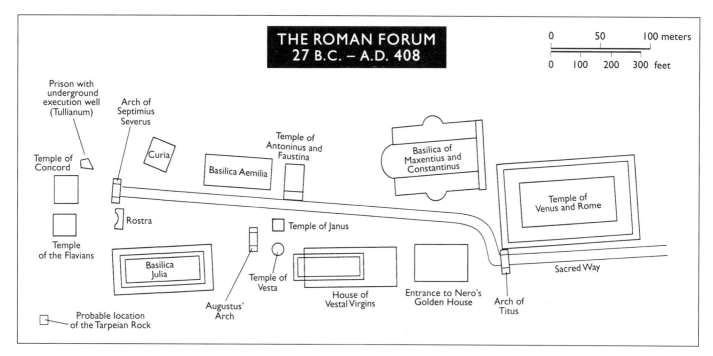

**THE ROMAN FORUM
27 B.C. – A.D. 408**

0   50   100 meters

0   100   200   300 feet

Prison with underground execution well (Tullianum)

Arch of Septimius Severus

Temple of Concord

Curia

Temple of Antoninus and Faustina

Basilica Aemilia

Basilica of Maxentius and Constantinus

Temple of Venus and Rome

Rostra

Temple of the Flavians

Temple of Janus

Basilica Julia

Temple of Vesta

House of Vestal Virgins

Entrance to Nero's Golden House

Arch of Titus

Sacred Way

Augustus' Arch

Probable location of the Tarpeian Rock

For Rome's subjects throughout the empire, the Roman Forum was the center of the world. Here statesmen were elected, laws passed, decrees issued, triumphal processions granted, and the deities petitioned for their protection.

ly stated, to avenge the murder of Pertinax.

But Severus was not the only contender for the title of emperor. In the East, Roman legions had pledged their allegiance to Pescennius Niger, the governor of Syria. However, the Senate threw its support behind Severus, and on June 9 he entered Rome unopposed. Recognizing that the powerful Praetorian Guard posed the only real threat to his authority, Severus immediately disbanded the Guard and began recruiting 15,000 men to replace them. Opening eligibility to all soldiers, Severus filled most of the positions with men from his loyal Danubian troops. The city of Rome was his; now all he needed was a strategy to win the empire.

Before setting out for the East to confront Pescennius Niger, Severus turned his attention to another potential trouble spot—Britain, where the powerful Clodius Albinus was governor. Unwilling to fight on two fronts at the same time, Severus awarded Albinus the honorary title of Caesar, thereby publicly suggesting that Albinus was

his designated heir. Believing that Albinus would be content with such a rank, Severus left for the East.

Meanwhile, Pescennius Niger confidently awaited Severus' approach. But his army contained many inexperienced recruits, whereas Severus' force was made up mostly of seasoned, loyal troops. At Issus (in modern Turkey) in 194, Severus decisively routed Niger's forces. Shortly afterward, Niger was caught and killed as he attempted to escape across the Euphrates River. To forestall further rebellion in Syria, Severus divided the area into two provinces, Coele-Syria and Phoenice (Phoenicia).

Meanwhile, in Britain, Albinus had rebelled and proclaimed himself emperor. After declaring his son Caracalla his heir and successor, Severus turned west to face Albinus. The two met in battle near present-day Lyon, France. Albinus' troops appeared to be on the verge of victory when reinforcements arrived for Severus. In the hard fighting that followed, Albinus' forces gradually lost their advantage and

Severus triumphed again. Just as he had used geographic division to weaken possible rivals in Syria, Severus now divided Britain into two parts.

Even with his two principal opponents dead, Severus did not feel secure until he had executed all of Niger's and Albinus' political allies. Believing that he had silenced all the opposition, Severus led his army east once again, this time to punish the Parthians for supporting Niger. In December 197, Severus took Ctesiphon, the capital of Parthia, and annexed Mesopotamia in 199. Again Rome's boundaries extended beyond the Euphrates River.

Aware that his power depended to a great extent on the strength of his troops, Severus increased the number of legions to approximately 33. And, for the first time in Rome's history, he stationed one of them inside Italy itself, at Albanum, not far from Rome. To win the soldiers' loyalty, he granted them special privileges and raised their pay. Severus also changed the rules forbidding frontier soldiers to marry and even allowed them to raise families away from camp quarters on land they had purchased for themselves.

Also for the first time in Roman history, Severus let Roman soldiers marry natives of the provinces to which they were assigned, and even allowed them to enter into business ventures. Severus hoped that such changes in the military would encourage provincials to enlist in the Roman army and aid in the defense of their own lands. Though the changes did produce the desired result, they also contributed to an increasing stubbornness on the part of the frontier soldiers, who now balked at leaving their families and homes for another post or province.

The Roman army, and not the constitution, had by now become the ruling force behind the emperor. The power of the Senate, on the other hand, had decreased considerably, especially as Severus preferred to choose his officials from the equestrian and not the senatorial class. However, the burden of ruling was too great for any one man, even the determined Severus, and he relied to a great degree on the head of his Praetorian Guard.

The first guard commander, Gaius Fulvius Plautianus, wielded considerable authority, but his tenure was cut short when others, jealous of his power, assassinated him. Succeeding as the emperor's right-hand man was Papinian, a distinguished Roman lawyer to whom Severus assigned the tremendous task of codifying and revamping the Roman legal system. For Severus, good government was possible only when there was a strong judicial system.

The public treasury also claimed much of Severus' attention, and he was adamant about collecting revenues. While many disagreed with his methods, no one objected too vehemently, for fear of touching off another civil war. In addition, most influential Romans recognized that Severus was neither a spendthrift nor a lover of luxury, and they believed that he sincerely wanted to revive the days of the Five Good Emperors, the last of whom had been Marcus Aurelius. Proof of Severus' fiscal responsibility came at his death when his successor inherited a surplus in the public treasury despite tremendous expenses, which had included an increase in soldiers' pay, honorariums awarded the people of Rome, and the reinstitution of the *alimenta* (public assistance to poor children).

Severus' extensive building program also weighed heavily on the treasury. For his hometown of Lepcis Magna (also spelled Leptis Magna) in

Septimius Severus

BORN

A.D. 146
Leptis Magna, Tripolitania

DIED

February A.D. 211
Eboracum, Britain

PROFESSION

Roman general and emperor

ACCOMPLISHMENTS

Ended the civil war that followed Commodus' assassination; weakened the power of the Senate and strengthened the military; expanded the eastern borders of the empire beyond the Euphrates River; divided Syria and Britain into two provinces each; rebuilt Hadrian's Wall; erected a series of magnificent buildings in his hometown of Lepcis Magna

"Keep on good terms with each other, be generous to the soldiers, and pay attention to no one."

—Severus' deathbed counsel to his sons, according to tradition

Tripolitania (part of present-day Libya), Severus commissioned a new forum, a basilica, a temple, and a colonnaded street leading to the harbor. Today the remains of Lepcis Magna are among the most magnificent that survive from ancient times.

In Rome, the Arch of Septimius Severus still graces the Forum. Records and engravings also describe the *septizodium*, another splendid structure Severus dedicated in the capital, in 203. A freestanding ornamental façade on the Palatine Hill in Rome, the *septizodium* had three tiers of porticos. Among the statues adorning the building was a representation of Severus as the sun god.

Severus' wife, Julia Domna, a Syrian, became extremely influential in Rome. Well educated and intelligent, she won recognition as a philosopher, establishing a circle of learned friends who met regularly to discuss the works of Greek and Roman thinkers.

Severus was not destined to spend his final years in the civilized atmosphere of Rome. Trouble was brewing again in Britain, with tribes from northern Scotland having broken across both Antoninus' and Hadrian's defensive walls. In 208, Severus marched north, accompanied by his sons, Caracalla and Geta. His plans were to focus all energies on restoring Hadrian's Wall and leave the Antonine wall, 100 miles to the north, as it was. Much of what remains today traces its origin to Severus' soldiers and workmen, not Hadrian's. In an effort to stop foreign infringement on Roman land,

Severus ordered an invasion of Scotland, but his forces met heavy resistance and suffered many losses. Severus persevered, however, determined to punish the Britons for daring to attack Roman positions. But declining health prevented him from accomplishing his goal.

By 210, Severus was too ill to lead his troops and ceded his position as general to his sons. In February 211, in Eboracum (modern York, England), Severus died at the age of 66, having just completed his 17th year as Roman emperor.

FURTHER READING

Birley, Anthony R. *Septimius Severus: The African Emperor*. London: Eyre & Spottiswoode, 1971.

Diocletian (Diocles)

NEW RULES FOR THE EMPIRE

U nlike most of the Roman emperors before him, Diocles was a man of humble origins. Born in A.D. 245, he entered the Roman army at an early age and steadily worked his way up through the ranks. His military career reached its apex when he became a leading general under the emperor Numerian in 283. When Numerian died the following year—allegedly murdered by an army officer—the army proclaimed Diocles emperor.

According to tradition, a priestess in Gaul had once told Diocles, "You shall become emperor on the day you slay the wild boar!" As it happened, the officer said to have murdered Numerian was named Aper, which means wild boar in Latin—so when Diocles killed Aper with his own hands, the prophecy was apparently fulfilled.

Romans put great stock in omens and prophecies, which were often cited to explain historical events. In this case, the wild-boar prophecy neatly portrayed Diocles' ascent to power as the will of the gods. But not everyone in Rome was will-

The piercing eyes and tight lips indicate this is a realistic portrait head of Diocletian. His grim determination returned stability and order to the empire.

In 1757, the English architect Robert Adam spent five weeks surveying, measuring the ruins, and making drawings of the emperor Diocletian's enormous palace that once covered five acres on the Dalmatian coast, near the modern city of Split.

ing to accept this story, and certainly not Carinus, Numerian's brother and co-emperor. Carinus had taken command in Rome while Numerian prepared to battle the Persians in the East. When he heard what had happened, Carinus immediately gathered his army and prepared to intercept Diocles on his way back to Rome. As far as Carinus was concerned, Diocles had murdered Numerian and then framed Aper. The truth will never be known, but many historians believe that Numerian's sudden death was actually caused either by a stroke or a bolt of lightning.

In April 285, as the two armies fought a decisive battle near the Danube River, a group of soldiers who favored Diocles succeeded in assassinating Carinus. Diocles then took control of the empire and assumed the imperial name of Gaius Aurelius Valerius Diocletianus, from which came the name Diocletian. He had come a long way from his humble beginnings in Dalma-

tia, a Roman province on the east coast of the Adriatic Sea, where his father had been a scribe or a freed slave.

Diocletian had little time to savor his good fortune, because the empire was restless and revolts threatened to erupt everywhere. Choosing Maximian, a capable general and trusted associate, as his second in command, Diocletian granted Maximian control of the western empire while he took the East. Rome continued to be the official capital of the empire, but Maximian's principal residence was Milan, in northern Italy, and Diocletian's was Nicomedia, in western Anatolia (modern Turkey).

Between 286 and 293, Diocletian and Maximian suppressed revolts in Gaul, Germany, Scythia (near the Black Sea), and Egypt. Only Carausius, a Roman admiral who had seized control of Britain and northern Gaul, successfully opposed the co-emperors. Recognizing further conflict as a drain on the empire's resources, Diocletian and Maximian withdrew Rome's soldiers from the contested areas but refused to recognize Carausius as a co-commander.

Accepting the fact that there was little hope of a lasting peace throughout the empire, Diocletian turned his attention to reorganizing the government. After carefully assessing Rome's strengths and weaknesses, he concluded that internal strength was the key to stability and peace. Although he believed strongly in maintaining a fortified defense network along the frontiers, he knew that such a system acted as a deterrent only to foreign tribes. Defensive walls, he noted, were ineffective against upstart Roman generals who sought power for themselves.

For Diocletian, the solution was the Tetrarchy, a system that divided the government of the empire among four rulers, two in the East and two in the West. Diocletian decreed that two of the four would be the principal rulers and bear the title of augustus; their two subordinates would bear the title of caesar. In Diocletian's mind, the Tetrarchy would solve the problem of succession by providing for the peaceful transfer of power. According to the rules he established, the two caesars would succeed the augusti and then choose their own caesars.

In the first Tetrarchy, Diocletian named himself augustus of the East and retained Maximian as augustus of the West. As Maximian's caesar, Diocletian named Constantius and located his official residence in Trier, Germany. His own caesar was Galerius, who operated from Sirmium in Pannonia. To ensure the success of the system, Diocletian assigned specific areas of responsibility to each leader. Diocletian controlled Thrace, Asia, and Egypt; Maximian Italy, Sicily, and Africa; Constantius Gaul, Spain, and Britain; and Galerius

Illyria, the Danube provinces, and Achaea.

To further ensure cooperation among the four members of the Tetrarchy, Diocletian arranged for his daughter to marry Galerius and for Maximian's stepdaughter to marry Constantius. He then declared publicly that the people should consider the gods and not himself responsible for the revisions in government. To reinforce this idea, Diocletian reminded everyone of the prophecy of the wild boar and began calling himself Jovius (another name for Jupiter, the king of the gods) and Maximian Herculius (in honor of the legendary Greek hero Hercules). The centuries-old eastern tradition of considering the emperor a god was gradually becoming a reality in the West.

For much of the decade of the 290s, the tetrarchs kept their armies in the field, overpowering rebels and defeating invaders. A major victory was Constantius' defeat of Carausius in 296, after which England once again became a Roman province subject to the emperor. The following year Diocletian defeated usurpers who had declared Egypt independent and named themselves the new rulers.

With the empire in order and the Tetrarchy working, Diocletian turned his attention to civil matters. He proved to be a masterful administrator whose changes remained in effect for centuries after his rule.

To increase the efficiency of his officials, Diocletian divided the existing provinces into smaller units, almost doubling the total number of provinces. This measure also made it more difficult for an ambitious governor to rally enough troops to stage a revolt. Diocletian then reorganized the army, increasing the number of soldiers and opening the ranks to foreigners. In order to protect both soldiers and sub-

Diocletian

BORN

Around A.D. 245
Salonae, Dalmatia

DIED

A.D. 316
Salonae, Dalmatia

PROFESSION

Roman emperor

ACCOMPLISHMENTS

Restored order to the Roman world; established the Tetrarchy, a four-man ruling body; divided the Roman Empire among tetrarchs and established a scheme for orderly succession; strengthened defenses along Rome's frontiers; reorganized the army and divided the provinces into smaller units; regulated prices and wages and increased the size of Rome's civil service; undertook numerous building projects in the capitals of the tetrarchs

jects along the frontiers, Diocletian ordered a massive building program aimed at strengthening fortifications and defensive structures.

To pay for his army, his building programs, and the continuous battles waged throughout the Roman world, Diocletian was forced to raise taxes, but he tried to make them as fair as possible. Therefore, he took into account the differences in quality of soil and taxed individuals on the potential yield of their land as well as the type of crop produced. In addition, he based a portion of each landowner's tax on the number of people required to work the property. Since the tax officials adjusted the rate only every 5 years (later extended to 15), it was necessary to keep the same number of people working the lands at least until reassessment time. If workers left between assessments, the tax continued to be paid on the number of workers on record. Naturally, this created problems for the landowners, who sometimes used unfair practices to keep their workers on the job.

To halt inflation and price gouging, Diocletian established ceilings on transportation charges and the prices of some 1,000 marketable items. He also set the maximum salary for workers in every field. Because the existing number of government employees could not handle the implementation of so many regulations, additional people had to be hired. As a result, Rome developed a vast network of civil servants similar to the bureaucracies of modern nations.

Although Diocletian was in theory only one member of the Tetrarchy, there was no doubt that he was Rome's principal ruler. To further centralize control of the government he issued a series of rules and regulations. The consuls, once Rome's most powerful officials, were now to be appointed rather than elected. Because Diocletian and his co-tetrarchs established all policy, the Senate no longer helped to formulate new laws or revise old ones. Senators also found that fewer and fewer military and civil positions were open to them. The Praetorian commanders, who in recent years had been able to elevate a favored general to the post of emperor, also saw their powers curtailed.

In 303, Diocletian traveled to Rome to celebrate the 20th anniversary of his rule. This was a momentous occasion, because it marked the first time he had actually set foot in the city. He had always preferred the East, especially Nicomedia, his first capital, and Antioch, his capital after the formation of the Tetrarchy. He had adorned these cities—as well as the capitals of the other tetrarchs—with temples, baths, granaries, and other structures appropriate to the residence of an emperor. In Rome itself, his major contribution had been the Curia (Senate House), which he had had rebuilt after a devastating fire in 283.

When Diocletian celebrated his 20 years as emperor, he could justly claim credit for bringing relative peace and stability to a great part of the world, even though his detractors accused him of being miserly, haughty, and harsh. Although he abolished the practice of using torture to extract confessions from prisoners, he was certainly no friend to Rome's Christians. Between 303 and 304, Diocletian issued a number of anti-Christian edicts. He forbade Christians to assemble for religious services, ordered their churches and sacred books destroyed, and authorized the arrest of all Christian clergy in the East who refused to make sacrifices to Rome's gods. This was to be Rome's last major persecution of Christians. A decade later, Diocletian's successor Constantine decreed that Christian religious practices were to be tolerated throughout the Roman world.

In the midst of the persecution, Diocletian fell seriously ill. When he recovered, he began to question his ability to govern. Deciding that he was no longer up to the job, he took the unprecedented step of abdicating. On May 1, 305, he yielded the responsibility of the empire to the caesars, Constantius and Galerius. Diocletian's co-augustus, Maximian, also relinquished his title, albeit reluctantly.

Diocletian remained in Nicomedia for a while before retiring to his villa near Salonae on the eastern coast of the Adriatic. In 308, when several contenders for the title of emperor threatened to engulf the empire in another civil war, Diocletian responded to an appeal from the emperor Galerius and returned briefly to politics. But once the crisis passed, Diocletian retired again to Salonae, where he died quietly eight years later.

By then, the Tetrarchy Diocletian had so carefully organized had disintegrated, as had the measure of tranquility he had brought to the Roman world. However, many of Diocletian's policies remained in force, eventually to provide a firm foundation for the Eastern Roman Empire, which outlived Rome and the Western Empire by several hundred years.

FURTHER READING

Williams, Stephen. *Diocletian and the Roman Recovery.* New York: Methuen, 1985.

Constantine the Great (Constantine I)

CHRISTIANITY'S "THIRTEENTH APOSTLE"

I
n A.D. 293, when he was around 10 years old, Constantine went to live at the court of the emperor Diocletian in Nicomedia, Bithynia (now northern Turkey). The young boy's father, Constantius Clorus, had just been appointed caesar by Diocletian, elevating him to the ranks of the four tetrarchs who governed the empire. Diocletian had argued that Constantine would receive a better education at the royal palace than if he remained in Germany with his father. However, his true motive was to keep the boy hostage to ensure his father's loyalty, a time-honored technique employed by Roman emperors and other rulers.

Nevertheless, Diocletian treated Constantine well and groomed him as a future ruler. But Constantine's situation

The calm, reflective look of the portrait head of young Constantine gives little indication that his battle victories and decrees would change the course of history for the Western world.

"In hoc signo, vinces." (In this sign, you will conquer.)

—according to Constantine, the divine message that spurred him to victory over Maxentius

became more complicated in 305, when Diocletian abdicated and turned over control to the tetrarch Galerius, who had long been wary of Constantine's growing popularity. Now in his early 20s, Constantine had been slated for appointment to the ruling Tetrarchy, but Galerius passed him over in favor of two other candidates.

Constantius realized that his son's life could be in danger, so he requested that Galerius send Constantine to Gaul to help his ailing father invade northern Britain. Galerius, however, feared that if Constantius died with Constantine at his side, the troops might insist that Constantine fill his father's post in the Tetrarchy. He therefore decided to keep Constantine in Nicomedia, trying to placate Constantius by saying that it would only be for a little while.

Father and son publicly accepted Galerius' decision, but secretly they devised an escape plan. Knowing that Galerius enjoyed drinking wine with his meals, Constantine approached the emperor one evening after he had downed several glasses and asked for permission to join his father. His mind clouded by wine, Galerius gave Constantine a written order allowing him not only to leave Nicomedia but also to use government horses at the posting stations along the official highway.

Wasting no time, Constantine joined a few trusted companions and left the city immediately. Through the night they galloped west, changing horses at each station and cutting the hamstrings of all the horses left behind.

When Galerius awoke the next morning and realized what he had done, he ordered soldiers to overtake Constantine—which proved impossible, because they found no healthy horses to replace their exhausted mounts and soon had to abandon the chase.

In the spring of 306, Constantine and his father led their troops from Gaul into Britain and then marched north to Eboracum (present-day York). When Constantius died soon after the invasion, the troops immediately pledged their allegiance to Constantine, hailing him as the West's new augustus, a title that made him the equal of Galerius, the augustus of the East. Gaul followed Britain's example, though the other Western provinces held back. But Galerius refused to recognize Constantine's claim, appointing Licinius to be augustus of the West. He tried to placate Constantine by appointing him caesar, second in command to the augustus. Constantine took this as an insult and resolved to achieve mastery in the West.

After Galerius died, in 311, Licinius succeeded him as augustus of the East, which left rule of the West open. Constantine now had to vie for the position with Maxentius, son of former augustus Maximian. To secure his position, Maxentius reinforced Rome's massive walls, which the emperor Aurelian had built 30 years earlier. Scouts returning to Constantine reported that Maxentius' new defenses had made the city impregnable, but Constantine refused to consider this a possibility.

Convinced that perseverance and determination would overcome all obstacles, Constantine marched south into Italy and prepared to take the city. His troops numbered far less than those of Maxentius, because he had felt obliged to leave many in Gaul to protect the frontier's borders. But Constantine's soldiers were tough and well disciplined from many battles against invading German tribes, and they were fiercely loyal to their commander.

On October 27, 312, Constantine and his troops set up camp a few miles outside the city's walls. After making final preparations for the next day's battle, Constantine went to bed. That night, the figure of Jesus Christ appeared to him in a dream, telling Constantine that if he painted the Greek letters *chi* and *rho* (representing the name Christos) on his soldiers' shields, victory would be his. Constantine awoke in amazement. Convinced by his dream that the Christian Messiah must be more powerful than the gods of the Romans, he ordered the two initials (written X and P in the Greek alphabet) painted on his own helmet and on as many shields as possible.

On the morning of October 28, Constantine led his soldiers toward Rome. Rather than sheltering behind his fortifications, Maxentius decided to do battle outside the city, marching his troops across the Milvian Bridge and into the valley beyond the Tiber River. Responding to this maneuver, Constantine led his troops across the valley and then ordered them to outflank the enemy and drive them back to the river. He then closed his ranks, forcing Maxentius' troops to crowd onto the Milvian Bridge. Unable to support the weight of so many men, the bridge collapsed, plunging hundreds to their deaths. A short while later, Constantine's men retrieved Maxentius' own body from the Tiber, cut off his head, and brought the trophy to their leader. With Maxentius' head mounted on a spear and the symbol of Christ on his own helmet, Constantine marched into Rome, the new emperor of the West.

Though Constantine continued to honor the traditional Roman gods, he did not forget his dream. He resolved to build Christian churches that were worthy of the great God who had brought him victory. At the time, there were thousands of Christians through-out the empire, but most belonged to the poor and middle classes and wielded no political power. Less than 10 years earlier, in 303, under Diocletian, they had suffered horrible persecution.

Aware that he might stir up old antagonisms by building a Christian church near a Roman temple, Constantine looked beyond the walls of the city for appropriate sites and sometimes adapted unused structures for the new churches. As suitable living quarters for the Christian bishop of Rome, Constantine refurbished an old imperial palace. (In the years that followed, the bishop of Rome would become the most important figure in the Christian church, an office that would evolve into the papacy.) On Vatican Hill, site of the tomb of the martyred Saint Peter, one of Jesus' 12 apostles, Constantine ordered a great church built. In time, it would become the most important church in the Christian world. Known today as St. Peter's Basilica, it stands on the same site, though much enlarged and remodeled over the centuries.

Rome was not Constantine's favorite city, and after attending to pressing administrative matters he left in 313 for the place he considered home, Trier, in northwestern Germany. On the way north he met with Licinius, augustus of the East, in the northern Italian city of Mediolanum (Milan). As proof of his willingness to remain Licinius' ally, Constantine arranged a marriage between Licinius and his favorite sister, Constantia. Of much more lasting significance was the law Constantine and Licinius signed during their meeting. Known as the Edict of Milan, this measure granted all peoples throughout the Roman Empire the right to practice whatever religion they chose to follow. The edict also stated that any property taken from Christians during Diocletian's persecutions was to be returned immediately to the rightful owners.

Constantine the Great

BORN
Around A.D. 284
Probably Naissus, Dalmatia

DIED
May 22, A.D. 337
Nicomedia, Bithynia

PROFESSION
Roman emperor

ACCOMPLISHMENTS
Obtained sole command of the Roman Empire; brought unity, stability, and peace to the Roman world; ended the persecution of Christians and decreed toleration for all religions; established Christianity as the religion of the Roman Empire; convened the Council of Nicaea; ordered Christian churches to be built throughout the empire; reorganized the army; established his capital at Byzantium, renamed Constantinople

More than 200 years after Constantine's death, the basilica of Saint Apollinare in Classe was built in Ravenna, Italy. Decorating the walls and ceilings were huge, beautifully crafted mosaics honoring important events and figures in the history of the Christian church. This scene shows Constantine the Great (fourth from left) granting new religious rules to the bishops.

The alliance forged at Mediolanum broke down in 323, when foreign tribes invaded Licinius' lands to the north of Thrace. At the time, Constantine was living in Serdica (present-day Sofia, Bulgaria) and thus considered the invasion a threat to his territory as well. For this reason, Constantine crossed into Licinius' territory and drove back the invaders. However, Licinius believed that Constantine had committed an act of aggression and promptly declared war on him.

In order to cut off Constantine from his home base, Licinius blockaded the Hellespont (now known as the Dardanelles), the narrow strait separating Europe from Asia. In response, Constantine commanded his son Crispus to attack Licinius' fleet. Crispus

broke through and brought much-needed supplies to his father's land forces. As at the Battle of the Milvian Bridge, here too Constantine put his trust in the Christian God. He went into battle flanked by a bodyguard of 50 men, one holding high a gold cross marked with the initials of Christ. Licinius' troops proved no match for Constantine's battle-hardened men. Licinius fled to his palace in Nicomedia, where soldiers acting on Constantine's orders captured and executed him. In 324, Constantine became the first man since Diocletian to rule the Roman Empire alone.

Christian beliefs guided many of Constantine's decisions as emperor. He prayed regularly for guidance, and on military campaigns he traveled with a portable chapel. Constantine outlawed crucifixion, the branding of criminals for certain crimes, and, in observance of the belief that God rested on the seventh day, chose Sunday as a day of rest.

Determined to maintain peace and unity throughout the empire, Constantine began looking for a site where he could build a new capital, one that would be truly impregnable. He believed that Rome, for all its grandeur and tradition, was too far removed from critical areas of the empire such as the Rhine, Danube, and Euphrates rivers.

After much thought, Constantine chose Byzantium, a city founded centuries earlier by Greek colonists at the entrance to the Black Sea. Standing at the crossroads between East and West, Byzantium had become a thriving international trading port. Romulus, the legendary founder of Rome, had supposedly circled the site marked for his city with a pair of oxen; emulating this symbolic gesture, Constantine walked around Byzantium and traced the outline of his new capital with the point of a spear.

Like Rome, Byzantium took its founder's name and became known as Constantinople (Constantine's city). Now Istanbul, this ancient city continues to flourish as one of Turkey's major cities.

For six years (324–30), hundreds of artisans, laborers, and architects set to work on Constantinople. Sea walls and land walls were stretched two miles across the peninsula as a defensive guard against attackers from the north. Like Rome, the new capital had a forum, a senate house, many impressive avenues, a sumptuous palace, magnificent gardens, a gigantic race course, enormous public baths, and several Christian churches. Unlike Rome, however, Constantinople was to be a Christian city and thus have no temples dedicated to the traditional Roman gods. Because Constantine did not wish to abolish the ancient traditions completely, however, he included both Roman and Christian rites at the dedication ceremonies in 330.

As the years passed, Constantine privately and publicly considered himself Jesus Christ's 13th apostle. The other 12 had accompanied Jesus during his earthly life and preached his message after his death. Constantine believed that Christ meant for him to spread his teachings across the empire. Yet, as Christianity spread, problems arose because of different interpretations of it, with bitter disagreements springing up between different schools of thought. Just as he had brought unity to the empire, so Constantine felt the Christian God had ordained him to do the same with Christianity. To this end he invited all the bishops in the empire to come, at public expense, to

the city of Nicaea in Asia Minor. Approximately 250 bishops answered his summons for the Council of Nicaea, which convened in May 325.

Constantine himself attended the meeting—and lost his patience when the bishops argued at great length over matters of doctrine without coming to any conclusion. Finally, approaching the issue as he would a military battle, Constantine addressed the group, demanding that they agree to formulate a prayer that would include Christian beliefs acceptable to all. The result was the Nicene Creed, a statement of the basic Christian beliefs about God, which is still proclaimed by many Christians throughout the world today. It begins: "We believe in One God, the Father, the Almighty, maker of heaven and earth, of all that is, seen and unseen."

The year following the Council of Nicaea marked Constantine's 20th anniversary as emperor. Because the occasion seemed to warrant a special celebration, he decided to return to Rome. This venture was marked by disturbing and unexplained acts on Constantine's part. During the journey to Rome, Constantine murdered both his wife, Fausta, and his son Crispus, possibly because he believed they were plotting against him. Then, during the anniversary celebrations, Constantine suddenly launched into an angry tirade in a sacred procession and refused to continue. Soon after, he left Rome, never to return.

On his way back to Constantinople, Constantine met with his mother, Helena, and took her back with him to Constantinople. A devout Christian herself, Helena undertook a pilgrimage to Jerusalem, where she is said to have discovered a piece of the cross on which Jesus Christ had been crucified.

The years that followed Constantine's return to Constantinople were relatively peaceful ones. His soldiers quickly quelled any revolt or conflict that erupted, and few foreign tribes dared match their strength against his troops. Nor did the people object too much to his constant tax increases, for they preferred taxes to civil war and foreign invasions.

In order to assure a smooth succession, Constantine promoted his sons Constantine II, Constantius II, and Constans to the rank of caesar. As further assurance of continuity, the emperor also groomed two nephews for imperial rule.

In 337, as Constantine prepared for a military campaign in Persia, he fell ill. When all treatments failed to restore his health and death seemed imminent, Constantine asked to be baptized, for he had never formally become a member of the church. Now, on his deathbed, he exchanged the purple robe of royalty for the simple white one of baptism. Soon after, on May 22, 337, he died.

Constantine's final resting place was a magnificently carved tomb in the city's Church of the Apostles, an appropriate choice for the man who considered himself Christ's 13th apostle.

FURTHER READING

Grant, Michael. *Constantine the Great: The Man and His Times*. New York: Macmillan, 1994.

MacMullen, Ramsay. *Constantine*. New York: Dial, 1969.

Smith, John H. *Constantine the Great*. New York: Scribners, 1971.

Walworth, Nancy. *Constantine*. New York: Chelsea House, 1989.

Theodosius the Great (Theodosius I)

DESTROYER OF THE
ANCIENT GODS

When his father was executed for high treason in A.D. 375, Theodosius withdrew from public life and retired to his estates at Cauca, in the northwestern Spanish province of Gallaecia (later Galicia), where he had been born and raised. The military had been Theodosius' life for as long as he could remember. His father had risen through the ranks to supreme commander of the cavalry, and Theodosius was still a teenager when he first fought alongside his father against the Picts and Scots in northern Britain. In the years that followed, other campaigns had pitted father and son against the Gauls and the Danube's Sarmatians. Theodosius had proven himself an able and courageous young soldier. But with his father dead, these qualities brought him few privileges at first.

By A.D. 375, the Roman world had become a battleground within and without as foreign tribes took advantage of conflicts between would-be emperors to advance across the frontiers. Under such conditions, few emperors and other

Considering the gods of the ancient Romans of no importance, Theodosius effectively ended all worship of them. The ball he holds here symbolizes his power over the world.

> *"No one shall own any property that is exempt from taxes."*
>
> —Decree of Theodosius (around A.D. 382)

Theodosius the Great

BORN

January 11, A.D. 347
Cauca, Gallaecia

DIED

January 17, A.D. 395
Mediolanum, Italy

PROFESSION

Roman emperor

ACCOMPLISHMENTS

Settled the Danube frontier by signing treaties with various German tribes; decreed that Christianity was the true faith and effectively abolished the ancient religion of the Romans; defeated the emperor of the West and became the sole ruler of the Roman Empire

ranking leaders died a natural death. In fact, the unexpected seemed to happen more often than the expected. Thus, in 378 Gratian, the same emperor who, just three years earlier, had ordered Theodosius' father executed, now summoned Theodosius to his court.

Gratian recognized Theodosius' military abilities and saw him as the one leader capable of securing the Danube borders. Theodosius immediately accepted the challenge. Pleased with the victories that followed, Gratian appointed Theodosius to be augustus (co-emperor) of the East on January 19, 379, and placed under his control the provinces of Dacia (modern Romania) and Macedonia.

Theodosius set his priorities, the first being to train a well-disciplined army. Because he felt that the current eligibility rules would not allow him to enroll the number of recruits he needed, he changed the laws and opened the military to the Teutons (a Germanic tribe). He then promoted to leadership positions those "foreigners" who proved their worth on the battlefield.

Meanwhile, the Visigoths (another Germanic tribe) continued to raid the northern borders of Theodosius' territory. Recognizing that no amount of fighting would eliminate this problem, Theodosius opted for a diplomatic solution. In 381, he met with the Visigothic chieftain Athanaric; within a few months the two signed a treaty. The Visigoths would be allowed to settle in the Roman province of Thrace in return for military assistance and farm labor.

In the treaty, Theodosius also agreed to pay the Visigoths for their services. In order to obtain the needed funds, Theodosius resorted to raising taxes and decreed that no property was exempt from taxation. These measures had a powerful impact, for tenant farmers were considered slaves of the land to which they were born and landowners paid taxes according to the amount of land and number of slaves owned. Should any tenant farmers dare leave they were, in effect, stealing themselves from that land and were guilty of theft. Thus, while Rome's subjects appreciated the peace Theodosius brought to the empire, the repressiveness of his rule caused simmering discontent.

Meanwhile, turmoil erupted in the West when the general Magnus Maximus declared himself emperor and killed Gratian in battle. In 384, Maximus invaded Italy and forced emperor Valentinian II to flee. At first, Theodosius stood aloof from this conflict, but eventually he concluded that Maximus posed a threat to his own rule. Leaving his son Arcadius in command of the East, Theodosius headed west.

Relying heavily on the powerful tribes he had settled in his lands, Theodosius defeated Maximus in a series of battles. After granting Valentinian II command of the West, Theodosius remained in Mediolanum (now Milan) for some three years. While there he spent much time with the city's Christian bishop, Ambrose. The

Despite Theodosius' ban on all so-called pagan practices, many small bronze statues representing ancient household gods and spirits—known as *Lares* and *Penates*—have survived.

two men discussed many matters, both political and religious. Ambrose believed that although emperors might be all-powerful in civil, judicial, and military matters, they were still obliged to obey the Christian God at all times.

In February 380, Theodosius decreed that only those who accepted the doctrines set out in the Nicene Creed, which had been formulated under Constantine the Great, could be considered Catholic Christians. (This was the first time that the term "Catholic" was used in any document.) Theodosius then placed all the churches under the control of Catholic bishops, who would determine who was Catholic and who was not.

When Theodosius fell seriously ill a few months later, he asked to be baptized, thereby becoming an official member of the Christian faith. Upon recovering, Theodosius convened a second council of bishops to review the Nicene Creed and make any changes they felt necessary.

Because of Theodosius' devotion to the Church and the Christian faith, he became known to history as Theodosius the Great. Like his predecessor Constantine, Theodosius saw himself as the main enforcer of Christian doctrine. In 391, Theodosius officially prohibited the practice of sacrificing to the ancient Roman gods, closed all the temples, and banned all foreign cults.

Upon the death of Valentinian II, the emperor of the West, control there passed to Flavius Eugenius, a former teacher of Latin rhetoric. Because Eugenius adhered to the ancient Roman faith, the empire was now split between Christians and those they referred to as pagans. Theodosius was determined to settle this conflict, by force of arms if necessary. Accordingly, in 394 he left Constantinople for the West and confronted Eugenius' forces at the Frigidus River on the eastern border of Italy. In the fierce fighting that followed, Theodosius triumphed, a victory he attributed to the power of the Christian God. He then proclaimed himself the sole ruler of the Roman Empire. But his reign was brief, for he became ill shortly after the battle and died in Mediolanum in January 395.

Still, the unity of the Roman world seemed secure, for on his deathbed Theodosius had entrusted the empire and the care of his sons and successors, Arcadius and Honorius, to his trusted advisors Rufinus and Stilicho.

A few decades later, a Greek historian named Zosimus condemned Theodosius for his persecution of the ancient gods and attributed his forced Christianization of the empire as the direct cause of Rome's destruction in 410. A firm believer in the power of the deities of Mount Olympus, Zosimus believed the gods punished Rome for Theodosius' acts. Yet the eastern Roman Empire continued to flourish for centuries, with Constantinople as its political, economic, and cultural center.

FURTHER READING

Williams, Stephen. *Theodosius: The Empire at Bay.* New Haven: Yale University Press, 1995.

More Ancient Romans to Remember

Plutarch (Lucius [?] Mestrius Plutarchus) (around A.D. 46–around A.D. 120) was a Greek by birth, born in Chaeronea, in the district of Boeotia. Although Plutarch studied in Athens and taught in Rome, he preferred Chaeronea. He held several public offices there and ran a school that taught philosophy and ethics as its principal subjects. Yet it was not Plutarch's teaching ability or his political duties, but his writings, that won him fame.

Plutarch's most important work is *Parallel Lives*, a collection of 46 biographies of Greek and Roman personalities written entirely in Greek. (Although Plutarch knew Latin, he was not proficient in the language.) Plutarch's format differed from that used by other biographers in that he chose to arrange his "lives" in pairs. For example, Plutarch wrote

In Venice in January 1478, Nicolaus Jenson printed this beautifully clear copy of the Latin edition of Plutarch's *Lives*. The Italian artist Girolamo da Cremona designed the colorful first page of the life of the Athenian statesman Cimon.

about Theseus, the legendary hero of Athens, and then about Romulus, the legendary founder of Rome. He then followed the biographies with a comparison of the two heroes.

Plutarch did not try to philosophize in his essays or dwell on specific political or moral problems. He never intended this work as a history, dry and full of details. Rather, he aimed to please his readers and give them a piece that they would enjoy.

Second in importance to the *Lives* is the *Moralia* (Ethical Works), which includes Plutarch's surviving writings on ethical, political, religious, and literary subjects.

Suetonius (Gaius Suetonius Tranquillus) (around A.D. 69–after A.D. 111) belonged to the wealthy business class of Romans known as the *equites*. Around A.D. 121, Hadrian promoted Suetonius to the position of secretary of imperial correspondence. Soon after, Hadrian dismissed Suetonius on charges of improper conduct. No accounts survive that tell us what Suetonius did next, but he probably devoted himself to the pursuit he enjoyed most—writing.

Suetonius' earliest major work appears to have been *De viris illustribus* (On Distinguished Men), a series of biographical accounts of Rome's literary masters, including Horace, Lucan, Terence, and Virgil. Many of Suetonius' works were lost in the centuries after his death, but while they were available other writers drew upon them extensively when writing biography. As a result, much of what we know about the lives of Rome's writers actually traces its origin to Suetonius.

Suetonius' best-known work is his *De Vita Caesarum* (The Lives of the Caesars). Surviving almost intact, this work provides detailed biographies of the 12 emperors known collectively as the Caesars, from Julius Caesar through Domitian. Suetonius' approach was unique in that he wrote first about the emperor's ancestry, then of his life until his accession, followed by his accomplishments, personal life, appearance, personality, and manner of death.

Frontinus (Sextus Julius Frontinus) (around A.D. 30–104) had a distinguished career as a soldier in the Roman army and later served as governor of Britain under the emperor Vespasian. However, he is best known as the author of *De aquis urbis Romae* (Concerning the Waters of the City of Rome). In A.D. 97, Vespasian's successor, Nerva, appointed Frontinus superintendent of the city's aqueducts. Believing that a manual about the aqueducts and their maintenance would be highly useful—both for himself and his successors—Frontinus began writing his two-volume work. Completed under Nerva's successor, Trajan, the work describes the aqueducts, relates their history, and presents numerous technical details concerning distribution and supply, as well as regulations governing public and private use.

Plotina (Pompeia Plotina) (died around A.D. 122) won the respect of Romans throughout the empire for her loyalty, courage, dignity, and modesty. Married to Trajan before he became emperor in A.D. 98, she remained devoted to him until his death in A.D. 117. When Pliny the Younger addressed the Senate in A.D. 100 and praised Trajan, he spoke also of Plotina: "Your wife has brought you nothing but fame and honor. No other woman alive is more sincere or more perfectly represents the Roman tradition of womanhood." It was said that when Plotina first entered the imperial palace as the emperor's wife she remarked, "I hope that when I leave this place I shall be the same woman that I am today."

When Trajan's cousin Hadrian was left fatherless in A.D. 85, Trajan took the young Hadrian into his household. With no children of their own, Trajan and Plotina treated Hadrian as a son. Years later, Plotina was with her husband on a military campaign in the East when he fell seriously ill. As Trajan lay dying, Plotina is said to have persuaded him to adopt Hadrian, of whom she was very fond, as his successor and heir. When Plotina died, around A.D. 122, Hadrian ordered a temple built in her honor.

Antoninus Pius (Titus Aurelius Fulvius Boionius Arrius Antoninus) (A.D. 86–161) came from southern Gaul but moved to Rome when his grandfather and father were named to the office of consul. Around A.D. 134, Antoninus left Rome to become governor of the province of Asia. His upright conduct again brought him to Hadrian's attention and, in A.D. 138, the ailing emperor named Antoninus his heir and successor. When Hadrian died just months later, the succession was smooth and quick.

During his 23-year rule there were no major wars. When dissent threatened to spark armed conflict, Antoninus tried first to settle the situation peacefully. When revolts erupted in Britain, Dacia, Mauretania, Germany, and Egypt, Antoninus crushed them. He then set about strengthening the borders and establishing new policies in an attempt to forestall further discontent. His most renowned defense system was the so-called Antonine Wall in Britain, built in A.D. 142, 100 miles north of Hadrian's Wall.

Antoninus eliminated the costly gifts Italian cities gave a new emperor, cut public spending wherever he could, and increased the treasury's resources. In honor of his beloved wife, Faustina, who died in A.D. 141, he established a fund to support poor girls. As a tribute to his sincere devotion to duty (and to his adoptive father, Hadrian) the Senate honored him with the title *Pius* (devoted).

Quintilian (Marcus Fabius Quintilianus) (around A.D. 35–after A.D. 96) was born in Spain and most likely spent his youth studying rhetoric and oratory in Rome. By A.D. 70, he was presenting cases in the law courts and gaining a reputation for excellent defenses. But the classroom appealed to him far more than the courtroom, and Quintilian became the first Roman teacher to receive a government salary. After teaching for 20 years, Quintilian retired to private life and devoted his time to writing.

Quintilian's best-known work is the *Institutio Oratoria*, a series of 12 books published before A.D. 96. In Books 1 and 2 he focused on the training an orator should receive from in-

Uncovered during excavations, this piece of stucco, most likely from a wall or ceiling in an ancient Roman home, shows a defeated member of a foreign tribe entreating the emperor Antoninus Pius.

For the ancient Romans, the public baths were an essential part of everyday life and became increasingly larger with each emperor. Today, the ruins of those built by Caracalla bear witness to their enormous size. Excavations under the ruins have uncovered frescos, mosaic floors, and sculptures from pre-existing houses.

fancy into adulthood. Book 10 presents a critical survey of Greek and Latin authors, indicating why studying each would be useful to anyone desiring to be a great orator. In the last book, Quintilian offers advice to would-be orators on a great variety of topics, including the character traits an orator should develop, the most advantageous style of eloquence, and the necessity of knowing when to retire. Throughout the *Institutio*, Quintilian made clear his belief that a good orator was also a good citizen, with high standards and an upright character. As he wrote, "A liar should have a good memory."

Commodus (Lucius Aelius Aurelius Commodus) (A.D. 161–92) became emperor of Rome in A.D. 180, the first son to succeed his father in that office since Titus had followed Vespasian a century earlier. At first, Commodus listened to his father's advisors, but he gradually began to rely on others whose morals and values proved far less wholesome.

Tigidius Perennis was the first of Commodus' associates to wield great

power and he soon turned to murder and intrigue to stay in power. Only when Commodus became convinced that Perennis had too much power and might become a rival did he order Perennis murdered.

In the years that followed, Commodus resorted to murder several times. As a result, Romans who had once rejoiced that Marcus Aurelius' son had succeeded his father now feared him and turned away in disgust when Commodus proclaimed he was the legendary hero Hercules. And when Commodus renamed Rome *Colonia Commodiana* (Colony of Commodus), he aroused widespread resentment.

Just before his inauguration as consul on January 1, A.D. 193, Commodus announced his intention to dress as a Roman gladiator for the occasion. Murmurs of discontent rumbled across the city and within the palace walls. On the night of December 31, 192, Commodus' mistress, Marcia, and a number of imperial advisors arranged for a well-known athlete to visit the unsuspecting Commodus and strangle him to death. All Rome rejoiced at the news, but

Commodus had already caused irreversible damage. He had destroyed the stability secured by his predecessors, the five good emperors, and ushered in a period of civil conflict.

Papinian (Aemilius Papinianus) (died A.D. 212) was a native of Syria and became the leading authority on Roman law. Indeed, the Law of Citations, enacted in A.D. 426, stated that whenever a majority of jurists failed to agree on a particular point, the view expressed in Papinian's works would prevail.

The most important of Papinian's surviving writings are his *Quaestiones* and *Responsa*. Written in legal Latin, they show a keen, balanced mind that could arrive at original solutions to problems. Ready to change his opinion when another seemed more correct, Papinian did not tailor his judgments to suit those in power, a trait that led to his death.

After Septimus Severus died in A.D. 211, Caracalla and his brother Geta succeeded their father as joint heirs. Determined to be sole ruler, Caracalla killed Geta. When Papinian refused to supply a legal rationale for the murder, Caracalla ordered Papinian's execution.

Caracalla (Septimius Bassianus) (A.D. 188–217) became co-ruler of the Roman Empire when his father Septimus Severus died in A.D. 211. Soon after, he ordered first his brother Geta and then Geta's chief supporters killed.

Following his father's advice, Caracalla treated his soldiers well, raised their pay, and increased their benefits. In A.D. 212, Caracalla marched against the German tribe known as the Alamanni and defeated them. Soon after, rumors spread that the victory had not come on the battlefield but at the bargaining table. That is, Caracalla had given the Alamanni benefits and money in return for peace.

There was another factor in Caracalla's attitude toward the Germans: he liked them. He even wore a blond wig to make himself resemble the fair-haired people to the north. Caracalla's name was also a stylish invention, deriving from the long, flowing cloak he wore. Designed by Caracalla himself, this garment resembled more closely the cloaks worn in Gaul and Germany than in Italy.

The most sweeping change inaugurated by Caracalla was his *Constitutio Antoniniana de Civitate*. Perhaps the most famous legal measure of ancient times, this law granted the entire free population of the Roman empire the rights of Roman citizenship.

Caracalla's motives were anything but charitable. With expenses steadily increasing, Caracalla needed to increase tax revenues. Inheritance taxes were a prime source of income, but only Roman citizens had to pay them. By extending the rights of citizenship, he immediately and dramatically expanded the tax base.

One of Caracalla's chief expenditures was the great public bath complex he built in Rome. The largest ever constructed, the Baths of Caracalla measured 750 feet by 380 feet and included gardens, open-air sports-training areas, swimming pools, art collections, courtyards, and auxiliary rooms. The Baths of Caracalla are the only ancient baths to have survived in the city of Rome. Today the building hosts a variety of open-air summer programs, including operas and orchestral performances.

In A.D. 216, Caracalla left Rome to conquer Parthia. But his needless killings and treacherous ways made those around him wonder about their own security. Then came a message from a supporter in Rome that a high-ranking officer named Macrinus was not to be trusted. Fortunately for Macrinus, he was in charge of receiving all reports that day. Realizing that his life was at stake, Macrinus recruited a fellow officer and plotted Caracalla's death.

The opportunity came when Caracalla set out to visit a temple in northern Mesopotamia, and Macrinus accompanied him, as did Macrinus' accomplice. At some point along the way the accomplice stabbed Caracalla with a dagger when he dismounted and stepped away to relieve himself.

Macrinus' pretended grief deceived everyone, and the soldiers hailed Macrinus as Caracalla's successor.

Dio Cassius (around A.D. 155–after A.D. 229) wrote the history of Rome in 80 books, beginning with the landing of the legendary Aeneas in Italy and ending with the rule of Alexander Severus in A.D. 229. A native of Nicaea in Bithynia, in present-day northern Turkey, Dio Cassius left for Rome in A.D. 180, where he quickly advanced politically, becoming a member of the Senate, a praetor, and finally a consul. He also held several high-ranking administrative posts in the provinces.

Although much of Dio Cassius' original work has not survived, later historians often used his material. From their writings it is possible to obtain a fairly accurate idea of what Dio Cassius covered in his history.

Written in Greek, Dio Cassius' history is sometimes biased and lacks a deep sense of historical criticism. Details of earlier events are often brief and sometimes unreliable, but those of later times, especially his own period, show a good grasp of political events and are given in great detail.

Aurelian (Lucius Domitius Aurelianus) (around A.D. 215–275) became the emperor of Rome in A.D. 270 and immediately unleashed his troops on German tribes returning home from a raid on northern Italy. After a crushing defeat, the Romans quickly rallied and sent the invaders scrambling back across the Alps.

Upon learning that riots had broken out in Rome during his absence, Aurelian ordered his engineers to build a massive wall around the city, 12 miles long, 12 feet thick, and 20 feet high, much of which is still standing today.

Turning his attention to Asia Minor, Aurelius grappled with Zenobia, the queen of Palmyra in Syria, who insisted on acting as an independent monarch rather than a subject of Rome. Zenobia believed that the Romans would never cross the desert to attack her, but Aurelian soon marched his troops across the sands and laid siege to Palmyra. When Zenobia left the city to seek help from allies in Persia, Aurelian captured the brave queen and razed the city soon after.

In the grand triumphal march that followed in Rome, Zenobia marched as a prized prisoner of war. Unlike many previous Roman conquerors, who executed their prisoners after a triumph, Aurelian allowed Zenobia to live and even married her to a Roman senator.

In domestic matters, Aurelian proved himself an outstanding administrator. He increased the free food distribution to the poor, reorganized the coinage system, and slowed rampant inflation.

In A.D. 275, Aurelian again marched his legions toward the east. When he was encamped in Thrace, he caught his private secretary, Eros, in a lie and threatened punishment. Fearing the emperor's wrath, Eros deceitfully told several officers of the Praetorian Guard that Aurelian planned to kill them. Acting on this misinformation, the officers assassinated Aurelian.

Stilicho (Flavius Stilicho) (around A.D. 365–408) proved himself such an excellent military commander that the emperor Theodosius I gave him his

niece in marriage and later named him regent for his young son Honorius. Upon Theodosius' death in A.D. 395, Stilicho prepared to govern the Western Roman Empire until 12-year-old Honorius came of age.

Before Stilicho could settle into his new position, the Germanic people known as the Visigoths, led by the daring Alaric, invaded Thrace and Macedonia. Descended from another ancient Germanic tribe, the Vandals, Stilicho prepared to attack Alaric. At just that moment, Arcadius, Honorius' brother and the emperor of the East, ordered Stilicho to send some of his troops to Constantinople. Now lacking adequate manpower, Stilicho was forced to stand aside while the Visigoths invaded Greece. Two years later, Alaric invaded Greece a second time and Stilicho again avoided battle.

In A.D. 401, Alaric invaded Roman territory for a third time. This time Stilicho was able to capture the Visigoths' camp. Alaric, however, managed to retreat.

Following another Visigoth invasion in A.D. 405, Alaric demanded 4,000 pounds of gold from Honorius. The Romans were outraged, but Stilicho persuaded Honorius and the Senate to pay up.

As a result, some Romans began to suspect Stilicho's motives. Honorius, convinced that Stilicho could not be trusted, ordered his execution.

Less than two years after Stilicho's death, Alaric again invaded Italy. With Stilicho gone, there was no one to stop Alaric or negotiate with him. On August 24, 410, Alaric reached the walls of Rome. Then a traitor opened the gates and, for the first time since Camillus had forced the Gauls to retreat from the city 800 years earlier, a foreign enemy entered Rome and sacked the city.

Appendix 1
Legendary Heroes and Heroines of Early Rome

Through the centuries, Roman orators, writers, statesmen, and generals often recalled the brave deeds of their nation's legendary heroes and heroines as a way of instilling pride and patriotism in both citizens and subjects. Below are brief biographies, in chronological order, of the most famous of these people. Though many of the details may actually be based on fact, the stories are mostly legends, embellished and shaped by later generations. For more information on Rome's legendary figures, read Livy's *History of Rome*.

Aeneas

A Trojan by birth, Aeneas defended his homeland against the Greeks in the great Trojan War, which it is traditionally agreed ended in 1184 B.C. In the 10th and final year of the war, the gods advised him to flee west across the Mediterranean to found a new city. At first, Aeneas resisted the idea of deserting his fellow Trojans, but eventually he left Troy, taking his father, Anchises, his son Ascanius, statues of the ancestral gods, and a few loyal companions.

After a long and dangerous sea journey, a fierce storm dashed Aeneas' ships against the shores of northern Africa, forcing him to seek refuge with the Carthaginians and their queen, Dido. Aeneas seriously considered remaining in Carthage but abandoned such thoughts after the gods reminded him of his duty to found a new city. Leaving Dido, who committed suicide in her despair, Aeneas sadly set sail again.

When he arrived on the west coast of Italy—legend pinpoints his landing at Cumae, just north of Naples—Aeneas prepared to establish his claim to the area. Ancient accounts tell different tales of the events that followed, the best known being that found in Virgil's *Aeneid*. According to that epic, King Latinus welcomed Aeneas to Italy and offered him his daughter Lavinia in marriage. This greatly angered Turnus, the native hero to whom Latinus had previously betrothed his daughter. Turnus declared war on Aeneas, but Aeneas defeated him in hand-to-hand combat.

Aeneas' victory did not bring peace. The neighboring Rutuli and their allies, the Etruscans, soon declared war on Aeneas' forces. Aeneas mysteriously disappeared during the ensuing battle and was never seen again, nor was his body ever found. In the centuries that followed, the Romans revered Aeneas as the founder of their nation. They also believed that Aeneas was the son of Aphrodite, the goddess of love and beauty, giving credibility to the belief that the Romans were descended from the gIndexods, who had decreed that they should rule. Julius Caesar, whose Latin family name was Iulius, traced his ancestry to Aeneas' son Ascanius, also called Iulus.

The Cumaean Sibyl

Deep within a cave near Cumae, Italy, dwelt a very old woman wise in the knowledge of world events—past, present, and future. Understanding her utterances was a problem, because the cave had 100 passageways and 100 openings, so that the voice of the sibyl (prophetess) echoed and re-echoed as it passed from the depths within to the outside world. And her written prophecies were even more difficult to understand; she wrote them on palm leaves that could be scattered by the slightest breeze and never again be arranged in the proper order.

Before entering the underworld to consult his dead father, Aeneas met and spoke with the sibyl. In a haunting voice she prophesied the future, foretelling Aeneas' marriage to an "alien bride" (Lavinia) and revealing to him the secrets of entering and exiting the underworld alive.

Tradition also relates that years later, during the reign of Tarquinius Priscus, the Cumaean sibyl offered the king nine books foretelling the history of Rome. Tarquinius dismissed them as irrelevant and laughed at the exorbitant asking price. Undeterred, the sibyl burned three books and then asked the same price for the remaining six. When Tarquinius still refused to pay, the sibyl burned another three books and then asked the original price for the last three. This time, Tarquinius gave the sibyl her money and placed the last three in a vault beneath the Temple of Jupiter on the Capitoline Hill.

In times of disaster and impending danger, Rome's religious officials consulted the sibyl's books to learn how the Romans could make amends to the gods for the offenses that had caused the crisis. In 83 B.C., after a fire destroyed the books, the Senate ordered that prophecies housed at other sacred sites be copied and brought to Rome. In 12 B.C., the emperor Augustus transferred these new books to the Temple of Apollo on the Palatine Hill, where they remained until A.D. 405, when the Roman general Stilicho reportedly burned them.

Rhea Silvia

Rhea's father was Numitor, a descendant of Aeneas and the rightful heir to the throne. When Numitor's brother Amulius usurped the power for himself, he made Rhea a Vestal Virgin. This meant that she had to serve Vesta, Rome's goddess of the hearth, for 30 years. By law, she could not marry until after her term expired, and should she become pregnant the punishment was death. But Mars, the god of war, took no interest in Amulius' plans and fell in love with Rhea. When Amulius learned that she had given birth to twin boys, he ordered that Rhea be buried alive, as the law demanded, and that the boys be cast adrift in a basket on the Tiber River.

Romulus

When the current in the Tiber River pushed the basket with Rhea Silvia's abandoned twin infants to the riverbank, a passing she-wolf found them and treated them as her cubs. By chance, a shepherd named Faustulus saw the boys suckling at the she-wolf's side and, carefully taking the boys in his arms, brought them home to his wife. Naming them Romulus and Remus, the couple reared the boys as their own.

Years later, when Remus was charged with stealing cattle belonging to a man named Numitor, Remus had no idea that the judge, King Amulius, was really his great-uncle and that Numitor was his grandfather. However, there was something in Remus' appearance that made Numitor aware that the accused thief was actually his lost grandson. Upon learning of his true identity, Remus immediately told his brother, and the two made plans to overthrow Amulius and return the throne to its rightful owner, their grandfather.

Their goal accomplished, the twins decided to found their own city on the spot where they had washed ashore years earlier. They could not, however, agree about the exact location. Romulus said it was the Palatine Hill, Remus the Aventine. Believing that the gods would provide the answer, each brother stood on the hill of his choice and waited for a divine sign. Remus claimed victory when he saw 6 vultures fly directly above him. But when Romulus saw 12 of them fly over the Palatine, he claimed that the gods had chosen him. During the quarrel that followed, Remus tauntingly jumped over the stone boundary Romulus was building around his city. Enraged by this act of defiance, Romulus killed Remus.

Romulus then called his new city Rome, a derivation of his own name. Succeeding generations of Romans would celebrate April 21, 753 B.C., as the founding date of their city. A wise and forceful ruler, Romulus disappeared suddenly one day during a thunderstorm. Legend said that the gods lifted him from the earth to reside with them.

Tarpeia

During a bitter struggle between the Romans and the neighboring Sabines, the latter had managed to advance as far as the Capitoline Hill. Aware that breaking through the gates was almost impossible, the Sabines sought other ways of entry. By chance, they were able to take Tarpeia, the daughter of the fortress's commander, into their confidence, offering her gold collars and armlets in return for opening the gates to the city. Tarpeia listened to the Sabines' request and wondered what to do.

Unfortunately for the Romans, Tarpeia chose the role of traitor. Her wealth, however, was short-lived, for the Sabines did not trust or respect traitors. Rather than give her their gold bands, they crushed her with their shields. The cliff on the Capitoline Hill where Tarpeia betrayed her people came to be known as the Tarpeian Rock. In the generations that followed, criminals convicted of crimes against the state were often hurled to their deaths from this precipice.

The Sabine Women

During Romulus' early years as king, he welcomed anyone who wished to settle in Rome. Naturally, the great majority of those who answered his call were men, many of them runaway slaves and criminals. Romulus knew that for his city to prosper he needed to devise a plan that would also bring women to the city.

Romulus accordingly sent invitations to the surrounding communities, announcing that Rome was sponsoring a great festival. The great majority of those who came were members of a neighboring tribe known as the Sabines. Soon after the athletic contests began, Romulus gave a prearranged signal that told each Roman to seize a Sabine girl and take her to his home.

Because the Sabines had come unarmed, they could not oppose the Romans. But they did not forget the incident. Returning home, they mobilized their troops and marched out, armed and battle ready, to challenge their daughters' abductors. The Romans, meanwhile, prepared to defend their newly won wives.

As the two lines of battle faced each other, the Sabine women suddenly ran between the two armies. Defiantly proclaiming that if the Romans died they would be widows and if the Sabines died they would be fatherless, the women refused to move until either they were killed or a treaty was signed between the two peoples. Realizing that the women were not about to yield, the troops on both sides agreed to live together in harmony.

Mettius Curtius

"If Rome wishes to be eternal, the Romans must place what they value most in this great chasm." So spoke the ancient soothsayers when consulted about a great hole that had suddenly opened in the Forum. But what did the Romans value most?

Young Mettius Curtius, a brave and loyal Roman soldier, voiced his opinion clearly and forcefully: "We value most the individual courage of each Roman, for it is this trait that has allowed Rome to succeed." Having spoken, he then dressed himself in full armor, leaped onto his horse, and jumped into the hole. Immediately the earth closed above him.

Numa Pompilius

Appointed king a year or so after Romulus' death, Numa devoted himself to establishing the principles and precepts by which Rome would be ruled. He also ordered the construction of the Temple of Janus (the god of beginnings), the doors of which were to be kept closed in time of peace and open in wartime. During Numa's reign, the doors were never opened. Tradition also honored Numa as the originator of Roman religious worship, relating that he received Rome's religious rules and regulations from a nymph named Egeria.

Lucius Tarquinius Priscus

As Lucuma and his wife, Tanaquil, left Tarquinii in Etruria and set out on the road to Rome, an eagle swooped down and seized Lucuma's cap. After carrying it high into the air, the eagle replaced the cap on Lucuma's head. A respected soothsayer, Tanaquil interpreted the omen as a sign that her husband would attain the highest honors.

Her prediction proved correct, for once they arrived in Rome they received a warm welcome and were given the rights of Roman citizenship. Lucumo then took the name Tarquinius, from his hometown. The historian Livy later added the qualifying term *Priscus*, meaning "previous," because Tarquinius was the first by that name to become a leader in Rome. Tarquinius soon won the admiration of the king, Ancus Marcius, who appointed him guardian of his children. When Marcius died, the Senate named Tarquinius his successor, and thus he became the first foreign king to rule Rome.

In the years that followed, Tarquinius added many neighboring lands to Rome's territory and directed a great building program throughout the city, including the magnificent Temple on the Capitoline Hill dedicated to the three major deities, Jupiter, Juno, and Minerva. Tradition also credited Tarquinius with the construction of the Circus Maximus (where chariot races were held), the Forum, and the Cloaca Maxima or "great sewer," which is still in service today.

In the 38th year of Tarquinius' reign, Ancus Marcius' sons took action to right the wrong they felt Tarquinius had committed against their father. But even though they killed Tarquinius, they were unable to claim the throne, and Servius Tullius became the next king.

Servius Tullius

Servius Tullius, like Tarquinius Priscus, was a historical figure. However, no one knows which of his recorded deeds are fact rather than legend.

As the son of a prisoner of war, Servius began life as a slave in the royal household. However, because Queen Tanaquil foresaw future greatness for him, King Tarquinius raised him as a royal son and gave him his daughter in marriage.

When Tarquinius died, Tanaquil kept the news of her husband's death a secret until Servius was able to gain control of the government and win the confidence of the Senate. Then, when Tarquinius' death was announced, the Senate immediately recognized Servius as king.

A firm believer in peace, Servius devoted his time to establishing civil rights and a code of laws. Tradition credited Servius with formulating Rome's first constitution, including a provision that granted the common people political rights. Servius also divided the Roman people into classes according to the number of acres they owned and the amount of money they had.

Servius' daughter, Tullia, disliked her father. Conspiring with her brother-in-law, Tarquinius Superbus, Tullia plotted the death of her husband and sister. As soon as this was accomplished, she married Tarquinius and the two conspired to overthrow Servius.

Aware that Servius was considering a plan to abolish the monarchy, Tullia urged quick action against her father. Tarquinius therefore dressed himself in royal robes and haughtily assumed Servius' seat in the Senate, demanding that the senators acknowledge him as their king.

After hearing of the incident, Servius approached the Senate house and ordered Tarquinius to step down. Tarquinius did so immediately, but then advanced on Servius. With one forceful blow Tarquinius sent Servius tumbling down the Senate's stone steps. Hurt and dazed, Servius tried to reach the safety of his home but was killed by Tarquinius' servants along the way.

Tarquinius Superbus

The second Etruscan to rule Rome, Tarquinius won the surname Superbus, meaning "proud" or "haughty," because of his part in the murder of Servius Tullius and his subsequent actions as king of Rome. A ruthless leader, he abolished the rights Servius had granted the commoners and condemned or forced into exile the senators and other patricians who had opposed him.

Despite his indifference to the people and the cruelties he committed against conquered towns, Tarquinius Superbus increased Rome's influence and power in central Italy and initiated grandiose building projects.

For 24 years, Tarquinius ruled Rome with a steadfast, unyielding hand. His downfall came when his son's brutal actions against a respected lady named Lucretia so incensed the Romans that they drove Tarquinius from their lands.

Lucretia

In 510 B.C., the Romans under Tarquinius Superbus were at war with their neighbors, the Rutuli. One night as Tarquinius' son Sextus entertained his friends in his tent, each began boasting about his wife. After a young nobleman named Collatinus declared that his wife, Lucretia, was the most virtuous of all, the men decided to visit each other's homes and ascertain the truth. However, it so happened that every wife was out, feasting at a sumptuous banquet, except for Lucretia, who was at home spinning wool.

Deciding that he wanted Lucretia for himself, a nobleman named Sextus secretly left the military camp a few days later and went to visit Lucretia. Warmly received as a friend of her husband, Sextus took advantage of Lucretia's kindness and hospitality and tried to force himself upon her. When she refused, he threatened to kill her and leave a dead naked slave by her bed, adding that he would tell everyone he had discovered Lucretia with her lover and killed them both.

Knowing that there would be no one to prove her innocence if she lay dead, Lucretia yielded to the evil Sextus and then summoned her husband and father from the battlefield. When the two arrived, Lucretia told them what had happened and then, to prove her innocence, took a knife and committed suicide.

Enraged at the boldness of Sextus, Collatinus and his friend Brutus rallied the Romans against the Tarquins and drove them out of the city. Abolishing the monarchy by decree, Collatinus and Brutus established the Roman republic, with two consuls, elected annually by the people, as their leaders.

Horatius Cocles

Tarquinius Superbus was not one to admit defeat and, taking his cause to the neighboring Etruscan king, Lars Porsenna, he enlisted Porsenna's aid against the Romans.

As the two approached Rome with their armies, the Romans withdrew all their troops to within the city's walls, except for a small contingent led by Horatius Cocles. Horatius planned to guard the Sublician Bridge, which spanned the Tiber River and gave entrance to the city. However, when Horatius' men saw the huge Etruscan army advancing toward the bridge, many panicked and retreated within the walls.

Horatio then ordered those soldiers who had stood their ground to cut away the bridge's timbers while he marched with two faithful companions to the far end of the bridge. As the last timbers of the bridge were about to give way, Horatius ordered his companions to retreat safely to Rome, while he remained to slow the enemy's advance.

Fighting until he felt all strength ebbing from his limbs, Horatius then dove into the Tiber's waters. When he reached the opposite shore safely, Horatius gave thanks to the gods.

Mucius Scaevola

Horatius Cocles' brave stand at the Sublician Bridge slowed Porsenna's advance, but it did not force him to retreat. Instead, Porsenna laid siege to the city in hopes of starving the Romans into submission. Intent on preventing this tragedy, a young Roman named Gaius Mucius obtained the Senate's permission to sneak into the Etruscan camp. Armed only with a sword, Mucius stealthily slipped past the sentries and made his way to where he believed Porsenna was camped. However, Mucius had no idea what Porsenna looked like. When he saw two men in regal clothes, he stabbed the one he believed to be the king. Unfortunately, Mucius chose Porsenna's scribe and not Porsenna.

Porsenna asked this bold Roman his name and the reason for his actions. Mucius proudly replied, "I am a Roman citizen. They call me Gaius Mucius." Porsenna then threatened Mucius with punishment, but the Roman shrugged his shoulders and calmly placed his right hand in a nearby campfire. When Porsenna ordered his men to pull Mucius' hand from the fire, Mucius retorted that he knew 300 more Romans just as brave and willing to fight for Rome.

Knowing that his troops were not this loyal, Porsenna freed Mucius and led his own troops home. Hailed as a hero, Mucius won the right to use the surname Scaevola, meaning left-handed, for his right hand was no longer of any use.

Coriolanus

The story of Coriolanus is based much more on historical fact than those of the preceding individuals. He lived in the 4th century B.C. at a time when Rome was steadily expanding its power. Early in his career, Coriolanus had defeated Rome's archenemies the Volsci in central Italy and had won the right to use the surname Coriolanus for his conquest of the major Volscian town, Corioli.

Coriolanus was an arrogant aristocrat who looked down on the common people, even asking the Senate to withdraw some of the plebeians' rights. When famine threatened the Romans, Coriolanus advised that incoming supplies be given to the rich, not the poor. Provoked by this attitude, the people successfully persuaded Rome's officials to banish Coriolanus.

Even in exile, however, Coriolanus maintained his haughty attitude and, with little hesitation, marched into Volscian territory to offer his services to their king. Sometime around 491 B.C., Coriolanus led the Volsci against Rome. When surrender seemed Rome's only alternative, two women left the protected walls of Rome and entered Coriolanus' camp.

What Coriolanus thought when he saw his mother and wife approaching him is not known, but he listened to their pleas and said nothing. As they continued to beg for mercy for his native city, the city of his family, his friends, his children, Coriolanus turned to his mother and said, "Mother, you have saved Rome, but lost your son!"

What happened to Coriolanus after he retreated with his soldiers is not known. Some sources say the Volscians condemned him as a traitor. Others maintain that he lived for many years in exile.

Appendix 2
Ancient Roman Emperors

Traditional Name	Date of Reign	Original Name	Official Name
Augustus	27 B.C.–A.D. 14	Gaius Octavius	Gaius Julius Caesar Octavianus (honorary title: Augustus)
Tiberius	A.D. 14–37	Tiberius Claudius Nero	Tiberius Caesar Augustus
Caligula	A.D. 31–41	Gaius Caesar	Gaius Caesar Germanicus
Claudius	A.D. 41–54	Tiberius Claudius Nero Germanicus	Tiberius Claudius Caesar Augustus Germanicus
Nero	A.D. 54–68	Lucius Domitius Ahenobarbus	Nero Claudius Caesar Augustus Germanicus
Galba	A.D. 68–69	Servius Sulpicius Galba	Servius Galba Caesar Augustus
Otho	A.D. 69	Marcus Salvius Otho	Marcus Otho Caesar Augustus
Vitellius	A.D. 69	Aulus Vitellius	Aulus Vitellius Germanicus
Vespasian	A.D. 69–79	Titus Flavius Vespasianus	Caesar Vespasianus Augustus
Titus	A.D. 79–81	Titus Flavius Vespasianus	Titus Vespasianus Augustus
Domitian	A.D. 81–96	Titus Flavius Domitianus	Caesar Domitianus Augustus
Nerva	A.D. 96–98	Marcus Cocceius Nerva	Nerva Caesar Augustus
Trajan	A.D. 98–117	Marcus Ulpius Traianus	Caesar Divi Nervae Filius Nerva Traianus Optimus Augustus
Hadrian	A.D. 117–138	Publius Aelius Hadrianus	Caesar Traianus Hadrianus Augustus
Antoninus Pius	A.D. 138–161	Titus Aurelius Fulvius Boionius Arrius Antonius	Caesar Titus Aelius Hadrianus Antoninus Augustus Pius
Marcus Aurelius and Lucius Verus	A.D. 161–180 [d. 169]	Marcus Annius Verus	Caesar Marcus Aurelius Antoninus Augustus
Commodus	A.D. 180-192	Lucius Aelius Aurelius Commodus	Caesar Marcus Aurelius Commodus Antoninus Augustus
Septimius Severus	A.D. 193–211	Septimius Severus	Lucius Septimius Severus Pertinax
Caracalla and Geta	A.D. 211–217 [d. 211–212]	Septimius Bassianus (uncertain)	Marcus Aurelius Severus Antoninus Augustus Publius Septimius Geta
Aurelian	A.D. 270–275	(uncertain)	Lucius Domitius Aurelianus
Diocletian and Maximian	A.D. 284–305 A.D. 286–305	Diocles (uncertain)	Gaius Aurelius Valerius Diocletianus Marcus Aurelius Velerius Maximianus
Constantine I and Licinius	A.D. 312–337 [d. 324]	(uncertain) (uncertain)	Flavius Valerius Constantinus Valerius Licinianus Licinus
Theodosius I	A.D. 378–395	(uncertain)	Flavius Theodosius

Appendix 3
Julian and Claudian Families

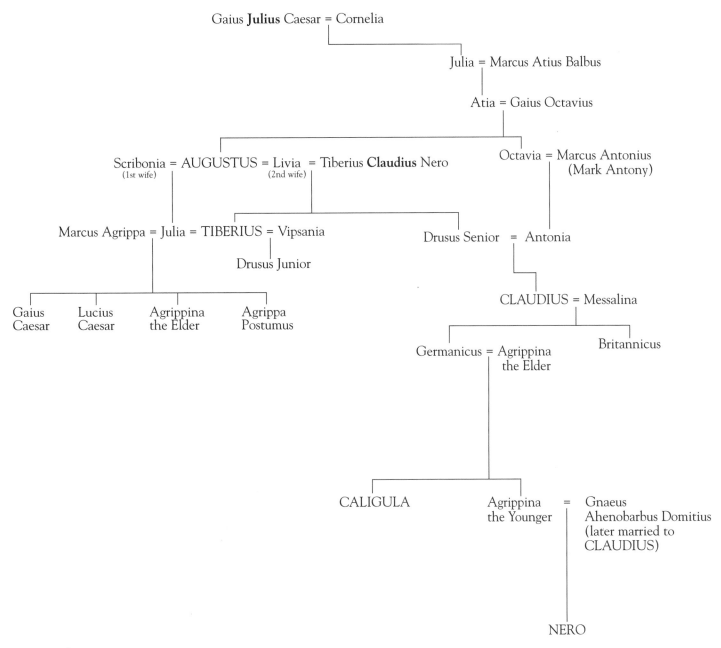

= married to
names in CAPITAL LETTERS indicate Roman emperors
names in **bold** indicate the Julian and Claudian ancestors

Note: The family name—the name through which a family traced its ancestry—
was the middle name, known in Latin as the *nomen*.

Appendix 4

Timeline of Events in the Roman World

B.C.

1184
Traditional date for the end of the Trojan War.

APRIL 21, 753
Traditional date for the founding of Rome.

510
Romans drive the Tarquins out of Rome and abolish the monarchy.

509
Roman Republic established.

396
Romans under Camillus capture the Etruscan town of Veii.

387
Gauls sack Rome.

264–41
First Punic War.

241
First Punic War ends.

218
Second Punic War begins.

216
Romans suffer a crushing defeat by Hannibal at the Battle of Cannae.

209
Scipio Africanus captures Carthago Nova (Carthage).

202
Scipio defeats Hannibal at the Battle of Zama; Second Punic War ends.

168
Greece falls to Rome after the Battle of Pydna.

149
Third Punic War begins.

146
Scipio Aemilianus takes Carthage and razes the city; Third Punic War ends.

100
Traditional birthdate of Julius Caesar.

91
Outbreak of Social War between Rome and Italian allies.

73
Spartacus and his band of gladiators lead a revolt against Rome.

71
Crassus and Pompey crush Spartacus' revolt.

63
Catiline conspires against Cicero and the republic; five conspirators are executed in Rome and the Roman army defeats Catiline in Etruria.

60
Pompey, Caesar, and Crassus form the First Triumvirate.

58
Caesar leaves to govern his province of Cisalpine Gaul; he subdues and conquers Gaul from 58 to 52.

56
Members of the First Triumvirate meet at Luca and renew their pact.

55 AND 54
Caesar invades Britain.

49
Caesar crosses the Rubicon River, thereby declaring war on Rome.

47
Caesar deposes Antony of his command in Rome.

46
Caesar defeats the pro-Pompey forces under Metellus Scipio at Thapsus in Africa.

45
Caesar defeats pro-Pompey forces in Spain and becomes dictator.

44
Caesar is assassinated on March 15.

43
Lepidus, Octavius, and Antony form the Second Triumvirate.

42

Antony and Octavius defeat Brutus and Cassius at Philippi.

31

Octavius defeats Antony at Battle of Actium.

30

Antony commits suicide.

Cleopatra commits suicide.

27

Octavius gains the title of Augustus and becomes Rome's first emperor.

A.D.

14

Augustus dies; Tiberius becomes Rome's second emperor.

37–41

Caligula reigns as emperor.

41

Gaius (Caligula) is assassinated on January 25; Claudius becomes emperor.

43

Claudius orders the invasion of Britain.

54–68

Reign of Nero.

60

Queen Boudicca leads a revolt in Britain.

64

Fire ravages much of Rome.

67

Vespasian and Titus quell a Jewish revolt in Judaea.

69

First Galba, then Otho, Vitellius, and finally Vespasian is named emperor.

70

Titus captures Jerusalem.

79

Mount Vesuvius erupts, burying Pompeii, Herculaneum, and other cities.

80

Fire destroys much of Rome, followed by a disastrous outbreak of plague.

81

Domitian becomes emperor.

93–96

"Reign of Terror" under Domitian.

96

Domitian is killed; Nerva becomes emperor.

98

Trajan becomes emperor.

101

Trajan invades Dacia.

102

Trajan invades Dacia a second time; he captures the Dacian capital of Sarmizagethusa.

106

Trajan annexes Dacia; he creates the province of Arabia.

114

Trajan captures Armenia.

117

Hadrian becomes emperor.

126

Hadrian's Wall completed in Britain.

138

Antoninus Pius becomes emperor.

142

The Antonine Wall built in Scotland.

161

Marcus Aurelius becomes emperor with Lucius Verus.

169

Lucius Verus dies and Marcus Aurelius is the sole emperor.

177

Christians are persecuted in Lugdunum (Lyon); Marcus Aurelius names his son Commodus his co-ruler and heir.

180

Commodus becomes emperor.

193

Septimius Severus becomes emperor.

199

Septimius Severus annexes Mesopotamia.

211

Caracalla is sole emperor.

285

Diocletian becomes emperor of the East and Maximian emperor of the West; empire is divided for the first time.

303

Diocletian orders the persecution of the Christians.

305

Diocletian abdicates and retires from public life.

306

Constantine and his father lead the Roman army into Britain.

311

Galerius, emperor of the East, dies; Licinius becomes emperor of the East.

313

Emperor Constantine issues Edict of Milan, forbidding the persecution of Christians.

324–30

Constantine defeats Licinius and becomes the sole ruler of the Roman Empire; Constantine rebuilds Byzantium, which becomes Constantinople.

325

Constantine convenes the Council of Nicaea.

380

Theodosius decrees that only those who believe in the Nicene Creed are to be considered Christians.

391

Theodosius prohibits sacrifices to the ancient gods, closes temples, and bans all foreign cults.

410

Rome falls to Visigoths led by Alaric.

Glossary

Literary Terms

eclogue—a short poem, usually pastoral in nature and often consisting of a dialogue between two shepherds.

elegy—a poem that expresses sorrow for the dead.

epic—a long narrative poem written in a dignified style detailing the deeds and achievements of a historical or legendary national hero.

epigram—a short poem with a witty or satirical point, that is, with a "sting in its tail."

lyric poetry—poems that express a poet's emotions; originally written to be accompanied by a lyre.

rhetoric—the art of using words effectively when writing or speaking.

satire—a literary piece that ridicules and condemns vices, foolishness, wickedness, and other human foibles.

Stoicism—a school of philosophy that teaches that the wise person should seek only virtue and be indifferent to pain and pleasure.

Political Terms

aedile—originally priests, the aediles became officials in charge of the streets and public buildings, trade markets, and public games.

augustus—member of the Tetrachy, the four rulers of the Roman Empire; there were two augusti—one was the head of the Western Empire and one of the Eastern.

caesar—member of the Tetrachy, the four rulers of the Roman Empire; there were two caesars—one was the assistant to the augustus of the Western Empire and one was the assistant to the augustus of the Eastern Empire.

censors—always two in number, these elected public officials determined the value of a Roman citizen's property and possessions every five years (sometimes 15) and assigned each Roman to his proper class in society; they had the right to lower a person's rank and deprive him of his right to vote if they judged his conduct improper.

consuls—always two in number, these elected leaders were the highest-ranking civil and military officials during the centuries when Rome was a republic. Under the empire, the office of consul gradually became honorary, with the emperor appointing those whom he wished to honor or those who would approve of his course of action.

cursus honorum—"the course of honors," or traditional succession to public offices; rules governing the cursus required that any Roman citizen seeking election to these offices be worth a specified amount of money, have senatorial rank either as a birthright or as a special privilege granted by the chief senator or emperor, and become a candidate for each in ascending order of importance. By tradition and law, the term of each office was one year.

dictator—a person nominated to be the sole ruler in times of military and domestic crises by a presiding consul upon the recommendation of the Senate. A dictator had sweeping powers but was required to surrender them immediately after the crisis was averted.

fasces—literally, a bundle of rods tied together with a red strap, enclosing an axe with its head facing outward. Men called lictors carried the fasces before consuls, dictators, and other high officials as a symbol of their power. Traditionally, 6 lictors walked before a consul and a praetor, 12 before a dictator.

imperator—originally, the honorary title given to a victorious general by his soldiers and, sometimes, the title with which the Senate would honor a general after an outstanding victory. The general could then use the title until either his command ended or he celebrated a triumph commemorating the victory. Gradually, the title became synonymous with military authority. Under the empire, an emperor affixed it to his official name.

praetor—an officer chiefly in charge of judicial matters.

Praetorian Guard—originally, Roman soldiers who acted as the personal bodyguard of a Roman general; in 27 B.C., Augustus created a permanent troop of Praetorians consisting of nine cohorts, or units, of specially chosen soldiers; more were added later.

pro-praetor, pro-consul—after completing a one-year term in Rome as praetor or consul, public officials usually served in the same capacity in the provinces as pro-praetor or pro-consul; the length of the assignment varied from one year to three or even five years.

proscription—a procedure employed first by Sulla in 82–81 B.C. and later by Octavius (Augustus), Antony, and Lepidus whereby they declared certain personal opponents enemies of Rome, listed their names on a public "wanted" notice, and then confiscated their land and possessions.

quaestor—originally in charge of judicial and financial matters, a quaestor became a financial officer of the Roman world.

senatus consultum ultimum—literally the "final decree of the Senate," it was an emergency decree that granted consuls the power to use whatever means necessary to safeguard the state against a public enemy.

Tetrarchy—the name historians have given to Diocletian's "rule of four," under which the eastern and western halves of the Roman Empire each had a commander in chief, or tetrarch, with the title of augustus, and each augustus had an assistant called a caesar. By plan, the caesars were to follow the augusti as commanders in chief.

tribunus, tribuni plebis (tribunes of the people)—an office first created in the early 5th century B.C. to protect the rights of the people, the plebeians. Forbidden by law to travel more than one mile from Rome, these tribunes kept their homes open to any plebeian who sought protection from unjust treatment. By law, a tribune had the right to veto any measure he deemed unfair to the plebeians, and no tribune could be prosecuted for any crime while in office.

tribuni aerarii (tribunes of the treasury)—officials responsible for collecting tribute from Rome's subjects and distributing it to Rome's soldiers.

tribuni militum (tribunes of the army)—elected by the people during the republic, they were the senior offi-cers of the legions, with six tribunes assigned to each legion.

triumph—a solemn procession the Senate awarded a general for an outstanding victory over a foreign enemy; on the appointed day, the general entered Rome in a chariot driven by four horses, preceded by the spoils and captives of war; the procession traveled along the Via Sacra (Sacred Way) to the Temple of Jupiter on the Capitoline Hill.

triumvirate—known in Latin as *triumviri* (or *tresviri*)—literally, "three men"—it was a board of three people officially appointed to rule over specific matters by the people or public officials. The triumvirate of Caesar, Crassus, and Pompey, however, was unofficial; the triumvirate of Octavius, Antony, and Lepidus was officially approved by the Senate in accordance with a law called the Lex Titia.

Religious Terms

augur—a person who interpreted omens.

basilica—a public building with court-rooms and public meeting places; the design of the basilica was adapted by Christians for important places of worship.

omen—an occurrence sometimes accepted as a forecast of future events.

oracle—the place or means by which a god or goddess may be asked for advice; also used to denote the advice given.

Pontifex Maximus—the title of the chief priest of the college of pontiffs, the priests who oversaw all religious observances. Under the empire, the emperor assumed the title and responsibilities of the Pontifex Maximus; with the rise of Christianity, the chief Christian bishop in Rome (known today as the pope) assumed the title.

Sibylline Books—a collection of prophetic sayings by the Cumaean sibyl, three of which were bought by Tarquinius Superbus; in times of crisis, Roman officials consulted these books to discover how they might make amends for actions that had caused the crisis.

Vestal Virgins—six in number, they were the priestesses of Vesta, the Roman goddess of the hearth; chosen as young girls, Vestal Virgins served for 30 years, during which time they were forbidden to marry. Their chief duty was to tend the sacred fire in Vesta's great temple in Rome.

Social Terms

alimenta (food)—the system for free distribution of corn, oil, and money to the poor.

clientes—poor Romans who allied themselves with a wealthy and powerful Roman (known as the *patronus*); clientes pledged their support for the patronus in public and private life in return for a daily portion of food or money plus legal assistance when necessary; by custom, the cliens went to his protector's house early each morning to greet him.

eques (plural: equites)—a member of the wealthy business class of Romans.

nomen—traditionally, Romans had three names: the *praenomen*, a first name, given at birth; the *nomen*, a family name indicating the ancestor to whom a person traced his or her roots; and the *cognomen*, the immediate family name. Thus Gaius Julius Caesar's praenomen was Gaius; his nomen, Julius, indicated that he traced his ancestry back to Iulus, the son of Aeneas, the traditional founder of the Roman nation. His family name, Caesar, he took from his father.

novus homo—a "new man," that is, the first one in a family to reach the Senate and attain senatorial privileges.

optimates—the name given to the conservative group within the Senate that favored the interests of the upper classes.

patrician—a member of the privileged class of Romans; the name is a derivative of the Latin word *pater* (meaning "father"), which, in the political sense, meant "a member of the Senate."

patronus—a person who agreed to help and protect another person (his *cliens*) financially and legally and to provide a minimum amount of food in return for public and private support.

Pax Romana—"Roman Peace" (also known as the Pax Augusta, "the Peace of Augustus"): the period when Augustus' rule brought a lasting peace to the Roman world and fostered a so-called golden age.

plebeian—a member of the less privileged class of Romans, which included the vast majority of Roman citizens.

populares—Roman political leaders who supported the people and worked with them (rather than with the Senate) to challenge the rights and privileges of the *optimates*.

toga—the traditional, official outer garment worn by Roman male citizens. White in color, the toga of boys and public officials had a purple hem along the straight edge.

Further Reading

Each of the major entries in *Ancient Romans* includes a list of readings. Refer to the index for page references to specific Roman individuals.

Although the following books vary in level of difficulty, none are too technical for the interested reader. Titles preceded by an asterisk (*) are especially geared to younger readers.

Magazines

Archaeology is published bimonthly by the Archaeological Institute of America, 135 William Street, New York, NY 10038.

Calliope: World History for Young People is published nine times during the school year by Cobblestone Publishing, 7 School Street, Peterborough, NH 03458.

General History

*Baker, Charles F. III, and Rosalie F. Baker. *The Classical Companion*. Peterborough, N.H.: Cobblestone, 1988.

Boardman, John, Jasper Griffin, and Oswyn Murray, eds. *Oxford History of the Classical World*. New York: Oxford University Press, 1986.

*Burrell, Roy. *Oxford First Ancient History*. New York: Oxford University Press, 1994.

*———. *The Romans*. New York: Oxford University Press, 1989.

Cary, Max, and H. H. Scullard. *A History of Rome*. New York: St. Martin's, 1975.

*Caselli, Giovanni. *The Roman Empire and the Dark Ages*. New York: Bedrick, 1985.

*Corbishley, Mike. *The Ancient World*. New York: Bedrick, 1992.

*Cornell, Tim, and John Matthews. *Atlas of the Roman World*. New York: Facts on File, 1982.

Cotterell, Arthur, ed. *Penguin Encyclopedia of Classical Civilizations*. New York: Viking, 1993.

*Dineen, Jacqueline. *The Romans*. New York: New Discovery, 1992.

**The Eyewitness Visual Dictionary of Ancient Civilizations*. New York: Dorling Kindersley, 1994.

Fantham, Elaine, et al. *Women in the Classical World*. New York: Oxford University Press, 1994.

Ferrill, Arthur. *The Fall of the Roman Empire: The Military Explanation*. London: Thames & Hudson, 1986.

Grant, Michael. *Atlas of Classical History*. New York: Oxford University Press, 1994.

———. *History of Rome*. New York: Scribners, 1978.

———. *The Roman Emperors: A Biographical Guide to the Rulers of Imperial Rome, 31 B.C.–A.D. 476*. New York: Scribners, 1985.

———. *The Twelve Caesars*. New York: Scribners, 1975.

Heichelheim, Fritz M., Cedric A. Yeo, and Allen M. Ward. *A History of the Roman People*. Englewood Cliffs, N.J.: Prentice-Hall, 1984.

Hooper, Finley A. *Roman Realities*. Detroit: Wayne State University Press, 1979.

Hornblower, Simon, and Antony Spawforth, eds. *The Oxford Classical Dictionary*. 3rd ed. New York: Oxford University Press, 1996.

*James, Simon. *Ancient Rome*. New York: Viking Penguin, 1992.

Plutarch. *Makers of Rome: Coriolanus, Fabius Maximus, Cato the Elder, Tiberius Gracchus, Gaius Gracchus, Antony*. Translated by Ian Scott. Baltimore, Md.: Penguin, 1965.

Potter, Timothy W. *Roman Italy*. University of California Press, 1987.

Scarre, Chris. *Smithsonian Timelines of the Ancient World*. London: Dorling Kindersley, 1993.

Starr, Chester G. *A History of the Ancient World*. New York: Oxford University Press, 1991.

Roman Life

Adkins, Lesley, and Roy A. Adkins. *Handbook to Life in Ancient Rome*. New York: Facts on File, 1994.

*Caselli, Giovanni. *A Roman Soldier*. New York: Bedrick, 1991.

*Coolidge, Olivia. *Lives of Famous Romans*. North Haven, Conn.: Linnet, 1992.

*Corbishley, Mike. *What Do We Know About the Romans?* New York: Bedrick, 1992.

*Macdonald, Fiona. *First Facts about the Ancient Romans*. New York: Bedrick, 1996.

*———. *The Roman Colosseum*. New York: Bedrick, 1996.

*———. *A Roman Fort*. New York: Bedrick, 1993.

*Morley, Jacqueline, and John James. *A Roman Villa*. New York: Bedrick, 1992.

Peck, Harry Thurston, ed. *Harper's Dictionary of Classical Literature and Antiquities*. New York: Cooper Square, 1965.

Roebuck, Carl, ed. *The Muses at Work*. Cambridge, Mass.: MIT Press, 1969.

*Steele, Philip. *Food and Feasts in Ancient Rome*. New York: New Discovery, 1995.

Roman Mythology

*Baker, Charles F. III, and Rosalie F. Baker. *Myths and Legends of Mount Olympos*. Peterborough, N.H.: Cobblestone, 1992.

*Flaum, Eric. *The Encylopedia of Mythology: Gods, Heroes, and Legends of the Greeks and Romans*. Philadelphia: Courage, 1993.

Martin, Richard, ed. *Bulfinch's Mythology*. New York: HarperCollins, 1991.

Morford, Mark P. O., and Robert J. Lenardon. *Classical Mythology*. New York: Classical Mythology, 1991.

Arts and Sciences

*Baker, Charles F. III, and Rosalie F. Baker. *Classical Ingenuity*. Peterborough, N.H.: Cobblestone, 1993.

Sutton, Dana F. *Ancient Comedy*. New York: Twayne, 1993.

Archaeology

*Cork, Barbara, and Struan Reid. *The Young Scientist Book of Archaeology*. London: Usborne, 1984.

Grant, Michael. *The Visible Past: Greek and Roman History from Archaeology 1960–1990*. New York: Scribners, 1990.

McIntosh, Jane. *The Practical Archaeologist*. New York: Facts on File, 1986.

McMillon, Bill. *The Archaeology Handbook: A Field Manual and Resource Guide*. New York: Wiley, 1991.

*Moloney, Norah. *The Young Oxford Book of Archaeology*. New York: Oxford University Press, 1997.

Perring, Stefania, and Dominic Perring. *Then and Now*. New York: Macmillan, 1991.

Words and Their Roots

*Fifer, Norma, and Nancy Flowers. *Vocabulary from Classical Roots*. Cambridge, Mass.: Educators Publishing Service, 1990.

Weiler, Susan K. *Mini Myths and Maxi Words: English Vocabulary from Classical Mythology*. White Plains, N.Y.: Longman, 1986.

Index of Ancient Romans by Profession

Emperors
Augustus
Claudius
Constantine the Great
Diocletian
Domitian
Hadrian
Marcus Aurelius
Nero
Septimius Severus
Theodosius the Great
Tiberius
Trajan
Vespasian

Financier
Crassus

Generals
Agrippa
Caesar
Camillus
Marius
Mark Antony
Pompey
Scipio Africanus
Sulla

Gladiator
Spartacus

Historians
Cato the Elder
Livy
Tacitus

Lawyers
Cicero
Pliny the Younger

Orator
Cicero

Playwrights
Plautus
Seneca
Terence

Philosopher
Seneca

Poets
Catullus
Horace
Martial
Ovid
Virgil

Satirist
Juvenal

Statesmen and administrators
Caesar
Camillus
Cato the Elder
Cicero
The Gracchi Brothers
Marius
Mark Antony
Pliny the Younger
Pompey
Scipio Africanus
Sulla

Wives of emperors
Agrippina the Younger
Livia

Writers
Cato the Elder
Cicero
Pliny the Younger

Index

Acknowledgments

Special thanks are owed to the staff of the John D. Rockefeller, Jr., Library at Brown University in Providence, Rhode Island, for its invaluable assistance in helping us search and locate so many of the books used in preparing *Ancient Romans*. We would also like to extend our thanks to the reference librarians at the New Bedford and South Dartmouth libraries in Massachusetts for their assistance in researching information used in writing this book.

Picture Credits

Rosalie F. and Charles F. Baker are the editors of the magazine *Calliope: World History for Young People*, which in 1991 was named one of the nation's 10 best magazines by *Library Journal*. They are the authors of *Ancient Greeks: Creating the Classical Tradition*, also part of the Oxford Profiles series; *The Classical Companion, Myths and Legends of Mount Olympos*; and *Classical Ingenuity: The Legacy of the Ancient Greek and Roman Architects, Artists, and Inventors*. Both are former teachers, and Charles Baker is currently an administrator for the New Bedford public schools in Massachusetts. He is also the author of *Struggle for Freedom*, 13 plays on the American Revolution for classroom performance. The Bakers live in New Bedford with their son, Chip.